THE KEY

STUDENT STUDY GUIDE

Social Studies 30

THE KEY

THE KEY series of student study guides is specifically designed to assist students in preparing for unit tests, provincial achievement tests, and diploma examinations. Each ***KEY*** includes questions, answers, detailed solutions, and practice tests. The complete solutions show problem-solving methods, explain key concepts, and highlight potential errors.

TABLE OF CORRELATIONS

Castle Rock Research has designed ***THE KEY*** by correlating every question and its solution to Alberta Education's curriculum outcomes. Each unit of review begins with a Table of Correlations that lists the General and Specific Outcomes from the Alberta curriculum along with Related Questions that correspond to the outcomes. Usually the emphasis placed on outcomes, concepts, and skills within each unit varies. Students and teachers can quickly identify the relevant importance of each outcome and concept in the unit as determined by the number of related questions provided in ***THE KEY***.

For grades 3, 6, 9, and 12, the weighting of each unit and concept is determined by analyzing the blueprint for the respective provincial achievement tests and diploma examinations. Based on this analysis, the Related Questions for outcomes and concepts are organized on a proportionate basis. For grades other than 3, 6, 9, and 12, the breakdown of each course is determined by consulting with experienced teachers and by reviewing curriculum guides and textbooks.

The Table of Correlations is a critical component of ***THE KEY***. For students, it offers a visual cue for effectively organizing study time. For teachers, the Table of Correlations indicates the instructional focus for each content strand, serves as a curriculum checklist, and focuses on the outcomes and concepts that are the most important in the unit and the particular course of study. Students become "test wise" by becoming familiar with exam and question formats used most often in provincial examinations.

Canadian Cataloguing in Publication Data

Rao, Gautam, 1961 –
THE KEY – Social Studies 30

1. Social Studies – Juvenile Literature. I. Title

Published by
Castle Rock Research Corp.
2340 Manulife Place
10180 – 101 Street
Edmonton, AB T5J 3S4

5 6 7 FP 07 06 05

Printed in Canada

Publisher:
Gautam Rao

Editors:
Mun Prasad
Shirley Wacowich

Contributors:
Greg Plouffe
Greg Robinson

Print Production:
Phil Beauchamp
Alesha Braitenbach
Tory Braybrook
Nishi Chadha
Mark Chan
Collin Goodman
Kevin Huenison
Lorraine James
Shawna Kozel
James Kropfreiter
Julie May
David Moret
Suzanne Morin
Jackie Pacheco
Tara Pratt
Abhinav Rastogi
Diana Seguin
Jan Witwicky
Gary Yaremchuk
Richard Yeomans

Dedicated to the memory of Dr. V. S. Rao

THE KEY – SOCIAL STUDIES 30

THE KEY is a student study guide specifically designed to assist students in preparing for unit tests and provincial diploma examinations. It is a compilation of questions and answers from previous diploma examinations, complete with detailed solutions for all questions. Questions have been grouped by concepts so that students can use the resource throughout the year to study for all unit tests and to prepare for their provincial diploma exams. An overview of the main sections of ***THE KEY*** follows.

I ***KEY Factors Contributing to School Success*** provides students with examples of study and review strategies. Information is included on learning styles, study schedules, and developing review notes.

II ***Unit Review***, includes questions from the 2001 (June) and 2000 (January and June) diploma exams. All questions are classified according to the units studied in class and are correlated to the specific concept(s) being tested. In *Unit Review*, questions considered to be more difficult are labelled as *Challenger* questions. ***THE KEY*** **provides detailed solutions for all questions.**

III ***KEY Strategies for Success on Exams*** explores topics such as common exam question formats and strategies for responding, directing words most commonly used, how to begin the exam, and managing test anxiety.

IV ***Unit Tests*** have been created for each unit to provide students with a sample test that covers the breadth of the curriculum. These tests are comprised of the relevant diploma exam questions from January and June 1999.

V The ***Diploma Preparation*** section contains the diploma examinations that were administered in June 2001 and January 2002. The questions presented here are distinct from the questions in the previous section. It is **recommended** that students work through these exams carefully because they are reflective of the exam format and level of difficulty that students are likely to encounter on their final. **Complete solutions are provided for all questions in this section.**

THE KEY *Study guides* are available for Biology 30, Chemistry 30, Physics 30, English 30-1, English 30-2, Mathematics 30 (Applied), Mathematics 30 (Pure), Social Studies 30, and Social Studies 33. A complete list of the ***THE KEY*** *Study guides* for Grades 3 to 12 is included at the back of this book.

For information about any of our resources or services, please call Castle Rock Research Corp. at 780.448.9619 or visit our web site at http://www.castlerockresearch.com.

At Castle Rock Research, we strive to produce a resource that is error-free. If you should find an error, please contact us so that future editions can be corrected.

CONTENTS

KEY FACTORS CONTRIBUTING TO SCHOOL SUCCESS

UNIT REVIEW

ANSWERS AND SOLUTIONS

KEY STRATEGIES FOR SUCCESS ON EXAMS

DIPLOMA EXAM PREPARATION

Answers and Solutions – Diploma Exam Preparation

Appendices

NOTES

KEY FACTORS CONTRIBUTING TO SCHOOL SUCCESS

NOTES

KEY FACTORS CONTRIBUTING TO SCHOOL SUCCESS

You want to do well in school. There are many factors that contribute to your success. While you may not have control over the number or types of assignments and tests that you need to complete, there are many factors that you can control to improve your academic success in any subject area. The following are examples of these factors.

- **REGULAR CLASS ATTENDANCE** – helps you to master the subject content, identify key concepts, take notes and receive important handouts, ask your teacher questions, clarify information, use school resources, and meet students with whom you can study
- **POSITIVE ATTITUDE AND PERSONAL DISCIPLINE** – helps you to come to classes on time, prepared to work and learn, complete all assignments to the best of your ability, and contribute to a positive learning environment
- **SELF-MOTIVATION AND PERSONAL DISCIPLINE** – helps you to set personal learning goals, take small steps continually moving toward achieving your goals, and to "stick it out when the going gets tough"
- **ACCESSING ASSISTANCE WHEN YOU NEED IT** – helps you to improve or clarify your understanding of the concept or new learning before moving on to the next phase
- **MANAGING YOUR TIME EFFICIENTLY** – helps you to reduce anxiety and focus your study and review efforts on the most important concepts
- **DEVELOPING 'TEST WISENESS'** – helps to increase your confidence in writing exams if you are familiar with the typical exam format, common errors to avoid, and know how the concepts in a subject area are usually tested
- **KNOWING YOUR PERSONAL LEARNING STYLE** – helps you to maximize your learning by using effective study techniques, developing meaningful study notes, and make the most efficient use of your study time

KNOW YOUR LEARNING STYLE

You have a unique learning style. Knowing your learning style – how you learn best – can help you to maximize your time in class and during your exam preparation. There are seven common learning styles. Read the following descriptions to see which one most closely describes your learning preferences.

- **Linguistic Learner** (sometimes referred to as an auditory learner) – learns best by saying, hearing and seeing words; is good at memorizing things such as dates, places, names and facts
- **Logical/Mathematical Learner** – learns best by categorizing, classifying and working with abstract relationships; is good at mathematics, problem solving and reasoning
- **Spatial Learner** (sometimes referred to as a visual learner) – learns best by visualizing, seeing, working with pictures; is good at puzzles, imaging things, and reading maps and charts
- **Musical Learner** – learns best by hearing, rhythm, melody, and music; is good at remembering tones, rhythms and melodies, picking up sounds
- **Bodily/Kinesthetic Learner** – learns best by touching, moving, and processing knowledge through bodily sensations; is good at physical activities
- **Interpersonal Learner** – learns best by sharing, comparing, relating, cooperating; is good at organizing, communicating, leading, and understanding others
- **Intrapersonal Learner** – learns best by working alone, individualized projects, and self-paced instruction

(Adapted from http://snow.utoronto.ca/Learn2/mod3/mistyles.html)

Your learning style may not fit "cleanly" into one specific category but may be a combination of two or more styles. Knowing your personal learning style allows you to organize your study notes in a manner that provides you with the most meaning. For example, if you are a spatial or visual learner, you may find mind mapping and webbing are effective ways to organize subject concepts, information, and study notes. If you are a linguistic learner, you may need to write and then "say out loud" the steps in a process, the formula, or actions that lead up to a significant event. If you are a kinesthetic learner you may need to use your finger to trace over a diagram to remember it or to "tap out" the steps in solving a problem or "feel" yourself writing or typing the formula.

SCHEDULING STUDY TIME

Effective time management skills are an essential component to your academic success. The more effectively you manage your time the more likely you are to achieve your goals such as completing all of your assignments on time or finishing all of the questions on a unit test or year-end exam. Developing a study schedule helps to ensure you have adequate time to review the subject content and prepare for the exam.

You should review your class notes regularly to ensure you have a clear understanding of the new material. Reviewing your lessons on a regular basis helps you to learn and remember the ideas and concepts. It also reduces the quantity of material that you must study prior to a unit test or year-end exam. If this practice is not part of your study habits, establishing a study schedule will help you to make the best use of your time. The following are brief descriptions of three types of study schedules.

- **LONG-TERM STUDY SCHEDULE** – begins early in the school year or semester and well in advance of an exam; is the **most effective** manner for improving your understanding and retention of the concepts, and increasing self-confidence; involves regular, nightly review of class notes, handouts and text material
- **SHORT-TERM STUDY SCHEDULE** – begins **five to seven days prior to an exam**; must organize the volume of material to be covered beginning with the most difficult concepts; each study session starts with a brief review of what was studied the day before
- **CRAMMING** – occurs the night before an exam; is the **least effective** form of studying or exam preparation; focuses on memorizing and reviewing critical information such as facts, dates, formulas; do not introduce new material; has the potential to increase exam anxiety by discovering something you do not know

Regardless of the type of study schedule you use, you may want to consider the following to maximize your study time and effort:

- establish a regular time and place for doing your studying
- minimize distractions and interruptions during your study time
- plan a ten minute break for every hour that you study
- organize the material so you begin with the most challenging content first

- divide the subject content into smaller manageable "chunks" to review
- develop a marking system for your study notes to identify key and secondary concepts, concepts that you are confident about, those that require additional attention or about which you have questions
- reward yourself for sticking to your schedule and/or completing each review section
- alternate the subjects and type of study activities to maintain your interest and motivation
- make a daily task list with the headings "must do", "should do", and "could do"
- begin each session by quickly reviewing what you studied the day before
- maintain your usual routine of eating, sleeping, and exercising to help you concentrate for extended periods of time

KEY STRATEGIES FOR REVIEWING

Reviewing textbook material, class notes, and handouts should be an ongoing activity and becomes more critical in preparing for exams. You may find some of the following strategies useful in completing your review during your scheduled study time.

READING OR SKIMMING FOR KEY INFORMATION

- Before reading the chapter, preview it by noting headings, charts and graphs, chapter questions.
- Turn each heading and sub-heading into a question before you start to read.
- Read the complete introduction to identify the key information that is addressed in the chapter.
- Read the first sentence of the next paragraph for the main idea.
- Skim the paragraph noting key words, phrases, and information.
- Read the last sentence of the paragraph.
- Repeat the process for each paragraph and section until you have skimmed the entire chapter.
- Read the complete conclusion to summarize each chapter's contents.
- Answer the questions you created.
- Answer the chapter questions.

Creating Study Notes

Mind Mapping or Webbing

- Use the key words, ideas or concepts from your reading or class notes to create a *mind map or web* (a diagram or visual representation of the information). A mind map or web is sometimes referred to as a knowledge map.
- Write the key word, concept, theory or formula in the centre of your page.
- Write and link related facts, ideas, events, and information to the central concept using lines.
- Use colored markers, underlining, or other symbols to emphasize things such as relationships, information of primary and secondary importance.
- The following example of a mind map or web illustrates how this technique can be used to develop an essay.

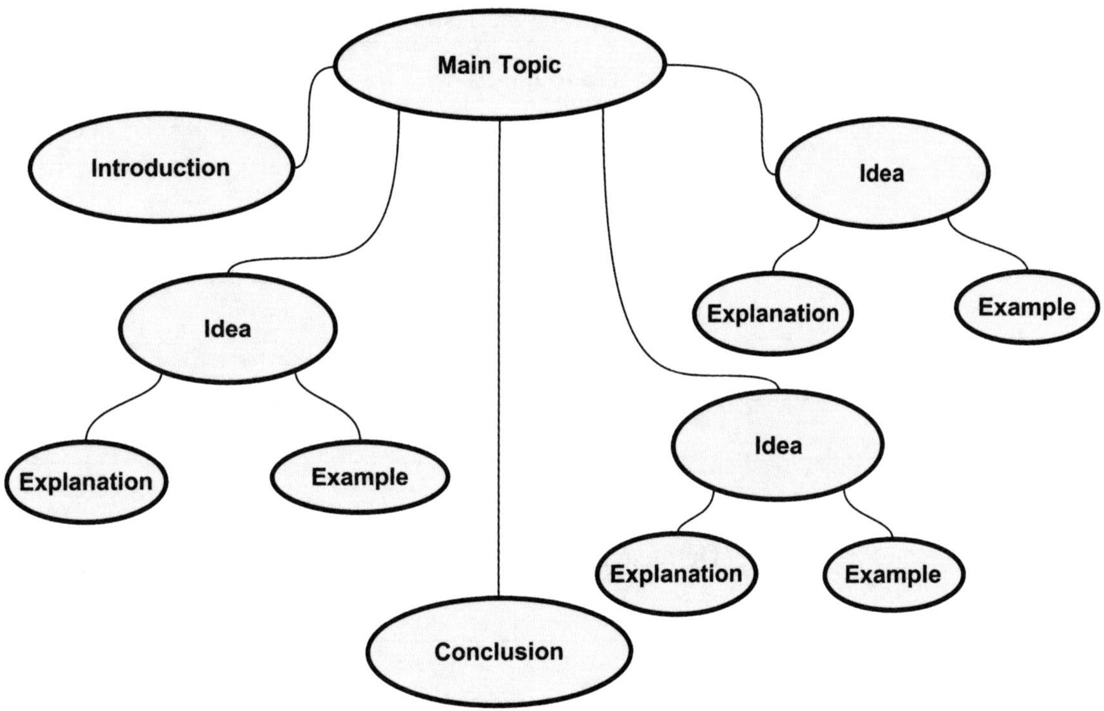

Charts

- Use charts to organize your information and relate theories, concepts, definitions, applications and other important details.
- Collect and enter the information in key categories.
- Use the completed chart as a composite picture of the concept or information.

The following is an example of how a chart can be used to help you organize information when exploring an issue in subjects such as Social Studies, the Sciences, or Humanities.

<table>
<tr><th colspan="6">Define Key Words</th></tr>
<tr><td colspan="6">1.</td></tr>
<tr><td colspan="6">2.</td></tr>
<tr><td colspan="6">3.</td></tr>
<tr><th colspan="6">Explore the Issue</th></tr>
<tr><th colspan="2">Yes to the Issue</th><th colspan="2">No to the Issue</th><th colspan="2">Maybe to the Issue</th></tr>
<tr><td colspan="2">1.</td><td colspan="2">1.</td><td colspan="2">1.</td></tr>
<tr><td colspan="2">2.</td><td colspan="2">2.</td><td colspan="2">2.</td></tr>
<tr><td colspan="2">3.</td><td colspan="2">3.</td><td colspan="2">3.</td></tr>
<tr><th colspan="6">Case Studies and Examples</th></tr>
<tr><td colspan="3">1.</td><td colspan="3">1.</td></tr>
<tr><td colspan="3">2.</td><td colspan="3">2.</td></tr>
<tr><td colspan="3">3.</td><td colspan="3">3.</td></tr>
<tr><th colspan="6">Defense of Your Point of View</th></tr>
<tr><td colspan="6">1.</td></tr>
<tr><td colspan="6">2.</td></tr>
<tr><td colspan="6">3.</td></tr>
</table>

Index Cards

- Write a key event, fact, concept, theory, word or question on one side of the index card.
- On the reverse side, write the date, place, important actions and key individuals involved in the event, significance of the fact, salient features of the concept, essence and application of the theory, definition of the word or answer to the question.
- Use the cards to quickly review important information.

International System of Units (SI)

International System of Units (SI)

SI base unit

Base quantity	Name	Symbol
length	metre	m
mass	kilogram	kg
time	second	s
amount of substance	mole	mol

Derived Measures

Measures	Unit	Symbol
Volume	cubic metre	m^3

SI Prefixes

Factor	Name	Symbol
10^6	mega	*M*
10^3	kilo	*k*
10^{-2}	centi	*c*
10^{-3}	milli	*m*
10^{-6}	micro	*μ*

Symbols

- Develop your own symbols to use when reviewing your material to identify information you need in preparing for your exam. For example, an exclamation mark (!) may signify something that "must be learned well" because it is a key concept that is likely to appear on unit tests and the year-end exam. A question mark (?) may identify something you are unsure of while a star or asterisk (*) may identify important information for formulating an argument. A check mark (✓) or an (×) can be used to show that you agree or disagree with the statement, sentence or paragraph.

Crib Notes

- Develop brief notes that are a critical summary of the essential concepts, dates, events, theories, formulas, supporting facts, or steps in a process that are most likely to be on the exam.
- Use your crib notes as your "last minute" review before you go in to write your exam. You can not take crib notes into an exam.

MEMORIZING

- **ASSOCIATION** relates the new learning to something you already know. For example, in distinguishing between the spelling of 'dessert' and 'desert', you know 'sand' has only one 's' and so should desert.
- **MNEMONIC DEVICES** are sentences you create to remember a list or group of items. For example, the first letters of the words in the sentence "**E**very **G**ood **B**oy **D**eserves **F**udge" helps you to remember the names of the lines on the treble clef staff (E, G, B, D, and F) in music.
- **ACRONYMS** are words formed from the first letters of the words in a group. For example, **HOMES** helps you to remember the names of Canada's five Great Lakes (**H**uron, **O**ntario, **M**ichigan, **E**rie, and **S**uperior).
- **VISUALIZING** requires you to use your mind's eye to "see" the chart, list, map, diagram, or sentence as it exists in your textbook, notes, on the board, computer screen or in the display.

SOCIAL STUDIES 30

Unit Review has been developed to aid students in their study throughout the term. Students can prepare for unit exams while gaining exposure to previous diploma exam questions. This section of ***THE KEY*** is a compilation of questions from the diploma exams that were administered in 2000 (January and June) and 2001 (January). Since many Social Studies 30 diploma exam questions are based on copyrighted material, considerable time and resources have been spent in either securing the consent of the copyright holders or adapting the material from its original form. All questions have been categorized by content strand to correspond to the units in Social Studies 30. Students will find questions for *Political and Economic Systems* and *Global Interactions in the Twentieth Century*.

A **Table of Correlations** at the beginning of each unit lists the curriculum outcomes and the questions that specifically test those concepts. To help students understand the curriculum, ***THE KEY*** provides explanations of the key concepts for each unit. After each explanation, students are directed to questions from previous diploma exams that are related to the underlying concepts. Sample unit tests are included at the end of each unit. The unit tests include the relevant questions from diploma exams administered in 1999 (January and June).

THE KEY **contains detailed solutions for all questions**. Solutions show the processes and/or ideas used in arriving at the correct answers and may help students gain a better understanding of the concepts that are being tested.

In *Unit Review*, certain questions have been categorized as *Challenger Questions*. *Challenger Questions* represent the more difficult questions that a student is likely to face, as illustrated in the following example.

CHALLENGER QUESTION	**DIFFICULTY: 41.1**

35. The Second World War event that resulted in extensive civilian casualties and, consequently, raised moral and ethical questions about the conduct of war was the

A. bombing of Pearl Harbor, 1941
B. Dieppe Raid, 1942
C. Battle of Midway, 1942
D. bombing of Dresden, 1945

The *Difficulty* rating is based on the percentage of students that answered the question correctly when it appeared on the Diploma Exam. In the example, only 41.1% of students answered it correctly (Source: Alberta Education Examiner's Reports). *Challenger Questions* for Social Studies 30 include those with less than a 60% achievement rate, as indicated by *Difficulty*.

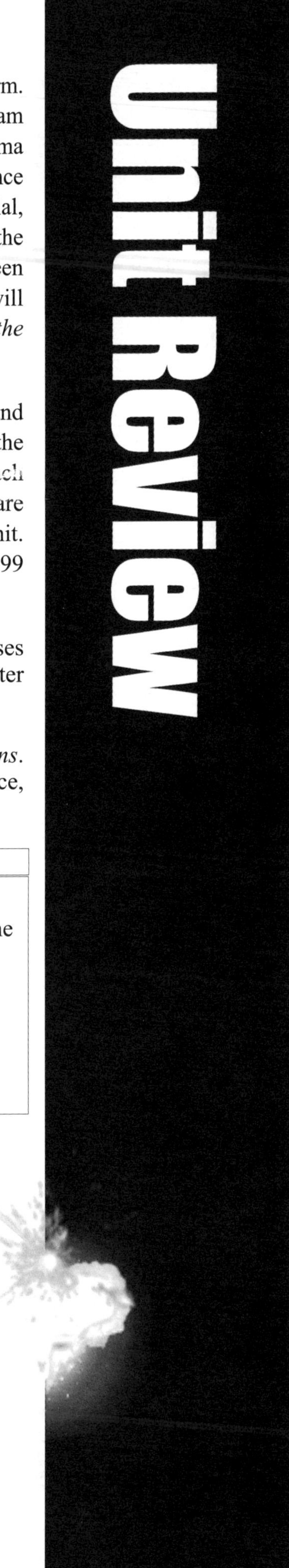

TOPIC A: POLITICAL AND ECONOMIC SYSTEMS
THEME I: POLITICAL AND ECONOMIC SYSTEMS IN THEORY

Table of Correlations

Generalizations	Concepts	Facts and Content	Questions
a. Ideologies contain beliefs and ideas about human nature and are used to explain and justify political and economic systems.	• ideology • individualism • collectivism	Identify the principle features of: • liberalism • conservatism • socialism • capitalism • fascism • communism • anarchism	1, 2, 3, 17, 27, 28, 29, 30, 48, 49, 73, 89, 90
b. Political systems are organized to allocate political power that involves the authority to make and to implement decisions in society.	• power • decision making	Examine the role of the following in the allocation of power and the organization and operation of political systems: • constitution – executive power – legislative power – judicial power – structure of government – federal – unitary • laws, rules, and regulations as they apply to: – political parties – voters – systems of representation – interest groups – media – dissemination of information – limits on dissent – role of the military, police, civil service	20, 21, 22, 24, 25, 26, 68, 69, 70, 75, 76, 77, 78, 86
c. Political systems may be organized in a democratic manner.	• democracy	Briefly identify the major types, characteristics, and features of democracy: • types – direct/representative – parliamentary – presidential • characteristics/features – majority rule – citizenship participation – accountability of government to the people – minority rights – guarantee of individual rights and freedoms – opposition – limits on dissent – provision for changes to the system – political parties – electoral systems	31, 62, 63, 67, 79, 83, 84, 87
d. Political systems may be organized in a dictatorial manner.	• dictatorship	Briefly identify the major types, characteristics, and features of a dictatorship: • types – autocracy – oligarchy – majority tyranny – minority tyranny – absolute monarchy – military dictatorship • characteristics/features – authoritarian – totalitarian – use of force – control of media – controlled participation – limits on dissent – lack of accountability – provision for changes to the system – indoctrination – direction of popular discontent	23, 55, 57, 58, 80, 81, 85, 88, 91
e. Economic systems are organized to deal with the production and distribution of goods and services in society.	• scarcity	Examine the basic economic questions that must be answered in any economic system: • what to produce? – limits – choices/opportunity costs • how to produce? – land/labour/capital • how to distribute? – allocation of goods/services – who makes the decisions about the allocation of resources, methods of production, and the distribution of goods and services?	44, 99, 100, 101, 102
f. Economic systems may be based on the principles of private enterprise.	• private enterprise • capitalism • market economy	Identify the major characteristics of a private enterprise system: • private property • competition • individual incentive • invisible hand • supply and demand • how the basic economic questions are answered	9, 10, 13, 43, 92, 93, 94, 98
g. Economic systems may be based on principles of public enterprise.	• public enterprise • socialism • centrally planned economy	Identify the major characteristics of a public enterprise system: • collective property • cooperation • group incentive • central planning • how the basic economic questions are answered	95, 97

THEME II: POLITICAL AND ECONOMIC SYSTEMS IN PRACTICE

Table of Correlations			
Generalizations	**Concepts**	**Facts and Content**	**Questions**
a. In practice, political and economic systems differ from theory.	• mixed economy • adaptation • tradition	Use Canada, the United States of America, the Soviet Union, Nazi Germany, and Sweden as examples to show how ideas and ideologies are used in practice. Refer to other current examples to illustrate how systems differ from theory.	12, 14, 53, 54, 61,104
b. Political and economic systems adapt to new ideas and changing circumstances.	• collectivization • privatization • nationalization • intervention • depression • business cycle • deregulation	Briefly examine political and economic changes in: • Canada – role of government – monetary policy – fiscal policy • the United States of America – Great Depression – New Deal – Keynesian economics/demand-side economics – Reaganomics/supply-side economics • the Soviet Union – under the leadership of Lenin and Stalin – under the leadership of Gorbachev (glasnost and perestroika) • an economy in transition; e.g.: – Russia, China • Sweden – welfare state	4, 5, 6, 7, 8, 15, 16, 19, 36, 37, 42, 45, 46, 47, 50, 82, 96, 103, 105
c. Political leaders achieve, exercise, and maintain power in different ways in democracies and dictatorships.	• majority rule • totalitarianism • elitism • accountability	Examine how political power was achieved, exercised, and maintained in democracies and dictatorships: • Canada; e.g.: – responsible government • the United States of America; e.g.: – separation of powers • the Soviet Union; e.g.: – the Russian Revolution and the role of the Communist Party • Nazi Germany; e.g.: – the role of Hitler and the Nazi Party	18, 32, 33, 34, 35, 38, 51, 52, 56, 59, 66, 71, 72, 74
d. The role of the individual in society is affected by the emphasis placed on collective good or individualism.	• individualism • collectivism • political rights • economic rights • minority rights • democratic socialism • neo-conservatism	Briefly consider the role of laws, rules, and regulations, and basic rights, as well as responsibilities of the individual in: • Canada • the United States of America • the Soviet Union • Sweden • Nazi Germany	11, 39, 40, 60, 64, 65
e. New issues and ideas challenge traditional political and economic beliefs and practices.	• human rights • justice • human survival • globalization	Identify recent issues that illustrate the need for change and adaptation in existing political and economic arrangements. These may involve issues drawn from: • environmental concerns • changing economic conditions • changing ideological perspectives	41

Political and Economic Systems

Theme I: Political and Economic Systems in Theory

Please refer to Appendix A - Image #1

Political and Economic Spectrum

It is essential for students to know the political and economic spectrum thoroughly. You can use the spectrum as a tool to determine the amount of government intervention into an economy, the primary focus of an economy, the method of change used in the economy, the ability for an economy to rapidly change and other key questions. For example, you can see the amount of government intervention increases from right to left on the spectrum, in theory. However, in practice, the amount of government intervention increases at two ends of the spectrum as economic powered concentrated in the hands of a ruler or ruling elite.

There are two competing values associated with **Generalization A: Individualism**, the belief that individuals must have the freedom to be *self-reliant* and *self-sufficient,* and **Collectivism**, which states that the will of the "collective or welfare of the entire society" must take precedence when making economic and political decisions. The application of these two values into theoretical models has assisted in the formation of the spectrum. As a student you should familiarize yourself with the level of **individual freedom or government control** at each theoretical/practical case study on the spectrums. This will promote insight into questions posed, which ask you **to predict if** government would **increase or decrease** its involvement in the event of fluctuations in the business cycle or to resolve other problems listed in **Theme I's generalizations E-G** and **Theme II's generalizations A and B**.

Please refer to Appendix A - Image #2

Related Questions: 1, 2, 3, 17, 27, 28, 29, 30, 48, 49, 73, 89, 90

Political Systems and Decision Making

Please refer to Appendix A - Image #3

The primary question to be asked when analyzing political systems is, "**Who has power**?" and "**How will change unfold**?" in these systems. As you can see in the spectrum at both extremes, governments work towards the creation of **dictatorships**. In theory, **Fascist governments** on the right promote **complete individual freedom** in the economy. In practice however these states are **racist** and therefore eliminate all **"undesirables"** from society regardless of their economic contributions. Contrasting Fascist behavior is their counterpart on the left of the spectrum, **Communist/Command states**.

These governments pledge to **protect the rights of all** and promise to work towards the creation of an **ideal, completely classless existence**. This was to be "[a life where individuals will live] from each according to their ability and each according to their need" in the words of Karl Marx. In reality these states historically employed **violence, slave labor** and other **inhumane** acts to **sanctify the interest of the state**, thereby creating a **class system**, the very thing that many of them were united against.

The primary goal of every dictatorship is to obtain and maintain political control at any and all cost. The difference between a dictatorship and a totalitarian state is totalitarian states have leaders with total control over society and simple dictatorships may or may not have power this far-reaching.

In democracies, there are numerous factors that have helped to shape the structure and scope of power found within the government. **Geography, cultural/ethnic makeup, resource distribution/availability and history** all influence the formation of democracies throughout the world. For many nations, the presence of a **ruling colonial power** has also exerted influence over how democracies have emerged.

The types of political/economic policies being implemented greatly affect the positioning of democracies on the spectrum. Those states working towards developing **egalitarian societies** are placed centre or centre left on the spectrum. Governments attempting to limit their input into the system to promote **individual freedom or self-reliance** are placed centre or centre right on the spectrum.

Note: It is essential to remember that the spectrum is elastic and as governmental policies change so too should the position of the nations listed.

You are responsible for a large amount of content in this section of the course. **Theoretical** elements, such as the **Branches, Levels and Types of Government, Types of Democracies** and **Elements of Democracies,** are studied. You will also review different governing rules, laws and regulations as they apply to the following in democracies and dictatorships: political parties, voters, systems of representation, interest groups, media, dissemination of information, limits on dissent, and the role of the military, police and civil service.

Note: This section correlates strongly with material learned during grade ten and eleven so do not hesitate to use your knowledge of **Canadian Government** or the **French Revolution.**

Related Questions: 20, 21, 22, 24, 25, 26, 68, 69, 70, 75, 76, 77, 78, 86

Democracies and the Political Spectrum

Please refer to Appendix A - Image #4

The primary focus of this section is on **Democracy**. You should know the various types of democracies: **direct, indirect/representative, proportional, republican/ presidential, and parliamentary/constitutional monarchies**. This information leads you to an examination of key features of democracies. This builds on concepts studied during Social Studies 20, which examined the roots of democracy.

On the graph in Appendix A you see that democratic nations fall at every point on the spectrum with the exception of the two extremes. It is significant that both ends of the spectrum attempt to *exploit democratic elements to obtain and maintain power,* but **quickly eliminate** any and all **"checks"** to their power. Further, the breadth of space occupied by democratic nations indicates a huge difference in attitude and practice by governments relative to economic activity. To effectively answer multiple choice questions based upon the positioning of government on the spectrum you may find it useful to focus on the following elements of democracy:

- Representation By Population
- Media or Free Press
- Periodic Elections
- Multiple Parties
- Lobby/Pressure or Special Interest Groups
- Power of the Purse
- Separation of Powers
- Rule of Law

You should also be aware of how these elements strengthen and weaken democratic practice and tradition. It is powerful to recognize how democracies and dictatorships alike have overstepped the freedoms permitted in democracies to ensure public order or welfare during times of crisis. Prime Minister Trudeau, during the FLQ Crisis, exemplified this as he turned to democratic practice to improve society after the end of the issue rather than to the progression towards dictatorial power entrenchment as evidenced by leaders such as Hitler and Mussolini.

As a critical thinker, you should review the process of dissenting in democratic states, protection of individual rights and freedoms and how governments "truly" become accountable. When writing multiple choices and essay exams, this is critical in the formation and use of arguments for and against democracies and, therefore, dictatorships.

ARGUMENTS FOR DEMOCRACY

- It is part of one's natural rights to have freedom and, therefore, one has the right to self-government.

- It is not a desirable goal to have absolute freedom because this does not protect one's freedom from those who are stronger.
- The interests of all citizens (general will) is considered in government decisions.
- The level of government intervention in the lives of citizens is limited.
- Democracy fosters general contentment in society.
- Democracy values self-help and self-reliance.
- Democracy provides citizens with the initiative to make changes.
- Democracy is based upon a collection of ideas and works to allow individuals to decide what works best for them and, therefore, promotes critical thinking and reflection.
- Citizens, not government, have 'true power' to control change.

ARGUMENTS AGAINST DEMOCRACY

- Democracy is based upon a collection of ideas and works to allow individuals to decide what works best for them and, therefore, promotes critical thinking and reflection.
- Citizens, not government, have 'true power' to control change.
- Those who are elected often gain the position for reasons other than merit.
- Democracy is seen as weak and slow and is, therefore, a poor choice to deal with big and/or pressing problems.
- A level of corruption takes place because representatives must support the party before attending to the needs of their constituents, i.e., Cabinet and Party Solidarity.

Related Questions: 31, 62, 63, 67, 79, 83, 87

Dictatorships and the Political Spectrum

Please refer to Appendix A - Image #5

In this section of the analysis a variety of dictatorships are examined. Classification of dictatorial rule comes in many forms: rule by one (**autocracy**), rule by an elite (**oligarchy**), **traditional absolute monarchy**, **nationalist one-party states**, **military dictatorships** or **ideological one-party states**.

Sometimes general classification takes the form of **majority tyranny** or **minority tyranny** when the **percentage of population** that is being represented by the state plays a role in the dictatorial decisions. More often than not a dictatorship may be referred to by two or more names, as it will meet the criteria of several classifications.

You should focus on **both the similarities and differences** between democracies and dictatorships. Often dictatorships have risen out of political instability in democracies. In many cases the dictator utilizes techniques like **periodic elections** and other **forms of citizen participation** to legitimize their leadership giving the illusion of democracy. However, these tools often lead to the **identification and elimination of dissenters**, **control over the media** and a gradual diminishing of leadership accountability.

Dictators see the loss of citizen control as essential for several reasons. Firstly, many of them justify their regime on the basis of **Machiavellian principles**, the **Great Man Theory** or via the **Crisis Theory**. These give dictators the illusion of being superior to the rest of society. Therefore, they do not wish to allow someone other than their choice to assume the leadership in the future.

To accomplish this dictators often employ **violence**, **force**, **indoctrination**, **scapegoating** and **tokenism**. Individuals do not matter in most dictatorships —it is only the **will of the state or the majority** that has meaning. These governments work to ensure this by normalizing the "**individual**" into the state; both are part of something far greater and should not be questioned. Dictators work towards the evolution of the

totalitarian dictatorship where the ruler/elite has total control over society.

Although dictatorships often reduce or eliminate many individual rights and freedoms, they do have supporters. Some of the key arguments used to support dictatorial rule are as follows:

- It is easier to administer to the country because one does not have to wait for consensus.
- The country is **completely unified** in its service of the state and, therefore, more effective.
- There is a strong sense of **nationalism**.
- Interest groups and opposition do not delay legislation and the 'inevitable'.
- The state is able to provide economic, social, political, and international **stability**.
- Dictatorships value the '**welfare of the state**', while promoting the growth of '**most individuals**' in society.
- Dictatorial rule provides citizens with the **initiative and direction** to make changes.

Despite these perceived benefits, strong cases against dictatorial rule often are made based upon one or more of the following arguments:

- There is no independent freedom of thought or action.
- Leaders believe that they have the only correct view of knowledge for all subjects and disciplines.
- Dictatorships do not allow for opposition to present alternative points of view.
- Dictatorships often arise during periods of economic, social and political instability and, at a later times are very difficult for citizens to remove.
- Dictatorships employ **violence** and **thought-control** to subjugate society.
- There is little or no room for '**citizen based**' political reform or change.
- Dictatorships exploit specific elements in society to obtain wealth or to facilitate a political end.

Related Questions: 23, 55, 57, 58, 80, 81, 85, 88, 91

Scarcity

Please refer to Appendix A - Image #6

Economics is nothing more than the study of how the question of **scarcity** is attended to in different economic systems. Scarcity results from a society's **unlimited consumer demand** and **limited resources** with which to meet this demand. Put simply, every economic system must create a system to determine "**what to produce,**" "**how to or how much to produce,**" and "**who gets what**." These three basic economic questions drive all economic activity in every nation.

Nations on the far right of the spectrum believe that the forces of the market will do the best job in determining appropriate answers to the three basic questions. In nations that move to the centre, government intervenes in the economy to promote a basic standard of living for citizens. The farther left one goes, the greater the level of guaranteed citizen support. This ultimately translates into economic decisions being made increasingly by the state and not the individual.

It is important to recognize that the spectrum is elastic and as policy changes are implemented to offset limitless economic forces, a nation's position is adjusted on the spectrum. Despite this, the spectrum provides a theoretical framework that allows you to postulate if government involvement will increase, decrease or remain the same based upon multiple choice scenarios that are presented.

Related Questions: 44, 99, 100, 101, 102

Private Enterprise

Please refer to Appendix A - Image #7

This component of learning requires the student to be familiar with terminology, terminology and more terminology. Private enterprise may be referred to by a variety of names: **capitalism**, **free**

enterprise, **market economy**, **price system** or **laissez-faire economics**. You will regularly have multiple choice questions with options that are disguised by these terms.

The "**Father of Capitalism**" was Adam Smith. He outlined capitalist theory in his 1776 ***An Inquiry into the Nature and Wealth of Nations*** or ***The Wealth of Nations***. He identified four key elements for the successful operation of a market economy.

1. **Profit Motive:** Smith believed that individuals work best when working for their own self-interest. He further advocated that individuals work primarily for extrinsic rewards and need to have something to show for their labour. This 'greed' or desire for reward would excite individual curiosity and help business to become more efficient as 'vested interest' took hold and people strove to do and make more out of their scarce resources.
2. **Private Property:** Smith argued that 'simple' reward was not enough. Individuals required the opportunity to select or determine their own reward. Individuals who were willing to sacrifice more or to take higher risks should have access to greater rewards. This would ultimately be manifested in one's property, which would not only impact quality of life and standard of living, but would also help to stratify society and give individuals an incentive to work more efficiently in the hope of social mobility.
3. **Competition:** Smith believed that in order to ensure that individuals and corporations were continually striving for increased efficiency, competitive markets were required. Competition would ensure that only the best producers/entrepreneurs would survive and, that to do so, they would have to promote maximum utility at all times.
4. **Laissez-faire:** According to Smith, the government did not have the resources to stay abreast of ever-changing consumer demand. Their interference would lead to regulation, which would result in waste as producers worked to facilitate the government's goals rather than doing what was best for the market. This was not acceptable because of scarcity. Smith further wrote that minimal government intervention would be required to ensure basic individual rights and freedoms or to provide supports such as infrastructure.

Smith's views revolved around the ability of every aspect of the market—land, labor and capital—to be continuously transferred to maximize efficiency. This was a great theory, but challenges have arisen in the complex market, as jobs require higher levels of education or greater degrees of specialization and are, therefore, not quickly transferable.

Related Questions: 9, 10, 13, 43, 92, 93, 94, 98

Public Enterprise

Please refer to Appendix A - Image #8

The Public Enterprise system is also commonly referred to as the **command system** or **communism**. This system values equality above all else. Many argue this is a wonderful system that attempts to create an environment where everyone flourishes because the individual is free to develop oneself fully since the individual does not have to worry about meeting life's basic necessities.

The "**Father of Communism**" was Karl Marx. He outlined communist theory in his **1848** work ***The Communist Manifesto*** and ***Das Kapital (*1867)**. Both of these prescribed a lifestyle that would revolve around the well-being of the community. Marx believed that it was not possible for anyone to truly "own" property—life was such that resources/property merely changed hands with time and utility. Therefore, property was actually owned by everyone or the "**collective**". Property distribution should revolve around the idea "from each according to their ability, to each according to their need", which means produce as much as your abilities permit and take only what you need to live.

Central to Marxist philosophy with its ever present undertone of sharing was the idea of cooperation. Marx did not believe that the divisive nature of capitalism would ever promote social stability. Through strong central planning and resource distribution, individuals would prosper most because resources could be distributed equitably and, therefore, people could live free of divisive greed. Ultimately the system would be above major market fluctuations because individual desire/demand would not matter as the state placed itself first. To achieve these ends, Marx advocated a "**Proletarian Revolution**". Marx saw capitalists, specifically the **Bourgeoisie,** as greedy, self-serving individuals who would never voluntarily turn over the ***means of production*** to the collective. If persuasion was not enough, Marx said that force should be employed. This was the only way to initiate the type of change that would allow an egalitarian solution to arise.

The **Revolution by the Proletariat** was to be the **first stage** in Marx's **four-stage revolution**. In the **second stage**, **Dictatorship by the Proletariat** (Government of the Working Class) would be established, which would work to restructure society around egalitarian principles. This stage would also see the elimination of capitalism throughout the world. As order was restored and society evolved, the **third stage** would be introduced. The was the **Withering of the State** where government slowly died away. The **fourth and final stage** would then be present—the **Classless Society**. In this manner Marx was hoping to end the cycle described in **dialectic** teachings and to create a classless society that operated in peace and harmony.

Related Questions: 95, 97

Topic A: Political and Economic Systems - Theme II: Political and Economic Systems in Practice

Please refer to Appendix A - Image #9

Practice Versus Theory

This area is one of the most difficult concepts because one is expected to take an ambiguous concept and apply it to an ever-changing and very abstract potential life situation. In reality, the nations in the centre of the spectrum are much closer together. Government policy has evolved to compensate or adapt to new consumer, ecological, technological, and political trends.

Out of the devastation of World War I and World War II came the writings of **John Maynard Keynes** and eventually the "**welfare state**". This has evolved into **democratic socialist states** and **mixed economies** throughout the world. These economic changes were often complemented by subsequent alterations to basic political philosophy as governments and entire governing systems tried to change quickly in order to remain in public favor.

In the United States and Canada, women gained **suffrage** or **franchise rights** and efforts were slowly made to extend **basic human rights and freedoms** to minorities or exploited groups in society. By the end of the twentieth century, democracies throughout the world were supposed to be moving closer to the ideals found in basic democratic theory, but little change had happened to the basic wealth distribution throughout the world. This continues to pose issues for governments who must deal with the fluctuations in the business cycle.

At the extremes of the spectrum, nations have been equally adaptive of theoretical underpinnings to serve the interests of the government. Communist states, such as Stalin's, often employed slave/forced labor to meet production quotas. Individuals were forced to suffer as the state bought military supplies to fight in the Cold War. Marx's four stage revolution did not progress much into stage two, "**Dictatorship of the Proletariat**", and this was fraught with corruption and self-serving political leaders.

These Fascist nations at the far right of the spectrum did marginally better. In theory, Fascist states were to revolve around capitalist principles in the economy, this did not happen as both Mussolini and Hitler developed **corporate states** to ensure that production targets supported political goals. The last pre-World War II Fascist state was quietly disbanded after the death of Franco of Spain in 1975.

Related Questions: 12, 14, 53, 54, 61

Adapting to Change

The ability to adapt to change has been of fundamental importance to the survival of every political and economic philosophy studied during this course. It is imperative that special attention be paid to the impact that socio-economic forces and the desire to obtain/maintain power have had on the evolution of political and economic systems.

One of the most powerful forces for change has been the fluctuating business cycle. Since the end of the nineteenth century, major powers, such as Britain and France, have been gradually moving from the **mercantilist system** toward **capitalism**. This has resulted in political autonomy for many states throughout the world, in particular (in Africa and Asia.) It often has occurred when they lacked the infrastructure or social stability to adopt change without violence.

Adding to these difficulties was the gradual linking together of economies into the global market. The development of the American industrial machine and the debilitating impact of the **Great Depression** contributed to socio-political instability in the United States and around the world. In the US itself, communist and Fascist platforms became attractive to many unemployed or poor during the 1930's because **Hoover's** right-leaning government believed that the market would correct itself. This forced **President Roosevelt** to introduce the **New Deal**, which was **Keynes' Demand Side Theory** in operation. With the New Deal, the US took a dramatic step towards the left of the political and economic spectrum.

Other states around the world did not fare as well as the US. In the **former Soviet Union**, by the end of World War I it was clear that Bolshevism would establish government policy. Mother Russia had little or no industrial development and was primarily agrarian. The social climate repressed social, economic and political change and the starving millions wanted hope for a better future. This interjection of small-scale private enterprise into the communist economy was a huge departure from **Marxist ideals** in practice but it still fit within theory by maintaining state ownership of the land.

In the late 1970's, **China** had some equally difficult choices to make and this time China become the model for the Soviets to follow. **Deng Xioping** introduced a similar element of "small scale" private enterprise into Chinese communism. He realized that incentives were required to produce more and that China's growing population was going to require more. Ultimately, his struggle and ensuing policies may have laid a foundation for Soviet leader **Gorbachev's Glasnost** and **Perestroika.** These political and economic reforms helped Russia move from **communism** in the **1980's into a market economy** in the **1990's** and until the present day. Over about 70 years, this would be an incredible journey for any economic system.

Communism has not been the only system to undergo substantial change. Both the **Canadian** and **Swedish** nations have floated between left and right leaning policies to compensate for socio-economic changes. At the end of the 1970's both nations were '**riding high**'. Their populations were happy due to the elevated level of social support provided by their governments. **Sweden** was openly touted as a **utopia** where anything was possible. By the late 1980's, changes in international business trends left the unproductive Swedes out in the cold.

In **Canada** more of the same was true. By the late 1980's, this state had huge debt issues and **Canada's** entry into '**freer trade**' with the **United States** (and later **Mexico**) meant that unproductive or more costly Canadian jobs would go 'south'. Unemployment rates started to climb. The result of this was a return to **supply-side fiscal and monetary** practices in the 1990's. **Privatization** took the place of **nationalization** in both **Canada** and **Sweden**. The **welfare state** had been systematically trimmed back, as **Reganomics** became a plausible first step for politicians concerned primarily with national and provincial debt.

Related Questions: 4, 5, 6, 7, 8, 15, 16, 19, 36, 37, 42, 45, 46, 47, 50, 82, 96, 103, 105

Political Leadership in Democracies and Dictatorships

Please refer to Appendix A - Image #10

There have been a variety of campaign slogans and platforms utilized by leaders to obtain power. Some of these have been very open while others have tended to focus on internal or party politics. It is clear that leaders in both democracies and dictatorships come to power when they are able to embody what a substantial portion of society wishes. From this perspective, you should tackle this element of the course, analyzing the position of nations on the political spectrum and what this means relative to political practice.

There are basically only two forms of government. The *first* is **democracies,** which is found in many different nations and with an equally diverse number of variations. You should know and understand the different applications of theoretical elements such as the "**separation of powers**" in **Canada** and the **United States**. One begins to recognize strengths and weaknesses for both systems and to critically form arguments essential to do well in higher-level multiple-choice questions or in essay writing.

The *second* form of government is **dictatorship**. This also comes with an array of national choices, but tends to be situated at the fringes of the political and economic spectrum. Dictatorships are placed into these slots because of their adherence to extreme economic practice and the desire to see holistic, profound and immediate change in their societies. This often translates to some form of violent revolution to gain power **or** plays upon social, political and economic turmoil to make policies more appealing to voters.

In either case, the effect is the same. The ruler comes to power and immediately works to eliminate political opposition while altering government structures and the constitution to strengthen their position. They become "**above the law**" and eventually work to have totalitarian control over every institution in society. This is why Hitler's elite very closely parallels Stalin's elite. This perspective is essential when critiquing theory and practice in this course.

With time and study, you are expected to recognize that often governing practices in democracies may cross over into those more readily employed in dictatorships to enable political leaders or parties to remain in power. President Nixon was involved in the Watergate scandal in the 1970's in an attempt to remain in power and Hitler/Stalin had secret police that kept track of "**subversives**". In both cases, the leaders believed that their actions were justified because they had the "**best interests of society at heart**". This raises some important questions about power, corruption and political change.

Related Questions: 18, 32, 33, 34, 35, 38, 51, 52, 56, 59, 61, 66, 71, 2, 74

The Role of the Individual in Society

Please refer to Appendix A - Image #10

The ***individual*** is ***essential to every political and economic system***. The difficulty is that citizens in most dictatorships lack the political power to protect their rights or to peacefully bring about change. In democracies, citizens have rights but the voice of those with power or influence may be used to persuade government to move away from what would be "best" for the collective.

If one examines basic rights in both democracies and dictatorships, patterns begin to emerge. In nations such as **Canada, Sweden** and the **United States**, individuals have used their democratic rights and responsibilities to work towards the **egalitarian application** of freedoms and benefits to all citizens. Sometimes this has taken time, but one can trace the gains being made towards **universality**. The protection of minority rights has risen to new levels over the twentieth century and more people than ever have access to the necessities and prerequisites of a basic standard of living. Democracies in developed nations appear to have found some balance to promote some peace and stability.

In other nations, the journey has evolved more slowly or has been impacted greatly by socio-economic shifts or influential political leadership. In the 1920's **Germany**, for instance, went from being a democratic state that protected the rights and freedoms of all to a full-fledged dictatorship with *virtually no guaranteed rights* for citizens under Hitler in the 1930's. Each time that neo-conservative supporters renew their call for "**days of past glory**", citizens the world over have been forced to account for their rights and freedoms and to decide if the political and economic gains being offered outweigh the potential for abuse.

The same has been true for citizens of nations with leaders who have flirted with both democracy and dictatorship before settling on one or the other. Ultimately, Castro's Cuba is a state where no citizen has all their basic rights and freedoms protected. The same was to be true of the Utopia promised after Lenin's Bolshevik revolution or Mao's seizure of power in 1949. In all three cases, citizens often lost their lives or were repeatedly denied basic rights and freedoms to while the power of the dictator was strengthened.

Related Questions: 4, 11, 39, 40, 60, 64, 65

Issues and Challenges to Political and Economic Beliefs and Practices

The most dynamic element of this course comes from this section. It contains numerous issues that range from basic human rights to philosophical and ideological innovations. It also raises the issue of justice and what it means to be a member of a society within the "**global**" context.

Related Question: 41

1. Citizens who support the principles of collectivism would accept a government policy that

A. privatized public services to encourage greater efficiency

B. instituted a guaranteed annual income to create economic equity

C. reduced the national debt through massive cuts to the civil service

D. reduced the child tax credit for citizens earning a certain income level

Source: January 2000

2. A supporter of a market-oriented economic system would favour controlling government deficits by

A. increasing personal income taxes

B. increasing corporate income taxes

C. reducing the level of social services

D. regulating the profits made by entrepreneurs

Source: January 2000

CHALLENGER QUESTION **DIFFICULTY: 54.2**

3. Which of the following statements illustrates a similarity between both the ideology and the practice of communism and fascism?

   A. We require the resolve and strength of an elite cadre of party faithful to achieve ultimate victory.

   B. We shall accomplish our common economic goals through the organization of a corporate state.

   C. We shall march together to overthrow the forces of Bolshevism that dominate our world.

   D. We require the unwavering support of the working class to crush the bourgeois menace in society.

Source: January 2000

CHALLENGER QUESTION **DIFFICULTY: 46.8**

4. The ideology of which of the following leaders is **inconsistent** with the action given?

	Leader	Ideology	Action
A.	Ronald Reagan	Supply-side economics	Deregulating the airline industry
B.	Margaret Thatcher	Neoconservatism	Privatizing utilities
C.	Franklin D. Roosevelt	Keynesian economics	Creating jobs in the Tennessee Valley
D.	Brian Mulroney	Global competitiveness	Raising protective tariffs

Source: January 2000

Use the following information to answer questions 5 to 7.

The Economic Problem
Runaway inflation is destroying the purchasing power of consumers

Possible Government Responses

I. Raise income taxes to slow the rate of economic growth

II. Allow the problem to correct itself through the normal fluctuations in the business cycle

III. Implement strict wage and price controls

IV. Lower interest rates to provide consumers with easier access to credit

5. Which of the possible government responses reflects a "market-oriented" approach to the problem?

   A. Response I

   B. Response II

   C. Response III

   D. Response IV

Source: January 2000

6. Which of the possible government responses would **most likely** intensify the problem of rising inflation?

   A. Response I

   B. Response II

   C. Response III

   D. Response IV

Source: January 2000

7. A Keynesian economist would criticize Response II because it would

A. absolve government from any responsibility in resolving economic problems

B. accelerate the amount of investment capital available to entrepreneurs

C. tend to shift purchasing power away from the wealthy to the poor

D. reduce the role of the individual in economic decision making

Source: January 2000

Use the following information to answer question 8.

Public services have, to use the economist's word, a strong redistributional effect. And this effect is strongly in favor of those with lower incomes.

—John Kenneth Galbraith
—from *Socialism: Opposing Viewpoints Series*

8. Supporters of the ideas reflected in the quotation would **most likely** accept which of the following actions taken by a government of a mixed economy?

A. Tax concessions to private corporations

B. Privatization of publicly owned businesses

C. Monetary incentives to profitable businesses

D. Transfer payments to economically depressed areas

Source: January 2000

9. According to Free Enterprise Theory, which of the following economic developments should **result** from the other three?

A. Increased profits

B. Decreased production costs

C. Decreased benefits to labour

D. Increased consumer demand

Source: January 2000

Use the following comment to answer question 10.

The operation of the market system relies on the motivation that results from increased corporate profits. Profits represent a return on capital and a reward for initiative. Profits not only generate dividends, but they also provide funds for much needed research and development. These funds contribute to the capital needed for future investments.

CHALLENGER QUESTION **DIFFICULTY: 52.5**

10. Given the point of view expressed above, this writer would support legislation designed to

A. limit foreign investment and takeovers

B. eliminate capital gains tax loopholes

C. nationalize unprofitable businesses

D. deregulate key industrial sectors

Source: January 2000

Use the following excerpt to answer questions 11 to 13.

There can only be one sane enlightened decision. It is a thousand times better to have a free market plan under fair and equitable laws democratically passed and enforced. First, we avoid the terrific burden entailed in maintaining a vast bureaucracy; and, second, the free market operates with a maximum of freedom and a minimum of force. The free market rewards efficiency and economy; it punishes laziness and waste, and thus provides incentive, the very mainspring of human progress.

— from *Vital Speeches of the Day, 1950*

11. A democratic socialist, in responding to the opinion expressed in this excerpt, would agree with the speaker's contention that

A. economic freedoms are valid goals, but would claim that the free market system makes little provision for the disadvantaged

B. expanding bureaucracies are valid pursuits, but would claim that personal incentive is the only "mainspring of human progress"

C. fair and equitable laws are valid goals, but would claim that some force is needed to motivate workers

D. efficiency and progress are valid pursuits, but would object to the high taxes demanded by a free market

Source: January 2000

12. Which of the following economic systems has traditionally been based on the ideas expressed by the speaker?

A. The British welfare state

B. The Canadian mixed economy

C. The Swedish democratic socialist state

D. The American capitalist-oriented economy

Source: January 2000

13. Given the point of view expressed in the excerpt, the speaker would likely agree that

A. government intervention in an economy is necessary under certain circumstances

B. free market economies must be regulated by key civil servants in a bureaucracy

C. individual initiative is essential for the successful functioning of an economy

D. public enterprise economies encourage the growth of investment capital

Source: January 2000

CHALLENGER QUESTION **DIFFICULTY: 59.4**

14. During the Second World War, the governments of Canada and the United States demonstrated that full employment could be generated by

A. restricting the power of trade unions

B. protectionist trade practices among Allied nations

C. privatizing major government-owned industries and departments

D. government planning and control within capitalist economic institutions

Source: January 2000

Use the following excerpt to answer questions 15 and 16.

Scandinavia may become "the most left-wing region of Europe," given the results of recent parliamentary elections in two countries and other political trends, according to *The Economist*. Shortly after the Swedes returned the Social Democrats to power in September 1994, the Danes voted to retain the coalition government, which will depend on left-wing parties. These votes reflect "a deep-seated determination to maintain the welfare state even at the cost of tax rates that would be unsustainable in other Western countries." But the resurgent welfare state is not out of danger in Sweden. Swedish voters can "expect at least another few years of austerity" as the new Prime Minister must present a convincing plan to reduce the huge budget deficit.

— from *World Press Review, 1994*

15. Given twentieth century political tradition in Scandinavia, is the information given in this excerpt surprising?

A. Yes, because most Scandinavian countries are very different from each other in their ideological beliefs.

B. Yes, because most Scandinavian countries have traditionally followed the principles of free enterprise.

C. No, because most Scandinavian countries have traditionally upheld the principles of the welfare state.

D. No, because most Scandinavian countries have followed ideological paths similar to those of Eastern Europe during the Cold War.

Source: January 2000

CHALLENGER QUESTION DIFFICULTY: 59.7

16. The excerpt implies that during the mid-1990s, Scandinavian governments and many other Western governments shared the problem of

A. unfavourable currency exchange rates

B. unstable minority and coalition governments

C. increased fiscal spending with decreasing revenues

D. increased labour unrest and inflationary wage increases

Source: January 2000

CHALLENGER QUESTION DIFFICULTY: 51.6

17. Which of the following ideologies is **most closely associated** with the idea that economic systems are based on exploitation and involve a constant class struggle?

A. Fascism

B. Marxism

C. Anarchism

D. Capitalism

Source: January 2000

18. The social and economic conditions that developed in Russia immediately following the collapse of communism **most closely resembled** those found in

A. Fascist Italy during the late 1920s

B. Weimar Germany during the early 1920s

C. Nazi Germany during the late 1930s

D. Imperial Japan during the mid-1940s

Source: January 2000

19. By the mid-1990s, many democratic governments led by political parties of the right were reducing budgetary deficits by

A. increasing the general rate of taxation

B. nationalizing major business enterprises

C. decreasing government spending on services

D. supporting wage increases to end labour disputes

Source: January 2000

Use the following chart to answer question 20.

The Year Various Countries Adopted Universal Suffrage	
Year	**Country**
By 1840	Australia, Canada, New Zealand, United States
By 1871	France, German Empire
By 1874	Switzerland
By 1884	Great Britain
By 1890	Spain
By 1893	Belgium
By 1896	Netherlands
By 1898	Norway
By 1912	Italy

— from *Approaches to Political and Economic Systems*

CHALLENGER QUESTION DIFFICULTY: 51.3

20. The title of the chart is inaccurate and misleading because it suggests that

A. universal suffrage means giving the right to vote to all adult men but not women

B. universal suffrage refers to the right to vote but not the right to periodic elections

C. 18-year-olds could vote in elections

D. voting was done by secret ballot

Source: January 2000

Use the following sources to answer questions 21 and 22.

Source I

"Caucus, dismiss!"

(Prime Minister Trudeau is represented by the figure on the right in this 1970s cartoon.)

Source II
Leadership in the party has to be established first with party members, and in the parliamentary caucus. … I used to encourage the frankest kind of questioning, however critical. That helped, I hope, to establish and maintain a leader's position with his parliamentary colleagues.
— former Prime Minister Lester B. Pearson
— both sources from *Challenge of Democracy*

21. Taken together, which of the following issues related to the Canadian parliamentary system do the sources raise?

A. To what extent should a prime minister be allowed to choose cabinet members?

B. To what extent should a majority government ignore opposition demands?

C. To what extent should parliamentary debates be dominated by ideological differences?

D. To what extent should party discipline be imposed on elected government members?

Source: January 2000

22. Within the context of representative democracy, the Source I cartoonist reveals a problem related to the

A. freedom of association extended to dissident minorities

B. domination of parliament by indecisive leaders and elected officials

C. inability of elected members to express the will of their constituents

D. lack of freedom by opposition members to express views different from those of the majority government

Source: January 2000

Use the following diagram to answer questions 23 and 24.

Allocation of Power and Authority

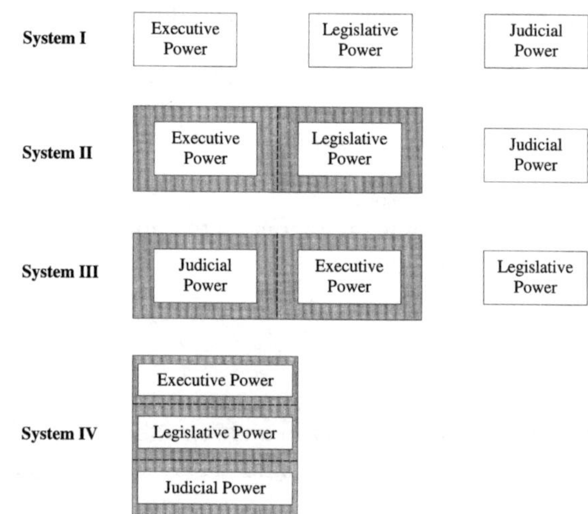

23. A totalitarian system is **best** illustrated by

A. System I

B. System II

C. System III

D. System IV

Source: January 2000

CHALLENGER QUESTION **DIFFICULTY: 59.6**

24. The system of checks and balances outlined in the American Constitution is represented by

A. System I

B. System II

C. System III

D. System IV

Source: January 2000

Use the following information to answer questions 25 and 26.

Statements Concerning the German System of Government

I. Germany is governed by a national government and 16 state governments.

II. The chancellor and cabinet are elected members of the *Bundestag*, the lower house of Germany's national legislative branch.

III. Three to five elected representatives from each state assembly are appointed by the state government to sit in the *Bundesrat*, the upper house of the national legislative branch.

IV. One-half of the members of the *Bundestag* are elected under a system of proportional representation.

25. Which statement **best** explains why German elections frequently result in coalition governments?

A. Statement I **B.** Statement II

C. Statement III **(D)** Statement IV

Source: January 2000

CHALLENGER QUESTION DIFFICULTY: 50.6

26. Which of the following significant changes would occur in the Canadian system of government if it were reformed to be more similar to that of the German system?

(A) The Senate would include members from the provincial legislatures.

B. The political stability of the national government would be increased.

C. The powers of the prime minister and cabinet would be greatly increased.

D. The prime minister and cabinet would be primarily responsible to the Senate.

Source: January 2000

Use the following information to answer questions 27 to 30.

The characteristics listed below are associated with different positions on the political spectrum.

Position I

- is willing to change the existing system through progressive reforms
- respects the concept of law and attempts to change it through legal means
- remains optimistic about people's ability to solve their own problems
- maintains faith in human reason and basic equality

Position II

- supports policies that will return society to a previous time, condition, or value system
- proposes retrogressive change to the status quo
- advocates any means (violent or non-violent) of restoring society to a former state
- reflects extreme dissatisfaction with existing institutions

Position III

- favours immediate and fundamental progressive change to the existing system
- indicates varying degrees of dissatisfaction with the status quo
- argues that revolution (violent or non-violent) is the only way to effect change in society
- challenges the basic values and institutions underlying society

Position IV

- supports the status quo and advocates very little change to existing systems
- places great emphasis on the importance of maintaining "traditional" values and institutions
- has an essentially cautious view of people's ability to reason and solve problems
- favours less control over individuals and opposes governmental remedies to society's inequities

— adapted from *Political Ideologies*

27. The **opposite** ends of the political spectrum are represented by

A. positions I and II

B. positions II and III

C. positions I and IV

D. positions III and IV

Source: January 2000

28. On the political spectrum, Position III would be located

A. on the extreme left

B. somewhat left of centre

C. somewhat right of centre

D. on the extreme right

Source: January 2000

29. *In 1994 in the United States, the Republican Party gained a majority in both houses of Congress, while President Clinton, a Democrat, held the chief executive office.*

A political consequence of this development was conflict between those holding the beliefs of

A. positions I and II

B. positions I and IV

C. positions II and III

D. positions II and IV

Source: January 2000

30. Position II reflects the characteristics usually associated with individuals labelled as

A. liberal

B. radical

C. reactionary

D. conservative

Source: January 2000

31. Political dissidents in democracies are generally free to express their views as long as they

A. refrain from endangering public order and stability

B. conform to the ideas held by the political leadership

C. propose ideas that are acceptable to the general population

D. advocate political moderation rather than political extremism

Source: January 2000

32. *Abuse of governmental authority is limited by the fact that all citizens enjoy a number of basic "civil rights" or "individual liberties."*

Proof that Adolf Hitler did *not* support this assertion is best revealed by his

A. enforcement of the Nuremberg Laws

B. use of massive propaganda campaigns and rallies

C. recruitment of the unemployed into military service

D. disregard for provisions of the Treaty of Versailles

Source: January 2000

33. The dictatorial technique of directing popular discontent to the advantage of the ruling elite is **best** illustrated by

A. Stalin's purges of political opponents

B. Hitler's persecution of "non-Aryan" races

C. Mussolini's March on Rome to gain widespread support

D. Lenin's support for mutinous troops during the Bolshevik Revolution

Source: January 2000

34. Which of the following explanations for Hitler's rise to power in Weimar Germany is historically **incorrect**?

A. Hitler cleverly used the dissatisfaction of war veterans as a subject for many of his speeches.

B. Hitler accepted President Hindenburg's request to assume the position of chancellor.

C. Hitler successfully appealed to various communist interests for support.

D. Hitler skillfully manipulated existing democratic structures for his own benefit.

Source: January 2000

CHALLENGER QUESTION DIFFICULTY: 46.5

35. In arguing against a parliamentary system, supporters of the American congressional system would insist that the advantage of the congressional system is that it

A. allows for the greater separation of powers

B. gives the strongest mandate to the executive branch

C. allows for the greatest responsiveness to special interest groups

D. gives citizens the strongest guarantee for their political participation

Source: January 2000

36. A government that promotes individualism over collectivism would favour

A. a steeply progressive income-tax structure

B. the bailout of failing private businesses

C. the nationalization of major industries

D. a deregulated business sector

Source: June 2000

CHALLENGER QUESTION DIFFICULTY: 59.7

37. For a Canadian who supports democratic capitalism, the **most acceptable** solution to the problem of growing government debt would be to

A. support extensive interventionist government fiscal and monetary policies

B. reduce federal government transfers to provincial governments in the areas of social welfare and health care

C. increase spending on job creation programs and increase progressive income taxes

D. adopt demand-side principles as guiding economic approaches

Source: June 2000

CHALLENGER QUESTION DIFFICULTY: 49.4

38. Which of the following statements is true of both Nazi Germany and the Soviet Union during the 1930s?

A. A state decree eliminated class differences.

B. The means of production were state-owned.

C. Citizenship was granted on the basis of race.

D. State planners set quotas for the production of many goods.

Source: June 2000

39. Concerns about growing income disparity and about increasing materialism in many Western economies are expressed by supporters of

A. laissez-faire economies

B. free enterprise economies

C. public enterprise economies

D. private enterprise economies

Source: June 2000

CHALLENGER QUESTION **DIFFICULTY: 58.7**

40. Contemporary neoconservative thinkers dispute the modern liberal belief that

A. economic growth is desirable and enhances quality of life

B. political authority should emerge through democratic processes

C. the civil rights and liberties of citizens should be guaranteed constitutionally

D. the state must play a greater role in ensuring economic security for all citizens

Source: June 2000

Use the following diagram to answer question 41.

Car Companies and Related Corporations

The following table lists three major car companies and some of the corporations in which they have an ownership interest or with which they have manufacturing or marketing agreements.

	Daimler Chrysler	Ford	GM
North America	Dodge Chrysler Plymouth Jeep	Lincoln Ford Mercury	Chevrolet Pontiac Oldsmobile Buick Cadillac Saturn
Europe	Mercedes-Benz Smart	Aston Martin Jaguar Volvo	Saab Opel Vauxhall
Asia / Australia	Mitsubishi	Mazda	Holden

41. This table effectively illustrates the

A. regulation of cartels by governments

B. international mobility of investment capital

C. high level of competition among automakers

D. similarity in car design across national borders

Source: June 2000

CHALLENGER QUESTION **DIFFICULTY: 57.3**

42. Critics of supply-side economics contend that the main reason that the "trickle-down" effect fails to spur business expansion is because

A. consumers are reluctant to commit themselves to credit expenditures

B. governments are willing to increase their current deficits or long-term debt

C. corporations often use increased profits to reward shareholders rather than to increase production

D. large labour unions often demand higher wages and more comprehensive benefits for their members

Source: June 2000

Use the following excerpt to answer question 43.

...free market capitalism is fundamentally *dependent* on the entrepreneur and his [or her] spirit of enterprise. That is to say on people such as *you*, as a democratic capitalist economy grows from the ground up, not the reverse. A pretty fair synopsis of why the entrepreneur is so important is that: Capitalism, in its essence, is a system of continuous change brought about by the innovative activities of entrepreneurs. Such characteristics of capitalism as interest, credit, profit and business cycles arise because of innovation. The entrepreneur is the central figure that distinguishes capitalism ... because he [or she] is the engine of innovative thought.

— from *Vital Speeches of the Day*

43. Which of the following government policies would be accepted by a person with this point of view?

A. Implementation of severe restrictions on foreign investment

B. Passage of laws to prevent the formation of monopolies

C. Centralized planning of economic production

D. Nationalization of key industries

Source: June 2000

Use the following excerpt to answer question 44.

Let welfare be a private concern. Let it be promoted by individuals and families, by churches, private hospitals, religious service organizations, community charities and other institutions that have been established for this purpose. If the objection is raised that private institutions lack sufficient funds, let us remember that every penny the federal government does not appropriate for welfare is potentially available for private use—and without the overhead charge for processing the money through the federal bureaucracy.
—from *Socialism: Opposing Viewpoints*

44. A proponent of this view would **most likely** support

A. an increase in pension and other social assistance benefits

B. the nationalization of industries as a means of job creation

C. a decrease in taxation rates for individuals and corporations

D. the discontinuation of gambling revenues to support charities

Source: June 2000

Use the following comments to answer questions 45 to 47.

I. The most generous [Canadian] tax breaks are those which allow corporations to defer their taxes. In theory the taxes saved this way are to be paid at a later date but they rarely are.

II. Ottawa has always justified tax breaks [for corporations] as a means of stimulating investment. …The federal auditor general reported that in 1985 corporations avoided paying $35 billion in taxes.

III. What is the difference [in Canada] between subsidies to corporations and welfare or unemployment payments? The former, largely hidden from public scrutiny, is called providing investment incentives, and the latter is called socialism.

IV. The Consumers' Association of Canada has noted a disturbing change in direction toward taxing money spent rather than money earned.
— from *The Edmonton Journal*

CHALLENGER QUESTION **DIFFICULTY: 56.3**

45. Which two comments directly suggest that the Canadian federal government was following a "Reaganomics" supply-side style of economic policy at the time these comments were made?

A. Comments I and II

B. Comments I and IV

C. Comments II and III

D. Comments III and IV

Source: June 2000

46. To support the trend noted in Comment IV, the Consumers' Association of Canada could point to

A. increases in corporate taxes

B. increases in personal income taxes

C. the introduction of a capital gains tax

D. the introduction of the goods and services tax

Source: June 2000

47. On the issue of reducing current federal and provincial government debt, the author of these comments would argue that

A. tax reform has become secondary to increased social spending

B. corporate taxation as a source of revenue has been largely ignored

C. the cost of social spending is lowering corporate investment revenue

D. the burden of reducing the national debt is borne primarily by corporations

Source: June 2000

Use the following economic spectrum to answer question 48.

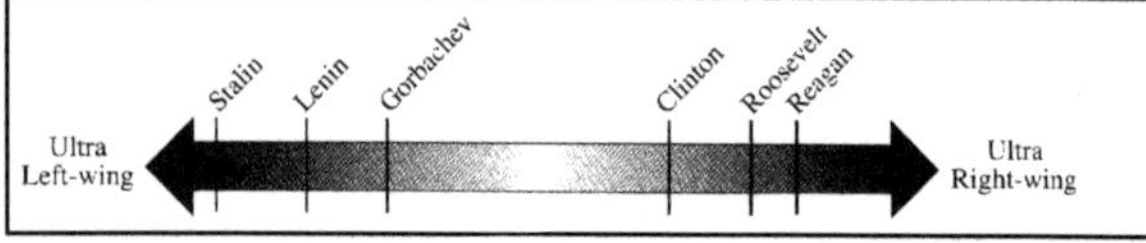

CHALLENGER QUESTION **DIFFICULTY: 57.0**

48. If it is assumed that the economic decisions made by leaders reveal their underlying beliefs, which leader has been **incorrectly** placed on the spectrum above?

A. Lenin **B.** Stalin

C. Reagan **D.** Roosevelt

Source: June 2000

49. Which philosophical assumption of Marxism would be considered naive and unrealistic by supporters of a laissez-faire economic philosophy?

A. A capitalist economic system will foster rapid economic expansion.

B. Economics play a major part in the evolution of human development.

C. Human creativity and productivity will flourish in a collectivist society.

D. Market competition leads to the growth of powerful businesses.

Source: June 2000

Use the following quotation to answer question 50.

> Perestroika is a revolution. A decisive acceleration of the socio-economic and cultural development of Soviet society which involves radical changes on the way to a qualitatively new state…
>
> — Mikhail Gorbachev
> — from *The Struggle for Democracy*

50. The "radical changes" to which Gorbachev alludes can **best** be categorized as the

A. increased use of government planning

B. privatization of all essential industries

C. increased emphasis on new technology

D. introduction of market-oriented reforms

Source: June 2000

In question 51, an economic policy is given, and in question 52, a political policy is given.

For each question, identify the policy as being

A. acceptable to Adolf Hitler but unacceptable to Josef Stalin

B. unacceptable to Adolf Hitler but acceptable to Josef Stalin

C. acceptable to both Adolf Hitler and Josef Stalin

D. unacceptable to both Adolf Hitler and Josef Stalin

51. Key industries are nationalized and agriculture is collectivized.

Source: June 2000

52. A multi-party elected legislature is constitutionally empowered to rule by decree for a limited period of time.

Source: June 2000

Use the following diagram to answer questions 53 and 54.

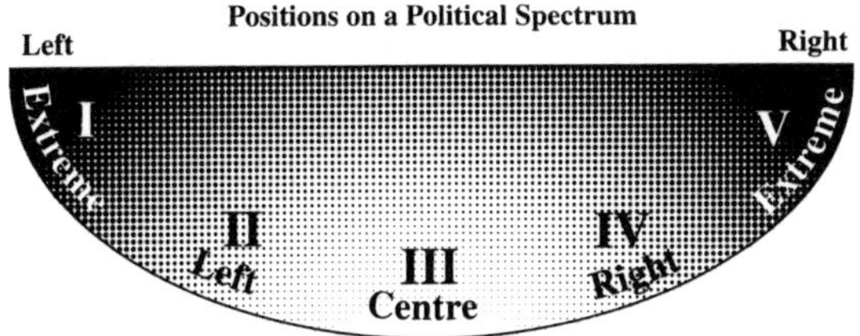

CHALLENGER QUESTION	DIFFICULTY: 58.9

53. In Canada, the ideology of democratic socialism is **most clearly** associated with

A. Position I

B. Position II

C. Position III

D. Position IV

Source: June 2000

54. An individual who believes in the strict preservation of "traditional family values," individualism, and the unfettered operation of the marketplace is associated with

A. positions I and II

B. positions II and III

C. positions III and IV

D. positions IV and V

Source: June 2000

CHALLENGER QUESTION	DIFFICULTY: 40.8

55. *The citizenry awoke to discover that they had only exchanged one form of dictatorship for another.*

This description **best** applies to which of the following historical situations?

A. Fascist Italy (1944) → Italy (1945)

B. Occupied Poland (1944) → Liberated Poland (1945)

C. Nazi Germany (1945) → West Germany (1946)

D. Imperial Japan (1945) → Liberated Japan (1946)

Source: June 2000

56. Adolf Hitler claimed that in terms of popular support, the Nazi party ultimately achieved political power through a

A. workers' revolution

B. democratic process

C. military junta

D. coup d'état

Source: June 2000

Use the following excerpt to answer questions 57 and 58.

Questions Taken from Nazi-Era Textbooks
The construction of a lunatic asylum costs 6 million RM [Reich marks]. How many houses at 15 000 RM each could have been built for that amount?

A modern night bomber can carry 1 800 incendiaries [bombs]. How long (in kilometres) is the path along which it can distribute these bombs if it drops a bomb every second at a speed of 250 km per hour? How far apart are the craters from one another? … How many fires are caused if 1/3 of the bombs hit their targets and of these 1/3 ignite?

— from *History at Source, Nazi Germany 1933–1945*

57. The intent of these questions, taken from school textbooks published in Germany during the 1930s, was to

A. strengthen student awareness of external enemies

B. encourage student acceptance of economic efficiency

C. desensitize students to the ideas of euthanasia and militarism

D. familiarize students with mathematics questions of a military nature

Source: June 2000

58. Which technique for maintaining power is illustrated by the excerpt?

A. The use of indoctrination

B. The use of force and terror

C. The glorification of the past

D. The identification of scapegoats

Source: June 2000

Use the following excerpts to answer questions 59 and 60.

What is Democracy?
Every citizen, it is said, must have equality, and therefore in a democracy the poor have more power than the rich, because there are more of them, and the will of the majority is supreme.

— Aristotle (384–322 B.C.)

The aim of government should be the greatest possible happiness of the greatest number; in a word, the common good is the right aim of government, and the proper task of a lawmaker is to discover regulations designed to bring about the greatest good to the greatest number of human beings.

— Jeremy Bentham (1748–1832)

We hold these truths to be self-evident, That all men are created equal, that they are endowed by their creator with certain inalienable rights; that among these are life, liberty, and the pursuit of happiness; that to secure these rights governments are instituted among men, deriving their just powers from the consent of the governed; that whenever any form of government becomes destructive of these ends, it is the right of the people to alter or to abolish it, and to institute new government, laying its foundation on such principles and organizing its powers in such form, as to them shall seem most likely to effect their safety and happiness.

— Thomas Jefferson (1743–1826)

…For democracy cannot be made to work in a country where a large part of the citizens are by status condemned to a perpetual state of domination, economic or otherwise. Essentially, a true democracy must permit the periodic transformation of political minorities into majorities.

— Pierre Elliott Trudeau (1919–2000)
— from *Inside World Politics*

CHALLENGER QUESTION	DIFFICULTY: 37.0

59. Which speaker issues an implied caution about the nature of democracy with which an elitist would agree?

A. Aristotle

B. Bentham

C. Trudeau

D. Jefferson

Source: June 2000

60. Individuals who support the point of view expressed by Jeremy Bentham would be alarmed by the current trend toward

A. developing government services and agencies

B. dismantling the liberal democratic welfare state

C. downplaying the superiority of a free enterprise system

D. devising new sources of tax revenue for government spending

Source: June 2000

CHALLENGER QUESTION	DIFFICULTY: 55.9

61. Which of the following alternatives identifies the distribution of Canada's four main political parties in 1999 along the traditional left-wing–right-wing political spectrum?

	Left-Wing Parties	Moderate Parties	Right-Wing Parties
A.	New Democrats	Liberal, Progressive Conservative	Reform
B.	Reform	Progressive Conservative, New Democrats	Liberal
C.	Progressive Conservative	Reform, Liberal	New Democrats
D.	Liberal	New Democrats, Reform	Progressive Conservative

Source: June 2000

Use the following diagram to answer question 62.

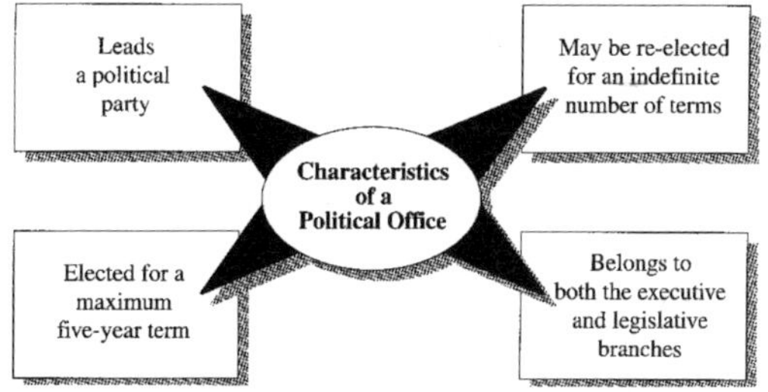

62. These characteristics describe a political office within the government of

A. Germany during the late 1930s

B. the Soviet Union during the early 1950s

C. the United States during the early 1980s

D. Canada during the late 1990s

Source: June 2000

CHALLENGER QUESTION **DIFFICULTY: 57.4**

63. Members of the House of Commons in Canada and the House of Representatives in the United States share the characteristic of being

A. chosen for fixed five-year terms

B. appointed by the executive branch

C. representative of the prevailing ideology

D. selected on the basis of representation by population

Source: June 2000

Use the following comments to answer questions 64 and 65.

Comments about Modern Government	
Government is so large that it is overwhelming us—its agencies and bureaucrats meddle in our lives.	Take away the heartbeat of the self-reliant individual and you take away the heartbeat of the nation.

CHALLENGER QUESTION **DIFFICULTY: 48.2**

64. These comments reflect a political position that is currently **most popular** with

A. liberal activists

B. socialist thinkers

C. conservative voters

D. left-wing economists

Source: June 2000

65. Which of the following comments is **most consistent** with those expressed above?

A. Rights to private property must be upheld.

B. Government must guarantee employment opportunities.

C. Every individual is entitled to a minimum standard of living.

D. Government is responsible for providing affordable health care to all.

Source: June 2000

CHALLENGER QUESTION **DIFFICULTY: 52.8**

66. Americans familiar with their nation's system of separation of powers may be surprised to discover that in Canada

A. members of parliament debate and vote on proposed laws

B. Supreme Court justices are appointed rather than elected to office

C. the prime minister is both a sitting and voting member of parliament

D. cabinet ministers discuss government policies with the prime minister

Source: June 2000

67. *True democrats have a suspicion that they may not always be right.*

This claim is related to which of the following statements?

A. Democracies function most effectively with an established two-party system.

B. Democracies rely on the free expression of alternative views and policies.

C. Democracies rely on the constitutional guarantee of periodic elections.

D. Democracies are hierarchical, with voters below and leaders at the top.

Source: June 2000

Use the following excerpt to answer questions 68 to 70.

> First-past-the-post is so named because a candidate has only to win more votes than his nearest competitor to take the riding, not an absolute majority of the votes cast. The most direct consequence is to exaggerate the majority enjoyed by the winning party, often grotesquely: with less than half the popular vote, governments have been formed with nearly all of the seats.
>
> — from *The Globe and Mail*

68. For a democratic theorist, the **most serious** weakness of the system described in the excerpt is its tendency to

A. deny interest groups an opportunity to influence decisions

B. undermine the authority of the executive branch

C. reduce the effectiveness of the governing party

D. distort the expressed will of the electorate

Source: June 2000

CHALLENGER QUESTION **DIFFICULTY: 46.4**

69. Those who defend the "first-past-the-post" system described in the excerpt claim that such a system ultimately preserves government

A. stability

B. frugalness

C. accountability

D. responsiveness

Source: June 2000

70. A practical solution to the problem described in the excerpt would be to adopt

A. direct democracy

B. representative democracy

C. proportional representation

D. representation by population

Source: June 2000

71. An important reason for the emergence of right-wing extremism in many parts of Europe during the 1920s and 1930s was the

A. popularity of emerging pacifist ideologies

B. decline in the attraction of nationalist fervour

C. fear of revolutionary communist movements

D. popular support for legitimate democratic institutions

Source: January 2001

CHALLENGER QUESTION **DIFFICULTY: 59.2**

72. During the last days of the Weimar Republic, the factor that **most strongly** contributed to the abandonment of democracy and any pretense of upholding parliamentary traditions was the

A. passage of the Enabling Act

B. election of Nazi deputies to the *Reichstag*

C. election of von Hindenburg to the presidency

D. plotting of the Night of the Long Knives

Source: January 2001

CHALLENGER QUESTION	DIFFICULTY: 57.4

73. Ideologically and historically, Marxists have envisioned a society that is based on the principles of

A. industrial growth and elitism

B. equality and humanitarianism

C. collectivization and nationalism

D. centralization and authoritarianism

Source: January 2001

Use the following statements to answer question 74.

Statement I
In the election campaigns of the early 1930s, Adolf Hitler promoted himself as an ardent supporter of state nationalization of key industries.

Statement II
When he became Soviet leader, Nikita Khrushchev denounced Josef Stalin as a despot who used excessive force to maintain his control over the Soviet Union.

CHALLENGER QUESTION	DIFFICULTY: 47.7

74. Which of the following observations regarding the above statements is accurate?

A. Both statements are true.

B. Both statements are false.

C. Statement I is true and Statement II is false.

D. Statement I is false and Statement II is true.

Source: January 2001

Use the following sources to answer questions 75 to 78.

Source I
1993 Federal Election Results

Political Party	Percentage of vote	Percentage of seats	Number of seats (295)	Number of seats if proportional representation
Liberal	41.3%	60.3%	178	122
New Democrat	6.9%	3.0%	9	20
Progressive Conservative	16.0%	0.7%	2	47
Reform	18.7%	17.6%	52	55
Bloc Québécois	13.5%	18.3%	54	40
Other	3.6%	0	0	10

— from *Citizenship and Democracy*

Source II
One of the world's oldest democracies, Canada is constantly on call to send its political experts to monitor elections in far-off fledgling nations, teaching newcomers how to climb the ropes of voting fairness. Yet back home in election after election, the most noticeable feature of the results is the unrepresentative nature of the governments created and how cheated some citizens feel.

Since 1921, with two exceptions, in 1958 and 1984, a sizable majority of Canadians have voted in federal elections *against* the political party which won enough seats in Canada's winner take-all electoral system to seize the reins of power

— from *The Edmonton Journal, April 1997*

Source III
Proportional representation almost guarantees a minority government, one that doesn't have enough seats to ensure it can pass its budgets and legislation. Or it leads to a coalition government; two parties teamed in a forced—and often shaky—alliance gain a majority in the legislature....
— from *The Edmonton Journal, April 1997*

75. According to the results shown in Source I, if the electoral system had been based on a system of proportional representation, which of the following political parties would have **benefitted most**?

A. Liberal

B. Reform

C. New Democrat

D. Progressive Conservative

Source: January 2001

76. Comments in Source II suggest that Canada's current electoral system

A. creates a political stalemate in parliament

B. creates disenchantment among some voters

C. provides a practical model for fledgling democracies

D. provides political extremists with excessive political influence

Source: January 2001

77. According to Source III, a system of proportional representation may result in a government that

A. promotes cabinet solidarity

B. produces unpopular legislation

C. experiences political instability

D. abandons democratic processes

Source: January 2001

78. Which of the following statements provides an accurate description of a relationship among the sources?

A. Information in Source I supports the contentions made in Source II.

B. Information in Source I contradicts the contentions made in Source II.

C. Source III provides evidence to support the ideas in Source II.

D. The three sources provide contradictory information.

Source: January 2001

79. In Canada, the **main** reason that the interests of local constituencies are not always addressed in the House of Commons is that

A. political agendas of opposition parties gain too much media attention

B. provincial politics have begun to dominate the national scene

C. representation by population does not adequately ensure voter equality

D. elected representatives often adhere to party discipline when deciding issues

Source: January 2001

Use the following information to answer questions 80 to 82.

Some Characteristics of Authoritarian Systems

1. The state owns and controls the means of production.
2. Mass communications and education are tightly controlled by the government.
3. National identity is considered to be of crucial importance. The state often promotes racist and discriminatory policies.
4. The stated goal of the system is to promote equality among all persons.
5. Opposition parties and dissent are not tolerated.
6. Economic decision making is centralized in many instances but decentralized in others.
7. A philosopher developed the statement of ideological principles that underlie the system.
8. Courts, police, and the military are subject to direct political control.

80. In practice, which characteristics have been common to both fascist and communist systems?

A. Characteristics 1, 6, and 8

B. Characteristics 2, 5, and 8

C. Characteristics 1, 2, and 7

D. Characteristics 4, 6, and 7

Source: January 2001

81. Which characteristics are unique to communist systems of government?

A. Characteristics 1, 4. and 7

B. Characteristics 3, 6, and 7

C. Characteristics 2, 5, and 7

D. Characteristics 1. 4, and 6

Source: January 2001

CHALLENGER QUESTION **DIFFICULTY: 54.0**

82. Reforms undertaken during the 1990s by the government of the People's Republic of China include

A. adopting characteristic 4 and devaluing the importance of characteristics 5 and 6

B. adopting characteristic 1 and devaluing the importance of characteristics 3 and 5

C. adopting characteristic 7 and devaluing the importance of characteristics 5 and 8

D. adopting characteristic 6 and devaluing the importance of characteristics 1 and 4

Source: January 2001

Use the following information to answer questions 83 and 84.

Some Characteristics of Parliamentary Democracies

1. An official and loyal opposition
2. Power of the purse
3. A bicameral legislative body
4. Responsible government
5. A public record of government debates
6. Question period
7. Judicial review

83. This list of characteristics indicates that in a parliamentary democracy, the **greatest** emphasis is placed on the

A. need for consensus and unanimity of opinion and action

B. effective and efficient operation of government bureaucracies

C. accountability of those representatives elected to serve in the government

D. centralization of political power in the hands of competent, elected leaders

Source: January 2001

84. The institutions of the "House of Lords," the "Senate," and the "House of Commons," within British and Canadian contexts, are related specifically to

A. Characteristic 1

B. Characteristic 3

C. Characteristic 4

D. Characteristic 7

Source: January 2001

Use the following excerpt to answer question 85.

In every move they made, the Nazis showed the advantage enjoyed by a political movement which refused to be bound by any rules, which … did everything it could to exploit surprise and shock, and [which] instead of repudiating violence in the streets employed… it to break down opposition.

— from *History of the 20th Century*

CHALLENGER QUESTION **DIFFICULTY: 58.9**

85. The technique of dictatorship illustrated in the excerpt is that of

A. using or threatening force and coercion

B. directing popular discontent at scapegoats

C. controlling participation at political rallies

D. using party propaganda and indoctrination

Source: January 2001

Use the following cartoon to answer question 86.

—from *Best Editorial Cartoons of the Year*, 1996 Edition

CHALLENGER QUESTION **DIFFICULTY: 35.7**

86. The point of view revealed by this American cartoon is critical of the

A. lack of consistent and principled leadership

B. undue influence exercised by elite lobby groups

C. unwillingness of government to respond to citizen concerns

D. electorate's inability to understand and participate in decision making

Source: January 2001

CHALLENGER QUESTION **DIFFICULTY: 58.1**

87. The development of representative democracy as an alternative to direct democracy challenges the underlying principle that

A. all minorities have political influence equal to that of the majority

B. universal suffrage is necessary in order to achieve responsible government

C. the primary purpose of government is to ensure the security of its citizens

D. all citizens have the same opportunity to participate in political decision making

Source: January 2001

CHALLENGER QUESTION	DIFFICULTY: 50.9

88. Which of the following characteristics of many democratic elections is **most likely** to be present in an election staged by a non-democratic regime?

A. Independent verification of election results

B. Free competition between rival political parties

C. Widely held electoral franchise with high voter-turnout

D. Freedom of speech and assembly during the campaign

Source: January 2001

Use the following commentary to answer questions 89 and 90.

The political left was built on a view of human life that was partly true, but not wholly true. People, the left argued, are not inherently unequal or inherently bad, but society can make them so.

By changing society, the left believed, you could remove the chains that oppress and distort people's lives. By redistributing income, you could create fairness. By improving the conditions of life, you could improve people. Crime, violence, greed, human misery-these were byproducts of an exploitive society. Humanize society and you humanize life.
— from The *Edmonton Journal, August 1994*

89. Which of the following generalizations reflects the characteristics attributed to the "political left" described in the commentary?

A. The left encourages individuals to take greater responsibility for their actions.

B. The left believes that people's lives have been overwhelmed by the intrusiveness of government.

C. The left advocates government involvement in people's lives to minimize social and economic disparity.

D. The left supports cautious changes to existing political traditions and institutions of government.

Source: January 2001

90. To right-wing thinkers, the methods that left-wing politicians would use to achieve the goal of "improving the conditions of life" are unacceptable because they involve

A. economically penalizing those who have demonstrated self-reliance and initiative

B. the creation of an economic system dominated by a small group of corporations

C. the elimination of state-financed programs that offer economic security for all

D. restricting the freedom of workers to organize and bargain collectively

Source: January 2001

91. *To stay in power, it is in the nature of authoritarian regimes to use the "stick" as well as to offer the "carrot."*

The "stick" in this statement **most likely** represents the dictatorial technique of

A. indoctrinating through media propaganda

B. using a secret police force to eliminate dissent

C. controlling and determining an election outcome

D. establishing paramilitary organizations to employ the jobless

Source: January 2001

Use the following sources to answer questions 92 to 95.

Source I

[Milton Friedman said], "(there) is one and only one social responsibility of business–to use its resources and engage in activities designed to increase its profits so long as it stays within the rules of the game. . . [and] engages in open and free competition, without deception and fraud. . . Few trends could so thoroughly undermine the very foundations of our free society as the acceptance by corporate officials of a social responsibility other than to make as much money for their stockholders as possible.". . . Friedman. . . [was] absolutely right, given the nature of the impersonal . . . institution that [human beings] created, the corporation.

Source II

The corporation is the dominant and dominating institution of our time. Governments identify growth and development with commercial corporations and shower them with subsidies, tax privileges, appropriate labor legislation and market protection to attract a commitment and investment.

...The primary objective of the corporate invader is to increase its own wealth and assets, not the level of community income. When communities enter into arrangements with corporations, it is important that the nature of this institution be clearly understood.

Source III

—all sources from *Policy Options*

92. The authors of sources I and II agree that corporations

A. have social responsibilities

B. contribute to community wealth

C. exist exclusively to make a profit

D. receive favourable government treatment

Source: January 2001

93. Friedman's point of view, as expressed in Source I, is based **primarily** on the assumption that

A. corporations will be law abiding and will follow the rules of fair competition

B. government intervention in any economy is often unplanned and haphazard

C. corporate decision making is often influenced by the needs of the community

D. governments will provide directly for the social-welfare needs of the community

Source: January 2001

94. The cartoon emphasizes the idea, cited in one of the other two sources, that

A. there is "one and only one social responsibility of business" (Source I)

B. "Governments identify growth and development with commercial corporations" (Source II)

C. the corporation has "the nature of the impersonal… institution that [human beings] created" (Source I)

D. "it is important that the nature of this institution be clearly understood" (Source II)

Source: January 2001

95. A social democrat would **strongly disagree** with

A. the Source III cartoonist's depiction of the Mega-Corp

B. the Source II idea that communities and corporations cooperate

C. Friedman's belief that corporations should make profits

D. Friedman's contention that corporations have only one social responsibility

Source: January 2001

CHALLENGER QUESTION **DIFFICULTY: 53.3**

96. Lenin's New Economic Policy and Gorbachev's perestroika were both characterized by

A. an increase in consumer goods production through greater central planning

B. a restructuring of government institutions to allow greater freedom of speech

C. a departure from dogmatic economic policy in order to increase individual initiative

D. an attempt to consolidate Communist party control in order to ensure political stability

Source: January 2001

Use the following information to answer questions 97 and 98.

Proposed Measures for Economic Reform

I. Sell all public utilities to private interests
II. Create a flat tax on all income levels
III. Establish a means test to determine old-age pension eligibility
IV. Apply user fees to all publicly funded medical services
V. Introduce lower consumption taxes on luxury goods and services

CHALLENGER QUESTION **DIFFICULTY: 53.8**

97. Which measure directly challenges the economic principle of the "universality" of social programs?

A. Measure I

B. Measure II

C. Measure III

D. Measure V

Source: January 2001

98. Given the context established by the above list, which of the following measures could be appropriately added?

A. Nationalize the transportation industry

B. Contract public services to entrepreneurs

C. Guarantee the continuation of transfer payments

D. Provide the education system with greater public funding

Source: January 2001

Use the following sources to answer questions 99 and 100.

Source I
Exchange Rates Over a Three-Year Period

Nov	£1=20 marks
May	£1=74 marks
Nov	£1=313 marks
Jan	£1=959 marks
June	£1=1,500 marks
Dec	£1=50,000 marks
Jan	£1=89,860 marks
Nov	£1=21,000,000,000 marks
Dec	£1=22,300,000,000 marks

Source II
The height to which prices have climbed may be shown by the fact that wholesale prices have risen on the average to 5,967 times the peacetime level, those of foodstuffs to 4,902 times, and those for industrial products to 7,958 times.

— both sources from *The 20th Century*

99. A government faced with the hyperinflation described in the sources could attempt to **reverse** the situation by taking steps to

A. increase workers' wages

B. decrease the money supply

C. encourage foreign borrowing

D. reduce consumer interest rates

Source: January 2001

100. Which of the following countries in the years given was affected disastrously by the economic problem shown in the sources?

A. The Soviet Union from 1942 to 1945

B. Great Britain from 1936 to 1939

C. The United States from 1930 to 1933

D. Germany from 1922 to 1925

Source: January 2001

101. Laissez-faire capitalists oppose the formation of unions **primarily** because they believe that unions

A. distort the labour market and increase the cost of production

B. encourage governments to spend lavishly on public works

C. fail to act in the long-term interests of their members

D. restrict consumer confidence and spending

Source: January 2001

Use the following excerpt from a newspaper commentary to answer question 102.

As subsidies work their way through the economy, they distort individual and corporate behaviour. Given an opportunity, individuals will accept a government subsidy and substitute leisure for work. Subsidies also distort corporate and government behaviour. To offset the subsidies, companies and institutions are forced to pay higher wages, driving up costs and rendering local economic activity less competitive.

— from *The Globe and Mail*

CHALLENGER QUESTION **DIFFICULTY: 58.0**

102. The writer of the above excerpt expresses beliefs that are **most consistent** with those of

A. Karl Marx

B. Adam Smith

C. John Stuart Mill

D. John Maynard Keynes

Source: January 2001

CHALLENGER QUESTION **DIFFICULTY: 54.2**

103. From the perspective of private enterprise economists, the **most effective** approach that western democratic governments use to eliminate deficit budgeting is to

A. place a surtax on corporate profits

B. introduce programs of fiscal restraint

C. nationalize high technology industries

D. increase public subsidies for low income earners

Source: January 2001

CHALLENGER QUESTION **DIFFICULTY: 54.1**

104. Which of the following theories is **correctly** matched with an example of its practice?

Theory **Practice**

A. Supply and demand → Wage and price controls

B. The invisible hand → Subsidies to small business

C. Interventionism → The New Deal

D. Demand-side economics → The Five Year Plans

Source: January 2001

105. During the 1980s and 1990s, individuals who criticized the implementation of "trickle-down," supply-side economic policies contended that such policies

A. caused income gaps to decrease significantly

B. created weaker competition within the corporate sector

C. challenged traditional free-market solutions to problems

D. concentrated more wealth in the hands of already wealthy citizens

Source: January 2001

Unit Test 1 – Political and Economic Systems

1. Which of the following statements would the majority of Canadians accept as being representative of their political beliefs?

   A. The goals of the political party in power should be promoted by all citizens.

   B. All eligible Canadians should be encouraged to vote in elections at all levels.

   C. Elected representatives should follow the ideology of their party on all issues.

   D. Canadians should encourage all other nations to adopt the parliamentary system of democracy.

2. In practice, the political and economic ideas of Adolf Hitler's Nazi Party were fundamentally in **opposition** to the idea of

   A. elitism

   B. equality

   C. nationalism

   D. free enterprise

3. Some historians have argued that Roosevelt's economic programs were less efficient and comprehensive than Hitler's because, ultimately, Roosevelt had to respect the

   A. advice of the political advisors in his cabinet

   B. importance of world trade in an interdependent world

   C. danger of high inflation accompanying government spending

   D. constitutional limitations imposed upon the executive branch

Use the following excerpt to answer question 4.

> Democratic freedom has failed in some countries because their people slept. It is commonplace for people who were fighting under the banner of tyranny to excuse themselves on two grounds: they didn't realize what was happening to their government, and there was nothing they could do but obey orders. Tyranny degrades both those who exercise it and those who allow it.
>
> — from *Royal Bank Newsletter*

4. The idea expressed in this excerpt could **most easily** be applied to citizens who allowed the

   A. Weimar Republic to become a fascist state

   B. Czarist empire to become a communist dictatorship

   C. former Yugoslavia to become a collection of quarrelling nationalities

   D. former Soviet Union to become a region of economic disintegration

Use the following to answer questions 5 to 7

Results of Canadian Federal Elections

Source I

1957 Monday, 10 June	Number of Seats	% of Seats	Votes (× 1 000)	% of Votes
Lib	105	39.6	2 702	40.9
PC	112	42.2	2 573	38.9
CCF	25	9.4	708	10.7
SC	19	7.2	440	6.7
Other	4	1.5	194	2.9
Total	265			
Eligible Voters		8 902	(× 1 000)	
Votes Cast		6 681		
Turnout (%)		74%		

Source II

1958 Monday, 31 March	Number of Seats	% of Seats	Votes (× 1 000)	% of Votes
Lib	49	18.5	2 448	33.6
PC	208	78.5	3 908	53.6
CCF	8	3.0	692	9.5
SC	0	–	188	2.6
Other	0	–	51	0.7
Total	265			
Eligible Voters		9 131	(× 1 000)	
Votes Cast		7 357		
Turnout (%)		79%		

Source III

1962 Monday, 18 June	Number of Seats	% of Seats	Votes (× 1 000)	% of Votes
Lib	100	37.7	2 847	37.0
PC	116	43.8	2 874	37.4
NDP / CCF	19	7.1	1 012	13.2
SC	30	11.3	899	11.7
Other	0	–	97	1.3
Total	265			
Eligible Voters		9 700	(× 1 000)	
Votes Cast		7 773		
Turnout (%)		79%		

Source IV

1963 Monday, 8 April	Number of Seats	% of Seats	Votes (× 1 000)	% of Votes
Lib	129	48.7	3 301	41.8
PC	95	35.8	2 561	32.4
NDP/ CCF	17	6.4	1 028	13.0
SC	24	9.1	945	12.0
Other	0	–	60	0.8
Total	265			
Eligible Voters		9 911	(× 1 000)	
Votes Cast		7 959		
Turnout (%)		79%		

— from *Canadian Political Facts 1945–1976*

5. The occurrence of four federal elections in the span of just six years, as shown by the sources, was the result of the

A. presence of voter apathy

B. inflexibility of cabinet solidarity

C. election of minority governments

D. ineffectiveness of government backbenchers

6. Which of the following conclusions can be supported by the sources?

   A. The size of the House of Commons was increased for the elections held in the 1960s.

   B. Voter turnouts in the 1960s were considerably higher than the voter turnouts in the 1950s.

   C. The platforms of the major political parties were far more conservative in the 1950s than in the 1960s.

   D. The election in 1958 was decisive, but the elections held in the 1960s failed to result in majority governments.

7. Despite the frequency of these elections, a supporter of parliamentary democracy would contend that the

   A. accountability of responsible government was preserved

   B. percentage of eligible voters who cast their votes increased

   C. effectiveness of a proportional representation system was upheld

   D. prime ministers elected succeeded in winning the support of the majority

8. Today in Europe and North America, many neo-Nazi groups are regarded by their opponents as politically

   A. liberal

   B. reactionary

   C. progressive

   D. conservative

9. One of the ways that fascist theory **differs** from communist theory is that in fascist theory,

   A. class differences are accepted

   B. economic planning is centralized

   C. agricultural production is collectivized

   D. state government is distinct from party structure

Use the following list of principles to answer questions 10 and 11.

Principles of Democratic Theory

A. Accountability
The belief that the cabinet is accountable to the legislature for its decisions and actions.

B. Constitutionalism
Limits are placed on the authority of government officials by the fundamental features a society sets out in its constitution.

C. Individualism
A main purpose of government is to foster the well-being of individuals and encourage the fulfillment of their potential.

D. Majority Rule
Decisions are based on majority rule, but minority rights are recognized and guaranteed, often in written human rights documents.

Choose the principle of democratic theory defined above that is ***most specifically*** *related to the statements about Canadian democracy given in questions 10 and 11.*

10. Responsible government has a long and well-grounded tradition within the Canadian parliamentary system.

11. The rule of law is firmly embedded in the Canadian political system as the basis for protection against abuses of power by government members.

12. Critics of proportional representation would argue that this type of representative democracy often leads to

    A. unstable minority or coalition governments

    B. undue influence by mainstream political parties

    C. domination of parliament by powerful lobby groups

    D. less cooperation in parliament among members of the same political party

Use the following information to answer questions 13 and 14.

Comparison of Principles Underlying the Traditional Liberal/Conservative Debate

	Liberals advocate:	Conservatives advocate:
A.	Progressive change	Maintaining the status quo
B.	Economic intervention	Minimal government intervention
C.	Redistribution of wealth	Protection of property rights
D.	Social and economic security	Individual self-reliance

*Choose the pair of underlying principles above that **best defines** the basis of the debate on the issues presented in questions 13 and 14.*

13. Should the Canadian government abolish the Senate?

14. Should the Canadian government legislate wage and price controls?

Use the following excerpt to answer question 15.

All the courts can do, really, is act like referees. They do not "make" laws. When they declare that a law violates the charter, they are saying that two laws created by politicians are in conflict.

If a law is so open to interpretation, the solution is to write a clearer law. And if a law isn't working well, write another.

— from *The Edmonton Journal, 1994*

15. According to this columnist, which of the following features would be **most necessary** to preserve democracy?

A. Minority rights

B. The secret ballot

C. Political competition

D. An independent judiciary

Use the following excerpt to answer questions 16 and 17.

The state parliaments were abolished and their functions taken over by the central government. ...all political parties, with the exception of the Nazis, were prohibited. Trade unions were banned, and strikes were made illegal, since... the interests of private individuals and [certain] sections of the population were sacrificed for the welfare of the whole community. The electorate was bombarded with Nazi propaganda ... and in the plebiscite of November 1933. ...96 per cent of the voters approved of all that he had done.

— from *International Affairs 1890–1939*

16. The **most** appropriate title for the excerpt would be

A. "Hitler Emphasizes Aryan Superiority"

B. "Hitler Enforces Indoctrination Program"

C. "Hitler Consolidates Nazi Power"

D. "Hitler Destroys Internal Party Opposition"

17. The 1933 results quoted above support which of the following generalizations?

A. An effective system of force and intimidation by storm troopers achieved national goals.

B. The techniques used by the Nazis were successful in creating the appearance of overwhelming support.

C. The German citizens believed that their military success depended on strong party support.

D. A strong national party achieved the goals of the German people more efficiently.

18. Provisions for the child tax credit, employment insurance, and old age security are **primarily** means by which the Canadian government

A. redistributes wealth

B. ensures individual rights

C. regulates monetary policy

D. encourages consumer purchasing

Use the following sources to answer question 19.

Source I

I am all in favour of **progress**... it's just **change** I can't stand.

Source II
In the last resort, the... position rests on the belief that in any society there are recognizably superior persons whose. ...inherited standards and values and position ought to be protected and who should have a greater influence on public affairs...

— from *The Political Spectrum: Opposing Viewpoints Series*

19. The comment made by the speaker in the cartoon and the content of Source II represent, respectively, moderate and extreme versions of

A. liberalism
B. radicalism
C. socialism
D. conservatism

20. Which of the following economic concepts is **correctly** matched with a corresponding action?

A. Deregulation → Creation of Crown corporations

B. Individualism resource → Nationalization of industries

C. Globalization → Formation of the WTO

D. Protectionism → Elimination of tariffs on Pacific Rim imports

Use the following economic goals to answer questions 21 and 22.

An individual believes in the following economic goals:

Goal I Government should spend more on social assistance
Goal II Government should raise corporate taxes
Goal III Government should nationalize certain key industries
Goal IV Government should provide universal health care
Goal V Government should subsidize failing businesses to preserve jobs

21. The goals above represent a point of view that would be **closest** to which position on the ideological spectrum below?

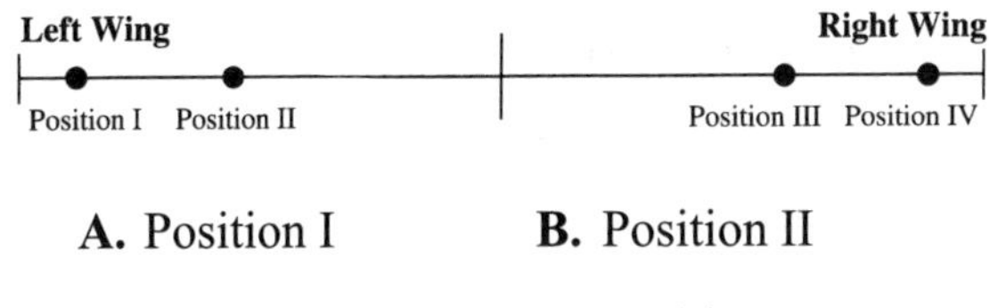

A. Position I
B. Position II
C. Position II
D. Position IV

22. Which two goals, if implemented, would have the **greatest** impact on the financial well-being of low income earners?

A. Goals I and II

B. Goals II and III

C. Goals I and IV

D. Goals IV and V

23. Individuals favouring the implementation of the five economic goals would be **most** opposed to the theories associated with

A. left-wing moderates

B. democratic socialists

C. Keynesian economists

D. laissez-faire capitalists

Use the following excerpt to answer questions 24 and 25.

> The expenditures of one group are the incomes of another. When one is without income because of unemployment, he or she is not the only loser; one's grocer and one's barber suffer too. If one is given unemployment insurance benefits, he or she is not the only person to gain. To spread the cost of the insurance more widely over those who benefit, the government uses its power to collect the money not only from employees but also from employers and the general public.
> — from *Political and Economic Systems*

24. This excerpt **best** illustrates the concept of

A. deficit financing

B. economic scarcity

C. supply and demand

D. economic interdependence

25. The main point made in this excerpt could **best** be used to support the affirmative position for which of the following debate resolutions?

A. Be it resolved that corporations should downsize to increase efficiency and productivity.

B. Be it resolved that governments should intervene in the economy to preserve economic security.

C. Be it resolved that corporations should move their capital and factories to nations with low labour costs.

D. Be it resolved that governments should lower their national deficits by cutting back on social programs.

26. A Canadian strongly committed to the principles of a model market economy would support a government policy that

A. provides subsidies to inefficient small businesses and corporations

B. decreases foreign investment through federal regulations

C. reduces transfer payments for social security programs

D. increases government contributions to pension plans

Use the following cartoon to answer questions 27 and 28.

— from *The Globe and Mail*

27. This cartoon depicts a point of view regarding the economic practice of

A. downsizing

B. deregulation

C. devaluation

D. decentralization

28. Supporters of supply-side economics would justify the action depicted in the cartoon by claiming that

A. business must help to fight government deficits

B. the social welfare net will take care of the unemployed

C. decreased overhead will create more investment capital for corporations

D. new technologies used by businesses today require more government regulation

Use the following information to answer question 29 to 31.

Government Actions in a Mixed Economy

1. Increase personal income taxes

2. Reduce social security benefits

3. Halt tax incentives to private industry

4. Raise the central bank interest rates for consumers

5. Decrease government transfer payment and equalization grants

29. These government actions are intended **primarily** to

A. revive a lagging economy

B. fight the effects of high inflation

C. increase foreign investment capital

D. raise the level of domestic production

30. Which actions would social democrats **most strongly** oppose?

A. Actions 1 and 3 **B.** Actions 3 and 4

C. Actions 2 and 5 **D.** Actions 4 and 5

31. A government taking these actions would risk creating an

A. overheated economy

B. increase in the national debt

C. overproduction of export goods

D. increase in recessionary pressures

32. Which of the following actions represents a government fiscal policy?

A. Minting a new coin

B. Regulating the stock market

C. Increasing the minimum wage

D. Decreasing the income tax rate

33. To maintain free competition in market-oriented economies, governments have traditionally established

A. higher tax rates for profitable corporations

B. regulations for the production of safe products

C. anti-combines legislation to prevent monopolies

D. quotas on the production of certain consumer goods

34. Prices in a model public enterprise economy are determined **primarily** by

A. labour costs

B. supply and demand

C. competitive markets

D. government priorities

35. Collectivism, in principle and practice, is a major component of ideologies founded on

A. socialism

B. liberalism

C. capitalism

D. conservatism

36. In a centrally planned economy, state regulation of supply has the **greatest** restrictive effect on

A. social control

B. class mobility

C. property ownership

D. consumer sovereignty

37. Adam Smith's description of the operation of the "invisible hand" applies to the economic practice of

A. redistributing wealth equally

B. implementing indicative planning

C. allocating resources by supply and demand

D. controlling inflation through taxes and interest rates

38. An underlying assumption about collectivism is that

A. individual consumer choice should be subordinate to the common good

B. a government should interfere as little as possible in the daily lives of its citizens

C. people function most effectively when they are responsible for satisfying their own needs

D. the economic success of a nation depends on the government's ability to adapt to fluctuations of the business cycle

Use the following quotation to answer question 39.

He opened the dam and hoped he could control the water flow. Instead, the dam burst.
— from *Twentieth Century Viewpoints*

39. This quotation is a metaphor for

A. Roosevelt's New Deal economic reforms

B. Reagan's "trickle-down" economic policies

C. Gorbachev's policies of glasnost and perestroika

D. Stalin's programs of industrialization and collectivization

Use the following cartoon to answer questions 40 and 41.

"It's people like you, Mr. Evers, constantly living beyond your means, getting hopelessly deeper and deeper in debt, to whom our industry owes eternal gratitude."
— from *Economics: A Search for Patterns*

40. The cartoonist is being **most critical** of the capitalist system's underlying

A. ethics

B. power

C. success

D. stability

41. To address the concern illustrated in the cartoon, a supporter of laissez-faire economic policies would propose

A. initiating a program by which the government assumes ownership of the banking institutions to provide low-interest loans

B. encouraging consumers to shop around for the best loan arrangements or to avoid borrowing

C. raising workers' wages to a level that would make borrowing largely unnecessary

D. enacting laws forbidding banks to grant loans to low wage earners

Use the following information to answer questions 42 and 43.

Economic Policies of the Soviet Union (from 1918 to 1988)

I. War Communism
II. The New Economic Policy
III. The Five Year Plans
IV. Perestroika

42. Which policies were associated with Lenin's leadership?

A. Policies I and II

B. Policies I and III

C. Policies II and III

D. Policies II and IV

43. These four policies indicate that, throughout its history, the Soviet Union's leadership

A. consistently supported the decentralization of control over the Soviet private enterprise economy

B. recognized the increasing importance of market forces within the Soviet private enterprise economy

C. recognized that adaptations needed to be made to the basic principles underlying the Soviet public enterprise economy

D. consistently supported the decentralization of decision making within the Soviet public enterprise economy

Use the following information to answer questions 44 to 47.

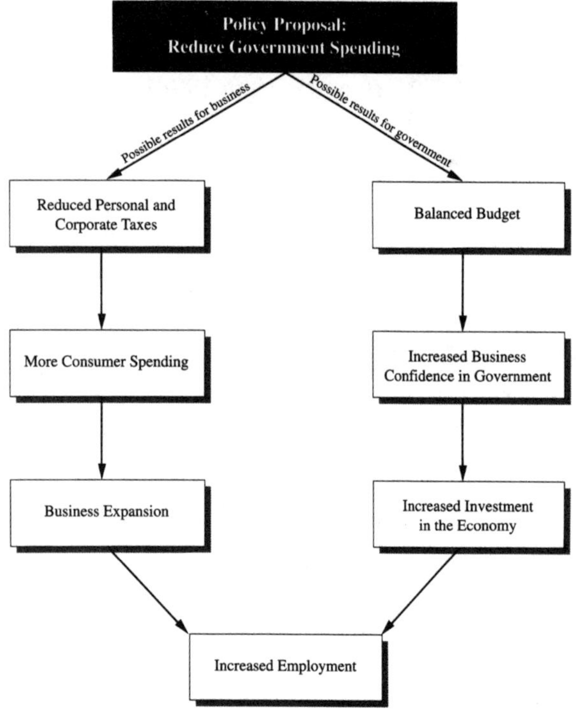

44. Canadian supporters of the economic theory underlying the policy proposal indicated in the diagram would also favour increased

A. spending on social programs

B. subsidies to large corporations

C. privatization of Crown corporations

D. transfer payments to poorer provinces

45. If this economic policy proposal were implemented, a democratic socialist would be **most** concerned that

A. social programs would be reduced

B. personal incomes would be greatly reduced

C. there would be a booming, out-of-control economy

D. new businesses would not receive government tax incentives

46. In theory, the economic policy proposal depicted in the diagram would be supported **most strongly** by

A. a government contractor

B. an old age pensioner

C. a factory worker

D. an entrepreneur

47. Which economic concern would **most likely** motivate the Canadian government to adopt this policy?

A. An increasing national debt

B. Shrinking revenue from taxation

C. A major increase in the unemployment rate

D. Large foreign takeovers of domestic industry

48. The economic theories of John Maynard Keynes were instrumental in the implementation of

A. Reagan's supply-side economics

B. Lenin's New Economic Policy

C. Mussolini's corporate state

D. Roosevelt's New Deal

Use the following graph to answer questions 49 and 50.

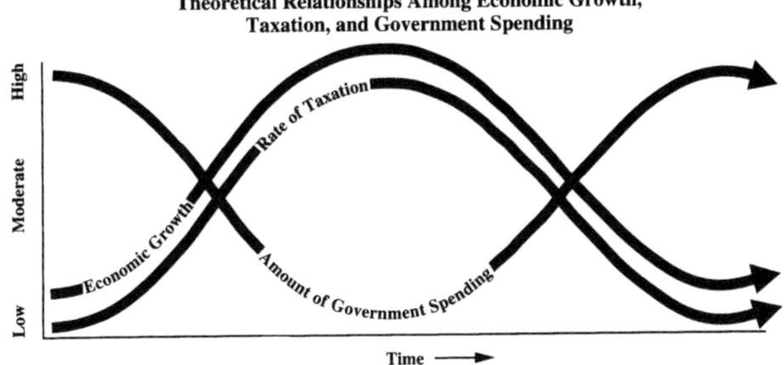

49. Assuming that the theoretical relationships in the graph are correct, government spending during times of increased economic growth should be low because

A. demands for public services are high

B. recessionary pressures are much less

C. taxation revenues are difficult to raise

D. unemployment rates are increasing

50. According to the theory underlying the graph, why should the rate of taxation be high during a period of high economic growth?

A. Because such a policy encourages greater consumer spending

B. Because increased taxation levels help to stop rising unemployment

C. Because increased government spending requires increased taxation levels

D. Because such a policy allows government to set aside revenues for future economic downturns

51. The belief that an economy must be based on the price system in order to function successfully places the **greatest emphasis** upon which of the following values?

A. Empathy

B. Cooperation

C. Individualism

D. Social consciousness

52. Historically, the primary reason for establishing Crown corporations in Canada was to

A. encourage increased entrepreneurship in the private sector

B. attract entrepreneurs from the private sector into the public sector

C. decrease the size of government bureaucracies through decentralization

D. provide services and products generally unavailable from the private sector

Use the following statement to answer questions 53 and 54.

The economic outline of the welfare state is as follows. If you work hard and save part of what you earn, you will have to support others. If you don't, they will support you. The inescapable conclusion is, therefore, that unemployment is the best policy.

53. Given the cynical tone of the statement, which of the following points of view would its writer support?

A. Despite its shortcomings, the welfare state is still the most viable economic system because it attempts to achieve collective goals.

B. In the welfare state, the lack of incentives and material rewards for hard work discourages self-sufficiency.

C. Hard work is the best policy because everyone in a welfare state is at least provided with basic subsistence.

D. The same income disparity that exists among individuals in a market economy also exists in a welfare state.

54. A proponent of a market economy would support the sentiment expressed in this statement. This support would be based on the belief that economic

A. freedom limits flexibility in achieving production goals set by government

B. competition results in the availability of a wide variety of goods and services

C. insecurity is necessary to produce a work force that exhibits self-reliance and initiative

D. choices made by individuals will lead inevitably to an increase in the standard of living for all

Use the following sources to answer questions 55 to 57.

Source I

Six years after the revolutions, it is time the West started thinking seriously about communism. There are still many people who assume that the experience of communism in Eastern and Central Europe was [one] of unmitigated tyranny, that all were victims except for the party bureaucrats and the secret policemen. Today, when democracy has returned neo-communist parties to power in [many former Soviet satellite countries], that view of history won't do.... The ideas put forward by the late communist governments were by no means all bad. From time to time, these governments created communities that were both securely employed and usefully productive, even innovative. None of these communities has survived. But those who lived in them now pass severe judgments on the social achievement of free-market economics and politics. Who can blame them?

—from *World Press Review, 1993*

Source II

55. According to Source 1, the stereotypical belief held by many Westerners regarding communist systems was that such systems were

A. accepted by a majority who valued autonomy over security

B. dominated by innovative and productive members of the party establishment

C. totalitarian régimes that neglected the well-being of citizens in favour of the advancement of the elite

D. authoritarian régimes that provided citizens economic prosperity at the cost of industrial production

56. The cartoon in Source II suggests that communist supporters in Russia wish to

A. eliminate the centralized economy

B. destroy the last traces of socialism

C. revive the attraction of patriotism

D. change the basis of their appeal

57. Sources I and II imply a growing dissatisfaction in Eastern Europe and Russia with the

A. consequences of market reforms

B. authoritarian rule of neo-fascist leaders

C. restrictions on freedom of speech and assembly

D. lack of opportunities to establish competitive businesses

58. In a parliamentary system, the principle of responsible government is **most clearly** demonstrated by

A. party discipline

B. cabinet solidarity

C. patronage appointments

D. a vote of non-confidence

59. In theory, the leaders of a totalitarian state consider opposition parties **unnecessary** because

A. individual and minority rights are protected by common law

B. political stability is assured through constitutional guarantees

C. multiparty systems are seen as too dictatorial and ideological

D. the elite knows what is in the best interests of citizens and society

60. The segment of German society that **most strongly** resisted the rise of Nazism during the early 1930s was comprised of

A. small business owners and farmers

B. wealthy industrialists and landowners

C. members of left-wing, socialist-oriented political parties

D. members of right-wing, capitalist-oriented political parties

Use the following events to answer questions 61 and 62.

Some Political Events In Germany, 1919–33

I. The National Socialist German Workers' Party was organized.

II. The Weimar Republic was established with a democratic constitution.

III. Adolf Hitler was appointed chancellor by President Hindenburg.

IV. Adolf Hitler attempted a coup d'état in the so-called Beer-Hall *Putsch*.

61. In what order did these events occur?

A. Events III, IV, II, I

B. Events II, I, IV, III

C. Events IV, I, III, II

D. Events I, II, III, IV

62. Which two events illustrate the effort of the Nazis to gain power through democratic means?

A. Events I and IV **B.** Events I and III

C. Events II and III **D.** Events II and IV

63. Multiparty political systems are **more likely** to reflect the fundamental principles of democracy than are two-party political systems because multiparty systems

A. produce stronger majority governments

B. ensure meaningful debate on political issues

C. inform voters consistently about political issues

D. represent a greater cross section of public opinion

Use the following excerpt to answer questions 64 and 65.

Yet it is in federal politics that first-past-the-post has done the most damage. In the [1993] election, it very nearly killed Canada. Take the three parties that won the lion's share of the non-Liberal vote: Reform, with 19 per cent of the popular vote, won 52 seats. The Bloc Quebecois, with 13.5 per cent, won 54. The Conservatives, with 16 per cent, took just two. Why did the Tories fare so poorly, when their popular vote was comparable? Because the other two parties' votes were more regionally concentrated. Reform won 36 per cent in B.C. and 52 per cent in Alberta. The Bloc, with 49 per cent of the vote in Quebec, gathered three-quarters of the seats in that province.

— from *The Edmonton Journal*

64. In claiming that the "first-past-the-post" electoral system "very nearly killed Canada," the author is emphasizing this system's tendency to

A. over represent parties with radical antidemocratic ideas

B. create political instability by preventing the formation of majority governments

C. reward regionally based parties at the expense of parties with broad-based national support

D. allow special interest parties to play a dominant role in the formation of coalitions

65. To solve the problem described in the passage, advocates of parliamentary reform would support adopting the system used to elect the

A. Swedish Riksdag

B. American Senate

C. British House of Commons

D. American House of Representatives

66. The principle of maintaining an independent judiciary in a democracy is based on the idea that

A. minority rights must be protected without fear of reprisal

B. majority views must prevail whenever there is a legal dispute

C. legal appeals must be left to the discretion of the executive branch

D. constitutional decisions must ultimately be approved by the legislature

67. In practice, the major difference between the ideologies of fascism and communism is **most evident** in the application of

A. propaganda

B. one-party rule

C. indoctrination

D. private ownership

Use the following excerpt to answer questions 68 and 69.

The true legislative role of parliament today is not to create legislation, but to scrutinize and ratify legislation introduced by the Government of the day. Although an occasional exception to this pattern of behaviour may exist, the general rule is clear: the legislature today does not actively initiate legislation. The legislature has a wide range of other functions. Among these are criticism of legislation, communication and representation of constituency concerns, and generally articulating the concerns of the public of the day.

— from *Comparative Politics 93/94*

68. According to this excerpt, the **main** function of elected members within the parliamentary system today is to

A. monitor the activities of the executive branch

B. attend to the needs of individual constituents

C. gauge popular opinion on major issues of the day

D. introduce legislation based on constituent demand

69. Which of the following examples represents "an occasional exception" to the general rule referred to in this excerpt?

A. Defeating a government bill

B. Monitoring riding business and concerns

C. Voting to support legislation approved by cabinet

D. Introducing a private member's bill concerning a key public issue

Use the following traditional political spectrum to answer question 70.

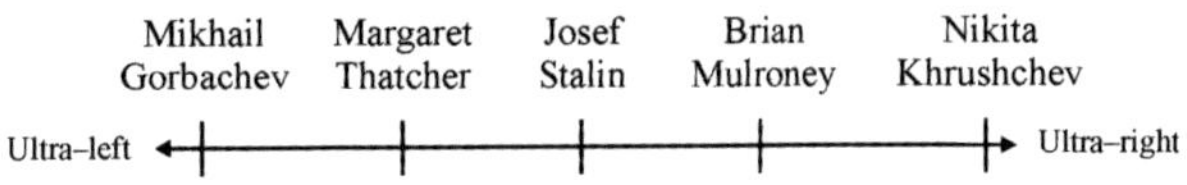

70. Which political leader has been **correctly** placed on the above spectrum?

A. Brian Mulroney

B. Margaret Thatcher

C. Nikita Khrushchev

D. Mikhail Gorbachev

TOPIC B: GLOBAL INTERACTIONS
THEME I: INTERNATIONAL CONFRONTATION AND COOPERATION: AN INTRODUCTION

Table of Correlations

Generalizations	Concepts	Facts and Content	Questions
a. International confrontations arise from a variety of motives and result in different types of interactions.	• confrontation	Briefly illustrate the following motives and forms of international confrontation: • motives– nationalism– self-determination – expansionism – ideology/beliefs • forms of confrontation – total war – limited war – guerrilla war – terrorism – brinkmanship – diplomatic – economic	
b. International cooperation arises from a variety of motives and results in different forms of cooperation.	• cooperation	Briefly illustrate the following motives and forms of international cooperation: • motives – collective security – internationalism – nationalism – balance of power – economic prosperity – humanitarianism – global survival • forms of cooperation – alliances – economic blocs – political groupings – regional organizations – international organizations – agreements – non-governmental organizations; e.g., cultural groups, popular movements	51, 67, 68, 69

THEME II: GLOBAL INTERACTIONS: INTERWAR PERIOD AND WORLD WAR II

Table of Correlations

Generalizations	Concepts	Facts and Content	Questions
a. International agreements may create the grounds for future confrontations.	• nationalism • national security • self-determination	Review the situation at the end of World War I and the *Treaty of Versailles* to illustrate how the settlements contributed to future confrontations: • territorial adjustments • arms restrictions • reparations • limitations on sovereignty • war guilt clause	1, 2, 5, 37, 73
b. Attempts at international cooperation are sometimes unsuccessful.	• internationalism	Identify various forms of international cooperation in the interwar period: • League of Nations • Treaties/agreements: Dawes Plan, Kellogg–Briand Pact, Locarno Pacts • conferences	71, 72
c. Security arrangements may strengthen or undermine global systems of collective security.	• regional security • global collective • security • alliances • appeasement	Examine the search for security in the 1920s and 1930s by referring to: • global collective security – League of Nations – regional security arrangements – Little Entente • isolationism – United States of America • treaties – Munich Agreement – Nazi–Soviet Non-aggression Pact	6, 7, 8, 9, 36, 39, 40, 41, 42, 43, 44, 74, 75, 77
d. Expansionist foreign policy may arise from a variety of motives or circumstances and elicit a variety of responses.	• economic security • ideologies • expansionism	Examine the policies and motives of nations who promoted or opposed expansionism in the 1930s by referring briefly to the circumstances faced by: • Germany • Italy • Japan • the Soviet Union • France • Great Britain • the United States of America	10, 76, 78, 79, 80, 84, 85
e. World War II altered both the nature of warfare and the international balance of power.	• conflict • total war • genocide • balance of power • justice • human rights	Briefly examine the impact of World War II: • brief overview of the war – the expansion of the Axis Powers – the Grand Alliance – the defeat of the Axis Powers and unconditional surrender • the changing nature of warfare – blitzkrieg – the Holocaust – civilian bombing – Hiroshima/Nagasaki • concern about justice and human rights – Atlantic Charter – war crimes • wartime conferences – Yalta – Potsdam	11, 12, 13, 45, 46, 47, 81, 82, 83, 86, 88

THEME III: THE RISE AND INTERACTION OF THE SUPERPOWERS (1945–1991)

Table of Correlations

Generalizations	Concepts	Facts and Content	Questions
a. A shift in the balance of power results in new alignments among nations.	• balance of power • spheres of influence • containment • cold war	Briefly describe the emergence of the cold war in Europe and Asia: • the Iron Curtain • Marshall Plan • Truman Doctrine • Berlin Blockade • NATO • COMECON • Warsaw Pact • Korean War • SEATO	14, 15, 16, 17, 28, 53, 54, 55, 56, 89, 90, 91
b. The emergence of new nation-states influenced the foreign policies of the superpowers.	• decolonization • guerrilla warfare • limited war	Briefly examine how issues raised by the emergence of new nations influenced the foreign policy of the superpowers: • Israel and the Middle East • China (1949) • Vietnam	48, 49, 92, 99
c. International arrangements for global peace and stability take into account the realities of power.	• global collective security	Describe the structure, procedures, and role of the United Nations in maintaining international peace: • General Assembly • Security Council • peacekeeping forces	87, 95, 96, 105
d. The superpowers have faced pressures of self-determination within their spheres of influence.	• terrorism • non-alignment • civil war • self-determination	Briefly examine the challenges faced by the Soviet Union in Eastern Europe and Afghanistan, and the United States of America in Cuba, Nicaragua, and the Middle East.	19, 24, 29, 60, 62, 100
e. The development of nuclear weapons has been viewed as both a stabilizing and a destabilizing influence in international relations.	• brinkmanship • deterrence • détente • peaceful coexistence • arms race • disarmament	Identify the following as examples of stabilizing or destabilizing developments: • nuclear arms control treaties: – Strategic Arms Limitations Talks (SALT) – Strategic Arms Reduction – Treaty (START) • nuclear arms confrontation: – Cuban Missile Crisis • nuclear arms technology: – cruise missiles – Strategic Defence Initiative (SDI) • international conferences; e.g.: – summit conferences – European security conferences	18, 50, 57, 58, 59, 93, 98

THEME IV: CONTEMPORARY GLOBAL INTERACTIONS

Table of Correlations

Generalizations	Concepts	Facts and Content	Questions
a. Global interactions are increasingly influenced by economic developments.	• interdependence	Briefly examine the impact on the international community of the following: • growth of multinational corporations • shifts in industrial production; e.g., Pacific Rim nations • international debt • globalization; e.g., WTO, IMF, G7/G8 Nations, World Bank, free trade agreements	35, 65
b. Nations form regional organizations to solve common problems.	• regional cooperation	Describe the purpose for regional cooperation by examining the European Union and one other organization; e.g., North American Free Trade Agreement (NAFTA).	23
c. Concern for global peace, human rights, and the environment has emphasized the need for international cooperation and understanding.	• humanitarianism • environmentalism	Identify the role of the following in international cooperation and understanding: • Universal Declaration of Human Rights • UN initiatives and agencies • Helsinki Agreements • Amnesty International • non-nuclear arms control	20, 22
d. Concern for global peace and stability has been heightened by the emergence of new states and the disintegration of others.	• self-determination • national sovereignty • supranationalism	Briefly examine the emergence and disintegration of states, as a challenge to world peace and security, resulting from: • 1989 revolutions in Eastern Europe • the re-unification of Germany • the disintegration of states; e.g., Soviet Union, Yugoslavia Briefly examine the following as examples of challenges to world peace and security and responses to them: • Gulf War • nuclear proliferation • ethnic conflict/civil wars/tribal conflict • peacekeeping • peace making • changing roles of alliances	3, 4, 20, 21, 25, 26, 27, 30, 31, 32, 33, 34, 38, 52, 61, 63, 64, 66, 70, 94, 97, 101, 102, 103, 104

Global Interaction in the 20th Century

Theme I: International Confrontation and Cooperation: An Introduction

International Confrontation

International confrontation has taken a number of different forms and has diverse causes. You should understand the following **four motives of confrontation** and be able to extrapolate to practical case materials:

Nationalism: During the twentieth century nationalist groups were present throughout the world. In the Middle East, conflict between Arab and Jew has nationalistic as well as religious underpinnings. In Canada, there has been the call for separation by French nationalists. What is true for both situations is that nationalist desire has led to conflict between two groups.

Self-determination: A particularly powerful example of self-determination came from the Sudeten Germans living in Czechoslovakia during the 1930's. Hitler had published the Hossbach document in 1937, which supported autonomy for large ethnic enclaves under the control of other states throughout Europe. In the spring of 1938, he began to demand autonomy for the Sudentenland from Czechoslovakia. Britain and France denied this and war appeared to be imminent until the Munich Pact was signed in September 1938.

Expansionism: In expansionism one nation tries to acquire new territory. There were countless examples of this in the last century. The ideological warfare between the US and the Former Soviet Union during the Cold War started over Germany and Eastern Europe. The Soviets wished to remain in control over lands that they had liberated during the course of the Second World War and the US wished to see these states become independent democracies. As both sides sought to expand their sphere of influence, confrontation culminated in what Churchill called "the Iron Curtain" descending on Eastern Europe.

Ideology/Beliefs: Rooted in the three motives listed above is ideology or belief. In an effort to protect, share or expand different ideologies, states have willingly confronted others. One of the best examples of this was Japan's declaration in 1931 before invading Manchuria. At that time Japan stated that it was their rightful place to establish the "Greater East Asian Co-prosperity Sphere", which would make Japan the industrial heart of Asia and other Asiatic states suppliers of cheap raw materials and markets for expensive finished goods. Japan then went on to try and conquer all of Asia before capitulating in August 1945.

Regardless of the motive employed, the result of confrontation usually ends some type of warfare. Sometimes **total war** is necessary, such as that used to stop Hitler and his allies during the Second World War. In some cases, a **limited war** involving the citizens of one state may erupt. One portion of the country supports one side and the other part supports another side. The Rwandan conflict in the 1990's is an example. **Guerilla warfare** was employed by Fidel Castro when he wished to obtain power from Batista in Cuba. Finally, many states have employed **terrorism** to try to force change. The Palestine Liberation Organization or PLO used terrorism as one of their key strategies for confrontation in the 1970's. All these forms of confrontation are all violent and bloody.

Brinkmanship is a another type of warfare, which resembles direct military action but focuses upon the use of political resources to bring about change. In this form of confrontation, two or more competing elements attempt to bring their enemy to the brink of war with the belief the enemy will back down and greater conflict will be averted. The most notable example of this was the **Cuban Missile Crisis**.

When governments wish to avoid the use of military force altogether, they employ diplomacy. Henry Kissenger was known for his "**shuttle diplomacy**" in the 1970's as he attempted to build peace between the **Arabs and Jews** in the **Middle East**. This form of confrontation is less destructive because both sides try to reach a compromise. But when diplomacy fails, it has major consequences such as in the **Korean War** after the peace talks broke down in 1951. The war continued until 1953, claiming many lives and causing devastation to both sides.

Finally, confrontation can occur via economic measures. During the Cold War, the term "**dollar/economic imperialism**" was coined. This type of confrontation sees both sides attempting to expand their sphere of influence by providing monies to "buy" the allegiance of nations, thus undermining the opposing side. The **Marshall Plan of 1947** exemplifies this type of confrontation.

International Cooperation

In addition to confrontation, nations have numerous other means to bring about change or growth. One of the most powerful of these has been the growth of **collective security**. This started with the **League of Nations**, the brainchild of President Woodrow Wilson following the First World War, and has grown into the present day **United Nations**. In this form of cooperation an attack on one state is seen as an attack on all members. The focus is on the promotion of **internationalism** or the welfare and development of all members.

The growth of **regional alliances** has balanced this development. Nations are hesitant to give up too much sovereignty to an international organization. Therefore, they have developed economic and defensive agreements that focus on specific regions. The **European Union (EU)** and **Organization of American States (OAS)** are two examples that emerged during the Cold War to protect regional interests of social, economic, political, military, and ideological importance.

During the later half of the twentieth century, nations began to recognize that increasing cooperation was necessary to maintain peace and stability in the face of the arms build-up of the Cold War. Nations started to form **alliances** to fight injustices like **apartheid** in South Africa and to promote global **economic prosperity**. It was increasingly evident that global survival would require coordinated international effort.

The **Group of Seven/Eight (G-7 or G-8)** decided to take up this challenge. They examined the disbursement of technology and innovation in nations throughout the world while trying to find solutions to promote **humanitarian** behaviour in the face of economic growth and development. Their efforts have been assisted by **non-governmental organizations (NGO's)**, like **Amnesty International**, who work hard to bring international recognition to challenges and abuse.

Another form of cooperation is economic/social action to promote **global survival**. The "Green Revolution" arose out of the economic turmoil caused by **OPEC** in the 1970's. This first step triggered issues about pollution and polluters. Nations sought to identify solutions and to take first steps. Unfortunately this process is sometimes limited to the self-interest of those who have the power to say no. The **Kyoto Accord** was a step towards limiting greenhouse gas pollution, however it has met with limited success as nations rally to protect business profits or attempt to limit environmental regulations and penalties to make themselves more attractive to potential investors.

Related Questions: 51, 67, 68, 69

Theme II : Global Interactions: Interwar Period and World War II

International Agreements and Confrontation

The devastation that resulted from World War I served as a reminder of what would occur in the event of another war in the industrial age of the twentieth century. In this unit of study you need to focus on the causes of World war I: nationalism, militarism, the alliance system, and imperialism. Each of these played a major role during the Interwar period.

THE AFTERMATH OF THE FIRST WORLD WAR

Please refer to Appendix A - Image #11

Italy had switched sides because they were promised colonial lands. The other **Allied Nations** wanted nothing to do with **mercantilism** following the First World War and established the **mandate system** under the **League of Nations**. **Self-determination** became the slogan of the day. This was to haunt those who created the **Treaty of**

Versailles because they had divided and grouped ethnic groups in Europe to act as protection against German aggression. Hitler played upon this self-interest and acquired the **Sudetenland** in the **Munich Pact (1938)**.

Treaty of Versailles (1919–1921) → Paris Peace Conference

1) Germany was forced to sign the "**War Guilt**" clause, which made Germany solely responsible for World War I.
2) Germany was forced to pay **$33 billion** in reparations.
3) Germany lost all colonies.
4) Germany returned Alsace and Lorraine to France
5) Germany gave up mining considerations in the Saar basin.
6) Germany was forced to destroy its army, navy, and air force.
7) Germany was permitted only 100 000 soldiers.
8) The "**Rhineland Demilitarized Zone**" was established with an **international peacekeeping force** for fifteen years.
9) **Anschluss** was forbidden between Germany and Austria.
10) The **Polish Corridor** was formed, separating Germany and East Prussia and giving Poland access to the Baltic Sea.

In analyzing the Treaty of Versailles today we can see how **territorial adjustments** were made out of spite, that limits were placed upon Germany's ability to protect itself, and its **sovereignty**, and that the desire to be **punitive** outweighed the humanity as Germany was forced to accept the **War-Guilt Clause**. In hindsight, it is clear that these actions caused resentment and led to another catastrophic confrontation, World War II.

Related Questions: 1, 2, 5, 37, 73

International Cooperation and Failure

The idea of internationalism as a pervasive force to reduce tension between nations was apparent in the "fourteen points" written by **Woodrow Wilson** following the end of the First World War. His dream was to develop an organization with a structure that would promote **internationalism** in a *non-confrontational* **supranationalistic** manner. He wanted to see nations join and work together to end the problems of the world so that the devastation of World War I would never happen again. Unfortunately, this dream was not to be.

Part of the reason for this failure stemmed from the removal of Wilson as President of the United States in the 1919 election. The US decided that it would prefer an **isolationist** rather than an **internationalist foreign policy**. **The US did not join the League of Nations** and this was a major blow to the organization. Adding to this was the purposeful absence of Russia and Germany who were not invited to participate until much later. The League's membership quickly established that they would operate from a selfish perspective, choosing to become involved in larger conflicts to an extent that did not pose a threat to their own self-interest. For weaker nations like Abyssinia (Ethiopia) this spelled doom.

From a positive perspective, there were many examples during the interwar period when nations broke with prescribed policy to promote international peace and stability. The first major example of this came in 1924 under the **Dawes Plan**. The US recognized that European and international stability relied upon German reparation payments. Their loan to Germany would be money in the bank for the US, while promoting peace and stability internationally.

Please refer to Appendix A - Image #11

A series of treaties and pacts were signed during this time of prosperity that made citizens of the globe believe that internationalism was alive and well. Most of the significant agreements were signed during the mid-and late 1920's as the boom cycle rolled unchecked. Powerful examples to focus on include the **Locarno Pact** of **1925** and the **Kellogg–Briand Pact (1928).**

The **Locarno Pact (1925)** was a redefinition of Germany's western borders with France and Belgium. Britain and Italy agreed to act as "guarantors" in the event of aggression. This was significant because major members of the international community welcomed Germany back to international affairs. As a result of signing this agreement, Germany was granted a seat in the League of Nations one year later. Ultimately this was another step towards the revival of the Alliance System that gave rise to the First World War.

The **Kellogg–Briand Pact (1928)** was important because it gave the illusion of peace and security. Its signatory nations denounced acts of aggression and weapons of mass destruction. In this manner it hoped that nations would agree to be brotherly and benevolent, working to promote peace and harmony. In reality this treaty did not have the machinery necessary to enforce the will of the collective and, therefore, was doomed to fail.

Related Questions: 71, 72

International Arrangements and Global Security

World War I was the most destructive war that had befallen humanity and the desire to avoid this at any cost drove international arrangements and agreements during the Interwar period. To accomplish this, a variety of mechanisms were employed. These included, but were not limited to, **global collective security organizations, alliances, appeasement, and regional security**.

The most prominent global security organization was the **League of Nations**. This organization was undermined from its inception because of the removal of Wilson as President of the United States in the 1919 election. His famous "**fourteen points**", a guide to the establishment of lasting peace and security in the Interwar period, required American participation in the League for its success. Instead, the US decided to pursue an **isolationist foreign policy** and to leave Europe to fend for itself. This was a serious blow to **internationalism**.

In an effort to compensate nations were forced into a resumption of the **alliance system**. As nations entered the 1930's and economic depression struck, aggressor states began to test the **internationalist** resolve of nations. Conferences such as the **London Naval Conference** were established and rules/agreements were made to curb expansionism. By the late 1930's participatory states in the **Munich Pact** openly violated Czechoslovakian sovereignty in an effort to prevent widespread war. Internationalism had failed.

This prompted a chain reaction as the Russians sought to secure peace and stability against the aggressive Nazi Party with the **1939 Nazi–Soviet Non-Aggression Pact**. The strength of this agreement lay in the extra time that Stalin had to build Russia's military strength and the removal of Hitler's second front for World War II. This was a blow to the British and French war plans. This was far less than the suffering of lesser powers, such as Czechoslovakia and Yugoslavia, who had placed hope for their security in events such as the signing of the **Little Entente**.

Related Questions: 6, 7, 8, 9, 36, 39, 40, 41, 42, 43, 44, 74, 75, 77

Expansionism: Its Causes and Impact during the Interwar Period

"During periods of extreme economic, social or political upheaval individuals have a predisposition to extreme philosophies." This quotation captures the motives underlying the emergence of many expansionist states during the Interwar period.

The Interwar period gave birth to the first expansionist state in 1921/2 when Benito Mussolini came to power in Italy and brought fascism to life. Mussolini played upon the Italian democracy's fight against hyperinflation. To wealthy industrialists/capitalists, he served as a role model who openly fought communists, a plague established in Russia under Lenin. Inherent in Mussolini's political agenda was the reestablishment of the Roman Empire to rule the world.

Mussolini received the support of the Italians because he played to their sense of nationalism, as well as their sense of fear. The **Japanese**, with their invasion of **Manchuria in 1931**, mirrored this technique. Their focus was not anti-communists but foreigners such as the Britain and the United States. The Japanese wanted "***Asia for the Asiatics***" in an effort to establish the "***Greater East Asian Co-prosperity Sphere***", which would make Japan the industrial heart of Asia. They would be supplied with inexpensive raw materials from other Asian nations who would provide a market for expensive finished Japanese products.

Germany and Russia also expanded to acquire resources and national glory. They divided Poland along the Vistula River with the **1939 Nazi–Soviet Non-Aggression Pact**. This ultimately served as the beginning of World War I. It is interesting to note that Hitler violated this agreement in June 1941 through **Operation Barbarossa**. He believed that he needed to "**push to the East to find Lebensraum**" for his people. More specifically, he was after Russian oil in the Caucus oil fields. Next, it was Russia's turn to try to resist European Fascist expansion.

This moment of resistance was too long in coming for Britain and France. They had been counting upon Russian support up to August 1939. They tried to stop Japanese, Italian and German expansionism. Again and again, they called for **sanctions** against each state. They signed **agreements** like the **Munich Accord** under which dictators such as Hitler promised to limit their growth. They even attempted to curb fascism by supporting anti-fascist forces during the **Spanish Civil War**. All of these failed because the desire for peace and the pursuit of **appeasement** continued to fuel aggressor nations. By the time nations were willing to take concerted action, it was too late. The fascist powers had become too strong for a quick victory.

Adding to the overestimation of the effectiveness of appeasement was the reluctance of the United States to become involved in international affairs. Too much of their foreign policy focus had been on isolationism. By the start of the Second World War President Roosevelt's economy continued to struggle, and barely employed Americans were reluctant to go abroad and die. The new wealth being generated by the war in Europe was needed to turn things around. The US followed the folly of the other Allied states in choosing to do little or nothing in the face of aggression for fear of personal loss. Roosevelt was forced to wait until December 7, 1941 when Japan bombed Pearl Harbor. The consequences were felt in a war that to lasted for almost six years and culminated in the dawn of the atomic age.

Related Questions: 10, 76, 78, 79, 80, 84, 85

World War II

World War II was overwhelming conflict because of the huge loss of life, lengthy duration and the introduction of new technologies that contributed to the advent of the **Cold War**. This conflict was truly exceptional because of the devastation that bombing raids, tanks, and automatic weapons wrought upon society. However, the development of Nazi Germany's "**Final Solution**" in **1941** greatly contributed to the legacy of this conflict as an estimated six million Jewish people were killed in the **Holocaust**. Adding to this loss were millions more Slavs, Poles, Hungarians, Czechs, and other Europeans who were deemed undesirable by the Aryan Germans. The magnitude of this loss is truly horrific and literally beyond words.

A student of the war must examine the conditions that gave rise to these heinous acts. Clearly this was not behavior that typified the lives of most citizens prior to World War II. During the period leading up to the war, Hitler artfully began to create a society where people openly looked for **scapegoats**. This gradual process was accompanied by the development of a strong military and economic recovery. By the start of the war, all sides were beginning to understand their destructive capabilities.

The desire to expand ultimately brought together the members known as the **Axis Powers**. Their adherence to Fascist ideology made them hate both democrats and communists alike. Slowly they maneuvered to unite first in the **Rome-Berlin Axis**, then the **Anti-Comintern Pact** and finally as the **Rome-Berlin-Tokyo Axis**. To balance this power structure, the British and French attempted to forge relations with both the Americans and the Soviets, both of whom abandoned the other Allied nations at the advent of the war to satisfy personal issues. The **Balance of Power system** came crumbling down with **Hitler** and **Stalin's Nazi-Soviet Non-Aggression Pact** and their subsequent invasions of **Poland**.

Many question why it took the allies such a long period of time to take action against the Axis powers. The answer lay in the devastation that befell all of Europe during the First World War. Clearly nations such as Germany had new arsenals. **Blitzkrieg** helped the Nazi's to overwhelm the Poles in a frightfully short period of time. By 1940 warfare took on yet another face as the **German Luftwaffe** bombed civilian targets, such as London, during the **Battle of Britain**.

It was not only Germany that worked feverishly to develop new weapons. The United States led the charge to acquire **atomic weapons technology**. They utilized atomic weapons against the Japanese when they bombed **Hiroshima** with "***Little Boy***" and Nagasaki with "***Fat Man***". These were the names given to the world's first A-bombs utilized during a military attack. Their effect was immediately felt as approximately 200 000 people were killed or wounded. The Japanese unconditionally surrendered and an estimated 800 000 deaths and/or casualties were documented. The use of the atomic weapons by the US ultimately started the **Cold War**.

The Second World War not only brought devastation, it also gave rise to many important conferences and other changes. The **Yalta Conference**, at Yalta in the Russian Crimea, focused on the Allied strategies for the treatment of Germany after the cessation of the war. It was then that the ***four zones of occupation*** were created in Germany. It was also at this time that the British and Americans began to suspect that Stalin was not going to permit democratic elections in Soviet–liberated Eastern European states.

This conference was followed by the **San Francisco Conference**, which finalized **the United Nations**. Next came the **Potsdam Conference**, which called for the unconditional surrender of Japan to end the war in the Pacific. In between these three powerful events was the establishment of the **Nuremberg War Crimes** trials. The world heard testimony from captured Nazi's and survivors of **Nazi Genocide**. It was decided that the United Nations' membership must not permit this form of devastation against humanity again in the future. Only time would tell if it could fulfill this awesome burden.

Related Questions: 11, 12, 13, 45, 46, 47, 81, 82, 83, 86, 88

Theme III: Cold War Period

The Cold War: An Introduction

The Cold War developed unexpectedly for most of the world's citizens because it introduced "a weapon of unparalleled mass destruction," the **Atomic Bomb**. As a result, the period following the end of World War II was a tenuous one for many nations. Clearly the world had two major powers: the United States and the Soviet Union. However, these two nations had to proceed carefully for fear of initiating a major conflict that would benefit no one.

The first few months following the Japanese capitulation nations celebrated and enjoyed their new-found autonomy. This was to be short lived, as a new **Balance of Power** system emerged. This centered on a **bipolar world**, where the US led the charge for ***democratic and capitalistic freedoms*** throughout the world and the Soviets battled to spread communist ideology and practice. Spheres of influence emerged as early as 1946 and **Sir Winston Churchill** coined the phrase "**Iron Curtain**" to describe Soviet control over **Eastern Europe**. The world was never to be the same.

On a positive note, the atomic age spurred the development of non-military methods of confrontation. The US acted first with its policy of **containment** under the **Truman Doctrine**. It was not enough for the United States to talk about stopping the spread of the "***Red Menace***," they would have to attack the root of communism: poverty. To do this **dollar or economic imperialism** was concealed in the **Marshall Plan** in 1947. Nations were to be attracted away from the egalitarian principals of communism with American money to rebuild. The business of being "***one better than one's enemies***" had begun.

The Soviets strengthened control over their satellites by creating their own financial assistance program named the **Molatov Plan**. This was to be supported by the efforts of **COMECON**, which allowed Russia to lead its many satellites in economic, social and political pursuits. Here was a marvelous way for the Soviets to block dollar imperialism, while further entrenching themselves in Europe without military conflict.

The Korean War (1950–53) was the first major test for the **United Nations**. The UN's validity was to be challenged in 1949 when the US led the formation of **North Atlantic Treaty Organization (NATO)**. This **regional defense alliance** entrenched the American's sphere of influence and provided an alternative **collective security** measure. The US did, however, effectively utilize the UN's Security Council to engage a collective action to restore democracy in South Korea.

The advent of **NATO** was not the first **regional security alliance/organization** developed during the Cold War. As early as 1945, the US began to work on the **Organization of American States (OAS)** with the official agreement being signed in 1948. **Southeast Asian Treaty Organization, 1954 (SEATO)** emerged in Southeast Asia and later **CENTO (1955)** was signed to protect western interests in the Middle Eastern area. These new organizations and alliances were to help the world to take the "first steps" towards greater regional integration.

Today, this integration is cemented in organizations such as the **European Union (EU)** and in agreements like the **North American Free Trade Agreement (NAFTA)**. If it were not for the Cold War, this evolution may not have taken place.

Related Questions: 14, 15, 16, 17, 28, 53, 54, 55, 56, 89, 90, 91

The Rise of New Nation-States

The end of World War I was a step towards the end of the **Colonial System** throughout the world. The League of Nations introduced the **Mandate System**, which divided colonies into three categories: **"A" mandates** who were immediately ready for self-rule; **"B" mandates** who would be ready for autonomy in less than fifty years; and **"C" mandates** who would take more than fifty years to be ready for self-government. This system was abandoned at the end of the Second World War but it had sparked awareness in many nation-states that they had a right to freedom.

The second profound development for nations-states was the formation of and the mass migration to the nation of **Israel,** which was to be a Jewish haven. Instead, it has evolved into a model for prolonged conflict as Jews and Arabs have battled since the first day that Israel was a nation. The ongoing conflict has resulted in opportunities for the **Superpowers** to make money and avoid direct conflict with each other.

The need for expanding spheres of influence worked to prevent **total war** as many nation-states attempted to gain autonomy from their superpower protectorate. In particular, the Soviets supported **Mao** in his bid for control over **China** until the official **Sino–Soviet split** in **1966** and the US supported the **Nationalist Kuomintang (KMT)** which fled to **Formosa (Taiwan).** Through such **proxy conflicts,** the superpower nations were able challenge each other without the conflict evolving into a larger world issue.

Other nations saw this period as an opportunity to exploit the Superpowers' desire to acquire friendship. Both **India** and **Egypt** successfully played the US and Soviets against each other to get monies or weapons. This did, however, lead to increased tensions between the US and India. Other nations did not fare as well in their bid to deal with powerful states.

Vietnam, **Cambodia** and **Laos** were nations who suffered major losses because of their relationship with both Superpowers. The Viet Nam War took millions of Vietnamese lives and led to American "***carpet bombing***" of Cambodia and later the installment of the **Khmer Rouge** communist government in that state. Had the communist North Vietnamese capitulated after 1955 when North and South Vietnam were established, the large, prolonged conflict might have been averted.

However they did not capitulate as they wished to have autonomy from American influence. The United States believed that if communist **North Vietnam** were to topple the **democratic South Vietnamese** government the **Domino Effect** would happen and surrounding Asian states would become communist until the entire world embraced Marxist teachings. In the end, it was the much smaller Vietnamese nation that thwarted the powerful Superpower.

The American and Soviet responses to emerging states continued throughout the entire Cold War era. In the end, the presence of the Superpowers is seen as positive in its ability to maintain order and avoid events like the war in **Yugoslavia** in the **1990's**. But, they have also been chastised for supporting dictators like **Pinochet, Batista** and **Castro** to maintain friendly relations at the price of **human rights and dignity**.

Related Questions: 48, 49, 92, 99

Global Peace and Stability

This section addresses the subject of **international collective security**. You are expected to understand the evolution of this concept from the ***League of Nations,*** its beginning, and subsequent demise by the end of the Interwar Period, with the ***United Nations***. You should review the **Moscow Conference (1943)** and **San Francisco Conference (1945)** from the Second World War to acquire a better understanding of how this organization came into existence.

Students must recognize that the "***Big Three***" (the **US, Britain,** and the **Former Soviet Union**) were attempting to establish a balance of power between themselves in the **UN** and, at the same time, were trying to create a structure that would accommodate an exhalted position for themselves. This duality was embodied in the **Security Council/General Assembly** approach. The nature and implementation of the UN is a continued source for discussion to this day.

One of the problems that has emerged with the Security Council relates to the use of the "**Big Five's**" (***France, Britain, China, US and Russia***) **veto power** to stop legislation or action that does not enhance the welfare of a Security Council member(s). This was a problem in many instances with the Korean War (1950–3) and the War Against Terrorism (2001).

Some argue that the veto issue is indicative of the deeper challenge, which is the desire of leaders to be self-serving and nationalistic, instead of internationalist, in global affairs. They see the **UN's General Assembly** as weak and ineffective because it has repeatedly demonstrated that it has limited power to implement larger social change, like the elimination of unsanitary drinking water or polio, or to have members pay their outstanding membership dues. Their belief is that the UN has issues in its power structure.

Nevertheless the **United Nations** has evolved into a multifaceted organization that attempts to correct economic, social, legal, and military injustice throughout the world. Since 1956 and Lester B. Pearson's vision of **peacekeeping** and **peacemaking forces**, the UN has been involved in national conflicts the world over. From the Suez Canal, to Cyprus, the UN has been active in making changes to enhance human worth and dignity.

Others believe that the past and present efforts of the UN have been inadequate. They argue for the creation of a new global organization that would legally rule over all nations. The new organization would not lack the support to function effectively nor would it leave disadvantaged nations to deal with civil issues with inadequate or limited resources. It would be empowered to act as an **impartial and omnipresent third party** for the collective wellbeing. Others say this is far too idealistic and insist that nations must place national self-interest before all else to ensure international peace and stability.

Related Questions: 87, 95, 96, 105

Self-determination and Superpower Supremacy

Although the Cold War had many important issues that drove policy makers in the US and the Former Soviet Union, the primary issue was the need for a **balance of power**. This policy was evident along many fronts but in particular in competing **spheres of influence**. As early as 1946, Sir Winston Churchill identified an "***Iron Curtain***" that separated **communist Eastern Europe** from **democratic Western Europe**. Out of this division came the struggle between the Superpowers and middle/lesser powers.

In Eastern Europe, the Soviets had numerous nations that acted as insurgents. From 1949 onwards, the allies exerted pressure to introduce democracy into nations liberated by the Second World War. However by 1946, it became clear that Stalin had plans for Poland and other Eastern satellites. He resisted calls for democratic reforms in Poland and refused to relinquish control over Russian occupation zones in Germany. The Soviets moved next on the **Czechoslovakian** front, facilitating the insertion of a communist regime. In 1953 they crushed **East German** demands for reform and repeated the action with the **Poles** and **Hungarians** in 1956. In 1979, the Former Soviet Union invaded **Afghanistan**, only to have their forces defeated by Afghani rebels and international pressure.

The United States of America did not fare much better in the maintenance and expansion of its "quasi-empire" in the same time period. The US brought itself to crisis during the **Cuban Missile Crisis.** The US was being driven in this area and throughout the world by the fear that communism would spread if not contained. This fear was later embodied in the "**Domino Theory**", which was to be the dominant force in American foreign policy in the 1960 and 1970's.

The US too, suffered defeat during the Cold War. American forces were driven out of **Vietnam**. In **Central** and **South America**, American **puppet regimes**, with leaders like **Batista**, were violently driven from office. In **Nicaragua**, a communist government came to power during the 1980's. Despite the covert efforts of American upper-level military officials to supply resources to **Contra Rebels**, the **Sandinista Government** came to office. This was a blow to the US and their perceived sphere of influence.

Other American losses suffered during this time were more devastating. The 1983 bombing of American forces in Beirut took the lives of 241 American soldiers. Terrorist bombs threatened Americans and Soviets alike as ethnic groups struggled for self-determination during the Cold War. Often the Superpowers became targets after becoming engaged in a "**Proxy War**". They tested each other by supporting opposing sides of a **civil war**. Troops, advisors, and other officials from both nations were sent to countries like Korea, Cambodia, and Vietnam to facilitate both sides. In the end, civilians, as well as soldiers and the superpowers, paid dearly with life and limb.

Related Questions: 19, 24, 29, 60, 62, 100

Stabilizing and Destabilizing Influences in International Relations

Nuclear weapons technology came on the world stage with the Allied desire to end World War II and to stop Hitler and his Nazi supporters. The "***race for the bomb***" as it was called, created weapons of unparalleled mass destruction. Over the next fifty years, nuclear weapons had a profound impact upon both sides of the Cold War, in both positive and negative ways.

Nuclear weapons had a positive impact by creating **Mutually Assured Destruction (MAD.)** This was a doctrine that stated that, in the event of a nuclear attack by one side, their enemy would reciprocate. The weapons would pass in space and both sides could be assured of total annihilation. It is believed that the severity of this potential outcome greatly shaped relations between the two Superpowers during the Cold War.

One example of this thinking was the **Cuban Missile Crisis**. Instead of directly confronting **Premier Khruschev, the Soviet Leader**, who was building missile bases in Cuba and supplying missiles) with military force, **President Kennedy** of the US established a ***naval blockade*** and employed **brinkmanship**. In doing so, he peacefully resolved the issue without resorting to violence. Even though this event was the closest that the two Superpowers came to nuclear war, many historians saw this as a positive starting point for **détente** and the many changes that eventually led to the end of the Cold War.

The idea of **nuclear deterrence** created problems as well. Both the US and the Soviets had huge military budgets to ensure that they could compete in the "Arms Race". It was essential to let the enemy know that an attack would result in a response by superior forces. By the 1980's, spiraling costs forced **Premier Gorbachev** to implement ***Glasnost*** and ***Perestroika***. **President Reagan** left office in 1988 with a debt of approximately three trillion dollars. Disarmament via the **1985 Strategic Arms Reduction Talks/Treaty (START)** allowed the world to breathe a momentary sigh of relief when both Superpowers agreed to dismantle nuclear weapon stockpiles. It took many steps to achieve this end.

One of the most significant series of events in this evolution unfolded in 1972. **Communist China** was offered a seat in the **UN Security Council (1971)** and **President Nixon** visited the Chinese (1972). This step towards friendlier international relations was in keeping with the ***Eisenhower–Khruschev*** era of "**peaceful coexistence**". The monumental signing of the **Strategic Arms Limitation Talks (SALT I)** in September of that year found both Superpowers agreeing to limit their production of nuclear weapons. This came on the heels of test ban treaties, such as the **1963 Nuclear Test Ban Treaty**, the **Non-Proliferation Treaty (1968)** and the **Seabed Treaty (1971)**. The very idea of limiting production was instrumental in ending the Cold War.

To achieve this goal, it took many meetings and conferences between the Superpowers. International cities, such as Geneva, were popular because they provided neutral grounds for both groups to come together to work for mutual benefit with limited interference. Such meetings were not enough, however, to stop developments like the growth of American cruise missile testing or the introduction of the **Strategic Defense Initiative (SDI)**, nicknamed "**Starwars**". In the end, however, peace prevailed. It is unclear if nuclear weapons were a **greater stabilizing** or **destabilizing influence** during this period.

Related Questions: 18, 50, 57, 58, 59, 93, 98

Theme IV: Contemporary Global Interactions

Interdependence in the Global Village

Following the end of World War II nations began to cooperate on both international and regional fronts. Organizations like **Organization for African Unity (OAU), South East Asian Treaty Organization (SEATO)**, the **Organization of American States (OAS)** and **European Common Market (EC)** allowed nations in specific areas to work together, sometimes with the support of stronger states, for advancement. Their belief was that there was strength in numbers.

Slowly but surely as these first steps combined with changes to demographics and technology, the world began to think more "***globally***". This gave birth to **multinational/transnational** companies that are the giants of today, such as **General Motors, IBM** and **Nike**. These companies identified specific regions in the world where there could access resources and develop specific products at substantially diminished costs. The result was growing interdependence and new jobs in the developing world. It also meant a loss of employment in developed nations that were no longer competitive.

Helping to fuel this trend has been the work of the **G7/G8** nations. The **Group of Seven or Group of Eight** is seven/eight of the world's wealthiest democratic industrialized nations who come together to analyze technological development and disbursement internationally and to promote industrial growth. They have been actively working to promote **globalization** of both resources and trade. In many cases, concerns have been raised that this wealthy group sticks together to ensure what is best for themselves, ignoring issues of human rights abuses or dictatorial policy in nations like **China** for fear of economic consequences.

Other organizations do not have such a small membership. One example is the **World Trade Organization (WTO)**. This ones from the **General Agreement on Trade and Tariffs (GATT)**. The WTO is concerned with the following goals:

1. Improving free trade throughout the world.
2. Acting as a dispute-solving mechanism.
3. Collecting data on trade.
4. Aiding or attempting to stabilize nations experiencing financial difficulty.

In striving for these goals, the WTO attempts to prevent extreme exploitation in the market.

The **International Monetary Fund** (**IMF**) has a similar goal, but works in a different manner. The IMF prevents *competitive currency devaluation*. To accomplish this end, the IMF collects a percentage of each member state's **Gross National Product (GNP)**, which is then bought and sold on international money markets to increase or decrease its value. In this manner no one nation may completely exploit another and business is, therefore, promoted globally.

A third organization that has similar goals is the **World Bank**. This entity provides loans and aid to nations in need. It has both an economic and humanitarian focus, working with numerous organizations and nations to make the world a better place.

In examining free trade agreements such as **North American Free Trade Agreement (NAFTA)** or groups like **European Union (EU)**, it is clear that the world is globalizing. As nations become increasingly interdependent, labour and resources flow more freely between borders, debt shifts and new organizations and ideas come to fruition. Areas, such as the **Pacific Rim,** find new investors and wealth while, North Americans lose low-skilled employment and are forced to obtain greater education and to create new employment, demonstrating that the world is truly a dynamic and highly interdependent environment for business.

Related Questions: 35, 65

Regional Cooperation in the Global Village

During the twentieth century and beyond, nations have joined together out of mutual interest. These groupings have occurred on two levels: international and regional. Generalization A of Theme IV focussed primarily on those groupings with international aims. This section looks at the '***who***' and '***why***' of **regional organizations**.

At the turn of the last century the ***mercantilist system*** was coming to an end. The League of Nations was being formed and major powers were attempting to provide opportunities for some colonies to acquire independence. Their efforts in the League led to the development and institution of the ***mandate system***. This first step was doomed to failure as expansionist fascist states attempted to conquer most of the world during the 1930's and 1940's. With the advent of the Cold War, lesser powers took a united stand.

One of the forces that prompted the regional unification process came from the two Superpowers. The United States led the way with the the **Organization of American States (OAS.)** This regional organization helped the United States maintain control over Central and South American nations in the US sphere of influence. It also fostered economic and industrial development for these nations. Ultimately, this enabled the US to keep the Former Soviet Union out of this area of the world, while developing new markets for American multinational interests.

In other areas, such as Africa, nations were forming regional alliances for different reasons. The **Organization for African Unity (OAU)** had the primary goals of helping its members deal with ending ***colonialism*** and to ending colonialism throughout the world. It also attempted to coordinate cultural, economic, and political policy to present a united front to the world. This is a very different purpose than that of the OAS.

Another reason for regional cooperation comes from economics. The **North American Free Trade Agreement (NAFTA)** has united **Canada**, the **USA,** and **Mexico** to promote **economic growth** and **efficiency** among these nations. In theory, markets in all three nations coalesce to ensure their wealth and competitiveness throughout the world. This was necessary for North America to remain competitive against the powerful nations of Europe.

Regional cooperation in Europe has been evolving since the 1960's. At that time, the **European Economic Community (EEC)** was little more than a collection of states that began to develop common economic policy through tariff reduction and consistent application. As the organization grew in membership and experience, it transformed into the **European Community (EC)** and finally into the **European Union (EU)**. The EU is unique because it is much more than a economic organization. It now works toward the creation of a single **European parliament** and **atomic policy**. It has already integrated a common currency, which is known as the Eurodollar. The growth potential demonstrated by the EU since the inception of the new millennium has made nations throughout the world rethink traditional boundaries. Regionalism clearly is a powerful tool to remain competitive during the twenty-first century.

Related Question: 23

Humanitarianism and Environmentalism in the Global Village

Technology offers a means for the world to have a heightened awareness and knowledge of the events. Fueling the drive for global interconnectedness has been the recognition that individuals and nations may need help to protect their rights or the welfare of the globe may be threatened by the actions of a single nation. With this in mind, the framers of the **United Nations** took several steps to protect peace and the rights of all in the second half of the twentieth century.

A major step towards protecting the rights of all came via the **Universal Declaration of Human Rights**. This document was created in ***1948*** on the heels of the Second World War genocide. It is a series of articles and statements that outline what is important and should be protected for citizens of the world. However, it was also clear to the signatory nations that this was not enough.

The United Nations has more than the Universal Declaration of Human Rights to support the welfare of the world's citizens. In the UN's structure, one finds important humanitarian groups. These include the **Food and Agriculture Organization(FAO), International Labor Organization (ILO), United Nations International Children's Emergency Fund (UNICEF)** and **United Nations Education, Scientific and Cultural Organization (UNESCO)**. These groups provide support to nations and individuals throughout the world to promote human rights, the acquisition of basic needs, and to overcome environmental issues. However, the challenges that they are facing still require more support.

When examining how to tackle these challenges from an **Non-Governmental Organization (NGO)** perspective, one may study **Amnesty International's** efforts. This is a non-profit organization that campaigns the world over to end human rights abuses, advocates for fair trials, and tries to obtain freedom for political prisoners. It provides a non-partisan perspective for citizens to weigh world events or to gauge human rights abuse.

The **Helsinki Agreements** supports the mandate of Amnesty International. First signed in **1975**, this UN initiative called for the universal protection of basic human rights and freedoms. These included, but were not limited to the right to marry a different national, the right to work anywhere in the world and the right to be free from wrongful imprisonment. This was an important step towards protecting the citizens of the world and it continues to be built upon.

Signing agreements is not the only way for nations to bring about change. The United Nations has employed economic and cultural sanctions many times to pressure nations with poor human rights records to change. Unfortunately, this often has a debilitating short-term effect on the general populations and does not guarantee a quick resolution of the issue. On a positive note, economic and cultural sanctions did help to end ***apartheid*** in South Africa.

In the wake of the Cold War, many nations have expressed concerns about the lack of human rights and the potential danger of nuclear proliferation. The inability of nations to create and agree to international policies, such as the **Kyoto Accord**, indicate that there will be problems with both environmentalism and human rights for years to come.

Related Questions: 20, 22

Peace, Security and the New Nation-State in the Global Village

The twentieth century began with the First World War because of **Serbia's** demands for autonomy. The **mercantilist** and **colonial systems** were gradually abandoned due to increasing pressure from **nationalistic groups** for self-rule. The League of Nations, via the "**mandate system**", directly addressed the idea of **self-determination** in the Interwar Period. Yet, to the present day, the world continues to lack the ability to quickly and peacefully solve demands for **national sovereignty**.

The cost of these demands has been high. During the Cold War, Eastern European nations, like **Poland, Hungary** and **Czechoslovakia**, who were struggling for self-rule, suffered at the hands of **Stalin** and other Soviet leaders. In the west, information is now surfacing about American activities that supported leaders in **Central and South American** states and **South East Asia** because they were friendly to the US. These same leaders **violated fundamental human rights** and **resisted democratic reforms**. The result was instability the world over.

Out of this turmoil came the disintegration of the Soviet Empire in the late 1980's and early 1990's. The destruction of the **Berlin Wall** in **1989** and subsequent reunification of Germany was a powerful first step in ending Soviet rule. Soon after other Soviet satellites, such as **Latvia, Lithuania** and **Estonia** announced their independence. For these nations the change to self-government was relatively smooth. For others, such as **Georgia**, ending Russian control over their state was a bloody and violent struggle.

The efforts of these groups seemed to trigger a desire for freedom in other European nations as the mid-1990's saw ethnic groups engage in civil conflict in the **former Yugoslavia**, and in **Rwanda** and **Somalia**. Some of these conflicts sprang from ancient tribal issues; others were fought over religious grievances from the past. It is difficult to isolate a single cause, but they all ended with similar results, the loss of thousands of innocent citizens' lives and bloodshed between the warring factions.

To address these grievances **supranationalistic** and **international organizations**, like the United Nations, were called upon to act. In some cases, **Cyprus** for instance, the United Nations has been involved for decades. Their job is peacekeeping between the Greek and Turkish communities so that the communities can work toward peace and harmony. Peacekeeping has been an important role for the UN.

The second major role that the UN has fulfilled has been that of **peacemaker.** In 1990–1, the United Nations engaged in the **Gulf War** to force Saddam Hussein to withdraw Iraqi forces from subjugated Kuwait. After Hussein's refusal to respect **UN mandates** to leave, a battle of approximately two months ensued. Ultimately, the international force was far too large and powerful. The Iraqis were easily defeated but their war tactics caused concern that a more ominous weapon was in hiding.

That potential threat was **nuclear weaponry**. By the end of the 1990's, it was clear that the fear had become reality in and around the globe. Developing nations, like **China, India** and **Pakistan**, detonated nuclear weapons in a show of internationalist "***saber rattling***". Ancient conflicts revolving around land and religion appeared to have the potential to result in conflicts of a magnitude unparalleled in human history. New solutions would have to be developed and old ones revisited to ensure peace; **alliances** would have to be forged and revised. Organizations like the **European Union**, with its desire for membership growth through mutual benefit, set a pattern for other alliances to follow as time unfolds.

Related Questions: 3, 4, 20, 21, 25, 26, 27, 30, 31, 32, 33, 34, 38, 52, 61, 63, 64, 66, 70, 94, 97, 101, 102, 103, 104

Use the following sources to answer questions 1 and 2.

Source I
The Democratic party favors the League of Nations as the surest, if not the only practical means of maintaining the peace of the world and terminating the insufferable burden of great military and naval establishments. It was for this that America broke away from traditional isolation and spent her blood and treasure to crush a colossal scheme of conquest.

Source II
The Republican party maintains the traditional American policy of non-interference in the political affairs of other nations. This government has definitely refused membership in the League of Nations and to assume any obligations under the covenant of the League. On this we stand.

— both sources from *Internationalism: Opposing Viewpoints Series*

1. The statements in these sources, in historical context, relate specifically to the

A. efforts to rebuild a war-torn Europe following the Paris Peace Conference

B. attempts by world leaders to establish an effective European alliance system

C. inability of nations to secure a "just" peace through the provisions of the Treaty of Versailles

(D) decision by the American Senate to reject collective security despite President Wilson's Fourteen Points

Source: January 2000

2. The two sources draw attention to a historical conflict in the United States that arose from the opposing ideas of isolationism and internationalism. This conflict centres around which of the following questions?

A. When is the most appropriate time for the United States to intervene in civil wars?

B. Why do nations in Europe depend upon American military aid during times of conflict?

C. Which foreign policy would best serve American national interests at any given time?

D. How can American diplomatic relations with other countries best be established?

Source: January 2000

Use the following sources to answer questions 3 to 5.

Source I
The statesmen [at the Paris Peace Conference] created separate, vulnerable states, whose peoples had long histories of mutual dislike and whose very creation gave them new grievances to quarrel over. To their west lay Germany, deeply offended but by no means crippled. To the east was massive, unpredictable Bolshevik Russia, whose interests had been ignored by the Big Three.

Source II

—both sources from *Twentieth Century History: The World Since 1900*

CHALLENGER QUESTION **DIFFICULTY: 54.7**

3. Sources I and II illustrate a central problem associated with the implementation of the principle of

A. isolationism

B. appeasement

C. collective security

D. national sovereignty

Source: January 2000

4. In the 1990s, which area of the world today experienced heightened tensions similar to those described in the first sentence of Source I?

A. Latin America

B. The Balkan States

C. South East Asia

D. The Baltic States

Source: January 2000

5. An appropriate title for the map in Source II would be

A. *Poland Marches West: Territorial Demands Settled*

B. *Europe after the Second World War: the New Frontiers*

C. *The Polish Land Grab: New Frontiers in Eastern Europe*

D. *Europe Deals with Aggressive Nations: New Alliances Signed*

Source: January 2000

Use the following diagram to answer question 6.

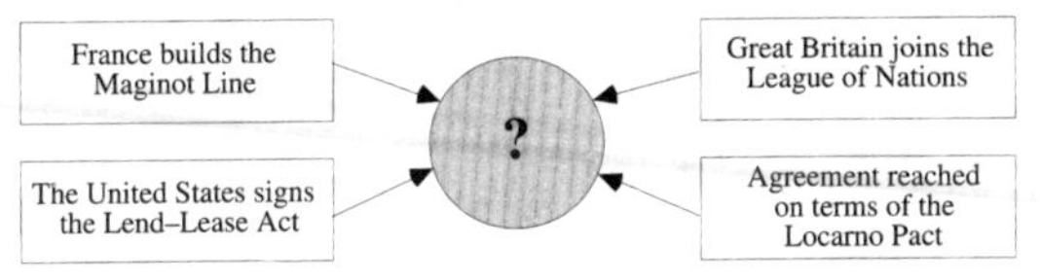

6. Taken together, the events shown in the diagram represent attempts to

A. enforce collective security between 1930 and 1940

B. ensure the security of nations between 1919 and 1941

C. eliminate fascism as a force in Europe during the 1930s

D. exclude Germany from diplomatic negotiations during the 1920s

Source: January 2000

7. Evidence that the United States was not completely isolationist during the interwar period is **best** illustrated by American involvement in the

A. Munich Pact

B. Little Entente

C. League of Nations

D. Dawes and Young plans

Source: January 2000

8. *The League of Nations' reaction to the Japanese invasion of Manchuria differed from its reaction to the Italian invasion of Ethiopia.*

This statement is accurate in that the League of Nations

A. achieved the withdrawal of Japanese forces

B. gave its official approval to the Japanese invasion

C. applied no economic sanctions against the Japanese

D. used peacekeeping forces to stop Japanese aggression

Source: January 2000

CHALLENGER QUESTION DIFFICULTY: 54.4

9. *Before us stands the last problem which must be solved and will be solved. It is the last territorial claim I have to make in Europe, but it is the claim from which I shall not recede.*

This "last territorial claim" made by Hitler before meeting with other European leaders at Munich refers to the

A. Polish Corridor

B. Sudetenland

C. Saar Basin

D. Rhineland

Source: January 2000

Use the following information to answer question 10.

Political Slogans
— Nothing has ever been won without bloodshed!
— Believe! Obey! Fight!
— A minute on the battlefield is worth a lifetime of peace!
— He who has steel has bread!

CHALLENGER QUESTION **DIFFICULTY: 58.5**

10. These political slogans achieved their greatest popularity in

A. Italy during the 1930s

B. France during the 1940s

C. the United States during the 1950s

D. the Soviet Union during the 1960s

Source: January 2000

11. Following the launch of Hitler's Operation Barbarossa against the Soviet Union, Stalin's main diplomatic objective was to

A. orchestrate the creation of neutral satellite states in Eastern Europe

B. expand Soviet involvement in the war against Japan in the Pacific

C. renegotiate the terms of the Nazi–Soviet Non-Aggression Pact

D. convince the Western Allies to open a second European front

Source: January 2000

12. The Japanese motivation for establishing the Greater East Asia Co-Prosperity Sphere during the Second World War was ultimately to

A. liberate former European colonies in the Pacific region

B. establish a Japanese empire encompassing the United States

C. counteract the growing influence of the Soviet Union in Asia

D. ensure Japanese access to the resources and markets of the Pacific region

Source: January 2000

13. The Nazis' systematic genocide of ethnic and religious groups during the Second World War provided impetus for the

A. creation of new autonomous states in central Europe

B. establishment of a war crimes tribunal at Nuremberg

C. exclusion of Germany from the original membership of NATO

D. establishment of agencies fostering European economic and political cooperation

Source: January 2000

CHALLENGER QUESTION **DIFFICULTY: 48.7**

14. Territorial adjustments and political changes in Eastern Europe immediately following the Second World War were most influenced by the fact that the

A. Allied wartime commitments to former Nazi-occupied states were honoured and enforced

B. principles of self-determination and national sovereignty were of primary concern to the victorious Allies

C. Soviet Union wished to create a buffer zone between itself and the non-communist West

D. United Nations' negotiated settlements were accepted by nations with conflicting interests

Source: January 2000

Use the following cartoon to answer questions 15 and 16.

—from *The World This Century*

15. The cartoon focuses on events in Europe occurring

A. immediately after the First World War

B. during the Second World War

C. immediately after the Second World War

D. during the final years of the Cold War

Source: January 2000

16. During the period illustrated by the cartoon, the "comfortable accommodation" offered by President Truman in the "Liberty Hotel" included the benefits associated with the

A. United Nations **B.** Marshall Plan

C. Atlantic Charter **D.** Common Market

Source: January 2000

Use the following diagram to answer question 17.

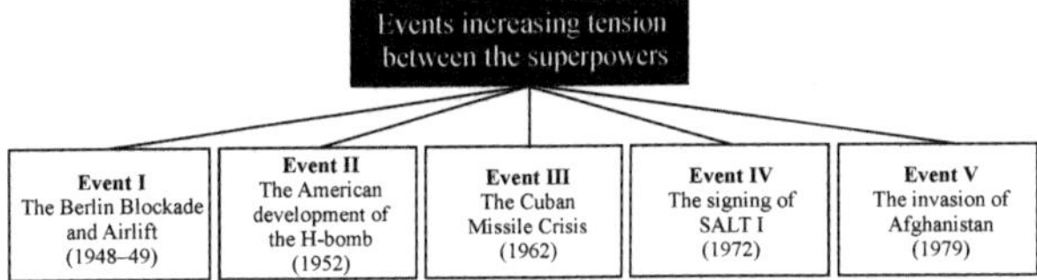

17. Given the focus of the diagram, which of the following events has been **incorrectly** included?

A. Event I **B.** Event II

C. Event III **D.** Event IV

Source: January 2000

Use the following information to answer question 18.

Developments in Nuclear Disarmament
— Partial Test Ban Treaty
— Nuclear Non-Proliferation Treaty
— Seabed Treaty
— Outer Space Treaty

18. The success of these developments depended **mainly** upon the signatories' willingness to promote

A. regional alliances

B. international prosperity

C. supranational cooperation

D. technological advancement

Source: January 2000

19. The Soviet invasion of Czechoslovakia in 1968 demonstrated to the West that

A. United Nations' peacekeeping forces were ineffective at enforcing truces

B. NATO forces were inferior to Warsaw Pact forces in conventional warfare

C. Soviet leaders were promoting the spread of communism beyond the Iron Curtain

D. Soviet leaders would not tolerate political liberalization in their sphere of influence

Source: January 2000

Use the following information to answer questions 20 to 22.

Source I

In 1991, expenditures on the United Nations Development Program and on refugee programs reached about US $1.5 billion each, triple that of the US $500 million cost of peacekeeping operations. The year 1993 showed a decline in contributions to the UNDP, while refugee programs rose to US $2 billion and costs of peacekeeping skyrocketed to US $3.6 billion. The UN spent less than US $4 billion on peacekeeping missions during the first 47 years of its existence. An administrator of the UNDP commented, "Surely it would be more humane, more effective, and less expensive to act preventively to meet threats to human development upstream rather than to have them confront us as crises downstream. We must recognize the need to increase allocations for preventive development as a complement to the more costly and more difficult curative peacekeeping."

— from *World Eagle, 1994*

Source II

Expenditures of UN Agencies (in billions of $US)

Year	Development Program	Refugee Operations	Peace-keeping
1990	1.2	1.0	0.5
1991	1.5	1.5	0.5
1992	1.4	1.8	1.6
1993	1.2	2.0	3.6

CHALLENGER QUESTION **DIFFICULTY: 45.1**

20. The United Nations' administrator quoted in Source I would **most likely favour** the

A. provision of United Nations' observer teams monitoring free elections in Haiti

B. withdrawal of United Nations' humanitarian assistance from Central Africa

C. withdrawal of United Nations' monitors of weapons installations in Iraq

D. provision of United Nations' ground forces in the Balkan region

Source: January 2000

21. The trends in the expenditures shown in Source II can be **primarily** attributed to the

A. increase in world poverty on a scale previously unimagined

B. breakup of the Soviet Union into many independent republics

C. movement toward a new world order after the Persian Gulf War

D. increase in the number of regional conflicts since the end of the Cold War

Source: January 2000

22. Taken together, the focus of the sources is on which of the following challenges currently facing the United Nations?

A. Financing the escalating costs of peacekeeping and refugee operations

B. Getting members to cooperate in sending peacekeepers to trouble spots

C. Changing the membership of the Security Council to reflect shifts in power

D. Restraining the escalating costs of the United Nations' bureaucratic structure

Source: January 2000

CHALLENGER QUESTION DIFFICULTY: 45.3

23. During the Cold War period, the prediction that the forces of nationalism would become less dominant in world affairs was supported by the

A. formation of the Warsaw Pact as a response to the NATO alliance

B. creation of defensive alliances to counter the threat of ethnic conflict

C. decolonization of Africa and the resulting creation of many new nations

D. formation of the Common Market in a movement toward a unified Europe

Source: January 2000

CHALLENGER QUESTION DIFFICULTY: 57.0

24. During the Cold War, Soviet Premier Khrushchev's desire for peaceful coexistence in conjunction with his suggestion that there are "many roads to socialism" **unintentionally** brought about

A. an end to East-West hostility

B. unrest in certain satellite states

C. crisis over oil in the Middle East

D. an end to the Sino-Soviet ideological split

Source: January 2000

Use the following sources to answer questions 25 to 27.

Source I

In the Balkans, the collapse of communism—the policeman on the corner—unleashed many demons. And does anyone really believe the West could have coaxed or bombed them into submission without a vastly greater loss of life, including the lives of many western soldiers? How many more deaths, precisely, would the interventionists have accepted as justified by the circumstances?

There will be a million standard ways of writing the history of the Yugoslav war. Unfortunately, there may be occasions for writing similar histories in other parts of Europe, east and west, because the nationalist demon—the nationalist disease—is reasserting itself everywhere .... The Communist policeman is missing from the block and a familiar and murderous pattern has reasserted itself .... Somehow "the West" is supposed to take the old policeman's spot .... [but] there is no vital great power interest at stake in the region that calls for more bloodshed. The United States ... wants to order bombing missions but has no intention of sending ground soldiers to an area where deaths would mount quickly. European states ... can see no compelling reasons to send their own soldiers to deaths in the hills of former Yugoslavia.

— from *The Edmonton Journal, 1993*

Source II

—from *Best Editorial Cartoons of the Year, 1992*

25. The author of Source I suggests that the foreign policy of Western nations is ultimately determined by

A. humanitarian concerns

B. a concern for national self-interest

C. a desire for national aggrandizement

D. resolutions passed by the United Nations

Source: January 2000

26. Which of the following statements from Source I **best** represents the underlying message illustrated by the details of the cartoon in Source II?

A. "the collapse of communism—the policeman on the corner—unleashed many demons"

B. "does anyone really believe the West could have coaxed or bombed them into submission"

C. "There will be a million standard ways of writing the history of the Yugoslav war"

D. "there is no vital great power interest at stake in the region that calls for more bloodshed"

Source: January 2000

27. Taken together, the sources suggest that the conflicts in Eastern Europe and the Balkans during the 1990s were caused **mainly** by

A. ongoing superpower competition in the area

B. long-standing nationalist rivalries and tensions

C. the failure of diplomacy to achieve a compromise

D. the deliberate policies of previous communist regimes

Source: January 2000

28. American military involvement in South Korea and South Vietnam during the Cold War illustrated the United States' commitment to

A. a policy of containment

B. the power of deterrence

C. upholding the NATO alliance

D. strengthening domestic national unity

Source: January 2000

29. The actions of international terrorists have been motivated **primarily** by the desire to draw world attention to

A. the abuses of authoritarian rule

B. the abuses of capitalist exploitation

C. demands for national self-determination

D. demands for increased global economic equality

Source: January 2000

Use the following sources to answer questions 30 to 32.

Source I
Liberalizing World Trade
Nations that trade with each other are less apt to quarrel. This, and the idea that peace has a better chance in a prosperous world, led 23 countries, including Canada, to found the General Agreement of Tariffs and Trade (GATT) in 1947. Almost half a century later, GATT completed the most important round of trade talks in its history. In April 1994, the Uruguay Round of Multilateral Trade Negotiations went a long way toward securing the fair and stable trading environment that is crucial to the development and prosperity of all nations. The Uruguay Round produced the most complete set of international trade agreements to date. Negotiations were long and difficult, but they were successful.

Source II
Post-Cold War Experience [Peacekeeping]
The end of the Cold War has changed peacekeeping in several important ways. First, there are fewer limits on where UN peacekeeping missions can be sent. Troops from the great powers can now be used, as has been the case in the former Yugoslavia, Somalia and Rwanda. New types of peacekeeping missions have been launched which go well beyond monitoring ceasefires. These operations have involved ensuring that humanitarian relief gets to those who need it, and have even included the use of military force. Regional organizations, mostly such bodies as the North Atlantic Treaty Organization (NATO) and the Conference of Security and Cooperation in Europe (CSCE), have become involved in peacekeeping activities.

Source III
Enforcing International Law
Within a nation, the law can be enforced by police. For the international legal system to be effective, it must rely on the voluntary compliance of member states. But the UN is not a toothless tiger. If a member state violates the UN Charter, it may have sanctions applied against it. This means that other UN member states are required to stop all trade with the offender. If trade sanctions fail, the UN can move on to military action.

Source IV
Nuclear Non-Proliferation
The end of the Cold War changed the world. With the superpower rivalry no longer dominating affairs, the way was open for regional tensions to increase. The way was also opened to resolving many regional conflicts. As local stability has declined, some states have become more interested in acquiring nuclear weapons as a means of ensuring their security. Controlling the spread of such weapons has become a major goal for Canada and most of its international partners.

— all sources from *Canadian Reference Guide to the United Nations*

30. Collectively, the sources support the generalization that the

A. need for nation states is disappearing as the United Nations moves toward becoming a world government

B. increased global nature of problems has created a trend toward greater supranational cooperation

C. United Nations is in dire need of major revisions so it can become an effective world force

D. end of the Cold War has created a host of new and unsolvable world problems

Source: January 2000

CHALLENGER QUESTION **DIFFICULTY: 45.5**

31. Events that developed during 1990 and 1991 as a result of the relations between Iraq and Kuwait are **most closely** associated with the actions described in

A. Source I

B. Source II

C. Source III

D. Source IV

Source: January 2000

CHALLENGER QUESTION **DIFFICULTY: 52.3**

32. The concern raised in Source IV has been heightened by renewed potential for hostilities between

A. Israel and Egypt

B. India and Pakistan

C. North and South Korea

D. the United States and Iran

Source: January 2000

Use the following time-line to answer questions 33 and 34.

A Warsaw Pact Time-Line

May 14, 1955 The Warsaw Treaty of Friendship, Cooperation, and Mutual Assistance is signed by Albania, Bulgaria, Czechoslovakia, East Germany, Hungary, Poland, Romania, and the Soviet Union. A joint command, based in Moscow, is established.

1956 Hungary announces that it is withdrawing from the Pact; Soviet troops are sent in to crush an uprising.

1968 Czechoslovakian reform is halted by an invasion by Pact troops. Romania refuses to take part, and Albania formally withdraws from the Pact.

1988 Soviet leader Gorbachev announces the withdrawal of 50 000 troops from Eastern Europe.

1989 Communist governments in Czechoslovakia, East Germany, and Romania collapse; Berlin Wall is torn down.

June–September 1990 Hungary and East Germany withdraw from the Pact.

June–July 1991 Withdrawal of Soviet troops from Czechoslovakia and Hungary is completed. The remaining members of the Pact meet in Prague to formally dissolve the alliance.

33. A Western diplomat examining the above time-line could infer that the **most critical event** that contributed to the dissolution of the Warsaw Pact was the

A. initiation of political reforms in the Soviet Union

B. reduction of NATO's military presence in Western Europe

C. reluctance of Pact members to modernize their armed forces

D. increase in nuclear weaponry initiated by the Reagan administration

Source: January 2000

34. Which of the following conclusions about the nature of military alliances is reinforced by the information provided in the time-line?

A. Alliances last only as long as other alliances oppose them.

B. Successful alliances require the willing participation of their members.

C. The success of alliances depends on the achievement of common economic goals.

D. Alliances are maintained most easily in a variable climate of détente and confrontation.

Source: January 2000

Use the following cartoon to answer question 35.

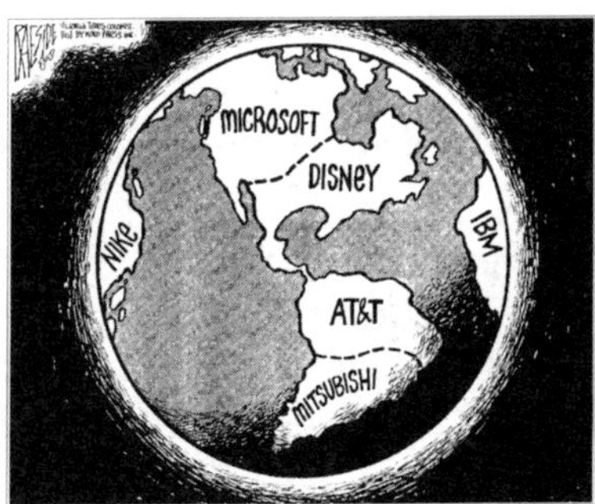

—from *The Edmonton Journal*

CHALLENGER QUESTION **DIFFICULTY: 51.7**

35. Which of the following issues is **not** suggested by the details of the cartoon?

A. To what extent are multinational corporations replacing governments?

B. To what extent has traditional sovereignty ceased to exist for most nations?

C. To what extent are national boundaries being redefined by protectionist policies?

D. To what extent have multinational corporations challenged the concept of self-determination?

Source: January 2000

CHALLENGER QUESTION **DIFFICULTY: 57.0**

36. Following the conclusion of the First World War, the architects of peace at Versailles did not consider provision for

A. creation of an international peacekeeping force

B. recognition of an independent Austria and Poland

C. reparation payments as compensation for destruction

D. demobilization and reduction of Germany's military forces

Source: June 2000

Use the following maps to answer question 37.

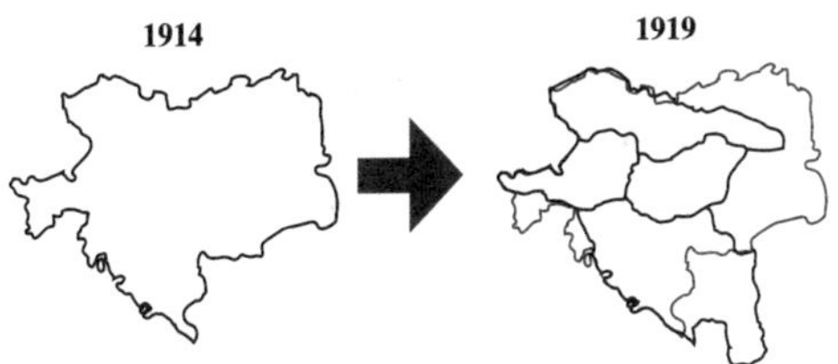

CHALLENGER QUESTION **DIFFICULTY: 48.8**

37. The maps above illustrate the disintegration of which European empire following the First World War?

A. The Ottoman Empire

B. The Russian Empire

C. The German Empire

D. The Austro-Hungarian Empire

Source: June 2000

38. *In areas with mixed ethnic populations, it is impossible to draw boundaries that satisfy all of the parties concerned.*

The truth of this statement was demonstrated during the

A. Sudetenland Crisis, 1938

B. Suez Crisis, 1956

C. Soviet invasion of Afghanistan, 1979

D. British action in the Falkland Islands, 1982

Source: June 2000

Use the following excerpt to answer questions 39 and 40.

[Czech] President Benes believed that Hitler was bluffing and would give way if faced with a firm, united opposition. When Hitler did not give way, even Benes in the last resort preferred surrender to war. The Czechs, Benes held, were a small people, who must preserve their lives for a better future. Their country had been occupied before and they had survived. They would survive again. In a sense, his arguments were justified by events. The Czechs were abandoned by the Western powers. Their country fell under German tyranny for six years. But only one or perhaps two hundred thousand of them lost their lives. Prague, their capital, was the only great city of Central Europe to remain undamaged in the Second World War, and Czechoslovakia emerged with unbroken spirit, at the end. In contrast, Poland was guaranteed by the Western powers, who went to war for her sake. As a result six million Poles were killed. Warsaw was reduced to a heap of ruins, and Poland, though restored, lost much of her territory and her independence.

— Historian A.J.P. Taylor
— from *The World This Century*

39. The comment, "The Czechs were abandoned by the Western powers" refers to the

A. Rome–Berlin Axis, 1936

B. Munich Pact, 1938

C. Nazi–Soviet Pact, 1939

D. Lend Lease Agreement, 1940

Source: June 2000

40. The author's comments could be interpreted as justifying a policy of

A. détente

B. militarism

C. appeasement

D. armed deterrence

Source: June 2000

Use the following table to answer questions 41 to 43.

**League of Nations –
Attempts to Resolve International Disputes**

1.	Finland and Sweden	1920
2.	Germany and Poland	1921–22
3.	Turkey and Iraq	1924–25
4.	Italy and Greece	1923
5.	Peru and Colombia	1933
6.	Bolivia and Paraguay	1933–34
7.	Japan and China	1931–32
8.	Abyssinia and Italy	1935

41. The table shows an early attempt by the League of Nations to promote peace based upon principles of

A. appeasement

B. brinkmanship

C. alliance systems

D. collective security

Source: June 2000

42. Considering the League of Nations' successes and failures in those areas listed in the table, the League was **most** successful in solving

A. minor territorial disputes that did not directly involve Great Power interests

B. distant colonial disputes that emerged among the major European imperialist powers

C. disputes emerging out of conflicting interpretations of the terms of the Treaty of Versailles

D. disputes resulting from the aggressive expansionist policies of right-wing nationalist regimes

Source: June 2000

CHALLENGER QUESTION **DIFFICULTY: 59.3**

43. The League's credibility and stature were undermined by its failure to address effectively

A. disputes 1 and 2

B. disputes 2 and 4

C. disputes 4 and 7

D. disputes 7 and 8

Source: June 2000

Use the following declaration to answer questions 44 and 45.

The Republican party maintains the traditional American policy of noninterference in the political affairs of other nations. This government has definitely refused membership in the League of Nations and to assume any obligations under the covenant of the League. On this we stand.
—from *Internationalism: Opposing Viewpoints*

44. On what principle was this declaration **most likely** made?

A. Containment should come before neutrality.

B. Deterrence should come before appeasement.

C. Sovereignty should come before collective security.

D. International cooperation should come before national interests.

Source: June 2000

45. Which American president and which event abruptly ended support for the philosophy underlying this declaration?

A. Harry S. Truman and the dropping of the first atomic bomb

B. Franklin D. Roosevelt and the bombing of Pearl Harbor

C. Richard M. Nixon and the evacuation of Saigon

D. John F. Kennedy and the Cuban Missile Crisis

Source: June 2000

46. The Nazi philosophy of *lebensraum* moved from theory to practice when Hitler

A. invaded the Soviet Union

B. sent soldiers and equipment to Spain

C. formed the Rome-Berlin-Tokyo Axis

D. withdrew from the League of Nations

Source: June 2000

CHALLENGER QUESTION **DIFFICULTY: 52.3**

47. British success in the Battle of Britain has historically been viewed as an important turning point during the Second World War because this success

A. forced Germany to withdraw from territories it occupied in Belgium and the Netherlands

B. persuaded the United States to immediately enter the war against Germany

C. motivated the Soviet Union to attack Germany's eastern frontiers

D. preserved an Allied base for attack on Nazi-occupied Europe

Source: June 2000

Use the following description to answer questions 48 and 49.

[The insurgents] must be keenly aware of both the physical and the cultural environment. They are usually less well-armed than their adversaries. Therefore, if they do not know the land they are moving across, they will be trapped and destroyed ....

[They] need not be numerous, but they need the sympathy of a sizable segment of the population. The first stage . . . is mobile warfare, in which small . . . bands are unable to seize permanent control over a territory and are constantly on the move to avoid capture. These bands confine their operations to specific, carefully chosen regions . . . where [they] can easily conceal themselves. At the same time, this chosen area should be largely self-sufficient economically, discontented politically, and located near key military objectives, such as cities and transport lines.

—from *The Human Mosaic*

48. This description refers to military tactics associated with

A. terrorist attacks

B. guerrilla warfare

C. covert operations

D. conventional warfare

Source: June 2000

49. These tactics are **best** illustrated by the conflict between

A. Palestinians and Israelis in the Middle East

B. Coalition and Iraqi forces in the Gulf region

C. Protestants and Catholics in Northern Ireland

D. Americans and the Viet Cong in South Vietnam

Source: June 2000

Use the following proposals to answer question 50.

Proposals for Averting Nuclear Confrontation	
I.	The number of nuclear weapons should be restricted to a certain level.
II.	Nuclear powers should be encouraged to protect their arsenals by using "Star Wars" technology.
III.	The United Nations should establish a force equipped with the military power to stop nuclear aggression.
IV.	Nuclear powers and their allies should agree to not deploy nuclear weapons in the event of war.

50. Which of the above proposals formed the basis for the SALT talks?

A. Proposal I **B.** Proposal II

C. Proposal III **D.** Proposal IV

Source: June 2000

CHALLENGER QUESTION DIFFICULTY: 54.2

51. The principle of internationalism is demonstrated when nations attempt to establish

A. colonial empires

B. isolationist policies

C. spheres of influence

D. multilateral agreements

Source: June 2000

52. *Nationalism is, by its very essence, dynamic rather than static. It is an explosive force, not a factor of stability.*

The historical development that **best** supports this contention is the

A. turmoil in the Balkans during the 1990s

B. the collapse of apartheid policies in South Africa during the 1990s

C. absorption of Hong Kong into the People's Republic of China

D. agreement to include Poland, Hungary, and the Czech Republic in NATO

Source: June 2000

Use the following cartoon to answer questions 53 to 55.

"NOSES LEFT!"
—from *Low's Cartoon History 1945–1953*

CHALLENGER QUESTION DIFFICULTY: 54.4

53. In this 1947 cartoon, the "American Hot Dog Stand" symbolizes the

A. protective alliance established by NATO

B. economic assistance offered by the Marshall Plan

C. economic appeal of joining the Common Market

D. national security assured through membership in COMECON

Source: June 2000

54. The "school girls" depicted in the cartoon represent

A. satellite states of the Soviet Union

B. members of the North Atlantic alliance

C. ethnic minority groups within the Soviet Union

D. founding states of the European Economic Community

Source: June 2000

55. Which of the following aspects of superpower relations during the Cold War is **best** illustrated by the cartoon?

A. The search for national unity and prosperity

B. The quest for détente and mutual coexistence

C. The competition to form and maintain spheres of influence

D. The conflict between national security and collective security

Source: June 2000

Use the following cartoon to answer question 56.

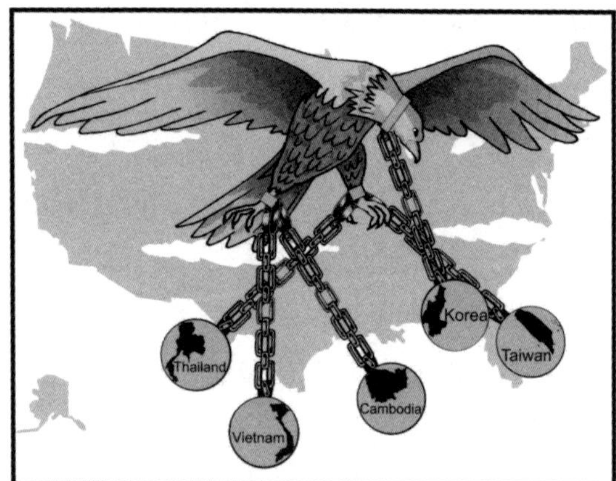

56. In this cartoon about the Cold War era, the cartoonist is commenting on a negative consequence of the American foreign policy of

A. détente

B. deterrence

C. containment

D. brinkmanship

Source: June 2000

Use the following sources to answer questions 57 to 59.

Source I
President John F. Kennedy's Attitude Toward the Cuban Crisis
President Kennedy dedicated himself to making it clear to Khrushchev by word and deed … that the United States had limited objectives and that we had no intention of accomplishing those objectives by adversely affecting the national security of the Soviet Union or by humiliating her.…

During our crisis talks he kept stressing the fact that we would indeed have war if we placed the Soviet Union in a position she believed would adversely affect her national security or such public humiliation that she lost the respect of her own people and countries round the globe. The missiles in Cuba, we felt, vitally concerned our national security, but not that of the Soviet Union.

This fact was ultimately recognized by Khrushchev, and this recognition, I believe, brought about this change in what, up to that time, had been a very adamant position. The President believed from the start that the Soviet Chairman was a rational, intelligent man, who if given sufficient time and shown our determination, would alter his position. …

— Robert Kennedy

Source II
Khrushchev's Recollection of the Cuba Crisis
…We were quite sure that the Americans would never reconcile themselves to the existence of Castro's Cuba. They feared, as much as we hoped, that a socialist Cuba might become a magnet that would attract other Latin American countries to socialism.…

The fate of Cuba and the maintenance of Soviet prestige in that part of the world preoccupied me. …We had to establish a tangible and effective deterrent to American interference in the Caribbean. But what exactly? The logical answer was missiles. ...

> I want to make one thing absolutely clear: when we put our ballistic missiles in Cuba, we had no desire to start a war. On the contrary, our principal aim was to deter America from starting a war. ...
>
> We sent the Americans a note saying that we agreed to remove our missiles and bombers on the condition that the President give us his assurance that there would be no invasion of Cuba by the forces of the United States or anybody else. Finally Kennedy gave in and agreed to make a statement giving us such an assurance. ...
>
> It had been, to say the least, an interesting and challenging situation. The two most powerful nations in the world had been squared off against each other, each with its finger on the button... It was a great victory for us, though...
>
> The Caribbean crisis was a triumph of Soviet foreign policy and a personal triumph in my own career... We achieved, I would say, a spectacular success without having to fire a single shot!
>
> —Nikita Khrushchev
>
> — both sources from *The Cold War*

57. Taken together, the two sources suggest that the key to the peaceful resolution of the Cuban Missile Crisis lay in

A. pursuing the policy of collective security to its logical conclusion

B. finding a face-saving solution that would allow both superpowers to claim victory

C. ensuring that the United States was fully aware of the capabilities of Soviet military forces

D. abandoning the principle of armed deterrence and embracing the principal of regional security

Source: June 2000

58. Khrushchev's rationale for placing ballistic missiles in Cuba is consistent with the doctrine of

A. coexistence

B. appeasement

C. balance of power

D. collective security

Source: June 2000

59. According to Source I, President Kennedy's "limited objectives" during the Cuban Missile Crisis included the

A. overthrow of Castro's regime by an airborne invasion

B. promotion of American democratic and capitalist ideas

C. abandonment of brinkmanship during a diplomatic crisis

D. preservation of the national security of the United States

Source: June 2000

60. During the Cold War, the experiences of the Americans in Vietnam and of the Soviets in Afghanistan illustrated that

A. military strength alone is not sufficient to guarantee victory

B. great powers often use total war to achieve their national objectives

C. the great powers felt less need to maintain spheres of influence because of their nuclear capabilities

D. collective security through the United Nations is the best way to resolve conflicts

Source: June 2000

Use the following chart to answer questions 61 and 62.

Incentive	Leader who initiated action	Action
To buy time to prepare for an inevitable German invasion	Stalin	Signed a non-aggression pact
?	Khrushchev	?
To maintain a communist sphere of influence on the Soviet border	Brezhnev	Invaded Afghanistan
To revive the Soviet economy	Gorbachev	Introduced perestroika
To prevent the secession of a region in Russia	Yeltsin	Attempted to subjugate Chechnya

61. The actions identified in this chart specifically span the years

A. 1919 to 1989

B. 1929 to 1989

C. 1939 to 2000

D. 1949 to 2000

Source: June 2000

62. The **Incentive** and **Action** that could be used to complete the chart above are given in row

	Incentive	Action
A.	To prevent West Germany from occupying Danzig	Ordered the closing of the Polish Corridor
B.	To maintain a Soviet sphere of influence	Ordered the invasion of Hungary
C.	To provoke a military confrontation with the United States	Sealed off the city of Prague
D.	To rapidly modernize the Soviet Union	Initiated the first Five Year Plan

Source: June 2000

63. Relations between the Israeli and Palestinian authorities improved significantly in 1993 when Israel

A. increased Jewish immigration from territory formerly under Soviet control

B. allowed limited Palestinian autonomy in lands under Israeli occupation

C. annexed territories that were formerly part of Egypt and Syria

D. dramatically reduced the size of its armed forces

Source: June 2000

64. Despite the end of the Cold War and the creation of the INF Treaty, the threat of global catastrophe is still present because of the

A. formation of new military alliances backed by massive conventional armies of the superpowers

B. continued buildup of sophisticated nuclear weapons in Russia and the former Soviet republics

C. increased possibility of nations other than the superpowers obtaining nuclear capability

D. growing power of transnational corporations to dictate and control the international supply of arms

Source: June 2000

CHALLENGER QUESTION DIFFICULTY: 46.5

65. Which of the following statements characterizes the role that transnational corporations have assumed in geopolitics?

A. Transnational corporations have reaffirmed their commitment to fairer corporate taxation and greater environmental protection.

B. Transnational corporations have become able to challenge the sovereign decision-making power of national governments.

C. Transnational corporations are now the object of intense regulation by national governments throughout the world.

D. Transnational corporations have avoided investing in developing nations with lax labour regulations.

Source: June 2000

CHALLENGER QUESTION DIFFICULTY: 49.3

66. The collective actions taken against Iraq during the Gulf War in 1991 were unique in that they represented the first time that the

A. United Nations used armed force against an aggressor

B. United Nations became actively involved in a Middle East dispute

C. former Cold War superpowers cooperated to confront a major act of aggression

D. former Cold War superpowers ignored a resolution of the UN Security Council

Source: June 2000

Use the following excerpt to answer questions 67 to 69.

Palm Pilot in one hand, cellular phone in the other, Jean-Marc Routiers, 26, was juggling business calls halfway between London and Paris. When his phone went dead as the high-speed Eurostar train pulled into the underwater tunnel that links England to the Continent, the London-based French banker loosened his Italian silk tie and introduced himself.

“I definitely describe myself as a European,” he said in the fluent English he perfected working at an Australian bank. “I may get sentimental when they play the Marseillaise, but for all the practical things, I see myself as a citizen of Europe. I like the lifestyle in France, but I don't make my living there.” . . .

Mobile, fluent in several languages and aggressively non-nationalistic, [the new generation of Europeans] are already living the kind of borderless, cosmopolitan existence that the single European currency is supposed to advance.

They do not share their parents’ memories of the Second World War or their parents’ sense of national identity.

"People worry when they hear talk of a common European defence policy because it suggests that at the end of the day, we have one government," said Kleon Papadopoulos, a Greek banker based in London.

"Countries are afraid to lose their sovereignty, but I don't see it as a bad thing. If a government is good, stable and efficient, who cares if it is based in Berlin or Athens?"

— from *The Edmonton Journal*

67. The excerpt suggests that when compared with the new generation of Europeans, former generations were

A. more willing to support international collective actions

B. less willing to serve their government without question

C. less concerned with global political affairs

D. more loyal to their ethnic heritage

Source: June 2000

68. The excerpt suggests that many young Europeans today are willing to sacrifice national sovereignty if, in exchange, Europe becomes more

A. culturally diverse

B. global in outlook

C. politically left-wing

D. conservative in ideology

Source: June 2000

69. Which of the following titles is **most appropriate** for this excerpt?

A. *Europe: A Model for Future Supranationalism*

B. *Europe: A Superpower to Rival the United States*

C. *Europe: Democracy Triumphs over Authoritarianism*

D. *Europe: Political Security Sacrificed for Economic Power*

Source: June 2000

70. *Regional security alliances and global collective security often have the same goals and objectives.*

The truth of this assertion is **best** illustrated by the

A. United Nations and UNICEF providing aid to Rwanda

B. United Nations and NATO sending peacekeepers to Bosnia

C. League of Nations organizing mandates from former colonial empires

D. League of Nations applying sanctions against Italy when Ethiopia was attacked

Source: June 2000

Use the following cartoon to answer questions 71 and 72.

Some day they'll come crawling back to her.

—from *A Cartoon History of United States Foreign Policy*

CHALLENGER QUESTION	**DIFFICULTY: 54.1**

71. This 1919 cartoon ridicules American political party members who supported the idea of

A. containing the spread of communism

B. appeasing aggressive European dictators

C. maintaining a balance of power through European alliances

D. employing collective security through the League of Nations

Source: January 2001

72. Advocates of the policy followed by the "America–Last Republicans" and "America–Last Democrats" would have said that "Americanism" was just another word for

A. idealism **B.** isolationism

C. ultranationalism **D.** supranationalism

Source: January 2001

Use the following map to answer questions 73 to 75.

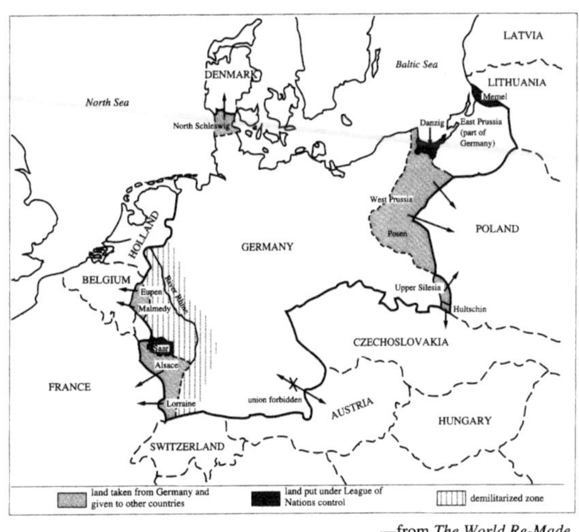

—from *The World Re-Made*

73. The territorial and other changes illustrated on the map can be attributed to Germany's

A. defeat at the conclusion of the First World War

B. failure to meet deadlines for reparation payments

C. acceptance of decisions made by the League of Nations

D. acceptance of specific provisions of the Locarno Pact

Source: January 2001

CHALLENGER QUESTION **DIFFICULTY: 58.5**

74. From a historical perspective, one could argue that the major result of the changes illustrated on the map was

A. the formation of a defensive alliance between Germany and Austria

B. internal strife in Germany along with bitterness toward neighbouring states

C. the abandonment of a defeated Germany to supervision by the League of Nations

D. a reinforcement of the belief that Germany had largely gone unpunished for past aggressions

Source: January 2001

75. If the legend for this map had included: *land ceded by terms of the Munich Agreement*, the shading would have been placed on

A. eastern Austria

B. western Poland

C. eastern Belgium

D. western Czechoslovakia

Source: January 2001

76. As a result of overlapping foreign policy interests during the interwar years, Japan and the United States came into conflict over their interest in

A. Northern Europe

B. the Middle East

C. Central Asia

D. the Pacific

Source: January 2001

Use the following diagram to answer question 77.

77. Chronologically and thematically, the event that completes the diagram is the

A. Italian invasion of Ethiopia

B. Japanese seizure of Manchuria

C. signing of the Nazi–Soviet Pact

D. outbreak of the Spanish Civil War

Source: January 2001

Use the following definition to answer questions 78 and 79.

Irredentism: The desire of the people of a state to annex those [neighbouring] territories of another country that are inhabited largely by linguistic or cultural minorities of the first state.
—from *The International Relations Dictionary*

78. Given this definition, which claims from the interwar years are the **best** example of irredentism?

A. Italy's claims on Ethiopia

B. Japan's claims on Manchuria

C. The Soviet Union's claims on Poland

D. Germany's claims on the Sudetenland

Source: January 2001

79. During the 1930s, the claims of European irredentists were largely addressed by a foreign policy of

A. collective security by the League of Nations

B. appeasement by Great Britain and France

C. containment by the United States

D. aggression by the Axis powers

Source: January 2001

Use the following excerpt to answer question 80.

More than four years have passed since China, failing to comprehend the true intentions of our Empire, and recklessly courting trouble, disturbed the peace of east Asia and compelled our Empire to take up arms. Eager to dominate the Orient, both America and Britain, by giving support to the Chunking regime, have aggravated the disturbances in east Asia. They have obstructed by every means our peaceful commerce, and finally resorted to a direct severance of economic relations, menacing gravely the existence of our Empire.

— from *Case Studies in Twentieth-Century History*

CHALLENGER QUESTION **DIFFICULTY: 51.8**

80. In which of the following historical contexts was this excerpt from a speech **most likely** given?

A. The Japanese government declaring war on Great Britain and the United States, 1941

B. The South Korean government condemning China for its invasion, 1950

C. The Soviet premier commenting on the Sino-Soviet split, 1969

D. The North Vietnamese president claiming victory over the United States, 1975

Source: January 2001

Use the following comments to answer questions 81 and 82.

Source I
The dropping of atom bombs without specific warning may have been inexcusable; but the decision to do so was taken by harassed men in the extremity of a life and death conflict. It aroused immediate feelings of revulsion. The mass murder of Jews and Russians was a deliberate policy made possible by the war but had nothing to do with the winning of it. It was carried out systematically and in cold blood by men who knew what they were doing and watched their victims die.

Source II
...the cruelties were not all on Hitler's side. We all became fascists, in certain respects, in the Second World War, and, indeed, in later, less extensive struggles such as the Korean War. We condemned vast numbers of personally innocent men, women, and children to horrible, flaming deaths, because they happened to be on other side. The atomic bomb merely systematically perfected a technique of mass slaughter with which we were already doing very well before that.

— both sources from *The Rise of the Nazi Horror*

81. The focus of the sources is reflected in which of the following questions?

A. Did the Allied powers turn a "blind eye" to Nazi atrocities?

B. Should nations continue to pursue and prosecute war crimes?

C. Which actions taken in times of conflict should be considered "criminal" ?

D. Can collective security organizations effectively monitor human rights abuse?

Source: January 2001

CHALLENGER QUESTION **DIFFICULTY: 58.7**

82. Which of the following statements **best** summarizes the point of view expressed in Source I?

A. It is impossible to agree upon what acceptable behaviours are during wartime.

B. In times of international conflict, the only rule is that victory must be achieved.

C. When battling an evil enemy, no actions should be considered improper or excessive.

D. Extreme measures, taken during wartime, are more justifiable if the intent is to end the conflict.

Source: January 2001

83. During the Second World War, the Atlantic corridor supply route was effectively disrupted by the submarine activity of

A. Germany

B. Great Britain

C. the Soviet Union

D. the United States

Source: January 2001

Use the following excerpt to answer questions 84 and 85.

The [economic] collapse of 1929–1933 put an end to the high hopes for a shared prosperity which had marked the post-war years. Now, as world trade fell, each nation determined to hang on to what was left, and at any rate to keep its own trade intact. This was a policy of 'economic nationalism'–a far cry from the economic internationalism of which President Wilson had dreamed.

— from *The 20th Century*

84. Which of the following strategies is inconsistent with the policy of "economic nationalism" described in the excerpt?

A. Negotiating multilateral trade agreements among nations

B. Erecting protectionist barriers to international commerce

C. Increasing tariffs on foreign goods

D. Imposing quotas on imported goods

Source: January 2001

CHALLENGER QUESTION **DIFFICULTY: 44.3**

85. The ironic consequence of the efforts made by nations to keep their "own trade intact" was

A. the adoption of Lenin's NEP in the Soviet Union

B. decreasing productivity and employment worldwide

C. the formation of regional and global common markets

D. increased inflationary pressures in Western and Central Europe

Source: January 2001

CHALLENGER QUESTION **DIFFICULTY: 54.5**

86. During the last days of the Second World War, the east-west Cold War split began to emerge in the proceedings and discussions surrounding the

A. Marshall Plan and COMECON

B. Potsdam and Yalta agreements

C. Truman Doctrine and Berlin airlift

D. Warsaw Pact and NATO agreements

Source: January 2001

87. The United Nations was originally formed in the belief that

A. conflict among the great powers can be avoided through mutual deterrence

B. global peace can be achieved through the actions of democratic powers

C. nations can achieve security by joining regional organizations

D. global stability can be achieved through collective security

Source: January 2001

Use the following map to answer question 88.

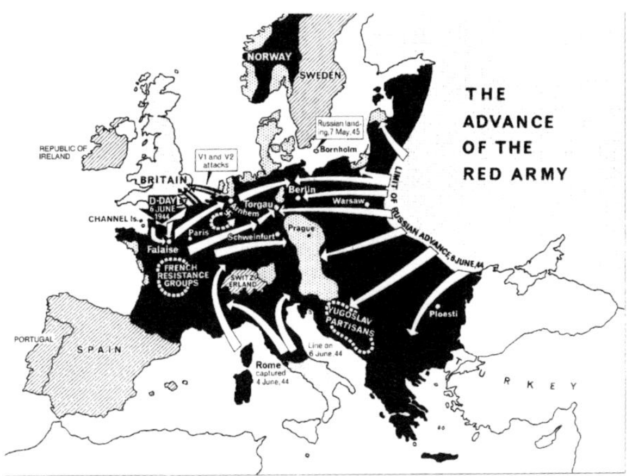

—from *A Map History of the Modern World*

88. The **best** title for this map is

A. *The Collapse of Nazi Germany*

B. *Stalemate on the Western Front*

C. *The Second Front in Central Europe*

D. *Nazi Forces Launch Eastern Blitzkrieg*

Source: January 2001

CHALLENGER QUESTION	DIFFICULTY: 57.9

89. Historically, which of the following alternatives demonstrates the greatest shift in a nation's foreign policy?

A. From appeasement to non-intervention

B. From deterrence to brinkmanship

C. From isolationism to containment

D. From détente to peaceful coexistence

Source: January 2001

Use the following cartoon to answer questions 90 and 91.

Starting Something?

—from *A Cartoon History of United States Foreign Policy Since World War I*

90. In this 1950s cartoon, the wasps symbolically portray the role taken by the

A. Great Powers in refusing to apply the principle of collective security

B. United Nations' members in responding to a specific act of aggression

C. People's Republic of China in providing military aid to an ideological ally

D. Soviet Union in militarily attacking a small and largely undefended Asian nation

Source: January 2001

91. Within the context of the cartoon, which nation is the swarm of wasps, represented as "Enraged World Democracies," attacking?

A. The People's Republic of China

B. The Soviet Union

C. North Korea

D. Japan

Source: January 2001

92. *"You have a row of dominoes set up; you knock over the first one, and what will happen to the last one is the certainty that it will go over very quickly."*

–Dwight D. Eisenhower

The idea given in this statement formed the basis of an American foreign policy of

A. détente with rival military superpowers

B. deterrence based on nuclear arms capability

C. containment of communism in southeast Asia

D. isolation from international conflicts and disputes

Source: January 2001

Use the following chart to answer question 93.

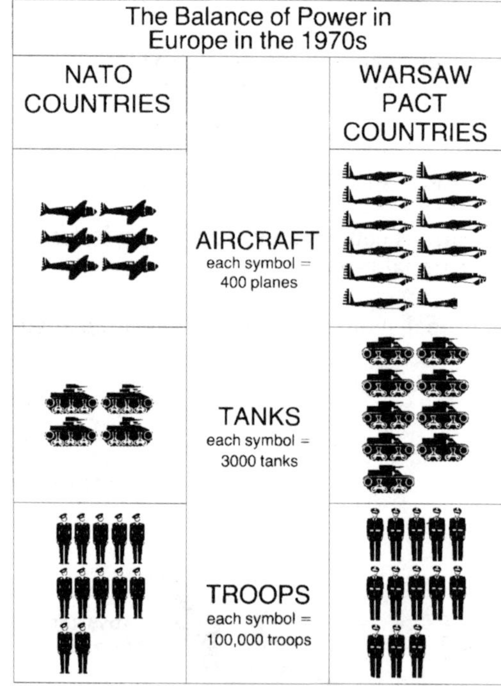

—from *The Modern World Since 1917*

93. During the Cold War, the military imbalance indicated in this chart was kept in check through the

A. threat of nuclear weapons

B. pressure of summit conferences

C. threat of all-out conventional warfare

D. pressure exerted by the United Nations

Source: January 2001

Use the following observations about the United Nations to answer questions 94 to 97.

Observation I
... the United Nations has undertaken 13 peacekeeping operations in the last four years–as many as it attempted in the previous 40 ... $2.7 billion will be spent on peacekeeping this year alone.

Observation II
... after years of near-irrelevance, the United Nations, "has almost too much credibility now." It is suddenly free to use its collective security powers. And people suddenly expect it to.

Observation III
The United Nations is broke... Members owe the United Nations $1.8 billion in overdue assessments; the United States, as the worst deadbeat, owes $555 million.
— I, II, and III from *The Edmonton Journal*

Observation IV
The changed world apparently is strengthening the rote of the [United Nations] to the benefit of all peoples everywhere. However, the [United Nations] also faces the increasing need to reform itself to effectively serve the newly emerging world order . . .. Obviously, the current organization does not fairly represent today's respective shares of international responsibility.
— IV from *World Press Review*

94. The expanded world role of the United Nations that is referred to in observations I, II, and IV resulted **primarily** from the

A. increase in the number of nations defaulting on IMF payments

B. emergence of a United Europe with superpower status

C. magnitude of world population growth

D. end of the Cold War

Source: January 2001

95. In commenting on the need for United Nations reform, the writer of Observation IV is **most likely** drawing attention to the

A. restricted permanent membership of the UN Security Council

B. admission rules for countries wishing to join the United Nations

C. shortage of funds available to support United Nations humanitarian agencies

D. failure of the United Nations to maintain a peacekeeping function

Source: January 2001

CHALLENGER QUESTION DIFFICULTY: 59.9

96. Which of the following statements regarding all four observations is **accurate**?

A. Observations I and III are making a similar point.

B. Observation I contradicts the point made in Observation IV.

C. Observation II provides a key reason explaining why the argument made in Observation IV is illogical.

D. Observation III reveals a situation that is potentially threatening to the expectations suggested in observations I, II, and IV.

Source: January 2001

97. Given these four observations, which of the following positions would an internationalist offer as an approach to maintaining global peace and security?

A. Nations should adopt foreign policy strategies that protect their vital interests.

B. Nations should demand a world police force composed of troops exclusively from the United States and Russia.

C. Nations should equip their militaries with the most recent high-tech weapons to ensure their national security in a dangerous world.

D. Nations should support decentralized collective security while regional organizations take more responsibility for mediation and preventive diplomacy.

Source: January 2001

CHALLENGER QUESTION **DIFFICULTY: 56.0**

98. The doctrine of peaceful coexistence initiated by Soviet leader Khrushchev indicated that the Soviet Union had

A. recognized that new strategies were needed because of nuclear threat

B. accepted the increased power of the United States in world affairs

C. placed greater confidence in nuclear weapons for security

D. lessened direct control over its European satellite states

Source: January 2001

CHALLENGER QUESTION **DIFFICULTY: 42.5**

99. During the Cold War, many nations achieved independence as a result of

A. decolonization in Africa and Asia

B. liberation movements in Latin America

C. struggles for power among ethnic groups in the Balkans

D. spheres of influence being established in the Middle East

Source: January 2001

100. Faced with the Hungarian uprising in 1956, the Soviet government was confronted with the dilemma of whether to

A. accept United Nations' peacekeepers or employ third-party mediation

B. utilize an appeasement policy or negotiate a settlement

C. preserve collective security or create a balance of power

D. maintain a sphere of influence or respect national sovereignty

Source: January 2001

Use the following sources to answer questions 101 to 103.

Source I

Despite obvious analogies, Serbian leader Milosevic is no Adolf Hitler, and Serbia is not 1930s Germany . … Yet historical analogies are relevant, for today's Western politicians labour under the same mentality that produced the disaster of the 1930s . … Every institution, from the Conference on Security and Co-operation in Europe to the European Community, the Western European Union, and NATO, has tried to handle an utterly predictable war, and all have been disgraced for one simple reason: they tackled a post-communist conflict with instruments best suited for a previous age.

— from *The Independent, London. May 1993*

Source II

—from *The Edmonton Journal*, May 1994

CHALLENGER QUESTION **DIFFICULTY: 59.2**

101. The phrase "Yet historical analogies are relevant" (Source I) refers to the dilemma that confronted those who attempted to stop the conflict in the former Yugoslavia. This dilemma was whether to

A. employ containment or deterrence as a diplomatic tactic

B. use armed force or conciliation in the face of aggression

C. apply sanctions or an arms embargo to topple a dictator

D. demand peace talks or a cease-fire through the United Nations

Source: January 2001

CHALLENGER QUESTION **DIFFICULTY: 43.5**

102. The historical event alluded to by both sources is the signing of the

A. Munich Pact

B. Locarno Pact

C. Nazi–Soviet Pact

D. Kellogg–Briand Pact

Source: January 2001

CHALLENGER QUESTION **DIFFICULTY: 50.4**

103. Both the writer (Source I) and the cartoonist (Source II) would **most likely** have supported which of the following international responses toward Serbia in 1993?

A. Armed neutrality

B. Mediated cease-fires

C. Direct confrontation

D. Negotiated land settlements

Source: January 2001

104. Throughout the history of conflict in the Middle East, the underlying issue that has remained constant is whether or not the opposing sides will

A. resolve their ongoing arms race

B. resolve their territorial claims

C. allow their oil resources to be conserved for the future

D. allow United Nations' peacekeepers to supervise democratic elections

Source: January 2001

105. According to a supporter of the principles of the Charter of the United Nations, international tensions have been lessened since 1945 by the

A. proliferation of military alliance systems worldwide

B. use of brinkmanship to resolve conflicts

C. creation of supranational organizations

D. strength of competing ideologies

Source: January 2001

NOTES

Unit Test 2 – Global Interaction in the 20th Century

Use the following cartoon to answer questions 1 and 2.

THE ACCUSER

— from *Internationalism: Opposing Viewpoints Series*

1. The slain figure labelled "Treaty of Peace" could be **most closely** associated with the

   A. Charter of the United Nations

   B. provisions of the Munich Accord

   C. Covenant of the League of Nations

   D. text of the Locarno Agreement

2. The purpose of this cartoon was to provide

   A. unqualified support for an American foreign policy of isolation during the 1920s

   B. a scathing indictment of American refusal to support the principle of collective security

   C. a strong criticism of American refusal to provide loans to war-ravaged European nations

   D. solid support for American reluctance to become involved in disputes between democracies and dictatorships

3. The collapse of the Romanov and Hapsburg dynasties during the First World War created a power vacuum that led to

   A. the failure of appeasement policies

   B. a weakening of the League of Nations

   C. a general European disarmament treaty

   D. the emergence of many, new independent states

4. In the view of many Germans, the political credibility of the government of the Weimar Republic during the 1920s was seriously damaged by its

   A. reluctance to join the League of Nations

   B. high level of spending on military rearmament

   C. acceptance of the terms of the Treaty of Versailles

   D. signing of a non-aggression pact with the Soviet Union

Use the following quotation to answer questions 5 and 6.

All is over. Silent, mournful, abandoned, broken, Czechoslovakia recedes into the darkness ... our loyal, brave people ... should know that we have sustained a defeat without a war, the consequences of which will travel far with us along our road; they should know that we have passed an awful milestone in our history ... And do not suppose that this is the end. This is only the beginning of the reckoning. This is only the first sip, the first foretaste of a bitter cup which will be proffered to us year by year unless, by a supreme recovery of moral health and martial vigour, we arise again and take our stand for freedom as in the olden time.

— Winston Churchill

5. Churchill's speech was a commentary on the consequences of the

   A. Yalta Conference

   B. Munich Conference

   C. Potsdam Conference

   D. Casablanca Conference

6. Churchill's statements indicate that he was an opponent of

   A. brinkmanship

   B. appeasement

   C. collective security

   D. peaceful coexistence

7. *The League of Nations lacked one avenue of power that was later available to the United Nations.*

   This "avenue" was the willingness to

   A. raise a military force to enforce decisions

   B. apply sanctions against an aggressor nation

   C. openly debate international issues with member nations

   D. involve members in making decisions to condemn aggression

8. Which of Hitler's goals is **correctly** paired with a corresponding response?

	Goal	**Response**
A.	Attain racial purification →	Enabling Act
B.	Eliminate possible rivals →	Night of the Long Knives
C.	Improve sluggish economy →	Nuremberg Laws
D.	Achieve territorial expansion →	The Final Solution

9. Which objective was common to the Casablanca (1943), Tehran (1943), Cairo (1943), and Yalta (1945) conferences?

   A. To establish a successor organization to the League of Nations

   B. To condemn Soviet expansion and aggression in Eastern Europe

   C. To develop and approve Allied plans to defeat the Axis powers

   D. To approve financial resources for the development of atomic weapons

10. By 1949, the existence of the North Atlantic Treaty Organization, the Marshall Plan, and the Truman Doctrine indicated

    A. an end to the dangerous Soviet policy of expansionism

    B. an end to the traditional American policy of isolationism

    C. the beginning of détente between the Soviet Union and the United States

    D. the failure of the Soviet Union to consolidate control over Eastern Europe

Use the following cartoon to answer questions 11 and 12.

— from *Evidence in Question*

11. This 1936 Soviet cartoon suggests that

A. Hitler's ideology was threatened by the wealth classes

B. western diplomats genuinely intended to contain Nazi Germany

C. western capitalists were responsible for the rise of Nazism in Germany

D. Hitler turned against neighbouring capitalist countries early in his career

12. The Soviet press suddenly **stopped** publishing cartoons such as this because of

A. the signing of the Munich Pact

B. the signing of the Nazi–Soviet Pact

C. Hitler's invasion of the Soviet Union

D. Stalin's plans to invade Nazi Germany

Use the following map to answer questions 13 and 14.

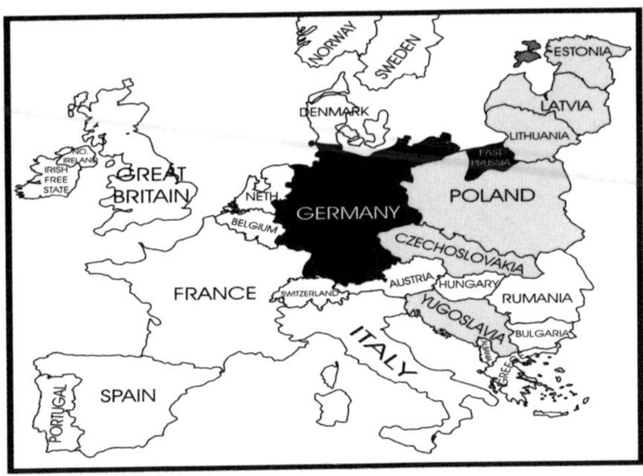

13. This map indicates the boundaries of Europe as they were in

A. 1929 **B.** 1940

C. 1955 **D.** 1991

14. According to historical context of the map, the areas shaded grey were

A. behind the Iron Curtain

B. allied against Nazi Germany

C. governed by pro-German fascist governments

D. newly independent states immediately following the First World War

15. Stalin refused to remove his troops from Eastern Europe following Hitler's defeat. Historians generally agree that this development **best** illustrated

A. the military superiority of Soviet conventional forces

B. an ideological commitment to destroy the last vestiges of Nazism

C. the desire to establish a strategic buffer zone against future aggression

D. a commitment to the economic restoration of formerly occupied territories

16. In which of the following conflicts did the United Nations assume a role that was **different** from a conventional peacekeeping function?

A. Korean War, 1950

B. Suez Crisis, 1956

C. Cyprus, 1974

D. Bosnia, 1995

17. In 1968, Soviet forces invaded Czechoslovakia in response to the Czechoslovakian government's

A. refusal to join the Warsaw Pact

B. attempt to democratize the state

C. refusal to collectivize agriculture

D. attempt to oppress its Russian minority

Use the following chart to answer question 18.

Belief	Goal	Policy	Means	Example
Sovereignty	National Security	?	?	?

18. Which three terms **best** complete this chart?

	Policy	Means	Example
A.	Deterrence	Arms Buildup	ICBM
B.	Deterrence	Arms Reduction	SDI
C.	Containment	Peacekeeping	The EU
D.	Containment	Regional Alliance	The UN

Use the following diagram to answer questions 19 to 21.

The Cold War in Europe, 1960's

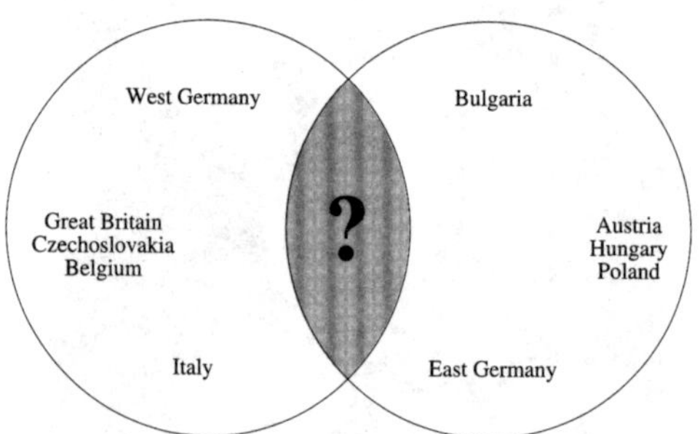

19. Which nations have been placed **incorrectly** in this diagram?

A. Italy and Poland

B. Belgium and Hungary

C. Great Britain and Bulgaria

D. Czechoslovakia and Austria

20. According to its established diplomatic stance and foreign policy during this period, which nation belongs in the centre area of the diagram?

A. Norway

B. Greece

C. Denmark

D. Yugoslavia

21. Within the context of the diagram, which of the following nations could be placed to the right of the centre area?

A. Romania

B. Sweden

C. Turkey

D. France

Use the following information to answer questions 22 and 23.

Possible World Structure Models

Model I
Independent countries pursue policies according to their nationalistic interests.
World problems and issues are resolved as they arise by temporary groupings and alliances of countries united by common interest.

Model II
A bipolar world is created along ideological lines. A dominant state determines policy and monitors affairs within each sphere.

Model III
A multipolar world that contains major regional groupings evolves. Countries within each sphere practise friendly cooperation but view outsiders with suspicion and see them as a threat to national interests.

Model IV
A supranational global village develops to allow countries to exist as separate entities. Global issues such as security, environmental concerns, economic prosperity, and human rights are addressed through mediation and diplomacy rather than through confrontation.

22. Which model **best** describes the world structure associated with the Cold War?

A. Model I

B. Model II

C. Model III

D. Model IV

23. The formation of a coalition force to counter the aggression of Iraq in the Gulf War fits **best** with

A. Model I **B.** Model II

C. Model III **D.** Model IV

Use the following list to answer question 24.

Difficulties Faced by the United States Government in Waging the Vietnam Conflict
Length of the conflict
Inhospitable terrain and climate
Lack of public support for the military effort
Reports of military atrocities against civilians
Highly mobile guerrilla soldiers

24. These difficulties were also experienced by the Soviet Union during its military involvement in

A. Cuba **B.** Hungary

C. Afghanistan **D.** Czechoslovakia

25. An examination of the principles underlying the domino theory would be useful in explaining the motivation for much of

A. British imperialist policy in Africa during the 1930s

B. French imperialist policy in the Pacific during the 1950s

C. Israeli foreign policy in the Middle East during the 1970s

D. American foreign policy in Latin America during the 1980s

26. Some historians contend that American President Reagan contributed greatly to ending the Cold War by

A. preserving American strategic interests in the Middle East

B. reducing the scope of America's military commitment NATO

C. placing greater reliance on the United Nations to maintain world peace and security

D. pushing the arms race to a point where the Soviet Union could no longer afford to compete

27. The shape and scope of economic and political power in Western Europe have been **most significantly** altered in recent years by the

A. reunification of the German states

B. division of Czechoslovakia into two separate states

C. ethnic strife gripping many newly independent nations

D. continued acts of terrorism used by radical nationalists

Use the following sources to answer questions 28 to 30.

Source I
The most aggressive nationalists in the Balkans were the Serbs. The kingdom of Serbia had been set up late in the previous century when its people had fought for independence from the decaying Turkish Empire. But that was not enough for Serbian nationalists: they planned to create a Yugoslavia (South Slavia) by joining all the Slav peoples who lived in the southern part of the Austrian Empire. To Vienna, this would mean the end of their empire: if the Southern Slavs were allowed to break away, it would only be a matter of time before the Czechs, Poles, Hungarians, and Slovaks went their separate ways as well.

— from *Twentieth Century History: The World Since 1900*

Source II

Yugoslavian Nationalists

Source III
Yugoslavia might survive as an entity in international law. This Yugoslavia would consist of a loose confederation of six sovereign nation-states....

It is assumed that Serbia, Montenegro, Bosnia and Herzegovinia, and Macedonia would remain within Yugoslavia. The most important disputed issue in this case would be that of Serbian people living in Croatia, who have declared that they would refuse to remain within an independent Croatian state. Furthermore, Serbia is willing to accept only a solution that enables all Serbs to live in one state. Thus, this option could be translated into reality by peaceful means only with difficulty and might well become a reason for civil war in Yugoslavia....

Finally, the armed forces, strictly observing the country's constitution, might seize power to prevent the disintegration of Yugoslavia.

— from *World Press Review, 1991*

28. The underlying message in each of these three sources supports the generalization that

A. aggressive nationalism is a destabilizing force

B. self-determination is a catalyst in solving ethnic conflict

C. ethnic divisions can be resolved through the United Nations

D. superpower intervention can no longer prevent boundary disputes

29. In addition to the problem caused by the death of Marshall Tito, the problems depicted in Source II and Source III were intensified by the

A. interference of UN peacekeeping forces

B. disintegration of the former Soviet bloc

C. threatened use of force by the superpowers

D. strong diplomacy of the Western European powers

30. Given subsequent events, the author of Source III, commenting in 1991, was quite correct in observing that

A. "Yugoslavia would consist of a loose confederation of six sovereign nation-states."

B. "Serbia is willing to accept only a solution that enables all Serbs to live in one state."

C. "all Serbs [living] in one state .... might well become a reason for civil war."

D. "the armed forces ... might seize power to prevent the disintegration of Yugoslavia."

Use the following statements to answer question 31.

Statement I
The Soviet Union blockaded Berlin in response to a United States naval quarantine of Cuba.

Statement II
The Hungarian Uprising of 1956 was resolved when UN peacekeepers began monitoring a cease-fire.

31. Which observation regarding the above statements is correct?

A. Both Statement I and Statement II are false.

B. Statement I is false and Statement II is true.

C. Statement I is true and Statement II is false.

D. Both Statement I and Statement II are true.

Use the following sources to answer questions 32 to 34.

Source I
A record 29 major wars raged around the world last year [1992], bringing to more than 23 million the death toll in conflicts since the end of the Second World War... "The 1990s opened with great promise... [but by] the beginning of 1993, ...peace seemed a grand illusion." In place of the Cold War between two giants, a troubled world was faced with an epidemic of ethnic violence and civil conflict.... [The report] defined a major war as one involving one or more governments and causing the deaths of 1,000 or more people a year.... Since the Second World War, there have been 149 wars and 23.14 million people killed in them. These figures represent a population almost the size of Canada....
— from *The Edmonton Journal, 1993*

Source II

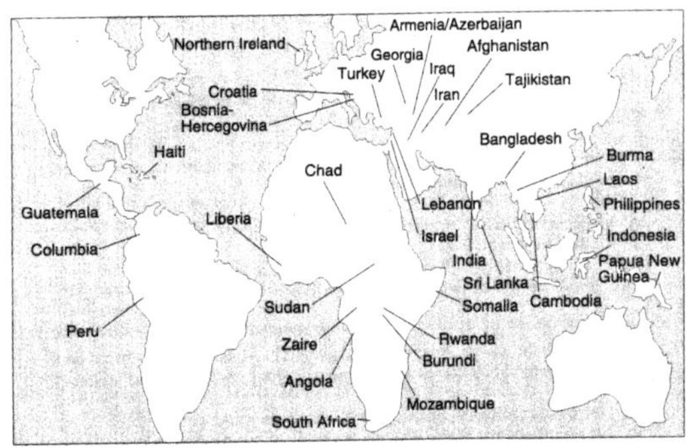

Source III
D-Day: landing boats, dramatic action, a known and evil foe, full power, victory. Nothing has changed more in 50 years than the way in which we tend to the global stability that was bought by massive commitment and sacrifice in the Second World War. The United Nations peacekeeping operations now scattered around the world are everything that D-Day was not: marginal, ambivalent, ragged, controversial. We must deal with the world we live in, and we live in a world where peacekeeping in its various forms is unavoidable and important to us. We have not done it well enough and as a result we face a certain crisis of internationalism.
— from *The Edmonton Journal, 1994*

32. Which fundamental question about global affairs since the end of the Cold War do the three sources raise?

A. Why have today's local conflicts involved higher casualty rates?

B. Why are there more unresolved conflicts today and how can the world deal with them?

C. Is the United Nations more effective in dealing with peacemaking than it is with peacekeeping?

D. Is the role of the superpowers in maintaining world stability based primarily on the use of force?

33. Which is the **best** title for the map in Source II?

A. New Democracies: 1993–94

B. Military Dictatorships: 1993–94

C. Armed Conflicts: 1993–94

D. United Nations' Peacekeeping Operations: 1993–94

34. The "crisis of internationalism" referred to in Source III can be illustrated by the decision that currently faces many nations about whether or not to

A. involve themselves in conflicts that do not directly affect their national interest

B. continue their membership in military alliances formed during the Cold War

C. support serious efforts to monitor and limit environmental degradation

D. rebuild their armed forces to protect national security

35. A journalist is being held without charge in a country known to use torture as a means of interrogation. The non-governmental agency that would be directly concerned with this situation is

A. Greenpeace

B. the Red Cross/Red Crescent

C. Amnesty International

D. the World Health Organization

Use the following comments to answer questions 36 and 37.

Source I

I can never be anything else but an American, and I must think of the United States first.... National I must remain, and in that way I like all other Americans can render the amplest service to the world. The United States is the world's best hope, but if you fetter her in the interests and quarrels of other nations, if you tangle her in the intrigues of Europe, you will destroy her power for good and endanger her very existence. Leave her to march freely through the centuries to come as in the years that have gone.

— Senator Henry Cabot Lodge, August 1919

Source II

The arrangements of this treaty are just, but they need the support of the combined power of the great nations of the world. And they will have that support.... I believe that [people] will see the truth, eye to eye and face to face. There is one thing that the American people always rise to and extend their hand to, and that is the truth of justice and of liberty and of peace. We have accepted that truth and we are going to be led by it, and it is going to lead us, and through us the world, out into pastures of quietness and peace such as the world never dreamed of before.

— President Woodrow Wilson, September 1919

— both sources from *Twentieth-Century Speeches*

36. These excerpts were taken from speeches that are both characterized by

A. fear that the United States would be torn apart by partisan politics

B. emotional appeals regarding the issue of America's entry into the League of Nations

C. skepticism regarding the feasibility of using collective security as a basis for the League of Nations

D. optimism about the United States following a policy of isolationism after the First World War

37. At the time of his speech, Lodge's position would have been strongly supported by

A. Republicans who believed that the United States should revert to isolationist policies

B. Democrats who believed that the United States should join the League but limit its involvement to matters of security

C. Congress, which believed that the United States should use force to protect its interests in any future European conflict

D. Senators who believed that the United States should adopt principles of collective security in its relations with foreign governments

Use the following sources to answer questions 38 to 41.

Source I

Nations have a natural resistance to any agreement that infringes on their sovereignty as an international disarmament treaty by its very nature must do.

The end of World War I brought limited arms control in the form of reductions that penalized defeated countries. Other limited disarmament measures followed.

Disarmament was a major objective of the League of Nations during the 1920s and 1930s—an objective, as it turned out, that was not attained. A starting point was the fourth of President Woodrow Wilson's Fourteen Points of 1918, which proposed that adequate guarantees be given that "national armaments be reduced to the lowest point consistent with domestic safety..."

Eventually, a disarmament conference was held from 1932 to 1934, but there was little unity of purpose. An agreement was worked out to prohibit air attacks against civilian populations, limit the size of artillery and tanks, and abolish chemical warfare. This agreement had little meaning, however, because Germany and the Soviet Union—two great powers of the era—refused to accept it. After Hitler took over in 1933, Germany walked out of the disarmament conference—and out of the League of Nations.

Source II

Peace, At Last!

—both sources from *The Bumpy Road to Disarmament*

38. Which statement could be used **most effectively** as a conclusion for Source I?

A. Disarmament proposals put forward by American President Wilson were largely ignored by the League of Nations.

B. Rearmament rather than disarmament became the dominant theme, as nations moved relentlessly toward the Second World War.

C. In 1938 and 1939, France, Italy, Japan, Britain, and the United States agreed to limit the number, size, and guns of their battleships for 15 years.

D. The League's efforts to secure a disarmament agreement went unheeded until nations were forced to agree on the eve of the Second World War.

39. In Source II, "The World" represents nations that support the

A. principles of supranationalism

B. preservation of global economic prosperity

C. ideas underlying an economic balance of power

D. governments that undermined the League's success

40. Personification is used in the cartoon in Source II to convey the ironic idea that the League of Nations

A. was able to gain compliance for major initiatives from its key members

B. accomplished its mandate only with great difficulty and suffering

C. was successful in maintaining "peace" by sacrificing itself

D. achieved "peace" only through its own demise

41. Which generalization about the interwar period do the two sources support?

A. The powers defeated in 1918 were reluctant to join the League, which led to its eventual downfall.

B. Most nations were more interested in bolstering their recessionary economies than in serious disarmament.

C. Isolation by major democracies between the two world wars created a power vacuum that the fascist powers filled.

D. Global cooperation was too idealistic of a goal, given the tension and distrust created by the settlements arising from the First World War.

42. In retrospect, France's military preparations in the 1920s and 1930s for a war with Germany relied too heavily on the

A. assumption that the United States would aid French forces

B. immovable defensive fortifications built along the French border

C. ability of the French air force to destroy German industrial centres

D. ability of the French navy to blockade German overseas supply routes

43. The borders of Poland have been redrawn during the twentieth century by the terms of the

A. Munich Pact and the Truman Doctrine

B. Locarno Pact and the Helsinki Accords

C. Atlantic Charter and the Potsdam Agreement

D. Treaty of Versailles and the Yalta Agreement

44. In deciding to adopt a policy of appeasement toward the fascist dictators, the British and French governments largely ignored the

A. public wish that war must be avoided at any cost

B. collective security apparatus of the League of Nations

C. questionable military preparedness of their armed forces

D. public feeling that certain territorial claims were justified

45. Military aggression was used **primarily** as a means of securing badly needed natural resources in

A. Italy's invasion of Abyssinia in the 1930s

B. Japan's invasion of East Asia during the 1940s

C. North Korea's invasion of South Korea in 1950

D. The Soviet Union's invasion of Afghanistan in 1979

46. The official, public justification given by the United States for its use of atomic bombs on Hiroshima and Nagasaki in 1945 was that

A. such weapons would show the Soviet Union that the United States had superior military capabilities, thus discouraging Soviet imperialism

B. the demonstration of such terrible destructive force would weaken German resolve to continue fighting in Europe

C. such weapons would bring the war to a quicker end with fewer casualties for both sides

D. the Japanese had to be punished for their surprise attack on Pearl Harbor

Use the following map to answer question 47.

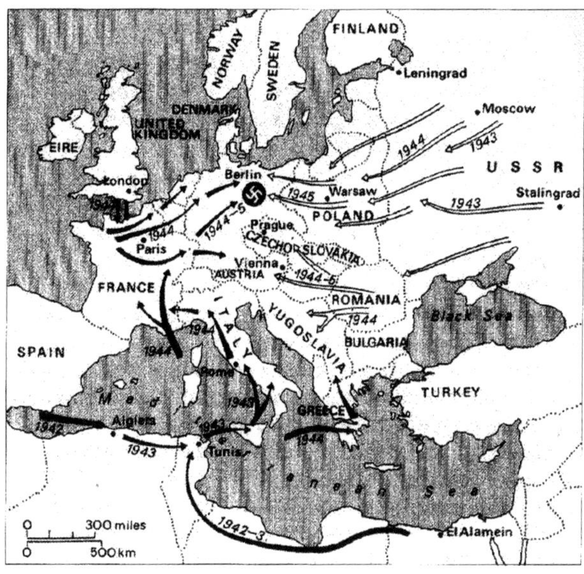

—from *The Twentieth Century*

47. The **best** title for this map is

A. "Hitler's Growing Empire"

B. "Operation Barbarossa is Launched."

C. "The Destruction of the Third Reich"

D. "American Successes in The Second World War"

48. An outline for future Cold War spheres of influence in Europe was established by provisions agreed upon

A. in the Marshall Plan

B. at the Yalta Conference

C. in the Versailles Treaty

D. at the Munich Conference

Use the following excerpt to answer questions 49 and 50.

Treaty Document Excerpt

Article 1
Japan recognizes and respects the leadership of Germany and Italy in the establishment of a new order in Europe.

Article 2
Germany and Italy recognize and respect the leadership of Japan in the establishment of a new order in Greater East Asia.

Article 3
Germany, Italy, and Japan agree to cooperate in their efforts on the aforesaid lines. They further undertake to assist one another with all political, economic, and military means if one of the three Contracting Powers is attacked by a Power at present not involved in the European War or in the Chinese–Japanese conflict.

— from *Landmarks of the Western Heritage*

49. Which of the following foreign policies is **most inconsistent** with the terms of the above treaty?

A. Creation of an alliance system

B. Support for collective security

C. Pursuit of territorial expansion

D. Establishment of spheres of influence

50. The governments of the nations named in the excerpt are **best** described as

A. fascist and militaristic

B. socialist and aggressive

C. capitalist and isolationist

D. communist and expansionist

51. Originally, the European Common Market was formed to

A. establish competitive trade rivalries

B. halt communist expansion in the area

C. encourage greater economic prosperity

D. compete with the North American Free Trade Agreement

Use the following time-line to answer question 52.

Some Important Events of the Cold War	
The Truman Doctrine	1947
The Korean War	1950
The Cuban Missile Crisis	1962
The SALT I Agreements	1972

52. The events in this time-line **best reflect** the shift in American foreign policy from

A. appeasement to détente

B. containment to détente

C. containment to brinkmanship

D. brinkmanship to appeasement

Use the following quotation to answer questions 53 and 54.

[The American Secretary of State], John Foster Dulles, at once made clear his basic Cold War outlook. His first official speech in January 1953 made this promise: 'To all those suffering under Communist slavery... Let us say: you can count on us.'... Dulles threatened 'massive retaliation' if any Communist boot stepped beyond the territory already held, and declared that America must be prepared to 'go to the brink' of war.
— from *World Powers in the Twentieth Century*

53. In the context of the Cold War, Dulles's foreign policy commitments, carried to their logical conclusion, were basically

A. dangerous because of the threat of nuclear war

B. misguided because Soviet expansionism was declining

C. unnecessary because European alliance systems already existed

D. unacceptable because nations relied heavily on UN collective security

54. During the 1950s, Dulles's promise of support was revealed as rhetorical bluster when the Soviet Union

A. exploded a hydrogen bomb

B. crushed the Hungarian Uprising

C. launched spy satellites into space

D. boycotted the UN Security Council

Use the following sources to answer questions 55 to 58.

Source I

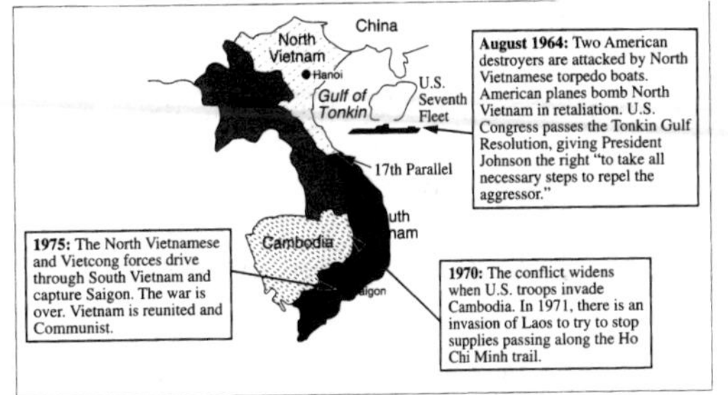

—from *The Modern World Since 1917*

Source II

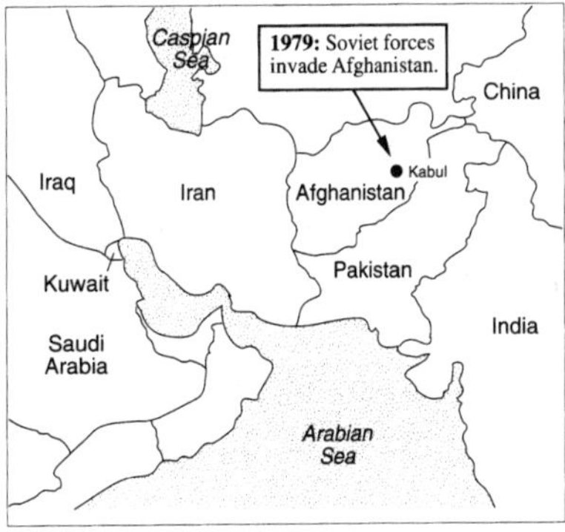

—from *The Contemporary World*

Source III

The theory of war demands that at the outset of a war its character and scope should be determined on the basis of its political probabilities. It is imperative that one does not take the first step without considering the last.
— Karl Von Clausewitz from *On War*

55. Which issue did the events described in sources I and II raise for all concerned at the time they occurred?

A. Should appeasement and diplomacy replace policies of neutrality?

B. Should the superpowers invite United Nations intervention to preserve peace on their borders?

C. Should the decision to continue armed conflict be determined by economic developments?

D. Should the superpowers violate the sovereignty of other nations in pursuit of their national interests?

56. The conflicts referred to in sources I and II were similar in that both were characterized by extensive

A. guerrilla warfare

B. naval and air force engagements

C. diplomatic efforts to resolve differences

D. military battles between the superpowers

57. The events identified in sources I and II were **primarily** attempts by the superpowers to

A. upset the balance of power

B. control important spheres of influence

C. appease each other's national interests

D. use alliances to achieve foreign policy objectives

58. The author of Source III would have criticized the actions described in sources I and II because

A. each action represents a selfish motive for foreign intervention

B. the actions are clear violations of the principle of national sovereignty

C. the actions illustrate a lack of consideration of their likely outcomes

D. each action allowed the superpowers to avoid confronting each other militarily

59. With the ending of the Cold War, which of the following terms best describe the issues facing nations regarding the future of nuclear weapons capability and technology?

A. Escalation and brinkmanship

B. Proliferation and disarmament

C. Détente and peaceful coexistence

D. Mutual deterrence and containment

Use the following to answer questions 60 and 61.

> [This policy] essentially intended to keep the post-war economies of the West Europe countries within the capitalist world, was also intended to dominate their economy. Every transaction was arranged to provide not only immediate profits ... for specific US banks, finance corporations, investment trusts and industries, but to make the European nations dependent on the United States.
>
> — from *The Cold War*

60. In expressing his point of view, the author is questioning the motives behind the establishment of the

A. Marshall Plan **B.** United Nations

C. NATO Alliance **D.** Common Market

61. Which of the following principles does the author feel was **most threatened** by the developments he describes?

A. The achievement of global prosperity

B. The enhancement of national prestige

C. The maintenance of national sovereignty

D. The advancement of international cooperation

62. Which action is **inconsistent** with the foreign policy goal with which it is paired?

	ACTION	FOREIGN POLICY GOAL
A.	The American Senate refuses to ratify the Treaty of Versailles.	Isolationism
B.	Many Western European nations join NATO.	Containment
C.	Warsaw Pact members send troops into Czechoslovakia.	Détente
D.	The American government funds SDI (Star Wars) research.	Deterrence

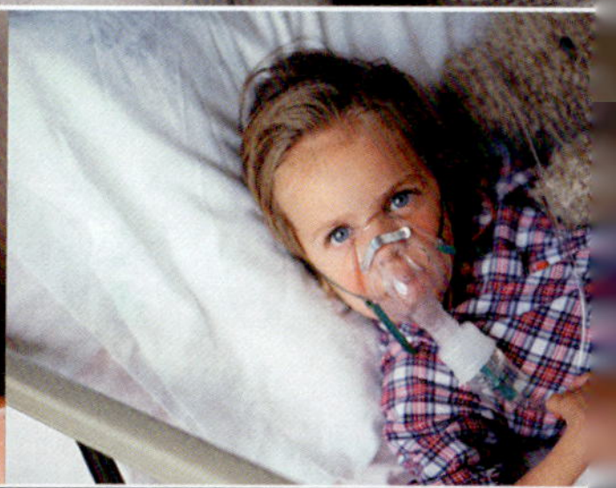

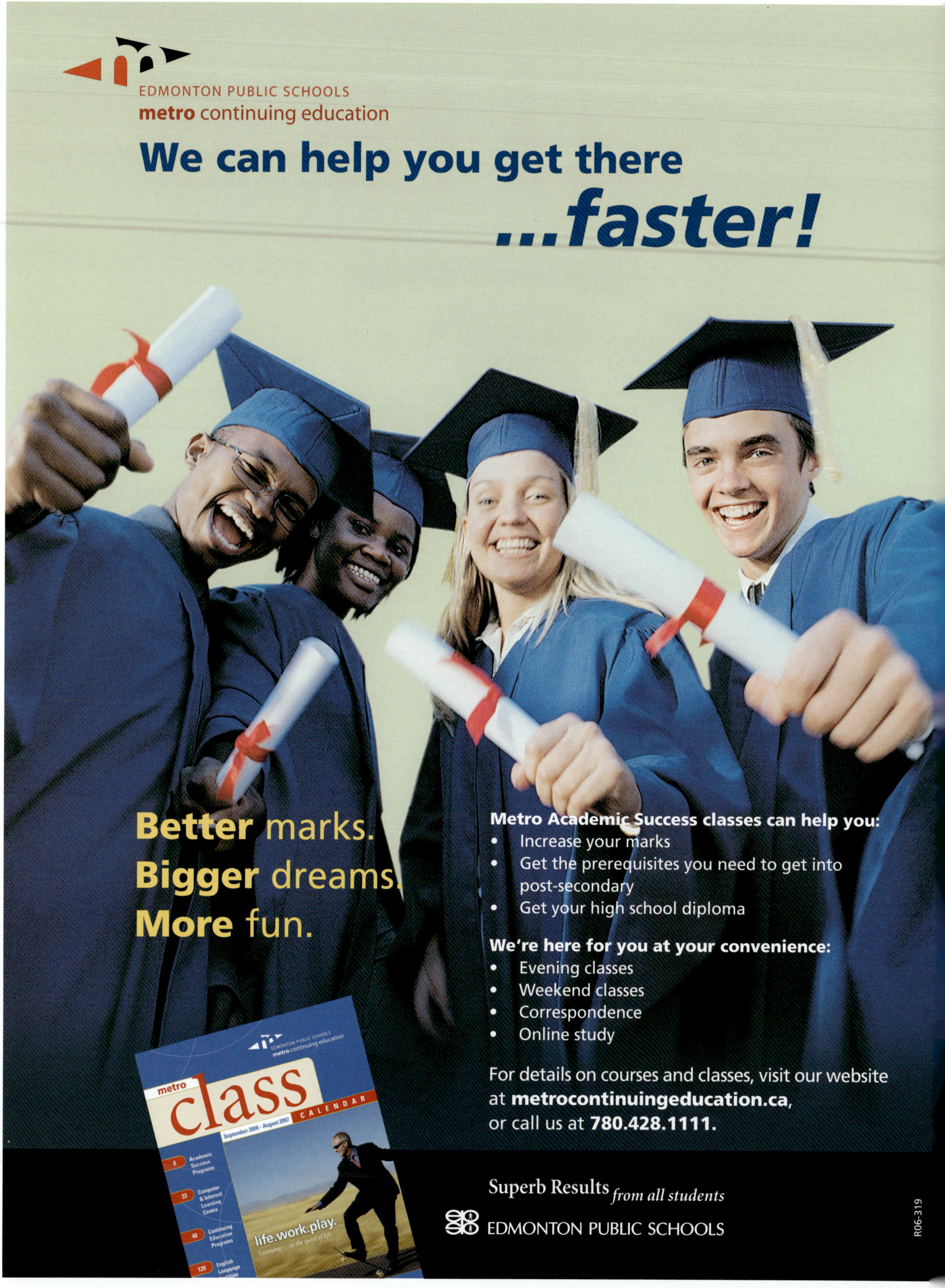
EDMONTON PUBLIC SCHOOLS
metro continuing education
We can help you get there
...faster!
Better marks.
Bigger dreams.
More fun.
Metro Academic Success classes can help you:
• Increase your marks
• Get the prerequisites you need to get into post-secondary
• Get your high school diploma
We're here for you at your convenience:
• Evening classes
• Weekend classes
• Correspondence
• Online study
For details on courses and classes, visit our website at metrocontinuingeducation.ca, or call us at 780.428.1111.
metro class CALENDAR
September 2006 - August 2007
life.work.play.
Superb Results from all students
EDMONTON PUBLIC SCHOOLS
R06-319

Use the following to answer questions 63 and 64.

Speaker I
NATO is no longer a useful alliance. With the end of the Cold War, there is no security threat worth justifying our continuing membership in the Atlantic alliance. We should instead focus our efforts on maintaining NORAD.

Speaker II
Our membership in NATO must be terminated. The resources spent in supplying soldiers and equipment could be better spent supporting the concept of collective security.

Speaker III
NATO must be disbanded. The end of the Cold War provides us with the opportunity to develop our own forces independent of other countries.

Speaker IV
NATO no longer serves our purpose. Threats to Western security now come out of the developing world, and another form of alliance is needed to respond to these concerns.

63. Which speaker would support expanding the peacekeeping role of the United Nations?

A. Speaker I

B. Speaker II

C. Speaker III

D. Speaker IV

64. Which pair of speakers would differ **most** concerning the foreign policy that should be followed if NATO were no longer in existence?

A. Speakers I and II

B. Speakers I and IV

C. Speakers II and III

D. Speakers III and IV

65. Since 1989, political and territorial changes in Eastern Europe have illustrated a global trend toward

A. increased acceptance of socialist ideologies

B. restoration of superpower spheres of influence

C. popular movements for autonomy along ethnic lines

D. government by authoritarian rather than democratic means

Use the following sources to answer questions 66 and 67.

Source I

I'LL STOP WHEN YOU DO!

— from *The Philadelphia Inquirer*

Source II
Proposals to Combat Terrorism
1. Boycott high-risk airports
2. Strengthen airport security
3. Safeguard possible targets
4. Expand intelligence operations
5. Intensify pressure on terrorists' allies

66. Those who support the point made by the cartoonist in Source I would question the proposals listed in Source II because

A. the proposals are not realistically achievable

B. terrorism is becoming increasingly indiscriminate

C. terrorists are often willing to give their lives for a cause

D. the proposals fail to address the underlying causes of terrorism

67. A basic assumption underlying the message in the cartoon is that terrorism is the

A. reaction of a group to political oppression

B. reflection of inadequate law enforcement

C. cause of much of the inequity found worldwide

D. cause of much of the conflict among ethnic groups

68. During the 1990s, the Russian government has reacted **most negatively** to the announcement that

A. EU members would begin to use a common currency

B. the UN selected a Ghanian diplomat as its new Security General

C. NAFTA members were considering including South American states in their trade agreement

D. the NATO alliance hoped to expand to include several central European states

69. Participation by Canadian soldiers in supervising the cease-fire that ended the 1980–88 Iraq-Iran War **best** illustrates Canada's ongoing commitment to the principle of

A. global prosperity

B. national security

C. collective security

D. international equality

70. In 1994, which of the following proposals would an internationalist **most** likely have advocated to end the civil strife in Bosnia-Herzegovina?

A. Worldwide recognition of Serbian claims in the area

B. Military intervention by the United States to establish a stable balance of power in the region

C. Intervention by a military power to bring a decisive halt to the conflict

D. UN arrangement of a cease-fire, followed by negotiation among belligerents

Answers and Solutions
Political and Economic Systems – Unit Review

1. B	19. C	37. B	55. B	73. B	91. B
2. C	20. A	38. D	56. B	74. D	92. C
3. A	21. D	39. C	57. C	75. D	93. A
4. D	22. C	40. D	58. A	76. B	94. C
5. B	23. D	41. B	59. A	77. C	95. D
6. D	24. A	42. C	60. B	78. A	96. C
7. A	25. D	43. B	61. A	79. D	97. C
8. D	26. A	44. C	62. D	80. B	98. B
9. A	27. B	45. A	63. D	81. A	99. B
10. D	28. A	46. D	64. C	82. D	100. D
11. A	29. B	47. B	65. A	83. C	101. A
12. D	30. C	48. D	66. C	84. B	102. B
13. C	31. A	49. C	67. B	85. A	103. B
14. D	32. A	50. D	68. D	86. A	104. C
15. C	33. B	51. B	69. A	87. D	105. D
16. C	34. C	52. D	70. C	88. C	
17. B	35. A	53. B	71. C	89. C	
18. B	36. D	54. D	72. A	90. A	

1. **B**

Collectivism is the belief that the welfare of the group (the collective) should be given priority over individual interests. In particular, collectivism seeks to create equality among all citizens. Therefore, collectivists would support a government policy that instituted a guaranteed annual income to create "economic equity" (a more fair distribution of wealth in society).

A, C, and D. Citizens who support the principles of collectivism would not accept these three individualistic policies. Collectivists support nationalization (government takeovers of industries)—not privatization (the sale or transfer of government-owned industries to private businessmen). Collectivists believe in an activist government with a large civil service; they would not support massive cuts to the bureaucracy. Finally, collectivists believe in universality (the principle that all citizens should receive exactly the same benefits from the government); they would want a child tax credit on earned income to equally apply to all citizens regardless of income level.

2. C

A market-oriented economic system is a mixed economy that emphasizes capitalism more than socialism. A supporter of this type of economy would favour controlling government deficits by reducing the level of social services. Capitalists believe in self-reliance and disapprove of social welfare programs.

A, B, and D. A supporter of a market-oriented economy would be less willing to control government overspending by increasing personal or corporate income taxes. Capitalists favour government cutbacks over tax increases as a means of balancing the government's budget. Capitalists also believe that the profit motive should not be eroded by high taxes or government regulation. Therefore, a supporter of a market-oriented economy would not support controlling government deficits by regulating the profits made by entrepreneurs (risk-taking, profit-seeking, capitalist businessmen).

3. A

In theory and practice, both communism and fascism rely on a key group of leaders (a cadre) to achieve power and attract new followers. Communism calls for a proletarian revolution to be led by "the vanguard of the proletariat" (the vanguard being an elite group of intellectuals with a comprehensive knowledge and understanding of Marxist theory). In practice, Vladimir Lenin and the other leading Russian communists (Leon Trotsky, Josef Stalin, and Sergei Kirov, for instance) served as the "vanguard of the proletariat" during the October Revolution and its aftermath. They used a private army (the Red Guards) to seize power and used a wider communist organization, the Bolshevik Party, to help them to maintain power after the Revolution. Communism also calls for "a dictatorship of the proletariat" in which the elite communist cadre would use authoritarian methods to transform all citizens into good communists and to convert the economy from capitalism to pure communism. In practice, the authoritarian rule of the Soviet Politburo could be viewed as "a dictatorship of the proletariat" in the USSR.

Fascists also believe that an elite cadre is necessary to achieve and maintain fascist power. They believe in a "leadership principle" (the Fuhrerprinzip) which maintains that the best form of government is a dictatorship headed by a leader with superior abilities (and by an elite group of his followers) whose commands the people must obey. In practice, Adolf Hitler and his immediate circle of followers (Hermann Goering, Heinrich Himmler, Joseph Goebbels, Rudolf Hess, Ernst Rohm, etc.) served as this Nazi cadre. Like the Russian Communists, the German fascists also used a political party (the National Socialist German Workers' Party) and a private army (the S.A. or "Brownshirts") to achieve power.

B, C, and D. The term *corporate state* refers to the economic organization of the fascist economy; communists do not believe in organizing the economy in this way. Only fascists would favour the overthrow of "Bolshevism" (Russian Communism). Only communists believe in the crushing of the bourgeoisie (wealthy capitalists) by the proletariat (working class); this is not a goal of fascism.

4. D

The belief in global competitiveness (free trade between nations/the globalization of trade) is inconsistent with raising protective tariffs (increasing taxes on foreign imports). Global capitalism would require the elimination of barriers to international free trade such as protective tariffs.

A, B, and C. Each of the others ideologies is consistent with the action given.

5. B

Market-oriented economic policies are those that emphasize capitalist economic ideas and strategies. In other words, these policies favour keeping government regulation of the economy to a minimum. Therefore, a market-oriented approach to runaway inflation would be to allow the problem to correct itself through normal fluctuations in the business cycle (the recurring cycle of economic booms and busts in a free market economy). According to this viewpoint, inflation (rapidly rising prices) would eventually be stopped by recessionary pressures such as decreased consumer spending.

A, C, and D. The three approaches involve government intervention (interference) in the economy. Given the choice between no government intervention (Response II) and some government invention (Response I, III, and IV), a supporter of a market-oriented (capitalist-style) economy would favour the former.

6. D

Inflation is a problem of rapidly increasing prices caused by too much consumer spending. Lowering interest rates to provide consumers with easier access to credit would definitely only worsen the problem. Governments generally raise interest rates to fight inflation.

A, B, and C. Responses I and III give effective ways to fight inflation. Response II, in the long term, would stop inflation—but in the short term, it would likely have no noticeable effect on rising inflation.

7. A

Demand-side economists (Keynesians) believe that a government must intervene in the economy to prevent recessions and reduce the human suffering that results from the boom-and-bust cycle. Therefore, a Keynesian economist would criticize Response II (allowing the problem of inflation to correct itself through the normal fluctuations of the business cycle) because it would absolve government from any responsibility in resolving economic problems.

B, C, and D. A Keynesian economist would not criticize Response II for any of these reasons because, in and of themselves, none would necessarily be the result of Response II.

8. D

John Kenneth Galbraith's quotation suggests that public (government-provided) services help the poor. Supporters of social services for the poor would likely also support transfer payments (welfare payments to individuals and/or government-to-government equalization payments) to economically depressed areas.

A, B, and C. People who believe in public (government) support for the poor would be less likely to favour tax breaks for private businesses, the privatization of publicly run programs, or government subsidies for profitable businesses. Such people would rather see tax dollars go toward helping the poor rather than toward benefitting wealthier businessmen. They would prefer tax breaks for the poor rather than tax breaks for the rich.

9. A

According to capitalism's laws of supply and demand, increased profits for the producer would result from lower production costs, cutbacks on workers' benefits, and increased sales of the producer's products.

10. D

The writer defends the capitalist (private enterprise) economy in his comment. As a capitalist, he would support legislation designed to deregulate key industrial areas. Capitalists favour reduced government control (regulation) of the economy.

A, B, and C. A capitalist would not support restrictions on investors, business takeovers, or the nationalization (government take-over) of unprofitable businesses. A capitalist would regard increased taxes on capital gains (investment income) as detrimental to the profit motive.

11. A

The excerpt is a defence of capitalism. A democratic socialist would agree with the capitalist speaker's contention that economic freedoms are valid goals; the democratic socialist, however, would claim that the free market system does not provide for the disadvantaged (the poor, unemployed, sick, or handicapped). Democratic socialists are strong defenders of social welfare programs for the poor; capitalists dislike such programs.

B, C, and D. A democratic socialist would not agree with any of these statements.

12. D

The American (capitalist-oriented) economy is based upon the capitalist beliefs found in the excerpt.

A, B, and C. The American economy is more market-oriented than the British welfare state, the Canadian mixed economy, or the Swedish democratic socialist state. Therefore, these three economic systems are not based on the ideas of the speaker as directly as the American economy is.

13. C

Given his capitalist views, the speaker would likely agree that individual initiative is essential for the successful functioning of an economy. The market economy depends on the "get-up-and-go" of entrepreneurs (the owners or managers of private businesses who, by risk and initiative, attempt to make profits).

A, B, and D. Capitalists oppose government intervention in the economy and bureaucratic control over private enterprises. They also reject the public enterprise system (communism).

14. D

During the Second World War, unemployment was virtually eliminated in Canada and the United States when the Canadian and American governments began to exercise greater control over their free market economies. For instance, both governments oversaw the production of armaments, ships, planes, and tanks during the war. Privately owned factories created employment and produced most of war material needed by Canada and the USA—but production in these private enterprises was directed and monitored somewhat by government planners.

A, B, and C. During the Second World War, full employment in Canada and the United States was not generated by any of these actions.

15. C

During the 20th century, Sweden, Norway, and Denmark established democratic socialist economies with the world's most generous social welfare programs. Therefore, the article's observation that Scandinavians wish to maintain the welfare state is not surprising.

16. C

The excerpt implies that Scandinavian governments—like other governments in Europe and North America—faced the problem of how to reduce huge budget deficits (massive government overspending) when citizens demand that governments continue to spend money on public services.

A, B, and D. The excerpt does not allude to these three problems.

17. B

Marxism (communism) is the ideology that holds that capitalists exploit workers in their quest for profits. Marxists also believe that the proletariat (wage workers) and the bourgeoisie (capitalist bosses) are locked in a class struggle for mastery of the economy.

A, C, and D. The ideas of class struggle and capitalist exploitation are not characteristic of fascism, anarchism, or capitalism.

18. B

Communism collapsed in Russia in 1991. During the following years, Russia's new market-oriented economy was plagued by runaway inflation, massive unemployment, and widespread poverty. These same conditions existed in Weimar Germany during the early 1920s.

A, C, and D. These economic problems were not particularly evident in Italy, Nazi Germany, or Japan during the given time periods.

19. C

The phrase "political parties of the right" refers to conservative, neo-conservative, or ultraconservative parties. During the 1990s, democracies governed by right-wing parties tried to reduce budgetary deficits by decreasing government spending on services. For instance, Premier Klein's Conservative government in Alberta took this approach during the decade.

A, B, and D. Conservatives support capitalist economic policies. They oppose tax increases, nationalization (government takeovers) of private enterprises, and higher wages for unionized labour.

20. A

The term *universal suffrage* refers to voting rights for all adult citizens—all male and female citizens, including those belonging to minority groups. The title of the chart is misleading because it suggests that universal suffrage means giving the vote to men only. The chart lists only dates when men were granted the franchise; in each case, women and members of some minority groups received the right to vote decades after the given year.

21. D

The issue raised by the sources is "To what extent should party discipline be imposed on elected government members?" Party discipline is the method used by a party leader in Canada's parliamentary democracy to ensure that the elected members of his party maintain a common front in the House of Commons, in the media, and in their public comments. Under party discipline, if a caucus member refuses to vote on a bill in the way demanded by his party leadership, he may be subject to various punishments—including expulsion from the party.

A, B, and C. The two sources do not focus on any of these three issues.

22. C

Source I shows Prime Minister Pierre Trudeau (leader of the governing Liberal Party) strictly controlling Liberal MPs through party discipline. Party discipline limits the ability of elected representatives to express the views of their constituents in debates and votes in the legislature. Instead of giving their first loyalty to the people who elected them, party members are required, through threat of party discipline, to give their first loyalty to their party's leadership.

A, B, and D. Source I does not focus on these three problems.

23. D

A totalitarian dictatorship is the most extreme form of dictatorship. Totalitarianism is "an authoritarian form of centralized government that regulates every aspect of state and private behaviour." A separation of powers would not exist in this type of dictatorship. A totalitarian dictator would totally control all branches of government; law-makers, judges, Cabinet members, and civil servants would all be dominated by him.

A, B, and C. System I is a democracy (like that of the USA) that has a strict separation of powers. System II represents a parliamentary system (like Canada's) in which a separation of powers exists—albeit with some overlap between the legislative and executive branch. System III represents a political system in which a separate legislative branch exists but where there is little division between the executive (law-enforcing) branch and the judicial (law-interpreting) branch.

24. A

In System I, government powers are strictly separated among three independent branches of government. This strict separation of powers is representative of the political system in the United States. The USA also has a system of checks and balances (a political arrangement whereby each branch of government supervises one or more of the other branches to ensure that none oversteps its constitutional authority). Checks and balances are the means by which the U.S. Constitution prevents any one branch of government from dominating another branch or the whole government.

B, C, and D. An American-style system of checks and balances does not exist in systems II, III, or IV, because each of these systems features a definite overlap between two or three branches of government.

25. D

German elections frequently result in coalition governments because Germany uses an electoral system of proportional representation to elect some member to the *Bundestag*. Under this system, a party receives a percentage of legislative seats that is roughly equivalent to its percentage of total votes cast in the election. It is more difficult for a party to earn a majority of the seats in a parliamentary system with a full or partial proportional representation electoral system.

26. A

Canada's Upper House of Parliament is the Senate. If Canada's Senate was made more similar to Germany's Upper House of Parliament (the Bundesrat), a few MLAs from each provincial legislature would be appointed to the Senate.

B, C, and D. These changes would not occur if the Canadian system of government was made more like Germany's political system.

27. B

Position I represents liberalism. Position II represents reactionism. Position III represents radicalism. Position IV represents conservatism. Reactionaries and radicals are located on opposite ends of the political spectrum.

28. A

Radicalism is located on the extreme left side of the political spectrum.

29. B

Democrats are liberals. Republicans are conservatives. This conflict in the government of the USA would have been between those holding the beliefs of Position I (liberalism) and those holding the beliefs of Position IV (conservatism).

30. C

Position II represents the views of a reactionary.

31. A

A political dissident is someone who disagrees with the established system of government and/or with the actions of the ruling party. In democracies, dissidents are allowed to freely express their views as long as they refrain from endangering public order and stability. Democratic governments do not allow dissidents to incite violence, provoke riots, agitate for the violent overthrow of the government, or promote hatred against identifiable groups. Democracies only defend speech that does not violate others' rights or lead to predictable and avoidable harm.

B, C, and D. In democratic nations, dissidents are allowed considerable freedom of expression. Most democracies allow them to express unpopular and even extreme views in speech and in writing. The only limits on freedom of speech in a democracy are laws regarding incitement, sedition, defamation, slander, libel, the expression of racial hatred, and conspiracy.

32. A

The Nuremberg Laws were a series of Nazi laws that discriminated against Jews in Germany. These laws proved that Hitler did not believe in respecting the civil rights and liberties of all citizens. Jewish citizens had no rights in Hitler's Germany.

33. B

A Dictator uses "the direction of popular discontent" (scapegoating) to maintain his popularity and dominance. This technique of dictatorship recognizes that citizens regularly get frustrated with the government and blame government officials for society's problems. Instead of letting these frustrations build, a dictator re-directs them by blaming societal problems and government shortcomings on scapegoats. Hitler's routine of blaming Germany's problems on people of "non-Aryan races"—particularly Jews, Gypsies, and Slavs—is a classic example of directing popular discontent.

A, C, and D. These actions are not examples of directing popular discontent.

34. C

Hitler was a staunch anti-communist who never attempted to appeal to German communists for support. In fact, Hitler's record as an anti-Marxist was an important factor in his rise to power in Weimar Germany.

A, B, and D. These three explanations of Hitler's rise to power are correct.

35. A

The American congressional system allows for a greater separation of powers than a parliamentary system. In a parliamentary system, the prime minister and cabinet ministers are members of both the legislative (law-making) branch and the executive (law-enforcing) branch. The government of the USA does not allow legislative power to be exercised by anyone from the executive branch—or vice versa.

B, C, and D. America's congressional system is not superior to the Canadian parliamentary system in these areas.

36. D

A government that is more concerned about individualism (the belief that individual freedom is more important than group needs) than collectivism (the belief that the welfare of the group should be given priority over the desires of individuals) would support a deregulated business sector. Individualism is most closely associated with the economic ideology of capitalism. A capitalist economy (the private enterprise system) affords the individual the greatest economic freedom. A private enterprise economy is a deregulated economy—virtually no regulation of private businesses occurs; in this type of economy, the government allows companies to operate more freely than in other economic systems.

A, B, and C. These three other policies are representative of economic collectivism (giving the economic welfare of society priority over the economic prosperity of individuals). Firstly, in a country with a steeply progressive income tax structure, richer citizens pay higher rates of income tax than poorer citizens; the government then shares some of the tax revenues from the rich with the poor to create more economic equality between citizens. Secondly, individualists believe in self-reliance, competition, and the economic survival of the fittest; therefore, they would not support bailing out failing private businesses. Thirdly, the nationalization (government take-over) of private businesses is a collectivist measure; it would not be supported by economic individualists (capitalists).

37. B

Democratic capitalism is the belief that a nation should have a democratic government and a market (private enterprise) economy. For a Canadian capitalist, the most acceptable solution for dealing with the debt problem would be to reduce government funding of social welfare programs and health care. Capitalists do not believe in providing economic assistance to the poor. Nor do they believe in public health care.

A, C, and D. A Canadian capitalist would not support these three ways of dealing with the government debt problem. Firstly, capitalists oppose government intervention (interference) in the economy through increased government spending during recessions, manipulation of the money supply, and/or manipulation of interest rates. Secondly, capitalists oppose job creation programs and increased progressive income taxes. Thirdly, capitalists do not favour demand-side (Keynesian) economic strategies because they believe that the marketplace should be left to operate freely without government intervention. They do not feel that the government should try to influence the economy through levels of government spending (deficit-spending during recessions and decreased spending during boom times).

38. D

A quota is a production assignment that, under official controls, must be manufactured. Both the governments of the USSR and Nazi Germany set quotas for the production of goods during the 1930s. In the Soviet Union, Stalin's Five Year Plans set economic production for targets for all industries. Managers and workers in state enterprises who failed to meet Stalin's quotas were severely punished. In Nazi Germany during the 1930s, the government set quotas for the production of armaments (weapons). By paying quota-fulfilling companies top dollar for military equipment, Adolf Hitler ensured that private enterprises would respond to his direction of this sector of the economy.

A and B. Only in the USSR did the state officially abolish class differences and nationalize all factories. C. Only in Nazi Germany was citizenship granted on the basis of race.

39. C

Supporters of public enterprise (government-owned and -controlled) economies would be most concerned about increased economic inequalities in Western economies because they believe in economic equality between citizens. Communists believe in government ownership and control of the economy. Communists are also materialists (people who consider material possessions and physical comfort more important than spiritual values), but they would oppose the blind pursuit of profit that can occur in private enterprise economies.

A, B, and D. Capitalists believe that economic inequality is natural and acceptable. They would not be bothered by growing income disparity. A capitalist is a supporter of a laissez-faire economy—also known as a free enterprise economy or a private enterprise economy.

40. D

There are two types of liberals—classical liberals and modern liberals. Neoconservatives are capitalists who share the economic views of classical liberals. For instance, both neoconservatives and classical liberals believe that each citizen should be responsible for his or her own economic well-being. Modern liberals, however, believe that the state must try to improve the economic status of the poor by providing them with some government assistance. Modern liberalism (together with democratic socialism) led to the creation of the modern welfare state.

A, B, and C. Present-day neoconservative (capitalist) thinkers probably would not disagree with any of these beliefs.

41. B

The table shows the international mobility of investment capital. It shows that automobile manufacturing corporations are increasingly investing in foreign car manufacturing operations and/or entering into global manufacturing or marketing partnerships with other corporations.

A, C, and D. The table does not focus on the regulation of cartels (associations of producers that engage in price-fixing by restricting output and competition), competition among automakers, or similarities in car designs.

42. C

Supply-side theory maintains that government subsidies and incentives for corporations will promote economic growth. Advocates of supply side economics believe that tax breaks for businesses will result in more investment in business expansion, increased production, and job creation. Critics of supply-side theory, however, point out that corporations can simply use increased profits (resulting from reduced corporate taxes) to reward shareholders rather than to increase production. Consequently, these critics argue that supply-side economics does not necessarily create jobs or lead to business expansion.

A, B, and D. Critics of supply-side economics— particularly supporters of Keynesianism—probably would not use these arguments to attack supply-side theory; they are not as directly relevant to the issue of whether or not trickle-down economics spurs business growth.

43. B

The speaker is clearly a supporter of entrepreneurship (the readiness to engage in bold, risky, innovative, private business ventures) and, therefore, is a capitalist. Capitalists generally oppose government intervention in the economy. One exception to this rule, however, is their support for government action to prevent the growth of monopolies.

A monopoly is defined as "exclusive control of a commodity or service in a particular market, or a control that makes possible the manipulation of prices." The term may also refer to "a company that exercises exclusive control over a commodity, service or industry." Capitalists oppose monopolies because they destroy economic competition (which is the foundation of the free market system) and hurt consumers (who are charged exorbitant prices in the absence of competition).

A, C, and D. Capitalists would not support government restrictions on foreign investment, central planning, or the nationalization (government take-over) of key industries.

44. C

The speaker supports the capitalist position that governments should not provide welfare to the less fortunate. Capitalists favour helping the less fortunate through private charities and seek to abolish social programs. The speaker notes that "every penny the federal government does not appropriate for welfare is potentially available for private use." This indicates that he would likely support a decrease in taxation for individuals and corporations.

A, B, and D. The capitalist speaker would oppose increases in social assistance benefits and the nationalization of industries as a means of job creation. The speaker favours private charities over the welfare state, but, while the speaker would not support government-run gambling operations or government-directed support for private charities, it is not stated whether the speaker favours discontinuing all funding from gambling revenues (e.g. bingos).

45. A

Supply-side economics favours tax breaks for corporations as a means of stimulating investment, encouraging business expansion, and creating jobs. Comments I and II mention corporate tax relief.

B, C, and D. Comment III mentions subsidies to corporations, which was not a part of Reaganomics. Comment IV has nothing to do with supply-side economics.

46. D

A goods and services tax (Canada's GST, for instance) is a means of "taxing money spent rather than money earned." In this method of taxation, consumers must pay money to the government each time they purchase a good or service in the marketplace.

A, B, and C. Corporate taxes, personal income taxes, and capital gains taxes, (taxes on investment income) are all taxes on money earned—not on money spent.

47. B

The author argues that the federal government is largely ignoring corporate taxation as a source of potential government revenue. He notes that corporations successfully avoid paying billions of dollars in taxes each year and that the government does nothing to force them to meet their tax obligations. The author would probably suggest that collecting taxes from deadbeat corporations would go a long way toward reducing Canada's national debt. He might also recommend ending subsidies and tax breaks for corporations as means of debt reduction.

A, C, and D. The author does not suggest any of these things in his comments.

48. D

Economically, Franklin Delano Roosevelt was a liberal—not a conservative. He should be placed more toward the centre of the economic spectrum.

A, B, and C. The other leaders are correctly placed on the economic spectrum.

49. C

Laissez-faire capitalists criticize the Marxist assumption that human creativity and productivity will flourish in a collectivist society. Laissez-faire capitalists are extreme economic individualists who believe that providing the individual with maximum economic freedom is always preferable to seeking to provide for the needs of society as a whole.

A, B, and D. A laissez-faire capitalist would agree with all of these assumptions.

50. D

Perestroika (Mikhail Gorbachev's 1985–1991 policy of economic restructuring) can best be categorized as "the introduction of market-oriented reforms" in the USSR. This policy involved relaxing government control over the economy, allowing private enterprises to compete with state enterprises, and inviting foreign companies to set up shop in the Soviet Union.

A, B, and C. Perestroika involved decreased government planning. It did not advocate privatizing all essential industries. Increased emphasis on new technology was not the main focus of Perestroika.

51. B

Government take-overs of private industries (nationalization) and private farms (collectivization) would have been supported by Josef Stalin but opposed by Adolf Hitler. Hitler was an anti-communist fascist who opposed these two communist policies. Stalin was a communist dictator who favoured these policies.

52. D

Although Adolf Hitler was given dictatorial powers through the Enabling Act in 1933, when a multi-party elected legislature (the Reichstag) gave him power to rule by decree for a limited period of four years, Hitler ultimately created a one-party state in which the constitution was ignored and the legislature was powerless. Stalin also led a one party state with similar conditions.

53. B

Democratic socialism is located slightly to the left side of the economic-political spectrum—between communism and liberalism.

A, C, and D. Position I represents to communism. Liberalism is placed at Position III. Conservatism is represented by Position IV. Fascism is placed at Position V.

54. D

Support for traditional family values and an unregulated marketplace are right-wing political values. On the spectrum, they are located at positions IV and V.

55. B

Poland was controlled by the dictatorial government of Nazi Germany in 1944. When the Soviet Red Army liberated Poland in 1944–45, Josef Stalin set up a communist puppet dictatorship in Poland that was controlled by him.

A, C, and D. 1944 Fascist Italy, 1945 Nazi Germany, and 1945 Imperial Japan had dictatorial governments. However, democracy was re-established in post-war Germany, Italy, and Japan.

56. B

Adolf Hitler claimed that the Nazi party achieved power through a democratic process. Hitler had been invited to become Chancellor by the democratically elected President (Hindenburg). Hitler's party was one of the largest parties in Germany's democratically elected parliament (the Reichstag).

A majority of democratically elected members of the Reichstag voted to give him dictatorial powers in the Enabling Act of 1933. And after coming to power, Hitler held several plebiscites in which close to 100% of German voters approved of his rule and policies.

A, C, and D. In the 1923 Beer Hall Putsch, Hitler attempted to forcibly overthrow the German government in a coup d'etat; but it was not a coup d'etat (nor the actions of a military faction or junta) that brought him to power in 1933. After his release from prison in December 1924, Hitler chose to enter electoral politics in an attempt to achieve power through legal means. He certainly did not claim to have achieved power through a communist-style workers' revolution; Hitler and the Nazis detested communists.

57. C

The intent of these Nazi textbook questions is clearly to make Germans indifferent toward euthanasia (the "mercy killing" of the diseased and handicapped) and war. In other words, the textbook excerpt sought to desensitize students to the ideas of euthanasia and militarism. The questions were a tool of indoctrination that attempted to instill Nazi viewpoints and values in school children. Hitler wanted children to embrace militarism (the love of war) and eugenics (the belief that one's race could be improved through selective breeding and the elimination of the weak and infirm). A major euthanasia program began in Nazi Germany in 1939 and resulted in the mass murder of more than 70,000 mentally and physically handicapped persons by the spring of 1945.

A, B, and D. These intents are not suggested by the excerpt.

58. A

The dictatorial technique illustrated by the excerpt is indoctrination (systematically teaching citizens to uncritically accept a dictator's ideas). The Nazis used textbook sections such as this one to win over a captive audience of students to Hitler's way of thinking.

B, C, and D. The excerpt does not illustrate the techniques of force, terror, or glorification of the past. Although scapegoating (blaming society's problems on a minority group) is evident in the first question about lunatic asylums—mental patients were clearly being blamed for being an economic drain on Germany—the second question about bombs is not an example of scapegoating (the direction of popular discontent). However, both of the excerpt's questions are good examples of indoctrination.

59. A

Aristotle implies that the rights of the rich will not be respected in a democracy by the majority of poorer citizens. An elitist (a supporter of leadership or dominance by a select group) would probably view democracy in the way that Aristotle did—as undesirable and unjust mob rule (a tyranny of the majority).

B, C, and D. Nothing in the comments of Jefferson, Bentham, and Trudeau suggests that these men had reservations about democracy or favoured rule by an elite over rule by the people.

60. B

Jeremy Bentham was a liberal who supported humanitarian reform in Britain during the late-eighteenth and the early-nineteenth century. Bentham's utilitarian ideas can be used to defend the modern welfare state. Among other things, he called for sickness benefits for workers, free public education, and minimum wage laws. Therefore, individuals who support Bentham's viewpoint of promoting "the greatest possible happiness of the greatest number" would be most alarmed by the dismantling of the liberal democratic welfare state. The eradication of social welfare programs would certainly reduce the happiness of the poorer classes.

A, C, and D. Benthamites would likely favour the creation of additional government services and agencies—provided that they increased the general happiness of society. Bentham was not a laissez-faire capitalist; he believed that the state should intervene in the economy to assist the unfortunate.

Bentham would not necessarily have opposed new taxes; he would have probably supported them if they enabled the government to promote the greater good of society.

61. A

Of the main political parties in Canada, the most left-wing party, both in the 1990s and today, is the socialist NDP (New Democratic Party). Centrist (moderate) parties in Canada currently include the Liberal Party and the Conservative Party (formerly, the Progressive Conservative Party). The most right-wing of Canada's mainstream political parties during the 1990's was the Reform Party.

62. D

The characteristics describe the office of the Prime Minister in Canada. The PM is the leader of the party with the most seats in the House of Commons. There is no term limit for the office of Prime Minister; a person may continue to serve as PM indefinitely—as long as voters and party members continue to support him. The maximum length of time between Canadian federal elections is five years. Canada's PM is a Member of Parliament in the House of Commons; therefore, he is a member of the legislative (law-making) branch of government. He is also the head of the Cabinet and of the government bureaucracy, therefore the PM is also a member of the executive (law enforcing) branch of government.

A and B. The characteristics do not describe political offices within the dictatorships of Nazi Germany and the Soviet Union.

C. No politician in the USA is elected for a five-year term (congressmen are elected for a term of two years; the president and vice president are elected for four year terms; senators are elected for six year terms). Moreover, no American government official may serve simultaneously in both the executive and legislative branches of government; the USA has a strict separation of powers in its democratic political system.

63. D

Representation by population is a system in which the number of representatives elected in a given area is proportionate to the number of people who live there. Both Canada's House of Commons and the USA's House of Representatives are selected on the basis of representation by population. According to this practice, provinces or states with larger populations are given more seats in the legislative assembly than provinces or states with smaller populations.

A. Canadian MPs (Members of the House of Commons) are elected for five-year terms, but these terms are not fixed; a general election in Canada may be called at any time the PM desires. Elections may also take place at irregular intervals as a result of the defeat of a government bill or a vote of non-confidence. American congressmen (Members of the House of Representatives) are elected for fixed two-year terms.

B. Neither Canadian MPs nor American congressmen are appointed by the executive branch. They are legislators who are chosen by voters in elections.

C. Members of opposition parties have always been elected to Canada's House of Commons and America's House of Representatives. Therefore, not everyone in these assemblies is representative of the prevailing ideology of the majority party.

64. C

The comments express positions of conservative voters. Conservatives feel that the size of government departments and the number of government bureaucrats should be kept to a minimum. They also believe that government social welfare programs erode self-reliance and the work ethic. Finally, conservatives generally oppose government restrictions on the political freedoms of individuals and the economic freedoms of businessmen.

A, B, and D. The comments are not typical of liberals, socialists, or left-wingers. Such persons are not as individualistic as the speaker. Nor are they as critical of government bureaucrats or "big government."

65. A

Conservatives strongly defend private property rights.

B, C, and D. Conservatives are individualists that would believe in self-reliance rather than social assistance. They do not support government job creation programs, welfare payments to the poor, or public health care.

66. C

The Canadian Prime Minister is a member of both the executive and the legislative branch. The PM not only runs government departments through his Cabinet, he is an elected MP who votes on proposed laws in the House of Commons. In the USA, the President is a member of the executive branch only. The President, therefore, does not sit in Congress and cannot vote on legislation.

A, B, and D. Members of Parliament (MPs) debate and vote on proposed laws just like American congressmen and senators. Supreme Court justices are appointed to office in both Canada and the USA. In both countries, the head of the government (the PM or President) discusses government policies with the members of his Cabinet (Cabinet Ministers or Secretaries).

67. B

Democracies rely on the free expression of alternative views as a means of correcting mistakes and righting wrongs. This concept is summed up well by the following quote by Pierre Trudeau.
"Democracy recognizes that one person may be right and ninety-nine wrong. That is why the freedom of speech is sacred: the one person must always have the right to proclaim his or her truth in the hope of persuading the ninety-nine to change their point of view."

A, C, and D. Free speech is more fundamentally important to the correction of mistakes in a democracy than a two-party system or periodic elections. Democracy must grant freedom of expression to all citizens—not just to elected politicians. A hierarchy (government by an elite group) is less likely to admit mistakes than an egalitarian democracy where the views of all citizens are respected and heeded.

68. D

The first-past-the-post system (plurality system) is sometimes criticized for distorting the expressed will of the electorate (voters). In this system, candidates often win an election with less than 50% of the vote. In fact, if votes are split rather evenly between several candidates, a politician could get elected with a very small percentage of the popular vote. If a similar voting trend occurs across the nation, a party can often win a majority of the seats in the legislature without having received a majority of the votes cast in an election. Critics of the first-past-the-post system generally favour an electoral system of proportional representation (PR); in this system, the percentage of seats that a party receives is roughly equivalent to its percentage of the popular vote.

A, B, and C. The first past-past-the-post system often produces majority governments. This would not undermine the authority of the executive branch or reduce the effectiveness of the governing party. In fact, the first-past-the-post system has the opposite effect on government authority and effectiveness. The first-pass-the-post system does not deny interest groups an opportunity to influence decisions.

69. A

Defenders of the first-past-the-post system maintain that this electoral system produces stable majority governments. They argue that electoral systems of proportional representation (PR), in contrast, generally produce unstable minority or coalition governments. A minority government is far more likely to fall prematurely because of the defeat of a government bill in the legislature or because of the passing of a motion of non-confidence. Governments change less frequently and elections are held less often in nations with a first-past-the-post electoral system.

B, C, and D. Defenders of the plurality system (the first-past-the-post system) could not claim that their electoral system was less costly, more accountable to voters, or more responsive to voters than the PR system.

70. C

In an electoral system of proportional representation, the percentage of seats awarded to a political party is based on the party's percentage of the total votes cast in the election. If a party received about 40% of the popular vote, it would receive roughly 40% of the seats in the legislative assembly. Adopting a PR system would ensure that no political party got more than its fair share of the seats in the legislature.

A, B, and D. Adopting a system of direct democracy would not be a practical solution to the problem. Direct democracy (allowing all citizens to thoroughly debate each proposed law before directly voting on it) is not a viable option for large countries with millions of citizens. The first-past-the-post system and PR system are both tools of representative democracy; in both systems, citizens elect representatives to make laws for the nation. Both electoral systems provide representation by population; both systems give each citizen an equal share of voting power.

71. C

Right-wing extremism (fascism) emerged in Europe during the interwar period partly as a result of a fear of communism. Fascism is an anti-communist ideology that tended to attract opponents of Marxism.

A, B, and D. Right-wing extremists (fascists) are militarists. The popularity of pacifist (peace-loving) attitudes during the interwar era does not help to explain the rise of fascist parties. Similarly, a decline in nationalist feeling and an increased support for democracy do not help to explain the rise of fascism; fascists are extreme nationalists (ultranationalists) who oppose democracy and favour authoritarianism.

72. A

The Enabling Act was the law passed by the Weimar Republic's Reichstag (parliament) on 23 March 1933; the act granted Hitler dictatorial powers. The Act was passed by a democratically elected parliament but marked the end of parliamentary democracy in Germany.

B, C, and D. The end of Germany's democracy was not brought about by the election of the first Nazi deputies to the Reichstag or the election of von Hindenburg to the presidency; both events took place years before the passing of the Enabling Act. The plotting of the Night of the Long Knives—the 1934 purge of Ernst Rohm and other leaders of the Nazi stormtroopers (SA)—was carried out by Hitler after achieving absolute power in 1933.

73. B

Marxism is an ideology that, in theory, supports total economic equality between human beings and the reduction of human suffering through social reform (humanitarianism).

A, C, and D. Marxists favour industrial growth, collectivization (the takeover of private industries by the state), or centralization of the economy (central economic planning). However, they are philosophically opposed to elitism and authoritarianism (rule by an elite rather than rule by the collective). Marxists also prefer internationalism to nationalism; they regard workers from all nations as proletarian brothers and sisters.

74. D

Statement I is false. Hitler believed in private ownership and never promoted the government takeover (nationalization) of privately owned industries. Statement II is true; in 1956, Khrushchev did condemn Stalin for his purges of communist officials; he also initiated a program of de-Stalinization, which ended Stalin's official personality cult in the USSR.

75. D

In a PR system, a party's share of seats in the national legislature is based on its percentage of total votes cast in the election. The PC party would have benefited most from a PR system; if a system of proportional representation had been in effect, the Progressive Conservatives would have received 47 seats instead of merely 2.

A, B, and C. Under a PR system, the Liberals would have received fewer seats (122 instead of 178). Both the Reform Party and the NDP would have received more seats under a PR system—but their gains would not have been as impressive as the Progressive Conservatives (2250% increase in seats).

76. B

The Source II comment suggests that Canada's first-past-the-post (plurality or winner-take-all) electoral system causes some voters to become disillusioned; the source states that Canadian elections usually give power to a party that was not supported by a majority of voters and leaves some citizens feeling "cheated."

A, C, and D. Source II does not suggest that Canada's winner-take-all-system creates political stalemate in parliament or provides political extremists with excessive political influence; actually, these two criticism are commonly made about the PR system. Finally, Source II does not maintain that Canada's current electoral system is a practical system that should be adopted by newly founded democracies; the source is very critical of the plurality system and suggests that it is an unfair electoral system.

77. C

Source III points out that a PR electoral system may produce shaky (unstable) coalition governments.

A, B, and D. Source III does not mention anything about cabinet solidarity (the principle that individual Cabinet Ministers should publicly support the decisions made by the Cabinet). It does not suggest that the PR system will result in unpopular legislation or disregard for democratic processes.

78. A

The information in Source I supports the contentions made in Source II. The 1993 Federal Election Results show that the Liberals received only 41.3% of the popular vote but won a majority of seats in the House of Commons; in other words, the Liberals received 60.3% of the seats in spite of the fact that 58.7% per cent of Canadian voters "voted against" the Liberals by supporting other parties. Source II points out that a sizable majority of Canadians usually vote against the political party that wins the most seats in Canada's winner-take-all electoral system.

B, C, and D. The information in Source I does not contradict the contentions made in Source II. Source III focuses on a PR system's tendency to produce minority and coalition governments; it does not provide any basis for the ideas in Source II that focus on the alleged unfairness of the winner-take-all (plurality) electoral system. The three sources do not provide contradictory information; no source contains ideas or information that conflicts with ideas or information in the other two sources.

79. D

Party discipline (compelling individual MPs to adhere to the party line on parliamentary votes and public statements under the threat of punishment or expulsion from the party) sometimes prevents a member of Parliament from expressing the actual views of his constituents in votes on bills, in debates in the House of Commons, and in public statements.

A, B, and C. Party leaders and whips do not enforce party discipline as strictly in opposition parties. Party discipline is more important for a government party that would fall from power if a government bill was defeated or if a non-confidence vote were passed. The media coverage devoted to the political goals of opposition parties is not the main reason why interests of local ridings are not always addressed in the House of Commons. Neither is representation by population (the principle that no voter should have more voting power than any other voter). Finally, provincial politics rarely, if ever, prevent federal MPs from addressing the interests of their federal constituents.

80. B

Both communist and fascist dictatorships are totalitarian regimes (dictatorships in which the government regulates every aspect of public and private behaviour). In a totalitarian dictatorship, opposition parties are not tolerated and an authoritarian government strictly controls schools and universities, judges, the police, and the military.

A, C, and D. Characteristic 1 (state ownership of factories and machinery) and Characteristic 4 (the promotion of economic equality) are representative of communist—but not fascist—dictatorships. Characteristic 7 holds true for communism (Karl Marx was a philosopher) but not for fascism (Benito Mussolini and Adolf Hitler are not generally described as philosophers in the formal sense; they were both politicians).

81. A

In communist systems, the state owns and controls factories and machinery (the means of production), tries to bring about complete economic equality between citizens, and attempts to implement the ideas of an economic philosopher (Karl Marx).

B, C, and D. State control of the mass media and crackdowns on opposition parties may occur in any type of dictatorship—not just in communist regimes. Nationalism and racism are not generally encouraged by communist governments; however, they would be promoted by fascist dictatorships. A combination of centralized and de-centralized economic decision making is more characteristic of a mixed economy than a communist economy.

82. D

During the 1990s, China adopted a policy of Red Capitalism in which it allowed the emergence of private enterprises and free market economics in special economic zones; in other words, it allowed some decentralized economic decision making to take place. Consequently, it devalued the importance of state ownership and strict economic equality.

A, B, and C. State control of the means of production had existed in communist China since 1949; it was not a new initiative of the 1990s. Similarly, economic equality had been promoted by the communist regime prior to 1990. Finally, Karl Marx's ideas had been promoted in China for more than four decades prior to 1990. In the 1990s, China continued to rigidly control the media, punish those who had criticized the government, and strictly control Chinese courts, police, and the military.

83. C

The list indicates that parliamentary democracies place a great emphasis on the accountability of elected representatives. The characteristics listed (opposition, question period, etc.) are means of holding MPs and/or bureaucrats responsible for their actions.

A, B, and D. These characteristics are not means of achieving consensus (general agreement) on issues. Most of the items listed are primarily strategies for holding elected officials (MPs/cabinet ministers) accountable; making government departments more efficient is, at best, a secondary objective of these techniques. The items listed are techniques for keeping political power decentralized—not methods of concentrating power in the hands of government officials.

84. B

The term "bicameral legislature" refers to a parliament with two houses (legislative chambers); the House of Commons in the Canadian parliamentary system is one of these chambers; the Senate is the second chamber. Canada's bicameral parliament is modelled after that of Britain; in Britain, the upper house of parliament is called the House of Lords—not the Senate.

A, C, and D. Judicial review, responsible government, and official opposition are terms that are not directly associated with the House of Commons, Senate, and House of Lords.

85. A

The dictatorial techniques of force (using violence or the threat of violence to gain the compliance of the general population) and coercion (persuading or restraining unwilling persons through the use of force) are mentioned in the excerpt. The excerpt states that the Nazis used street violence "to break down opposition."

B, C, and D. The excerpt does not directly refer to these other techniques of dictatorship.

86. A

The cartoon depicts US President Bill Clinton as a leader who lacks consistent principles and policies; Clinton is represented as a politician who lacks a distinct and coherent political vision and merely tries to retain his popularity by responding to public opinion polls.

B, C, and D. Pollsters are professionals who conduct public opinion polls. They are not lobby groups per se. The cartoon does not depict the unwillingness of government to respond to citizen concerns; in fact, it suggests that government is too willing to cater to public opinion. Finally, the cartoon does not suggest that voters (the electorate) are unable to understand or participate in government decision making.

87. D

In a direct democracy, citizens do not elect representatives to make decisions for them; they make decisions themselves by participating in a mass assembly. In a representative democracy, the people elect representatives who make decisions for them in a legislative assembly. Therefore, in a representative democracy, citizens surrender some control of the political decision-making process.

A, B, and C. In both direct and representative democracies, minorities are given a voice, majority rule is maintained, universal suffrage (the granting of voting rights to all adult citizens) can exist, and public security is protected. The idea, however, that the primary purpose of government is to ensure the security of its citizens is a founding principle of dictatorship—not democracy. In a democracy, the primary purpose of government is to preserve the freedoms and protect the rights of citizens.

88. C

Dictators commonly stage rigged elections with pre-determined outcomes. Even though citizens are allowed to vote in these elections, these elections are merely a form of controlled participation.

A, B, and D. Dictators will not allow independent officials to verify election results. They do not want to yield any control of the political process. For the same reason, dictators do not permit unrestricted political competition, freedom of speech, and freedom of assembly.

89. C

The newspaper excerpt maintains that leftists have advocated the redistribution of income as a means of eliminating economic unfairness and disparity (inequality).

A, B, and D. None of these three generalizations about leftists is made in the newspaper excerpt. Moreover, none of these generalizations is a typical characterization of the political left.

90. A

Right-wing economic thinkers (supporters of capitalism) believe strongly that each individual should take responsibility for his/her own well being; they are philosophically opposed to the welfare benefits and social services that are favoured by left-wing (socialist) politicians. They believe strongly in self-reliance, initiative and other capitalist values. They believe that is it unfair for the government to share the wealth of the richer members of society with the poorer members of society.

B, C, and D. Right-wing (capitalist) thinkers do not think that left-wing (socialist) economic policies would lead to the formation of monopolies, the elimination of welfare programs, or the restrictions of labour unions and collective bargaining. On the contrary, right-wing thinkers believe that left-wing politicians would be more active in restricting large corporations, expanding the welfare state, and encouraging labour union activities.

91. B

A secret police force is one "stick" used by dictators to maintain power. The term "the stick" refers to the use of violence and punishments.

A, C, and D. The direct use of force is not involved in these dictatorial techniques.

92. C

The authors of both sources agree that corporations exist exclusively to make a profit. In Source I, the writer maintains that companies should "'make as much money for their stockholders as possible.'" In Source II, the author declares that the primary objective of a corporation is to "increase its own wealth and assets."

A, B, and D. Source I does not suggest that corporations receive favourable government treatment; only Source II does. The authors of both sources argue that corporations should not have social responsibilities. Source I does not state outright that corporations contribute to community wealth.

Source II states only that "Governments identify growth and development with commercial corporations."

93. A

Friedman's support for a free market economy is based on the assumption that corporations will engage '"in open and free competition, without deception and fraud."'

B, C, and D. Friedman's right-wing economic views are not primarily based on these assumptions.

94. C

The cartoon represents a large corporation (Mega-Corp) as a smug, faceless, and impersonal institution—devoid of human warmth or sympathy.

A, B and D. The other quotations do not match the cartoon's message.

95. D

A social democrat (democratic socialist) would most strongly disagree with Friedman's contention that corporations have only one social responsibility.

A, B, and C. A social democrat tends to see corporations as profit-seeking institutions that can often be impersonal and inhumane; social democrats generally believe that corporations must be forced to live up their social responsibilities. Social democrats believe in extensive cooperation between communities and corporations. Social democrats are democratic socialists—not communists. They are not philosophically opposed to corporations making a profit; but social democrats do believe that a portion of corporate profits should be taxed and used for the development of a more just society.

96. C

Lenin's NEP and Gorbachev's perestroika were both economic policies that allowed more economic individualism (capitalism) within the Soviet economic system.

A, B, and D. Both the NEP and perestroika brought about some decentralization of the economy; neither policy brought about greater central planning. Gorbachev's policy of glasnost—not perestroika—promoted freedom of speech; the NEP did nothing of the sort. Both policies directly attempted to create more economic stability; they were only indirectly aimed at bringing about greater political stability.

97. C

The economic principle of "universality" holds that all citizens—rich and poor alike—should receive the same benefits from social programs such as unemployment insurance and public health care. If a means test is used to determine old-age pension eligibility, wealthier citizens will not be able to receive a government pension because they do not really need it. Such a means test would directly challenge the principle of universality of social programs.

A, B, and D. These three other measures do not directly challenge the economic principle of the universality of social programs. Privatization and taxation are not social programs.

98. B

The economic reforms on the list are right-wing (conservative) policies. Downsizing government by contracting out public services to private companies is another conservative policy.

A, C, and D. A supporter of economic conservatism (capitalism) would not support the government takeover of the transportation industry, transfer payments to less fortunate persons and regions, or public education. These economic policies are left-wing (socialist) economic policies.

99. B

A government could attempt to reverse runaway inflation (soaring prices and decreasing purchasing power) by decreasing the money supply.

A, C, and D. Increasing workers' wages, encouraging foreign borrowing, and reducing interest rates would all encourage increased spending and continued inflation.

100. D

Germany (the Weimar Republic) experienced hyperinflation during the 1922 to 1925 period. During this period, Germany's currency (the mark) became virtually worthless.

A, B, and C. The USSR, Great Britain, and the USA did not experience runaway inflation during the given periods.

101. A

Laissez-faire capitalists believe that labour unions distort the labour market (which they feel should be regulated only by the laws of supply and demand) and make it difficult for a capitalist businessmen to fire unproductive employees. They feel that unions also force companies to pay higher wages and, consequently, increase the costs of production.

B, C, and D. Laissez-faire capitalists do not generally oppose labour unions for these reasons.

102. B

The writer expresses beliefs that are consistent with those of Adam Smith—the founding father of the capitalist ideology. Capitalists are opposed to government intervention in the economy except when such intervention is necessary to preserve the free market. Therefore, a capitalist writer would oppose subsidies (money granted by the government to a private businesses) as unnecessary interference in the economy.

A, C, and D. The ideas expressed are not as consistent with the more-interventionist beliefs of Karl Marx's communism, John Stuart Mill's liberalism, or John Maynard Keynes' demand-side economic theory.

103. B

Private enterprise (capitalist) economists believe that the best way to eliminate government deficits is to practise fiscal restraint (by reducing government spending).

A, C, and D. Private enterprise economists are philosophically opposed to increased business taxes, government takeovers of industries, or grants of government funds to the poor.

104. C

The New Deal (FDR's economic reform program in the USA during the Great Depression) is a good example of interventionism (government involvement in the economy). In the New Deal, the American government intervened in the marketplace by creating jobs through public works projects and creating social welfare programs.

A, B and D. Wage and price controls are anti-inflation measures that do not allow prices to be determined by the free market (the laws of supply and demand); instead, the government imposes a cap on wage and price levels. The invisible hand refers to the beneficial impact that the profit motive has on the economy; this capitalist concept is not consistent with the liberal or socialist policy of providing government grants to private corporations. The Five Year Plans were Josef Stalin's program of industrialization in the communist USSR; demand-side economic theory is supported by economic liberals and democratic socialists; demand-side economics (Keynesianism) is not a communist approach to economics.

105. D

Supply-side (trickle-down) economic theory recommends that tax cuts be given to corporations and rich persons as a way of promoting increased economic production and job creation. Critics contend that supply-side economic policies concentrate more wealth in the hands of already wealthy citizens while putting greater economic burdens on the middle class and the poor.

A, B, and C. Critics of supply-side policies maintain that these initiatives have caused greater economic disparity—not greater economic equality. The suggestion that trickle-down policies have caused a less competitive marketplace is not a common criticism of supply-side economics. Finally, supply-side theory is associated with the right-wing (capitalist) side of the economic spectrum; therefore, it is not considered to be a significant challenge to traditional free-market economic theory.

NOTES

Answers and Solutions
Political and Economic Systems – Unit Test 1

1. B	11. B	21. B	31. D	41. B	51. C	61. B
2. B	12. A	22. C	32. D	42. A	52. D	62. B
3. D	13. A	23. D	33. C	43. C	53. B	63. D
4. A	14. B	24. D	34. D	44. C	54. C	64. C
5. C	15. D	25. B	35. A	45. A	55. C	65. A
6. D	16. C	26. C	36. D	46. D	56. D	66. A
7. A	17. B	27. A	37. C	47. A	57. A	67. D
8. B	18. A	28. C	38. A	48. D	58. D	68. A
9. A	19. D	29. B	39. C	49. B	59. D	69. D
10. A	20. C	30. C	40. A	50. D	60. C	70. A

1. B

The key words in this question are to a **majority of Canadians.** Students are expected to understand the basic principles of the Canadian political system.

B. Voting in elections is considered a basic responsibility of all citizens in a democracy.

A. The idea that a majority of citizens should support the goals of the political party in power is more typical of an authoritarian system of government, rather than Canada's democratic system.

C. This answer is similar to response A in that it is a more typical expectation of the majority in an authoritarian system than a democracy.

D. Even though some Canadians might believe that their system of government is best, it is hardly likely that they would seek to promote it as a worldwide system.

2. B

Students answering this question are expected to understand the characteristics of **Nazism.**

B. Hitler's Nazi Party was fascist. Fascists are strongly opposed to the concept of equality.

A. The political and economic ideals of parties like the Nazi Party usually support the concept of elitism.

C. Nazism is almost fanatical in its support of nationalism.

D. The concept of private property is part of the ideals of Nazism.

3. D

Students answering this question must understand the differences between economic intervention in a democratic system and an authoritarian system.

D. The American president is limited in his actions by the checks and balances placed on his power by the United States' constitution.

A. Due to the fact that the American president appoints and has complete control over members of his cabinet, he is free to disregard their advice.

B. As the leading industrial power of the 20th century, the United States was in a position to establish any economic programs that it saw fit.

C. Inflation created by government spending would have been a problem faced by both Hitler and Roosevelt.

4. A

Students answering this question are expected to recognize and understand the main events that occurred in the **Weimar Republic** during the 1920's and 1930's.

A. The collapse of the democratic Weimar Republic is a classic study of how the subversion of a weak democracy occurred as a result of the inaction of an apathetic electorate.

B. The Czarist empire of Nicholas II hardly fits the model of a democratic system of government that was undermined by an apathetic electorate.

C. The disintegration of Yugoslavia is a good example of turmoil caused by nationalistic agitation, rather than the rise to power of a dictator as a result of the inaction of the citizenry.

D. The disintegration of the Soviet Union was a result of an increase in democratic rights and privileges. It is not a good example of the failure of democracy, but rather of the rise of democracy.

5. C

The skill being tested in questions 5 to 7 is that of the ability to interpret data. Careful study of the election results should allow the student to discover the information necessary to obtain a correct answer to all of the questions. Key statistics to note are those dealing with **voter turnout, % of seats,** and **% of votes.**

C. Only in Source II is there evidence that any of the elections led to a stable majority government. Historically, this period was characterized by weak governments that were forced into frequent and indecisive elections.

A. Voter apathy is not likely to lead to more elections. Also, the data indicate a high voter turnout in these elections.

B. There are no data on the influence of cabinet solidarity on the number of elections shown.

D. Government backbenchers, ineffective or not, are unlikely to force frequent elections.

6. D

D. The election in 1958 was one of the most lopsided victories in Canadian history. The other elections shown all resulted in minority governments.

A. The data indicates that the total number of seats in the House of Commons (265) did not increase in the period covered.

B. The voter turnout in 1958 (Source II) was identical to voter turnout in 1962 and 1963 (Sources III and IV).

C. There is no way of determining the philosophies of the various political parties from the data.

7. A

A. Accountability in a democratic system requires that the government seek the support of the population through periodic elections. This principle is upheld by the data.

B. The data indicates that the percentage of eligible voters who cast their ballots (79%) was unchanged from 1958 to 1963.

C. The percentage of votes received and the percentage of seats won in the elections indicates that a system of proportional representation was not being used. If such a system were used, the percentage of seats won and the percentage of votes received would be identical.

D. The frequency of the elections suggests that the prime ministers of the day had difficulty in receiving the support of the majority.

8. B

Students are expected to understand the characteristics of modern **neo-nazi** groups.

B. Extreme right-wing groups, such as neo-Nazis, are usually considered reactionary. A reactionary is a person who hearkens back to a previous era that is perceived as being a more perfect time. A neo-Nazi seeks a return to the policies of Hitler's Third Reich.

A. Neo-Nazis are an extreme right-wing group. Those who are politically liberal are on the left of the political spectrum.

C. Neo-Nazi groups are not considered to have any progressive political ideas.

D. Although conservatives and neo-Nazis are both on the right side of the political spectrum, the extreme views of neo-Nazis distance them considerably from the more moderate views of ordinary conservatives.

9. A

Students are expected to understand the similarities and differences between the authoritarian systems of **fascism** and **communism.**

A. Class differences are not only accepted by fascists, they are usually promoted.

B. Both fascism and communism make widespread use of central planning; however, in communism, the entire economy is not only planned but also owned by the state. In fascism, ownership remains in private hands.

C. Fascism supports private property. Collectivization of agriculture would be a violation of fascist principles.

D. In both fascism and communism, the party controls the working of the government.

10. A

Students are expected to understand that the terms *responsible government* and *accountability of the cabinet* rafer to the same concept.

A. The principle of executive accountability is called responsible government. This principle has been a feature of Canadian democracy since the passing of the Rebellion Losses Bill in 1847.

B. Constitutional limits on the power of government are not the same as traditions that have developed in the Canadian parliamentary system.

C. The stress on individualism in Canada does not necessarily serve to limit the executive power of government.

D. Majority rule and acceptance of the rights of minorities may not effectively limit the power of the cabinet as much as the principle of executive accountability.

11. B

Students are expected to understand that the **rule of law** is a belief in the sanctity of the law and in the protection of individuals in society.

B. A constitution limits the power of government, forcing it to obey the laws that it has passed, and thus protecting citizens against the arbitrary power of government.

A. The principle that the executive (the Cabinet) is accountable to the legislature (the House of Commons) does not necessarily prevent Parliament from imposing its will on members of society, but a written constitution is intended to do exactly that.

C. The stated rights of the individual may be meaningless if they are not guaranteed by some sort of written constitution because otherwise the government can always take away such rights when it sees fit.

D. The concept of the rule of law is that the judicial system can be used to protect citizens against arbitrary or unfair decisions of government. Respect for minority rights does not always offer this protection, as it can always be removed in times of crisis.

12. A

Students are expected to understand the strengths and weaknesses of the various different democratic political systems.

A. Because seats are awarded in proportion (hence the name) to the number of votes received, it is rare for countries using a proportional system to have majority governments. This sometimes leads to political instability.

B. There is no evidence that mainstream political parties enjoy any advantages under proportional representation. On the contrary, fringe parties usually enjoy enhanced political importance under this system.

C. The influence of lobby groups can be a problem under any system of representation.

D. A result of the fact that minority or coalition governments are the norm in proportional systems is that there is usually greater cooperation between political parties.

13. A

Students are expected to interpret information about liberal and conservative principles. This question also is intended to determine if students can separate political principles from economic principles.

A. The abolition of the Senate is a political issue. The principles outlined in alternative A are political in nature. As a result, this is the best answer.

B. C. and D. The principles outlined in alternatives B, C, and D are economic in nature and are not related to the issue of Senate reform.

14. B

The clue in this question is the reference in alternative B to **intervention.** Wage and price controls are an intervention in the economy.

B. The issue of wage and price controls is related to the question of just how much governments should intervene in the economy.

A. The principles contrasted in alternative A are political in nature and are not related to the economic issue of wage and price controls.

C. The principles contrasted in alternative C are concerned with economic equality. Those who have property wish to protect it from those who wish wealth to be shared more equally.

D. The principles contrasted in alternative D are concerned with whether or not members of society should rely on themselves or depend on other members of society to help them out in time of need.

15. D

In the excerpt, the words **courts, referees,** and **interpretation** are clues to the correct answer. Students are expected to understand the role of courts in a democracy.

D. In the article, the words "courts," "laws," "charter," and "interpretation" all point to concern over an independent judiciary.

A. The excerpt does not refer to minority rights in any way. The laws being referred to could relate to any legal matter.

B. The secret ballot is not mentioned in the excerpt. The article is discussing the duty of the courts.

C. Political competition is not an issue in the excerpt. As a matter of fact, there is no reference to any sort of political action.

16. C

C. The references to elimination of state parliaments, the banning of trade unions, the use of propaganda, and the use of plebiscites all point to Hitler's consolidation of his power.

A. Hitler's fascination with the mythical Aryan race is not mentioned in the excerpt.

B. Although there are some elements of indoctrination in the excerpt, numerous other actions are mentioned as well. As a result, this is not the **most** appropriate title.

D. Nowhere in the article is there any mention of Hitler's destruction of political opponents in his own party.

17. B

B. The excerpt lists a variety of Nazi Party actions that culminated in the overwhelming victory in the plebiscite of 1933, which confirmed Hitler's power in Germany.

A. The actions of Hitler's storm troopers are not mentioned in the article and, in any case, the storm troopers were an instrument of the Nazi Party and not intended to achieve "national goals."

C. The only opinion expressed by German citizens in the excerpt is that of support for Hitler in the plebiscite. There is no reference at all to the importance of the military.

D. The excerpt does not mention any of the goals of the German people, whatever they might have been. After the rise of Hitler, the goals of the Nazi Party became the goals of the German people.

18. A

Students are expected to understand that the actions described in the question are all examples of transfer payments and ways of redistributing the wealth of society.

A. All of the actions described in the question refer to the Canadian government redistributing tax dollars to various segments of society.

B. Although individuals might be enriched by the redistribution of wealth, this does not ensure individual rights.

C. Monetary policy is not regulated. Monetary policy is the act of regulating. This answer makes no sense.

D. Although government transfer payments would serve to encourage consumer spending, such spending is not the main motive behind such government action.

19. D

The key to understanding the cartoon is that the speaker is opposed to change. In Source II, a number of key phrases such as **recognizably superior persons** and **values and position…should have a greater influence** point to conservatism.

D. Both of the sources express conservative ideals. Conservatives usually oppose change (Source I) and believe in elite leadership (Source II).

A. Liberalism espouses the ideas of change and of political equality. Both of these ideas are contradicted by the sources.

B. The term "radical" usually refers to ideas on the left of the political spectrum. The ideas in the sources belong on the right of the spectrum.

C. Socialism is a philosophy of the left. As mentioned, the political opinions expressed in the sources are on the right of the spectrum.

20. C

Students are expected to display knowledge of basic economic terminology.

C. The WTO (World Trade Organization) has as its goal the liberalization of world trade, a goal that fits into the theme of globalization.

A. Deregulation of the economy would usually be accompanied by the elimination of Crown corporations.

B. Stressing individualism would usually be accompanied by the selling off of government-owned industries, not their acquisition.

D. Protectionism involves increasing tariff barriers, not eliminating them.

21. B

Students are expected to understand the characteristics of left-wing economic ideas and display knowledge of the political spectrum. The key words that point to the left- wing position of the goals listed are **social assistance, raise…taxes, nationalize, universal,** and **subsidize.**

B. Democratic socialism would occupy Position II on the spectrum. This ideology would readily accept all of the above goals.

A. An ideology occupying Position I on the extreme left of the spectrum (communism) would support most of the goals listed above, but would advocate more extreme action such as the complete control of all industries.

C. Position III is that of conservatism. It would oppose all of the stated goals.

D. Position IV on the extreme right would adopt a position similar to that of Position III, but might advocate some government control over industry to accommodate national goals.

22. C

C. Goals I and IV would prove to be of great benefit to low- income earners. Goal I would provide them with higher incomes, and Goal IV would reduce their medical costs.

A. Goal I would help low-income earners, but Goal II would not necessarily have any impact.

B. Goal II would bring the government more revenue and Goal III would give the government more control over the economy, but neither would help out low-income earners.

D. Goal IV would be of benefit to low income earners by providing them with health care services, however, Goal V would only help low income earners if the businesses being subsidized employed low income earners, which might or might not be the case.

23. D

D. Laissez-faire capitalists would oppose any form of government intervention in the economy.

A. Left-wing moderates might support many of the goals listed.

B. Democratic socialists would definitely support most or all of the goals listed.

C. Keynesian economists would see nothing wrong with the selective implementation of certain of the goals, especially those dealing with the regulation of a market economy, such as Goal II.

24. D

Students are expected to understand that in a modern economy, a weakness of one sector of society has an impact on other areas of society. Students are also supposed to show that they can differentiate between the basic economic terms used in the answers.

D. The excerpt is attempting to point out that all members of society benefit when the weakest members of a society receive some sort of social benefit such as unemployment insurance.

A. Deficit financing is where the government spends more than it receives as revenue in a given fiscal year. There is no mention of this practice in the excerpt.

B. Scarcity is the reason for the existence of all economic systems. However, the excerpt makes no mention of scarcity.

C. Supply and demand determines the value of goods in a market economy. Once again, the excerpt makes no mention of this factor.

25. B

B. Programs such as Unemployment Insurance (or Employment Insurance) are classic examples of government intervention in the economy in order to preserve economic security.

A. Downsizing of corporations is not likely to contribute the general well-being of the population.

C. Moving capital and factories to nations with low labour costs is likely to have a negative impact on the society from which the factories and capital are removed.

D. Reduction of social programs is likely to have a strong negative impact on the lives of the poor.

26. C

The key words in this question are **model market economy**. Students are expected to understand the principles of such a system.

C. Supporters of a market economy believe that individuals should depend on their own resources in order to survive. Government support is seen as unnecessary, and, as a result, any attempt to reduce such payments would be strongly supported.

A. Supporters of the market system believe that inefficient businesses should be allowed to fail in accordance with the market principle of competition.

B. Supporters of the market system believe that there should be few, if any, restrictions on the flow of capital, such as foreign investment, across borders.

D. Supporters of a market economy believe that individuals should provide for themselves. Any pension plans that exist should come from the contributions of the recipients, without government help.

27. A

Students are expected to understand the reference to Adam Smith's **invisible hand** and to the modern practice of **downsizing**.

A. In the cartoon, the invisible hand of capitalism has crushed an unsuspecting worker while attempting to hand him a layoff notice.

B. The practice of deregulation occurs when government reduces its control over the economy. The cartoon does not hint at this process.

C. Devaluation is the deliberate reduction in value of a nation's currency in order to give it an advantage in foreign trade. Again, the cartoon is not concerned with this process.

D. Decentralization is the process of spreading government or corporate administrations to several locations from a single central location. This process is not depicted in the cartoon.

28. C

Students are expected to understand the principles of **supply-side economics**. This system requires a reduction or elimination of government regulation.

C. Decreasing overhead refers to cutting the cost of doing businesses. Elimination of unnecessary workers will achieve this goal.

A. Supply-side economics involves freeing up businesses from the high taxes associated with paying down government debt.

B. Advocates of supply-side economics do not believe in providing a social welfare net.

D. Supply-side economics advocates the reduction or elimination of government regulations.

29. B

Students are expected to understand the characteristics of a mixed economy and the basics of **Keynesian economics**.

B. All of the actions would reduce consumer demand and, therefore, slow the rate of inflation

A. All of the actions listed would slow down an economy.

C. Only Action 4 is likely to increase foreign investment by encouraging investors to put their money in domestic banks.

D. By lowering demand and by reducing incentives to industry, the government actions would actually decrease domestic production.

30. C

C. Except under extreme circumstances, few social democrats would be in favour of reducing social security benefits (Action 2) or decreasing transfer payments and equalization programs.

A. Social democrats might justify an increase in income taxes (Action 1) on the grounds that it is necessary to provide social services. They might also justify incentives to private industry (Action 3) on the grounds that this would create jobs.

B. As mentioned, social democrats might favour certain tax incentives to private industry. They would also favour increases in bank rates as a method of combating inflation.

D. Although Action 5 (decreasing transfer payments and equalization grants) would be opposed by social democrats, Action 4 (raising interest rates) could be justified as a measure to control inflation or slow down an overheated economy.

31. D

D. It is very likely that the actions taken would result in a recession as a result of a reduction in consumer spending and an increase in unemployment.

A. All of the actions described would slow down an overheated economy.

B. A result of the reduction in government spending is that the national debt would likely be decreased, not increased.

C. None of the actions taken would result in an increase in export goods.

32. D

Students are expected to understand what is meant by **fiscal policy**.

D. Fiscal policy involves government spending, the setting of levels of taxation, and the establishment of fees for government services.

A. Although the minting of a coin is connected with money, there is more to fiscal policy than this action.

B. The regulation of the stock market is not considered a part of fiscal policy; rather, it is considered a method of encouraging investment by adding stability to an inherently unstable institution.

C. Increasing the minimum wage does not involve any government spending. It may be considered an aspect of government social policy, but not fiscal policy.

33. C

The key words in the question are **free competition** and **market-oriented**. Students are expected to understand the principles that make a market economy function.

C. A paradox of the free market system is that without legislation to prevent the formation of monopolies, the free market system cannot function.

A. Setting a higher tax rate for profitable corporations would be considered a violation of the basic principles of free enterprise.

B. In a model market economy, consumers would be expected to determine the safety of products for themselves.

D. Introduction of quotas on the production of consumer goods is characteristic of a centrally planned economy, not a market economy.

34. D

Students are expected to understand the difference between **public enterprise** and **free enterprise**. Public enterprise refers to government ownership.

D. Government priorities are the overwhelming factor in the establishment of prices in a public enterprise economy.

A. Public enterprise is not influenced greatly by the price of labour.

B. Supply and demand in a public enterprise economy is often ignored in determining prices. What the government decides is what is important.

C. Competition in a public enterprise economy is usually ignored.

35. A

Students are expected to understand the principles of **collectivism**.

A. Socialism is based on the concept of a united society in which people work together to maintain and support the society. This fits the definition of collectivism.

B. Liberalism refers to the ideals of political reform and political freedoms. It is a policy of the left, but it is not a policy of collectivism.

C. Capitalism is opposed to the basic concepts associated with collectivism.

D. Conservatism is also opposed to collectivism, as it shares many of the same principles as capitalism.

36. D

The term *consumer sovereignty* refers to the idea that "production is determined by the demands and preferences of consumers rather than by state planners. In a centrally planned (communist) economy, the state controls production rather than let it be guided by the free market (the laws of supply and demand). That is, in a centrally planned economy, the government decides what goods will be produced; it does not base production on what consumers are buying. Consumer sovereignty exists only when consumers, through their buying and spending habits, decide what future goods will be produced. Consumer sovereignty is most fully present in a laissez-faire capitalist economy. It is eroded by governmental regulation of production. Consumer sovereignty is most severely restricted in a communist economy.

A. Social control (the government's control over society) would be increased by the state regulation of supply—rather than being restricted by it.

B. Class mobility (the ability of lower-class people to work their way up into higher-class society) is not a feature of a centrally planned economy—as only one class exists in a communist (classless) society.

C. The state owns all property in a centrally planned economy. This is an essential feature of communism—as is state regulation of supply. State ownership of property is not restricted by government direction of production in a communist economy.

37. C

The term "invisible hand" refers to the profit motive (greed), which is the guiding force of the free market (capitalist) economy. Adam Smith argued that by each person pursuing his own selfish advantage, individuals acted for the good of society as a whole, guided by a "hidden hand" made possible by the free play of economic competition. The "invisible hand" and the allocation of resources through supply and demand are both essential features of capitalism.

A. An equal distribution of wealth applies to communism, not capitalism.

B. Indicative planning (government direction of economic production through incentives or persuasion rather than by outright command and control) is a feature of democratic socialism rather than capitalism.

D. Adam Smith's economic ideas, including his concept of the invisible hand, favour laissez-faire capitalism. Laissez-faire capitalism is opposed to any type of government regulation of the economy—unless such regulation is necessary to preserve economic competition and the free market. This economic philosophy opposes government manipulation or regulation of the economy in any other way.

38. A

Collectivism advocates putting the welfare of the group ahead of the rights and freedoms of the individual. Consequently, this philosophy would favour the common good over the wants of individuals.

B. Collectivism actually supports interference in the daily lives of individual citizens to obtain more benefits for the citizenry as a whole.

C. A collectivist believes that people function most effectively when they try, above all, to satisfy the needs of the group. Collectivism aims to satisfy the needs of the collective rather than the needs of individuals. This philosophy promotes state paternalism (reliance on the government) rather than self-reliance. It believes that the government should take responsibility for the welfare of its people.

D. The business cycle is the succession of booms and busts that occurs in a capitalist (free enterprise) economy. Rather than trying to adapt to the fluctuations of the business cycle, collectivists would favour transforming a capitalist economy into a socialist or communist economy in which the peaks and valleys of the business cycle would be levelled out.

39. C

Gorbachev hoped to preserve Soviet communism by reforming it through economic and political restructuring (perestroika) and freer speech (glasnost). Instead, glasnost and perestroika became uncontrollable forces that caused the collapse of Soviet communism and the fall of the USSR.

A, B, and D. None of these other economic policies caused an economic or political collapse comparable to that experienced in Gorbachev's USSR in 1991.

40. A

Ethics refers to "a code of moral behaviour considered correct" or "the rules of conduct recognized as appropriate to a particular profession or area of life." The cartoon suggests that the capitalist banking system is immoral because it encourages individuals to overspend, borrow too much, and become impoverished.

B, C, and D. The cartoon criticizes the banking system for being corrupt and corrupting. It does not criticize it for being successful, powerful, or stable.

41. B

Laissez-faire capitalism encourages self-reliance, fiscal responsibility, and economic competition. Thus, it recommends shopping around for the best deal, pursuing greater prosperity, and avoiding insolvency (bankruptcy).

A. A laissez-faire capitalist would oppose any form of government ownership—particularly public ownership of banks.

C. Laissez-faire capitalists believe that wage levels should be determined solely by the laws of supply and demand within a free market. Supporters of laissez-faire would oppose any government regulation or manipulation of wages.

D. Laissez-faire capitalists oppose all forms of state regulation of banks, other than the passing of laws preventing crimes such as theft and embezzlement.

42. A

Lenin governed the Soviet Union from 1917 to 1924. War Communism (1918–21) and NEP (1921–28) were initiated by him.

B, C and D. The Five Year Plans were initiated by Stalin in 1928. Perestroika was the economic policy employed by Mikhail Gorbachev during the 1985 to 1991 era.

43. C

During the USSR's existence, Soviet leaders experimented with several different forms of communism. Each of their policies deviated somewhat from the principles of Marxism—particularly the NEP and perestroika.

A. War Communism and the Five Year Plans were attempts at centralization rather than decentralization. Moreover, the USSR never had a private enterprise (capitalist) economy—not even under the NEP or perestroika, which provided for limited economic decentralization. It always had a public enterprise (communist) economy.

B. War Communism and the Five Year Plans tried to eliminate market forces—not encourage them. Furthermore, the USSR did not have a private enterprise economy.

D. War Communism and the Five Year Plans were attempts at centralization rather than decentralization.

44. C

The economic theory underlying the economic policy in the diagram is "conservatism" or "neo-conservatism." The selling of public enterprises (government-run companies that Canadians call "Crown Corporations") to private businessmen is one of the actions favoured by Canadian neo-conservatives. The selling-off of state enterprises is called privatization.

A. (Neo-)Conservatives actually advocate reducing or eliminating spending on social programs.

B. (Neo-)Conservatives in Canada recommend reducing government spending. Increased subsidies to large corporations would involve increased government spending.

D. (Neo-)Conservatives actually advocate reducing or eliminating government transfers as a means of reducing government spending. They support cutbacks in both the areas of private transfers (social-welfare-program spending on disadvantaged individuals) and public transfers (such as equalization payments to poorer provinces).

45. A

Democratic socialists support the welfare state. They would worry that reduced government spending would directly result in an erosion of social welfare programs.

B. A democratic socialist would acknowledge that reduced personal taxes would result in increased, not decreased, personal incomes. This would concern him only indirectly—in the sense that such tax breaks might result in cutbacks in government social services.

C. Economic prosperity is a goal of democratic socialism.

D. The social safety net is a higher priority for democratic socialists than are tax incentives for corporations.

46. D

(Neo-)Conservatism encourages entrepreneurship and appeals to entrepreneurs (trail-blazing, risk-taking, profit-seeking "venture capitalists").

A. A government contractor (a person who agrees to provide materials or services to the government) would fear that reduced government spending would result in fewer and/or less-lucrative government contracts. This, of course, would cause an unwelcome reduction in his personal income.

B. An old age pensioner would worry that cuts in government spending would result in cutbacks to his old-age pension and/or to other social programs for seniors.

C. A factory worker is less likely to support (neo-)conservative economic policies than a capitalistic entrepreneur. Blue-collar workers tend to be supportive of the social welfare state and liberal or socialist economic policies.

47. A

Debt and deficit reduction are the main motivations for reduced government spending (fiscal restraint).

B. A shrinking tax base would make it more difficult for the government to reduce personal and corporate taxes (or balance the budget).

C. A major increase in the unemployment rate would put pressure on the Canadian government to spend more money (on job creation and social welfare programs such as employment insurance).

D. Large foreign takeovers of domestic industry would probably create strong public pressure for more government regulation and intervention in the economy. In contrast, the proposal indicated in the diagram favours deregulation and non-intervention.

48. D

Roosevelt's New Deal put Keynesianism (demand-side economic theory) into practice in the USA.

A. Reagan's supply-side economic policy was a rejection of Keynesianism.

B. Keynesianism favours a market-oriented economy but tries to regulate the business cycle and provide more economic stability and security. Lenin's New Economic Policy involved some deregulation of the Soviet economy, but, nevertheless, was still a communist policy. Keynesianism is an economic approach favoured by liberal economists and democratic socialists.

C. Fascist economic theory, not Keynesianism, was the inspiration for Mussolini's corporate state.

49. B

The graph represents Keynesian (demand-side) economic theory. Keynes maintained that during a period of economic growth, government spending should be reduced because job-creation and social-welfare programs are not needed as much as they are in a recession.

A. Demands for public services are lower during a period of economic boom.

C. Taxes are easier to raise in a period of economic growth.

D. Unemployment rates decrease during an economic growth period.

50. D

According to demand-side (Keynesian) economic theory, higher taxes during an economic boom can cover the costs of previous deficit-spending and/or may help pay for social welfare spending in a future recession.

A. Higher taxation would discourage consumer spending—not encourage it—as consumers would be left with less disposable income.

B. Increased taxation generally causes an increase—not a decrease—in unemployment.

C. As shown in the graph, Keynesianism calls for decreased—not increased—government spending during an economic boom-time.

51. C

The term "price system" refers to a capitalist (free enterprise) economy. Capitalism places a great emphasis on individualism and calls for maximal economic freedom for the individual.

A, B, and D. Empathy (concern, understanding, and sympathy for others), social consciousness (an awareness of societal problems and a desire to correct social injustices), and cooperation are values associated with collectivism, the social welfare state, socialism, and communism.

52. D

Historically, the Canadian government established Crown corporations (public enterprises) to provide services and products that the private sector was unable or unwilling to provide. For example, the Canadian Broadcasting Corporation was originally established to provide Canadians with a national radio network. Private investors were not willing to create this type of network as it did not promise to be profitable. In fact, since its creation, taxpayers have had to pay considerable sums of money to maintain coast-to-coast public broadcasting by the CBC.

A. The establishment of Crown corporations generally discourages entrepreneurship in a particular sector of the economy as it is often very difficult to compete with a government–owned, –operated, and –subsidized enterprise.

B. The creation of Crown Corporations is never intended to lure businessmen away from a private-sector job to a public-sector one. These public enterprises are intended to open up new economic areas or to preserve industries and services that would not survive without government support.

C. The establishment of a Crown corporation creates more government jobs and increases the size of the bureaucracy (civil service).

53. B

The statement suggests that the welfare state discourages self-sufficiency by supporting unemployed slackers and penalizing hard-working, gainfully employed taxpayers.

A, C, and D. None of the other viewpoints is directly supported by the statement. The statement supports individualism and is contradicted in some way by these three points of view.

54. C

A capitalist (proponent of a market economy) would support this defence of individualism because he believes in individualistic values such as self-reliance (reliance on oneself or one's own skills and resources) and initiative (the get-up-and-go that fuels entrepreneurship). He also believes that the social safety net erodes the work ethic by providing people with too much comfort and security.

A. A capitalist would actually believe that freedom enhances flexibility in reaching economic targets, but he would oppose having production goals set by the government.

B. Although a capitalist might believe that competition results in a wider range of goods and services, this belief does not serve as a basis of support for the given statement.

D. Although a capitalist might hold this viewpoint, it does not serve as a basis of support for the given statement.

55. C

The answer corresponds to the statement from Source I which reads "There are still many people who assume that the experience of communism in Eastern and Central Europe was [one] of unmitigated tyranny, that all were victims except for the party bureaucrats and secret policemen." Source I states that this view of history "won't do"—implying that it is an inaccurate, stereotypical belief.

A, B and D. None of the other answers directly corresponds with a statement made in Source I.

56. D

On the cartoon, the "hammer and sickle" insignia of the communist flag has been replaced by a "chicken leg and sickle" insignia. This suggests that communist supporters in Russia are changing the basis of their appeal by promising to provide food to desperate and hungry people. This tactic would appeal to the millions of impoverished Russians who are suffering in Russia's new market-oriented economy.

A and B. Communist supporters in Russia are believers in the centralized economy and socialist programs. They would not want to do away with these things.

C. The chicken leg is not a traditional national symbol that could be used to rally patriotic Russians.

57. A

Both sources imply that people are dissatisfied with the hardships of Russia's new market-oriented economy. Both suggest that the "social costs" of market reforms have been severe.

B, C, and D. None of the other statements directly matches the viewpoints expressed in the two sources.

58. D

Responsible government is "an unwritten idea in Canada's constitution that means a government may only remain in office or power for as long as it has the support of the legislative assembly (the House of Commons)." A motion of non-confidence is "a motion presented by an MP that a current governing party should not continue to govern." If a motion of non-confidence is passed, the governing party must resign and, usually, call for a general election. Thus, a non-confidence vote is a clear demonstration of the principle of responsible government.

A, B and C. The principle of responsible government is not demonstrated by the other three answers. They are all methods used by the prime minister to entrench or enhance his executive power.

59. D

A totalitarian state is "an authoritarian system of government that tolerates only one political party, to which all other institutions are subordinated, and that demands the complete subservience of the individual to the state." In a totalitarian dictatorship, the elite (dictator, oligarchs, or ruling party) attempts to indoctrinate the population into believing that only it knows what is best for the country. Totalitarianism sets out to eliminate any viewpoints that challenge those held by ruling party.

A. A totalitarian state does not respect individual and minority rights.

B. A totalitarian state attempts to maintain political stability through the crushing of all dissent. It does not respect constitutional guarantees.

C. A totalitarian state is dictatorial and ideological. It does not oppose alternative political parties because they might be dictatorial or ideological. A totalitarian dictator opposes them because he wants absolute and unchallenged control over society.

60. C

In Germany during the early 1930s, the strongest opponents of Nazism were leftists (social democrats and communists). Hatred of these two groups was one of the essential elements of German fascism. Contempt for fascism was a distinguishing feature of the German left during the inter-war period. Nazi supporters fought countless street battles with German communists and socialists throughout the 1920s and early 1930s. When Hitler became dictator of Germany, these long-time left-wing opponents became the first victims of Nazism.

A, B and D. All of the other groups either supported Nazism or did little to resist its rise.

61. B

In early 1919, the Weimar Republic was established and drew up a constitution. The Nazi Party was organized in the latter part of 1919 and adopted the name "National Socialist German Worker's Party" in April 1920. The Beer-Hall *Putsch* took place in November 1923. Adolf Hitler became chancellor of Germany in January 1933.

A, C, and D. The other answers are not arranged in the proper chronological order.

62. B

The formation of a political party and the legal (and constitutional) appointment of a government official are both regular occurrences in a democracy. There was nothing undemocratic about these efforts.

A, C, and D. The Beer-Hall Putsch was a coup d'etat in which the Nazis attempted to overthrow a democratically elected government by force. This was an illegal and undemocratic act. The Nazis played no role in the establishment of the Weimar Republic or in the writing of its constitution.

63. D

A multiparty political system is one in which more than two political parties compete in elections and have a reasonable chance of winning seats. Such a political system can better represent a population with a variety of political opinions. In other words, in a multiparty system, a citizen has a better chance of voting for a candidate whose views more closely correspond to his own. This makes it, at least theoretically, more democratic than a two-party system.

A. Providing for stronger majority governments might make a political system more efficient, but not necessarily more democratic.

B. Meaningful debate may occur — or not — on both two-party and multiparty systems. Even in Canada's multiparty democracy, most debate in the House of Commons involves only two parties—the government party and the Official Opposition.

C. Both multiparty and two-party systems are capable of consistently informing voters about political issues.

64. C

The author suggests that the first-past-the-post electoral system—a.k.a. the plurality system or the winner-take-all-system —unfairly favours regionally based parties like the Reform Party (a party supported mainly by Western Canadians) and the Bloc Quebecois (a party that runs only in Quebec). He observes that the Conservative Party (a national party with broad support throughout Canada) received a greater percentage of the popular vote than the Bloc Quebecois but received fewer seats in the House of Commons. This "very nearly killed Canada" because the separatist BQ became the Official Opposition and threw its new power and prestige behind the 1995 Quebec referendum campaign, which very nearly resulted in the break-up of Canada.

A. No radical, antidemocratic parties are mentioned in the excerpt. Moreover, no such parties were represented—never mind overrepresented—in the House of Commons at the time.

B. The first-past-the-post system actually has the tendency to create stable, majority governments. The author does not claim otherwise.

D. The excerpt doesn't mention the formation of a coalition government or any special interest groups. Moreover, special interest groups (pressure groups) are not political parties and cannot, therefore, play a dominant role in the formation of a coalition in the House of Commons.

65. A

In an electoral system of proportional representation, each political party's share of seats in the House of Commons would be based on the percentage of the popular vote it received in the general election. For example, if Reform received 19% of the popular vote, it would be given roughly 19% of the seats in the House of Commons. The proportional representation system is used to elect members of Sweden's parliament (the Riksdag).

B, C, and D. The first-past-the-post system is used to elect members of the American Senate, British House of Commons, and the American House of Representatives. The British and the Americans do not use the proportional representation system to elect legislators.

66. A

An independent judiciary (independent courts that are not interfered with by the legislative or executive branches of government) provides for the protection of individual and minority rights. Independent judges prevent democracy from turning into "a tyranny of the majority."

B. An independent judiciary is guided by the constitution, existing laws, legal precedents, and legal principles—not by public opinion.

C. Legal appeals are handled by the judicial branch (the judiciary)—not the executive branch.

D. The legislative branch (legislature) is responsible for creating and amending (changing) the constitution. This, however, has nothing to do with the principle of maintaining an independent judiciary. It is, however, the responsibility of the judicial branch to determine whether controversial new laws are constitutional.

67. D

The ideology of communism seeks to abolish private property and private ownership. Fascists, however, permit private ownership and private property.

A, B, and C. Both fascism and communism are totalitarian ideologies. Not surprisingly, both communists and fascists make use of the following techniques of dictatorship: propaganda, indoctrination, and one-party rule. For example, the communist dictator, Stalin, and the fascist dictator, Hitler, both employed these three techniques.

68. A

The excerpt is correct in stating that the initiation of new legislation is an executive power—not a legislative one. In Canada, it is the Prime Minister and his Cabinet that decide what new bills, if any, will be introduced in the House of Commons. Criticism and ratification of the bills that are introduced, however, is a responsibility of legislators, especially the members of opposition parties. The excerpt suggests that the true role of the House of Commons, then, is to monitor the activities of the executive branch—especially the chief executive officers in the Cabinet.

B. Although the excerpt does mention the legislative duties of "communication and representation of constituency concerns"—it does not present these as the main functions of elected members. It identifies "scrutinizing and ratifying legislation" as their chief duties.

C. The excerpt does mention the gauging of popular opinion, but does not claim that this is the main function of legislators.

D. The excerpt actually maintains that legislators do not generally create or introduce legislation; this is an executive function exercised by the prime minister and his Cabinet ministers.

69. D

A private member's bill is a piece of legislation that is introduced to the House of Commons by an MP who is not a member of the Cabinet. The Cabinet rarely allows such bills to be presented to the House or to reach the Third Reading stage. Thus, private members' bills are "occasional exceptions" to the general rule referred to in the excerpt—namely, that the initiation of legislation is an executive function of Cabinet.

A, B, and C. None of the other answers represents "an occasional exception" to the general rule that the creation and initiation of legislation is a function of the executive branch of government.

70. A

On the traditional left–right political spectrum, Brian Mulroney (a conservative politician) is correctly placed.

B. Margaret Thatcher was a conservative politician; she does not belong on the left side of the spectrum.

C. Nikita Khruschev was a leftist, not an ultra-right political leader.

D. Mikhail Gorbachev was a leftist politician, but not an ultra-left one. Placing Josef Stalin in the spot occupied by Gorbachev would be a more appropriate placement. Stalin was a true radical extremist—as was shown by his willingness to use violence to accomplish his goals. Gorbachev sought non-violent means to bring about change.

Answers and Solutions
Global Interaction in the Twentieth Century – Unit Review

1.	D	19.	D	37.	D	55.	C	73.	A	91.	C
2.	C	20.	A	38.	A	56.	C	74.	B	92.	C
3.	D	21.	D	39.	B	57.	B	75.	D	93.	A
4.	B	22.	A	40.	C	58.	C	76.	D	94.	D
5.	C	23.	D	41.	D	59.	D	77.	C	95.	A
6.	B	24.	B	42.	A	60.	A	78.	D	96.	D
7.	D	25.	B	43.	D	61.	C	79.	B	97.	D
8.	C	26.	A	44.	C	62.	B	80.	A	98.	A
9.	B	27.	B	45.	B	63.	B	81.	C	99.	A
10.	A	28.	A	46.	A	64.	C	82.	D	100.	D
11.	D	29.	C	47.	D	65.	B	83.	A	101.	B
12.	D	30.	B	48.	B	66.	C	84.	A	102.	A
13.	B	31.	C	49.	D	67.	D	85.	B	103.	C
14.	C	32.	B	50.	A	68.	B	86.	B	104.	B
15.	C	33.	A	51.	D	69.	A	87.	D	105.	C
16.	B	34.	B	52.	A	70.	B	88.	A		
17.	D	35.	C	53.	B	71.	D	89.	C		
18.	C	36.	A	54.	A	72.	B	90.	B		

1. D

The two statements relate to the decision by the American Senate to reject collective security despite President Wilson's Fourteen Points. In January 1918, Woodrow Wilson, the US President, had publicly announced a fourteen-point peace plan for bringing World War I to an end and for preventing subsequent wars. The last of his famous Fourteen Points was a call for the formation of a global collective security organization (the League of Nations). At the Paris Peace Conference in 1919, Wilson (a member of the Democratic Party) managed to get other nations to agree to form the League of Nations, but because the American Senate was then controlled by a rival isolationist party (the Republican Party), the Senate vetoed the treaty (the Treaty of Versailles) that would have brought the USA into the League of Nations. One of the checking powers in the American system of checks and balances is that the Senate votes to ratify or reject any treaty that the President makes.

A, B, and C. The two sources do not directly relate to efforts to rebuild a war-torn Europe, attempts to establish a European alliance system, or the inability to secure a just peace through the Treaty of Versailles.

2. C

Isolationism is a foreign policy that advocates non-participation in alliances or in the affairs of other states. Internationalism is the belief that a nation should pursue the greatest possible cooperation between nations (in trade, culture, education, government, etc.) through its foreign policy. The conflict between these two conflicting foreign policy approaches centres on the question: "Which foreign policy would best serve American national interests at any given time?" This was the central question being debated by American politicians in 1919-20. At the end of their debate, they decided that isolationism was the best overall foreign policy approach for the United States.

A, B, and D. The two sources are not directly focused on and of these three questions.

3. D

The term *national sovereignty* refers to "the power of a nationality (people) to govern itself without outside interference." To achieve national independence, a nation forms its own state—a nation-state.

Sources I and II point out a central problem with the creation of nation-states: it is very hard to draw national boundaries that can satisfy separate nations on both sides of the border. The redrawing of the map of Europe after the First World War, which attempted to accommodate the demands for sovereignty of many nations, caused many Interwar-era border disputes. These disputes were one of the causes of the Second World War.

A, B, and C. The sources do not focus on a central problem related to isolationism (non-participation in alliances or in the affairs of other states), appeasement (giving into the demands of an aggressor-nation in the effort to placate it and avoid a confrontation), or collective security (a policy of discouraging aggression against any member of an alliance by presenting an aggressor-nation with the real threat of an armed response by all of the member-states of the alliance).

4. B

During the early 1990's, nationalist movements in Slovenia, Croatia, and Bosnia provoked three bloody wars in the Balkans (the mountainous region of southeastern Europe). Eventually, these territories broke away from Yugoslavia and achieved sovereignty. In the late 1990's, the Albanians in Kosovo (a region of Yugoslavia) also attempted to separate from Serbia. The Albanian Kosovars' desire for national sovereignty eventually led to two wars. The first one was a guerilla war between the Kosovar Liberation Army (KLA) and the army of Yugoslavia in 1996–99. The second was a larger-scale war between NATO and Yugoslavia in 1999; it was provoked by a Serbian attempt to forcibly drive out (ethnically cleanse) Albanians from Kosovo. These two recent conflicts have deepened mutual hatreds between Serbs and Albanian Kosovars—and created tensions between the Balkan nation-states of Yugoslavia and Albania.

A, C, and D. New nation-states have not emerged in these regions in recent years.

5. C

An appropriate title for the map (Source II) would be "The Polish Land Grab: New Frontiers in Eastern Europe." The map shows how Poland used military force to seize territories from Lithuania and Russia in 1920–21.

A, B, and D. "Poland Marches West" would not be an appropriate title for the map—the Poles marched east in their conflicts with Lithuania and Russia. The map shows central Europe after the First World War—not the Second World War. It does not show new alliances in Europe or how Europeans dealt with aggressive nations.

6. B

Taken together, the events shown in the diagram represent attempts to ensure the security of nations between 1919 and 1941. The Maginot Line (a line of defensive fortifications along the French–German border) was built to deter Germany from attacking France. One of the reasons Great Britain joined the League of Nations was to gain more security through the League's collective security commitment.
The United States entered into the Lend–Lease Agreement to safeguard the national security of Britain. European nations (Belgium, France, and Germany) recognized one another's existing national boundaries in the Locarno Pact in an effort to be secure from border wars with their neighbours.

A, C and D. Not all of the events were attempts at collective security, efforts to eliminate fascism, or attempts to diplomatically isolate Germany.

7. D

Isolationism is a policy of non-involvement in international affairs. The Dawes Plan (1924) and the Young Plan (1929) were two American-initiated schemes for reducing the burdens of Germany's war reparations payments. The USA's involvement in German and European affairs through these plans was a departure from America's Interwar-era isolationism.

A, B, and C. The United States did not participate in the Munich Conference, Little Entente, or League of Nations.

8. C

A sanction is "an economic action by a state (or international organization) to coerce a renegade state to conform to international norms of conduct." In 1935–36, the League of Nations applied economic sanctions against Italy in an unsuccessful effort to force invading Italian troops to withdraw from Ethiopia (Abyssinia). Previously, the League had not imposed sanctions on Japan for its invasion of Manchuria (northeastern China) in 1931.

A, B, and D. Although the League of Nations did not manage to get Japanese troops to withdraw from Manchuria, the organization certainly did not give its approval to the Japanese invasion. The League of Nations never created or deployed a peacekeeping force during its existence (1919–1946).

9. B

Hitler's famous quote comes from the 1938 Munich Crisis. He declared that the Sudetenland (an ethnically German region of Czechoslovakia) was his "last territorial claim" in Europe. In the Munich Pact of 1938, Britain and France gave their consent to Germany's annexation of the Sudetenland. Of course, when Hitler invaded Poland and the rest of Czechoslovakia in 1939, it became clear that he was after more than the Sudetenland all along.

A, C and D. The Polish Corridor, the Saar Basin, and the Rhineland were not the focus of the Munich Conference or Munich Pact of 1938.

10. A

The political slogans express the militarism (love of war and military conquest) and authoritarianism (belief in a dictatorial form of government) that are characteristic of 1930s Italian fascism.

B, C, and D. These slogans were never used in 1940s France, 1950s America, or 1960s Russia.

11. D

Operation Barbarossa was the codename for Nazi Germany's surprise invasion of the USSR in 1941. After the Soviet Union was attacked, Stalin's main diplomatic objective was to get the other major Allied powers (Britain, and after December 1941, the USA) to open up a second front against the Germans in Western Europe. He desired a second front to relieve some of the pressure on Soviet troops. The Western Allies eventually opened up two new fronts against the German army—in Italy (1943) and France (1944).

A, B, and C. Josef Stalin did not pursue these foreign policy objectives during the 1941–44 era.

12. D

The Greater East Asia Co-Prosperity Sphere was the label given by Japan to its empire in East and South-East Asia during the Second World War. This name suggested that Asian nations had become willing allies of Japan and belied the truth, which was that they had been conquered by Japan. In reality, however, Japan cruelly treated and viciously exploited the territories within the Sphere. Japan's true motive for establishing the Co-Prosperity Sphere was to ensure Japanese access to the resources and markets of the Asia-Pacific region.

A, B, and C. Japan did not establish the Greater East Asia Co-Prosperity Sphere in order to liberate former European colonies, bring the USA under its domination, or contain the growing influence of the USSR.

13. B

The victorious Allied Powers held war crimes trials at Nuremberg, Germany in 1945–46. Many surviving Nazi leaders (who were captured by the Allies) were put on trial for various charges—including the charge of perpetrating "crimes against humanity." The charge of crimes against humanity was developed mainly to deal with the Holocaust (the mass murder of 6 million European Jews) and with the 4 to 5 million other racially motivated murders (of Gypsies, Poles, Ukrainians, Russians, and other Slavs) committed by the Nazis in their concentration camps. Nazi leaders and followers who were proven to have killed, tortured, or mistreated a person because of his/her ethnic or religious identity were deemed guilty of committing a crime against humanity; additionally, anyone who planned, ordered or supervised such an action was also considered guilty.

A, C, and D. The Nazis' genocides (attempts to exterminate entire peoples) of Jews and Gypsies did not motivate the creation of new independent states in central Europe or the exclusion of West Germany from NATO. Nor did these genocides directly lead to greater economic and political cooperation in Europe.

14. C

Most of the political and territorial changes that occurred in Europe at the end of the Second World War were influenced by the USSR's desire to create a buffer zone between itself and the non-communist West.

Buffer zones are areas adjacent to and controlled by a state to better shield it from attacks by its enemies. Josef Stalin feared that the United States might attack the Soviet Union at the end of the Second World War. In response to this perceived threat, the Stalin established communist puppet dictatorships in several central European countries (Poland, Czechoslovakia, Hungary, Rumania, and Bulgaria) that had been overrun by his troops in 1944–45. He extended his control over these neighbouring states so that a surprise attack on the USSR by the USA would be more difficult. For instance, if the USA used western Europe as a base for an attack on the USSR, American troops would have to advance through Soviet-occupied East Germany and Poland before even reaching the frontiers of the Soviet Union. A divided Germany was also a result of Stalin's desire for a buffer zone. Britain, the USA, and France all wanted a united Germany after the Second World War. Stalin, however, decided to keep East Germany as a cushion against a surprise American attack via western Europe.

A. The USSR broke many of its commitments to former Nazi-occupied states at the end of the Second World War. For instance, the Soviets had pledged to respect the sovereignty of states like Poland, Hungary, and Czechoslovakia after the war; instead, the USSR oppressively controlled these countries between 1945 and 1989.

B. Most of the territorial and political changes that were made in Europe after 1945 were not influenced by the concept of self-determination (the belief that each nation should have independent control of its own affairs and its own national territory). For example, at the end of the Second World War, Stalin created new borders for Poland by ethnically cleansing Poles from eastern Poland and Germans from eastern Germany.

D. The newly formed United Nations had little or no influence on post-war political and territorial changes in Europe.

15. C

The cartoon represents the division of Europe into two spheres of influence—the American sphere in western Europe and the Soviet sphere in eastern Europe—immediately after the Second World War.

A, B, and D. Harry Truman was President of the USA from 1945 to 1953. Josef Stalin was dictator of the USSR from 1924 to 1953. The overlap between their periods of leadership was the 1945 to 1953 era—the years during which the Iron Curtain descended across central Europe. The First World War ended in 1918. The Second World War lasted from 1939 to 1945. The Cold War ended in either 1989 or 1991, depending on what is considered to be the final events.

16. B

The United States provided generous economic assistance to war-torn western European nations during the 1947–52 era. This aid was distributed through America's Marshall Plan (European Recovery Program).

A, C and D. In the aftermath of the Second World War, Marshall Plan assistance was much more generous than UN aid to western Europe. The Atlantic Charter was a 1941 joint British–American declaration that called for self-determination for European nations after the Second World War. It provided an ideological framework for Allied cooperation during the Second World War but offered no real benefits for post-war Europeans. The European Common Market (European Economic Community) was an economic free trade association that offered real economic benefits for its western European member-states; it did not come into being until 1958 by which time Stalin was dead and Truman was no longer President.

17. D

The signing of the SALT I treaty was an event that decreased—not increased—Cold War tensions between the USA and USSR. SALT I was a 1972 strategic arms limitation treaty that put a cap on superpower ICBMs (intercontinental ballistic missiles) and limited the deployment of anti-ballistic missiles. It slowed down the arms race between the two superpowers and was one of the opening events of the subsequent period of détente.

A, B, and C. Each of these events corresponds with the diagram's theme.

18. C

Supranationalism is the belief that nations should set aside national differences and cooperate for their mutual benefit. All of these arms control agreements are examples of supranational cooperation. In the 1963 Partial Test Ban Treaty, the USA, Britain, and the USSR agreed to not test nuclear weapons in the atmosphere, in outer space, or underwater. The treaty was an attempt to stop an alarming rise in worldwide radioactive pollution levels. In the 1968 Non-Proliferation Treaty, these nuclear powers committed themselves to preventing the spread of nuclear weapons technology to new countries. In the 1967 Outer Space Treaty and the 1971 Seabed Treaty, nuclear powers pledged to not deploy nuclear weapons in outer space or on the ocean floor.

A, B, and D. Arms control agreements do not depend on signatories' willingness to promote regional alliances, international prosperity, or technological advancement.

19. D

In 1968, Soviet and Warsaw Pact troops invaded Czechoslovakia to crush the "Prague Spring" liberalization movement. This invasion demonstrated that the Soviet leaders would not tolerate any departure from hard-line, Moscow-dominated communism within their sphere of influence.

A, B, and C. None of these things were demonstrated by the Soviet invasion. Firstly, UN peacekeepers were not involved in the events in Czechoslovakia in 1968. Secondly, NATO forces did not confront Warsaw Pact troops during the Czechoslovak crisis; NATO did not want to provoke a third world war by intervening in the crisis. Thirdly, the Soviet invasion aimed at maintaining communism in Czechoslovakia—not promoting the spread of communism beyond the Soviet bloc.

20. A

In the quotation, the UN administrator suggests that humanitarian efforts should focus more on preventing crises in the global community. He favours proactive rather than reactive humanitarianism. Therefore, he would most likely support the provision of UN observer teams for the monitoring of elections in Haiti. According to the administrator's viewpoint, it is better to take the initiative to ensure that elections are conducted fairly in Haiti—rather than later on having to take measures to get rid of an oppressive Haitian government that came to power through electoral corruption.

B and C. The UN administrator clearly favours humanitarian and developmental assistance; he would not support these actions.

D. The UN administrator would probably support deploying UN peacekeepers in a conflict, but he would prefer preventative deployments rather than interventions in war zones. As he supports proactive measures over reactive measures, he probably would prefer actions like that given in alternative A over this type of action.

21. D

The number of refugees has increased significantly since the end of the Cold War as a result of the outbreak of many ethnic wars and civil wars in southeastern Europe, Africa, and Asia. For instance, a huge refugee problem was created by regional conflicts in the Balkans (Serbs versus Slovenes, Serbs versus Croats, Serbs versus Bosnian Muslims, Bosnian Muslims versus Croats, and Serbs versus Albanian Kosovars). During the same period, regional wars such as these have created an enormous demand for UN peacekeepers.

A. World poverty has not significantly increased since the end of the Cold War; in fact, outside of Africa and eastern Europe, global poverty has probably decreased in the years since 1991.

B. The breakup of the Soviet Union did lead to fighting between some of the nationalities of the former USSR (Georgians versus Abkhazians, Armenians versus Azerbaijanis, Russians versus Chechens, etc.), but the UN did not deploy any peacekeepers in these war zones. Therefore, skyrocketing UN peacekeeping expenditures cannot be attributed to the breakup of the Soviet Union.

C. American President George Bush coined the term "New World Order" to refer to a new era of global peace and prosperity that was supposedly inaugurated by the victory of UN forces during the Gulf War. If the world had moved toward this a new world order after 1991, increased UN spending on refugee programs and peacekeeping operations would not have been required.

22. A

Both sources focus on the escalating costs of UN peacekeeping and refugee operations.

B, C, and D. These three challenges are not directly addressed by both sources.

23. D

The formation of the Common Market and other efforts to create a more unified Europe pointed to the fact that nationalism was becoming less dominant in world affairs.

The Warsaw Pact and the NATO alliance had little or no effect on nationalism. Further, defensive alliances were not formed during the Cold War to counter the threat of ethnic conflict. Therefore, A and B are not correct. During the Cold War, many nations in Africa and Asia gained their independence through the process of decolonization. The creation of new nations could make the forces of nationalism more dominant. Nationalism could play a role as competing forces within these new countries vie for power and neighbouring countries settle any disputes they may have over newly drawn borders.

24. B

During the Cold War, Premier Khrushchev's suggestion that there were "many roads to socialism" caused unrest in certain satellite states—particularly, in Hungary. His comments played an important role in provoking the 1956 anti-communist uprising in that country.

A, C, and D. Khrushchev did not bring the Cold War to an end or precipitate a Middle Eastern oil crisis. Furthermore, his "many roads to socialism" comment (and his de-Stalinization activities) actually angered the hard-line communist regime in China; Khrushchev's comment was one of the causes of the Sino-Soviet split.

25. B

The author of Source I suggests that Western nations have been reluctant to intervene in post-1991 Balkan conflicts because these Western powers would gain no real benefits from intervening. In other words, the author maintains that the foreign policy of Western nations is ultimately determined by a concern for national self-interest. He claims that the Western nations will not act in a region where their own narrow national interests are not at stake.

A, C and D. The author of Source I does not suggest that the foreign policy of Western nations is ultimately determined by a concern for the general welfare of the human race, the desire to increase national power or prestige, or UN resolutions.

26. A

The cartoon suggests that the former victims of communist repression are now victims of ethnic conflict. Therefore, the statement that best represents the cartoon's underlying message is: "The collapse of communism—the policeman on the corner—unleashed many demons." Both sources suggest that the chief demon that was released by the fall of communism was the nationalist demon.

B, C, and D. These statements do not represent the underlying message of the cartoon.

27. B

Taken together, the two sources suggest that long-standing nationalist tensions caused conflicts in Eastern Europe during the 1990s. Both sources suggest that ethnic nationalism is the root cause of recent wars in this region.

A, C, and D. Neither source suggests that the main cause of the Balkan conflicts was superpower competition, the failure of diplomacy, or communist policy.

28. A

The USA participated in both the Korean War (1950–53) and the Vietnam War (1964–75) in the attempt to stop the spread of communism in Asia. In other words, the United States went to war in these two countries because of a policy of containment. Containment is "a policy of preventing the spread of the power or influence of an enemy country (or ideology) beyond the existing boundaries of its influence."

B, C, and D. These two wars do not illustrate an American commitment to deterrence (a policy of attempting to control the behaviour of other countries by the use of threats) or to national unity. In fact, public opinion about both wars was sharply divided in the USA. The NATO alliance did not take part in either war. Therefore, neither conflict illustrates a US commitment to NATO. Actually, the Vietnam War strained relations between the United States and its NATO partners.

29. C

Over the past several decades, the actions of international terrorists have been motivated primarily by the desire to draw world attention to demands for national self-determination. For instance, the PLO (Palestinian Liberation Organization) staged terrorist bombings, assassinations, kidnappings and hijackings all over the world during the 1964–1993 period—in an effort to gain recognition for the nationalist aspirations of the Palestinian people.

A, B, and D. Most of the well-known terrorist organizations of recent years (the PLO, Irish Republican Army, the Kosovo Liberation Army, Hamas, etc.) have been motivated by nationalism. These organizations sought national independence—not democratic government, economic justice, or global economic equality.

30. B

All four sources contain examples of supranational cooperation (cooperation between nations for their mutual benefit—through the formation of international organizations, the negotiation of international agreements, and/or the creation of international laws). Supranationalism is "the recognition that the world's nations are interdependent and that individual nations all require some international and institutional cooperation."

A, C, and D. The sources do not, collectively, support these generalizations. The sources do not mention any drive for one-world government. They do not suggest that new global problems are unsolvable. Most sources suggest that the UN is already quite effective.

31. C

When Iraq invaded Kuwait in 1990, the United Nations Organization denounced this invasion as a clear case of aggression. It imposed economic sanctions on Iraq in the attempt to force it to withdraw from Kuwait. When Iraq still refused to quit Kuwait, the UN used military action in 1991 to force out the Iraqi army.

A, B, and D. The causes and events of the 1991 Gulf War do not directly relate to the actions described in these three sources.

32. B

Source IV mentions the problem of nuclear proliferation (the process whereby more and more nations join the "nuclear club" by acquiring nuclear weapons and/or nuclear-weapons capability). A recent example of proliferation was Pakistan's development of nuclear weapons in 1998. Because India, Pakistan's traditional enemy, also has a stockpile of nuclear weapons, both countries now live under the threat of nuclear war.

A, C, and D. At the present time, the possibility of nuclear warfare between these countries is remote.

33. A

Gorbachev's political reforms (Glasnost and Perestroika) stimulated liberalization in the USSR and within the Soviet bloc. Once freedom of speech and freedom of the press emerged in the satellite countries of eastern Europe, nationalists were inspired to free these countries from Russian control. Ultimately, anti-communist nationalists came to power in Poland, Hungary, Czechoslovakia, Romania, Bulgaria, and East Germany in 1989. Shortly thereafter, these nations withdrew from the Warsaw Pact.

B, C, and D. These events did not play a critical role in the dissolution of the communist bloc's military alliance.

34. B

The Russian-controlled communist nations of Eastern Europe were forced by Moscow to join the Warsaw Pact in 1955. These nations (Poland, Hungary, Czechoslovakia, etc.) were never willing partners in the military alliance. The major goal of the Hungarian Uprising of 1956, for instance, was to take Hungary out of the unpopular Warsaw Pact. The time-line shows that the communist bloc nations quickly withdrew from the Pact when they had the chance. Therefore, the information on the time-line reinforces the conclusion that "successful alliances require the willing participation of their members."

A, C, and D. These conclusions are not supported by information provided in the time-line.

35. C

The cartoon suggests that multinational corporations are becoming dominant in global affairs. The cartoon, though, does not imply that nationalist boundaries are being redefined by protectionist policies. Protectionism is "the doctrine or practice of restricting international trade to favor home producers—by tariffs (taxes on imported goods), quotas, or other trade barriers." The cartoon suggests that trade barriers between countries have been eroded—not that these barriers have been strengthened.

A, B, and D. Each of these three issues is suggested by the cartoon.

36. A

The authors of the 1919 Treaty of Versailles (chiefly Premier Georges Clemenceau of France, PM David Lloyd George of Britain, and President Woodrow Wilson of the USA) included the Covenant of the League of Nations in the treaty. They did not, however, create an international peacekeeping force to help the League of Nations keep the peace.

B, C, and D. Allied leaders at the Paris Peace Conference of 1919–20 recognized an independent Poland and ensured that Austrian Germans were kept isolated from the rest of Germany in a separate state. The Treaty of Versailles obligated Germany to make war reparations payments to Allied countries (primarily Belgium and France) for war damages. The treaty also reduced the size of the German army to 100,000 men.

37. D

The 1914 map represents the Austro-Hungarian Empire. The 1919 map shows how several new states emerged from the territory of the former empire—Czechoslovakia, Hungary, Austria, Poland, and Yugoslavia.

A, B, and C. The maps do not represent the collapse of the German, Russian, or Ottoman (Turkish) empires.

38. A

The difficulty of creating clear national boundaries in areas with mixed ethnic populations was demonstrated by the 1938 crisis over the Sudetenland. The Sudetenland is a region of northwest Czechoslovakia that was predominantly populated by ethnic Germans. Adolf Hitler used the threat of war to successfully pressure Britain, France, and Czechoslovakia to agree to Germany's annexation of the Sudetenland in the 1938 Munich Pact. The Czechs were reluctant to surrender the territory as it contained a minority of Czechs who were forcibly expelled (ethnically cleansed) from the territory shortly after the German takeover.

B, C, and D. A territory with a mixed ethnic population was not a source of conflict in the Suez Crisis, the Soviet invasion of Afghanistan, or the Falklands War.

39. B

The Czechs were abandoned by France and Britain in the Munich Pact. When Germany threatened to invade Czechoslovakia in 1938 in order to seize the Sudetenland, the Czechs were willing to resist the Germans militarily until they were abandoned by their Western allies. To appease Hitler, Britain and France agreed to allow Nazi Germany's annexation of the Sudetenland—the border region in which the Czechs had constructed most of their military defences against a feared German invasion. The region also contained the main manufacturing centres for Czech armaments. Once they had lost the Sudetenland, the Czechs had also lost the ability to defend themselves against a subsequent Nazi invasion in 1939.

A, C, and D. The comment does not refer to the Rome–Berlin Axis (the mutual pledge of cooperation between Mussolini's Italy and Hitler's Germany), the Nazi–Soviet Non-aggression Pact, or the Lend–Lease Agreement between USA and Britain.

40. C

The author suggests that the Czechs were ultimately better off for surrendering to German domination without a fight. He notes that the Poles were very badly treated by Nazi Germany after they took up arms in self-defence. Such comments could be interpreted as justifying a policy of appeasement (giving into an aggressor-state in the hope of avoiding a military conflict).

A, B, and D. The comments do not justify a policy of détente (reducing tensions between mutually hostile powers), militarism (increasing a nation's military might), or armed deterrence (using formidable weapons and/or armed forces to prevent an enemy from attacking).

41. D

The table lists efforts by the League of Nations to promote peace based on the principles of collective security. Collective security is "a system for maintaining world peace and security by the concerned action and agreement of all nations." According to the principle of collective security, the League of Nations had a duty to intervene in international conflicts and disputing nations had an obligation to submit their grievances to the League. The table shows some attempts of the League to promote peace. While the League was not successful in preventing or stopping Italian aggression in Abyssinia or Japanese aggression in Manchuria, it did succeed in resolving disputes in other cases (in South America and the Balkans, for instance).

A, B, and C. The table does not depict the League's use of appeasement (giving in to unreasonable demands or threats out of weakness or stupidity), brinkmanship (taking big risks, even to the brink of war, in the hope that one's adversary will back down), or alliance formation (establishing formal agreements for collaboration on mutual security issues).

42. A

The League of Nations was most effective in solving minor territorial disputes that did not directly involve Great Power interests. The League, for instance, successfully resolved disputes between Bolivia and Paraguay, Peru and Colombia, and Finland and Sweden. The League was least successful in dealing with the aggression of powerful nations such as Italy, Japan, and Germany.

B, C, and D. The table does not depict disputes between European imperialist powers over overseas colonies. Most of the disputes shown in the table have nothing to do with the Treaty of Versailles (the 1919 treaty between Germany and the Allied Powers that readjusted Germany's borders). The League was not successful in preventing or stopping aggression by right-wing nationalist regimes—namely, Japan, Germany, and Italy.

43. D

The League failed most miserably in its responses to the Japanese invasion of northeast China (Manchuria) and the Italian invasion of Abyssinia (Ethiopia). After member-states of the League neglected to protect the Chinese and Ethiopians from aggression, the League lost all credibility as a global collective security organization.

A, B, and C. These League actions were all more successful and less controversial than the organization's handling of the Manchurian and Abyssinian crises.

44. C

The declaration is an expression of isolationism. Isolationism is "the policy or doctrine that peace and economic advancement can best be achieved by removing one's country from alliances and commitments to other nations." Isolationism is a policy of narrow nationalism. The isolationist cares about his own country but has no real concern for the welfare of other nations. The declaration suggests that sovereignty (national independence) should take precedence over collective security (protecting weaker nations from aggression through participation in a global defensive alliance).

A, B, and D. The declaration does not express support for containment (preventing the spread of the power or influence of an enemy country, or ideology, beyond the existing boundaries of its influence), deterrence (maintaining vast military power and weaponry in order to discourage war), or international cooperation. It recommends giving priority to internal affairs and national interests. It goes beyond recommending neutrality (not taking part or giving assistance in a dispute or war between other nations) by suggesting that the USA should not participate at all in the affairs of other nations.

45. B

America's policy of isolationism ended with the bombing of Pearl Harbor. When Japan staged its sneak attack on the American naval base in Hawaii in December 1941, President Franklin Delano Roosevelt immediately declared war on Japan. Once the USA had entered the Second World War, allied itself with anti-Axis nations, and become greatly involved in international affairs, it had ceased to be an isolationist country.

A, C, and D. America's interwar-era (1919–1941) isolationism ended long before any of these events occurred.

46. A

***Lebensraum* was Hitler's idea that the Germans needed more "living space" in eastern Europe in order to develop into a more prosperous and healthy nation. In *Mein Kampf,* Hitler made it very clear that the living space that he desired was found in Poland and the European lands of the western USSR—namely, Ukraine, Belarus, and Russia. Hitler's invasion of the USSR in 1941 was an attempt to acquire *lebensraum*.**

B, C, and D. None of these actions was a Nazi German attempt to acquire *lebensraum* (living space).

47. D

The Battle of Britain was the air war between Britain's Royal Air Force (RAF) and Nazi Germany's Luftwaffe in the summer and autumn of 1940.

The Germans attacked the RAF as the first step in a planned invasion of England. When the Luftwaffe was defeated in the Battle of Britain, an invasion of Britain was no longer possible. The British victory preserved a base for an Allied attack on Nazi-occupied Europe. The eventual 1944 Allied invasion of German-occupied France (on D-Day) would not have been possible if Britain had been conquered in 1940.

A, B, and C. The British victory in the Battle of Britain did not force Germany to withdraw from Belgium and Holland; these countries continued to be occupied by Nazi Germany until 1944–45. The British victory did not persuade the USA to enter the Second World War —the 1941 Japanese attack on Pearl Harbor did. Germany attacked the Soviet Union in 1941 and pushed deep into Soviet territory. The USSR was not able to push Germany back to its eastern frontiers until 1945.

48. B

The description refers to guerrilla warfare tactics. Guerrilla warfare consists of hit-and-run attacks by small independent bands of guerrillas (irregular soldiers or partisans).

A, C, and D. The description does not refer to terrorist tactics, covert (spy) operations, or conventional warfare (military operations by regular armies equipped with non-nuclear weapons).

49. D

Guerrilla warfare tactics were used by the Viet Cong (communist guerrillas operating in South Vietnam) during the Vietnam War. The VC rebels staged effective hit-and-run attacks on the American Army and the South Vietnamese Army in this conflict.

A, B, and C. The Palestinians have used mainly terrorist tactics in their struggle with the Israelis. Terrorism has also been the preferred strategy in the conflict in Northern Ireland. Conventional warfare was employed during the Gulf War of 1991.

50. A

The Strategic Arms Limitation Talks (SALT) of 1969–1979 aimed at limiting the USA's and USSR's production and deployment of nuclear weapons. Therefore, Proposal I "(The number of nuclear weapons should be restricted to a certain level)" was the basis for the SALT talks.

51. D

Internationalism is "the belief that the greatest possible cooperation between nations in trade, culture, education, government, etc. is the best way to build peace." Therefore, internationalism demonstrated when nations enter into multilateral agreements (agreements or treaties in which three or more nation-states participate).

A, B, and C. Internationalism is not demonstrated when a nation conquers weaker nations, practices non-involvement in international affairs, or dominates other nations politically or economically.

52. A

Ethnic nationalism ignited turmoil and instability in the Balkans (the mountainous area of southeastern Europe) during the 1990s. During this decade, Serbs fought several wars in an unsuccessful attempt to suppress nationalist independence movements in Slovenia, Croatia, Bosnia, and Kosovo.

B, C, and D. Nationalism did not play much of a role in the collapse of the racist (anti-Black) policy of apartheid in South Africa. Nor was it a factor in the NATO's admission of Poland, Hungary, and the Czech Republic. Although China annexed Hong Kong for nationalist reasons (the Hong Kong people are part of the greater Chinese nation), this takeover was managed in a peaceful and orderly way.

53. B

The focus of the cartoon is the Marshall Plan of 1948–51. The American Hot Dog Stand symbolizes the American economic aid offered to impoverished and war-torn European nations through the plan.

A, C, and D. The American Hot Dog Stand does not symbolize the advantages of joining NATO, the European Common Market, or COMECON.

54. A

The school girls symbolize the satellite states of the USSR (Poland, Hungary, East Germany, Romania, Czechoslovakia, and Bulgaria). These Russian-controlled communist countries were offered economic assistance under the Marshall Plan but were prevented from accepting it by a disapproving USSR. Instead, the Soviet Union offered these Iron Curtain countries economic assistance through its own economic relief agency, COMECON.

B, C, and D. The school girls do not represent NATO member-states, nationalities of the Soviet Union, or founding states of the European Economic Community (EEC).

55. C

The cartoon illustrates the superpower competition to form and maintain spheres of influence. Through the Marshall Plan, the USA hoped to gain greater political and economic influence over European nations (including the Soviet satellite states). This was viewed by the USSR as interference with its sphere of influence in eastern Europe. A sphere of influence is "a territory or region over which an outside state claims control, influence, or preferential status." To preserve its sphere of influence in eastern Europe, the USSR created the Council for Mutual Economic Assistance (COMECON), forced communist bloc countries to join COMECON, and prevented Marshall Plan aid from reaching Iron Curtain countries.

A, B, and D. The cartoon does not depict détente (an easing of tensions between the superpowers), mutual coexistence (superpower tolerance for one another), or collective security (a mutual defence agreement among nations).

56. C

The cartoon depicts the USA being chained down in southeast Asia through its policy of containment. Containment is "an attempt to stop the spread of the power or influence of an enemy country (or ideology) beyond the existing boundaries of its influence." During the Cold War, the United States attempted to stop the spread of communism in southeast Asia by stationing and/or using its troops in the region. Although this policy proved to be very costly, involved the USA in bloody wars in Korea and Vietnam, and resulted in hundreds of thousands of Americans being stationed overseas, the USA persisted in its efforts to stop the spread of Marxism.

A, B, and D. The cartoon does not comment on the negative consequences of détente (seeking to reduce tensions between the superpowers), deterrence (maintaining a large army and advanced weaponry in the attempt to prevent the enemy from attacking), or brinkmanship (taking a nation to the brink of war in pursuit of foreign policy goals).

57. B

The two sources suggest that the key to resolving the Cuban Missile Crisis was finding a face-saving solution that would allow both superpowers to claim victory. Kennedy notes that the crisis was averted because the USA avoided humiliating the USSR. Khrushchev was able to claim victory in the showdown because at the end of the crisis, USA promised to never again invade Cuba. Consequently, the USSR could publicly declare that it had achieved its main objective in the confrontation; Soviet missiles had originally been placed in Cuba to prevent a US invasion. In the crisis, the USA was able to get the USSR to remove its missiles from Cuba; as a result, the American President could claim that his main goal had been achieved in the showdown.

A, C, and D. The two sources do not suggest that collective security, increased American awareness of Soviet military capabilities, abandoning a policy of armed deterrence, or embracing the principle of regional security helped to resolve the crisis.

58. C

Khrushchev placed ballistic missiles in Cuba to deter the USA from attempting another Bay-of-Pigs-style invasion of the Caribbean communist country. This is consistent with the doctrine of balance of power. This doctrine refers to "an observed principle of international politics, whereby any state which threatens to increase its power becomes at once subject to increases in countervailing power from opposing countries." Khrushchev suggests that he was motivated by the balance of power doctrine when he placed nuclear weapons in Cuba. When the USA attempted to increase its power in the Caribbean by invading Cuba, the USSR sought to deter the American threat by deploying defensive missiles in Cuba.

A, B, and D. Khrushchev's rationale for placing missiles in Cuba is not consistent with the doctrines of coexistence (the policy of living peacefully with other nations despite fundamental disagreements), appeasement (giving in to the demands of an aggressor-state in the hope of avoiding a military conflict), or collective security (the agreement that aggression by one state against another is the same as aggression against all, and should be defeated by the collective action of all).

59. D

In Source I, Robert Kennedy notes that during the Cuban Missile Crisis, President Kennedy was primarily concerned with protecting the national security of the USA.

A, B, and C. Kennedy does not state that the USA's limited objectives in the Cuban Missile Crisis included overthrowing Castro's regime, promoting democracy or capitalism, or abandoning brinkmanship.

60. A

One of the lessons of the Vietnam War and the war in Afghanistan was that military strength alone is not sufficient to guarantee victory. In both wars, military superpowers were defeated by Third World nations. Both the Afghan rebels and Viet Cong guerrillas had smaller armies and poorer weapons than their superpower enemy. In both of these wars, the weaker side won because it had greater will to win and a greater tolerance for suffering.

B, C, and D. Neither the Vietnam War nor the war in Afghanistan was a total war (a war in which all available weapons and resources were employed); nuclear weapons, for instance, were never used by either superpower in these two wars. Both wars were attempts to maintain spheres of influence; however, ultimately, they were unsuccessful attempts. Neither the Vietnam War nor the war in Afghanistan was resolved by the UN or by a UN collective security operation.

61. C

The events in the chart span the years 1939 to 2000. The Nazi–Soviet Non-aggression Pact was signed in 1939. Russia fought two wars against the Chechens in the 1990s. Yeltsin initiated the second war in 1999; the war continued into the year 2000 when Vladimir Putin became President of Russia.

A, B, and D. No event on the chart occurs before 1939. The 1939 Nazi–Soviet Pact took place ten years before 1949.

62. B

In 1956, Nikita Khrushchev ordered the invasion of Hungary in order to maintain Soviet control over Hungary and other Soviet satellite countries. In other words, Khrushchev crushed the 1956 Hungarian Uprising to maintain a Soviet sphere of influence in Eastern Europe.

None of the other actions was taken by Khrushchev during his period of rule in the USSR (1953–1964).

63. B

Israeli–Palestinian relations improved significantly in 1993 when Israel and the Palestine Liberation Organization (PLO) signed the 1993 Oslo Accord (the Gaza–Jericho Agreement). This agreement granted Palestinians limited autonomy over the Gaza Strip and parts of the West Bank.

A, C, and D. Increased Jewish immigration to Israel would not have improved Israeli–Palestinian relations. Israel did not seize territories from Egypt or Syria in 1993, nor did Israel dramatically reduce the size of its armed forces in that year.

64. C

The INF (Intermediate Range Nuclear Forces) Treaty was a 1987 USA–USSR arms control agreement that eliminated the superpowers' stockpiles of medium-range nuclear missiles. The INF Treaty and the subsequent end of the Cold War have not prevented nuclear proliferation (the development or acquisition of nuclear weapons by non-nuclear powers). For instance, in 1998, Pakistan joined the nuclear club when it developed and tested its own nuclear weapons. Nuclear proliferation means that the possibility of a global nuclear-weapons catastrophe is still possible.

A, B, and D. The superpowers have not formed new alliances since 1987. In fact, Russia's alliance (the Warsaw Pact) ceased to exist in 1991. Russia has not put much effort into further developing its nuclear arsenal since 1987. In fact, since then, it has repeatedly sought arms reduction and limitation agreements with the USA. Presently, there is no evidence that multinational corporations are sowing the seeds of global catastrophe through their control of the international arms trade.

65. B

Transnational corporations are companies that are based in a home country but that have branch offices, plants, resource extraction operations, and/or retail outlets in other countries. In recent decades, some of these TNCs (Mitsubishi, Microsoft, or General Motors, for example) have become more wealthy and powerful than many nation-states. During the same period, the globalization of trade has meant that national governments are no longer regulating these companies as closely as in the past. Consequently, transnational corporations appear to be challenging the sovereign decision-making power of national governments. For example, it is debatable who has more influence over the WTO (World Trade Organization)—government leaders of WTO member-states or CEOs of multinational corporations.

A, C, and D. TNCs have been criticized for tax-dodging, destroying the environment, and mistreating workers. These corporations have shown themselves to be willing to invest in developing nations with lax labour standards. They have also been successful in lobbying for more economic freedom and less government regulation.

66. C

The Gulf War was a turning point in superpower relations. It was the first time since the end of the Second World War that the USA and USSR cooperated to confront a major act of aggression. Although the USSR did not contribute troops to the UN's successful effort to liberate Kuwait from Iraqi occupation, the USSR did not use its veto power to stop the UN from using military force in the Persian Gulf.

In the past, the Soviet Union usually vetoed any UN Security Council action that was proposed or supported by the USA. Moreover, during the Persian Gulf Crisis, the USSR did serve the UN and USA's cause by diplomatically pressuring Iraq to withdraw its forces from Kuwait.

A, B, and D. The Gulf War was the second time that the UN used military force to defend a sovereign country from aggression (the Korean War was the first instance). The Gulf War was not the first time that the UN became actively involved in a Middle East dispute; for instance, the UN played a key role in ending in the 1956 Suez Crisis. Prior to the Gulf War, the superpowers had vetoed or ignored many UN Security Council resolutions.

67. D

The excerpt states that young Europeans do not share "their parents' sense of national identity." In other words, the excerpt suggests that former European generations were more loyal to their ethnic heritage than today's young Europeans. The Edmonton Journal article notes that young people in Europe are more cosmopolitan than their parents or grandparents. To be cosmopolitan means to be "free from national and/or ethnic attachments and prejudices."

A, B, and C. The excerpt does not suggest these things.

68. B

The excerpt suggests that many young Europeans are willing to surrender national sovereignty (freedom from outside control and interference) provided that Europe becomes more cosmopolitan (more international and/or global in outlook).

A, C, and D. The excerpt does not suggest these things.

69. A

The most appropriate title for the excerpt is "Europe: A Model for Future Supranationalism." Supranationalism is the belief that nations should set aside national differences and cooperate for their mutual benefit. It involves the creation of international organizations above the level of individual national governments—organizations such as the European Union. Supranationalism also involves the surrender of some self-determination— because it gives other nations some control over your nation's actions.

B, C, and D. The other titles do not match the theme of the excerpt.

70. B

NATO is an example of a regional security alliance. The UN is an example of a global collective security organization. NATO intervened in the civil war in Bosnia for humanitarian reasons. The UN intervened for the same reason. Both organizations sought to bring peace to the war-torn country by sending peacekeepers there.

A. UNICEF is neither a regional security alliance or a collective security organization; it is a UN agency that assists nations with improving the health and education of children and their mothers.

C and D. Neither of these statements about the League of Nations illustrates the truth of the assertion.

71. D

The 1919 cartoon shows the traditional America-first philosophy being abandoned by American politicians who have turned their attentions away from domestic politics to international affairs. This cartoon ridicules American politicians like Woodrow Wilson who placed great hope in the philosophy of internationalism (a concern for the general welfare of humanity), the League of Nations, and the concept of collective security (the principle that member-states of the League of Nations would act together to stop aggression).

A, B, and C. The cartoon does not ridicule communism, appeasement, or a balance of power system.

72. B

In the cartoon, "Americanism" refers to an "America-First Philosophy," which is a synonym for "isolationism."

A, C, and D. In the cartoon, the term "Americanism" does not refer to idealism (the pursuit of idealistic goals), ultranationalism (the willingness to go to extreme lengths to increase the power and prosperity of one's nation-state), or supranationalism (support for the creation of international organizations and international laws).

73. A

The border changes on the map resulted from Germany's defeat in the First World War. Through the Treaty of Versailles (1919), a defeated Germany was forced to surrender territories to France, Belgium, Poland, and Czechoslovakia.

B, C and D. The territorial changes shown on the map did not result from Germany's failure to make war damages payments, decisions made by the League of Nations, or provisions of the Locarno Pact of 1925.

74. B

The German people greatly resented being stripped of territories at the end of the First World War —particularly those that contained German nationals (the Sudentenland in Czechoslovakia, for example). This resentment of the territorial changes resulting from the despised Treaty of Versailles was one of the most important factors in the rise of Adolf Hitler and Germany's Nazi movement. The rise of Nazism caused great internal tensions in Germany during the Interwar period and popularized the idea of taking revenge against the countries who had seized German lands.

A, C, and D. The major result of the border changes shown on the map was not a defensive alliance between Germany and Austria or a reinforcement of the belief that Germany should have been more severely punished. A defeated Germany was not supervised by the League of Nations—although the lost German city of Danzig was.

75. D

The Sudentenland (a German-inhabited territory in western Czechoslovakia) was the territory given to Germany under the terms of the 1938 Munich Agreement.

A, B, and C. The Munich Pact did not result in Germany's annexation of territories in eastern Austria, western Poland, or eastern Belgium.

76. D

Japan and the USA came into conflict over their conflicting foreign policies in the Pacific. Japan wanted to expand its empire in the Pacific; the USA wanted to protect its territories in the Pacific and to block Japanese expansionism in the region.

A, B, and C. The USA and Japan did not have overlapping foreign policy interests in Northern Europe, the Middle East, or Central Asia. They did have conflicting foreign policy goals in southeast Asia—with regard to China in particular.

77. C

The dates of the events shown on the diagram are: Reoccupation of the Rhineland (March 1936), union of Austria and Germany (March 1938), Munich Conference (September 1938). The event that completes the diagram is the signing of the Nazi–Soviet Non-aggression Pact (August 1939).

A, B, and D. All of the other events took place prior to 1937 and, therefore, cannot complete the diagram. The dates for these events are as follows: Japanese invasion of Manchuria (1931), Italian invasion of Ethiopia (1935), outbreak of the Spanish Civil War (1936).

78. D

The Sudentenland was an ethnically German region in western Czechoslovakia. The German desire to annex Czechoslovakia was motivated by irredentism.

A, B, and C. Ethiopia was not inhabited by Italians. Manchuria was inhabited by Chinese —not by Japanese nationals. Poland was not inhabited by Russians. Therefore, none of the given territorial claims is an irredentist one.

79. B

During the 1930s, European irredentist claims were largely addressed by a foreign policy of appeasement (giving into the demands of an aggressor in the effort to avert a war). For instance, Britain and France tried to avert a war with Germany by signing the Munich Pact; this agreement allowed Hitler to annex the Sudentenland and satisfy German irredentism.

A, C, and D. The irredentist claims of Germany and other European nations were not addressed by collective security, containment, or aggression.

80. A

The excerpt is from a Japanese speech from 1941. In the excerpt, a Japanese government official is justifying Japan's declaration of war on the USA and Great Britain.

B, C, and D. The details of the speech are not consistent with these three scenarios.

81. C

Both sources deal with events that can be interpreted as war crimes: the dropping of atomic bombs on Hiroshima and Nagasaki, the Holocaust, the systematic mass murder of Russian civilians by the Germans in the Second World War, and the carpet bombing of civilians in the Second World War and the Korean War. According to definition, a war crime occurs any time that civilians are purposely targeted by military forces in a war.

A, B, and D. The sources do not merely focus on Nazi war crimes. Source II, for instance, condemns the Allies' firebombing of German cities in the Second World War. They do not deal with the pursuit and prosecution of war criminals. Nor do they focus on the monitoring of human rights abuses by collective security organizations such as the UN.

82. D

The statement that best summarizes Source I's point of view is "Extreme measures taken during wartime, are more justifiable if the intent is to end the conflict." The author of Source I expresses this viewpoint when he/she suggests that the decision to drop the atomic bombs on Hiroshima and Nagasaki was "taken by harassed men in the extremity of a life and death conflict."

A, B and C. The three other statements are not consistent with the point of view expressed in Source I.

83. A

In the Second World War, German submarines (U-Boats) attacked Allied transport and escort ships that were carrying supplies and armaments from North America to Great Britain. This naval conflict was known as the Battle of the Atlantic.

B, C, and D. The submarine war against the Allied powers was not carried out by Great Britain, the USSR or the USA. All three of these nations were Allied powers.

84. A

The term "economic nationalism" refers to an economic policy of protectionism (the policy of imposing tariffs and quotas to restrict the inflow of imports and to protect domestic industries from foreign competition). Negotiating a free trade agreement with other nations would open up a nation to increased foreign competition; this would be inconsistent with a policy of economic nationalism.

B, C, and D. All of the other strategies are examples of actions favoured by economic nationalists.

85. B

The result of the economic nationalism (protectionism) adopted during the Great Depression was decreasing productivity and employment worldwide. No nation was interested in buying products from nations that refused to buy its products. The result was a global decline in foreign trade, resource extraction, manufacturing, and employment levels.

A, C, and D. Firstly, Lenin's adoption of NEP took place in 1921—long before the adoption of protectionism during the Great Depression of 1929–1939. Secondly, common markets (free trade zones) did not (and could not) emerge in the protectionist climate of the Depression years. Finally, prices fell during the Great Depression; they did not rise.

86. B

The 1945 Allied conferences at Yalta and Potsdam witnessed the breakdown of friendly relations between the USSR and its western Allies (the USA and Britain).

A, C, and D. The beginning of the Cold War preceded the Marshall Plan, the formation of COMECON, the establishment of NATO and the Warsaw Pact, the Berlin Airlift, and the announcement of the Truman Doctrine.

87. D

The UN was intended to be a collective security organization in which member-nations would defend one another from aggression.

A, B, and C. Firstly, the UN did not encourage the great powers to adopt a policy of mutual deterrence (the buildup of military strength as a means of discouraging other nations from attacking); instead, it promoted the concept of collective security. Secondly, the UN was founded on the belief that world peace was only possible if all nations (both democracies and dictatorships) strove for peace. Finally, the founders of the UN hoped that if an effective global collective security organization was established, regional collective security alliances would no longer be needed.

88. A

The map shows the defeat of German military forces by the Allies in Europe. Therefore, the best title for the map is "The Collapse of Nazi Germany."

B, C, and D. None of the other titles matches the situation shown on the map.

89. C

An isolationist nation does not want to get involved in the affairs of other nations. In contrast, a country that adopts a policy of containment becomes actively involved in world affairs in the effort to stop the spread of the influence and ideology of an enemy nation.

A, B, and D. Firstly, nations that adopt a foreign policy of appeasement (a policy of placating aggressors rather than confronting them) tend to favour non-intervention (the principle of not becoming involved in other nations' affairs).

Secondly, a policy of deterrence (building up military strength as a means of forestalling an enemy attack) is not much different from brinkmanship (threatening to use force if another state does not meet the demands of one's nation); both policies are means of getting another nation to back down. Finally, détente (the easing of tensions between hostile nations) is similar to the policy of peaceful co-existence (an attempt by nations with extreme ideological differences to live together peacefully in the world by avoiding antagonism).

90. B

In the cartoon, the wasps represent the UN response to the unprovoked invasion of South Korea by communist North Korea. In the early 1950s, the UN sent military forces to Korea to defend South Korea from aggression.

A, C, and D. The wasps actually represent the forces deployed in Korea in a UN collective security operation. The enraged insects represent UN forces sent to defend South Korea—not the communist Chinese forces that fought against them on the side of North Korea during the Korean War. The USSR was not directly involved in the Korean War.

91. C

Initially, UN forces were sent to Korea to fight against the army of North Korea. Only later did communist China enter the Korean War on the side of North Korea.

A, B, and D. At the start of the Korean War, communist China, the USSR, and Japan were not involved in the conflict.

92. C

Eisenhower's "domino theory" suggests that neighbouring states are so interdependent that if one became communist, the others would too. The domino theory was used to justify American intervention in Vietnam to contain communism (stop it from spreading to new territories) in southeast Asia.

A, B, and D. The domino theory is not related to the foreign policies of détente (the easing of tensions between hostile nations), deterrence (a policy of maintaining powerful armed forces or advanced weaponry to discourage an enemy from attacking), or isolationism (a policy that advocates non-participation in alliances or in the affairs of other states).

93. A

During the Cold War, the Americans used the nuclear threat to deter the Soviet Union from using its superiority in troop numbers and conventional weapons (planes, tanks, etc.) to attack the USA or her allies.

B, C, and D. Summit conferences (face-to-face meetings between national leaders), the threat of conventional war (a war with non-nuclear weapons), and UN pressures were not the factors that created the balance of power between the superpowers. Ultimately, it was nuclear weapons that created a balance of terror between the USA and USSR.

94. D

The end of the Cold War greatly reduced tensions between the USA and Russia. Consequently, the two nations stopped using their veto power for ideological reasons to block UN peacekeeping missions.

A, B, and C. The number of peacekeeping missions did not increase after 1989 as a result of rapid population growth, unification in Europe, or failures to pay back loans to the International Monetary Fund.

95. A

Observer IV comments that the current UN organization "does not fairly represent today's respective shares of international responsibility." What he probably means by this is that important nations such as Japan and Germany do not have permanent membership in the UN Security Council as do Britain, France, the USA, Russia, and China.

B, C, and D. Nothing in Observation IV suggests that the writer is drawing attention to these things.

96. D

The UN's shortage of funds may prevent or impede it from carrying out necessary reforms and future peacekeeping and peacemaking missions.

A, B, and C. The three other statements are not accurate.

97. D

An internationalist believes in extensive cooperation between nations for the general benefit of humanity. Therefore, he/she would favour collective security agreements, mediation (intervention in international crises to promote reconciliation between the disputing nations), and diplomatic negotiation for the prevention of wars.

A, B, and C. Internationalists would not support these other approaches. They condemn the pursuit of narrow national interests at the expense of other nations. Internationalists also believe that no nation should be allowed to become too dominant in world affairs.

98. A

Khrushchev's doctrine of peaceful coexistence held that the USSR and USA could not afford to go to war with one another (because of the danger of mutual annihilation through nuclear exchanges)—and that, therefore, each side would have to learn to tolerate the other.

B, C, and D. Peaceful coexistence was a belief that the ideologically opposed superpowers should not concede defeat in the Cold War—only that they should refrain from antagonizing one another unnecessarily. Khrushchev's doctrine did not make way for increased American influence in world affairs, acknowledge a greater confidence in nuclear deterrence, or loosen Soviet control over eastern European satellite states.

99. A

During the 1945-1991 era, many European colonies in Africa and Asia gained political independence.

B, C and D. Latin America underwent decolonization in the nineteenth century. Nations in the Balkans (southeastern Europe) gained national sovereignty prior to World War I or during the 1990s. The establishment of a sphere of influence is a form of imperialism that erodes national sovereignty.

100. D

The Hungarian uprising in 1956 was an attempt to end Soviet control of Hungary and democratize the nation's oppressive communist regime. Faced with this situation, Soviet premier Nikita Khrushchev was confronted with the choice of maintaining Soviet domination of Hungary or allowing Hungarians to control their own affairs.

101. B

In deciding how to deal with Serbian aggression and ethnic cleansing in the 1990s, Western politicians had to decide whether to confront Serbian dictator Slobodan Milosevic or appease (conciliate) him.

A, C, and D. When the author of Source I declares that "today's Western politicians labour under the same mentality that produced the disaster of the 1930s," it is clear that he is criticizing Western politicians' appeasement of Adolf Hitler and Benito Mussolini in the 1930s. Therefore, Source I does not refer to these other dilemmas.

102. A

Both sources refer to (directly or indirectly) Neville Chamberlain's attempt to appease Adolf Hitler in the Munich Pact of 1938.

B, C, and D. None of other treaties is associated with appeasement or British PM Neville Chamberlain. The Locarno Pact was a 1925 series of agreements in which various European countries accepted their existing borders; the 1939 Nazi-Soviet Non-Aggression Pact was a Russo-German treaty in which each signatory promised not to attack the other; and, in the 1928 Kellogg–Briand Pact, many nations renounced war and promised to settle international disputes through peaceful means.

103. C

Both sources reject appeasement so forcefully that one can assume that they would favour direct confrontation over the other non-interventionist and conciliatory strategies (armed neutrality, mediation, and negotiation).

104. B

At the root of the Arab-Israeli conflict in the Middle East are conflicting claims to the territory of Palestine. Most Israelis believe that Palestine (Israel) rightfully belongs to them. The Palestinians are adamant that Palestine is their homeland. To achieve peace, both sides will have to settle this territorial dispute.

105. C

The UN Charter is the written constitution of the United Nations Organization. A supporter of the UN charter would believe in supranationalism (the belief that nations should cooperate through the creation of international organizations and international laws). Anyone who supports the UN must believe that it has, to some degree, lessened international tensions since 1945.

A, B, and D. The 1945 UN Charter created a global collective security organization that was intended to make regional military alliances unnecessary. In the Charter, nations pledged themselves to use only peaceful means to settle international disputes. The founders of the UN hoped that ideological tensions between its member-states would be reduced by the organization—not increased.

NOTES

Answers and Solutions
Global Interaction in the Twentieth Century – Unit Test 2

1. C	**11. C**	**21. A**	**31. A**	**41. D**	**51. C**	**61. C**
2. B	**12. B**	**22. B**	**32. B**	**42. B**	**52. B**	**62. C**
3. D	**13. A**	**23. A**	**33. C**	**43. D**	**53. A**	**63. B**
4. C	**14. D**	**24. C**	**34. A**	**44. B**	**54. B**	**64. C**
5. B	**15. C**	**25. D**	**35. C**	**45. B**	**55. D**	**65. C**
6. B	**16. A**	**26. D**	**36. B**	**46. C**	**56. A**	**66. D**
7. A	**17. B**	**27. A**	**37. A**	**47. C**	**57. B**	**67. A**
8. B	**18. A**	**28. A**	**38. B**	**48. B**	**58. C**	**68. D**
9. C	**19. D**	**29. B**	**39. A**	**49. B**	**59. B**	**69. C**
10. B	**20. D**	**30. C**	**40. D**	**50. A**	**60. A**	**70. D**

1. C

Students are expected to understand the **isolationist** sentiments of the United States following the First World War and the American reaction to the **Versailles Treaty**.

C. The United States Senate refused to ratify the Treaty of Versailles, thus preventing the United States from joining the League of Nations.

A. The United Nations was created following the Second World War, not the First World War.

B. The Munich Accord was signed in 1938, and the United States was not a participant in this accord.

D. The Locarno Agreement was concluded in 1925 and did not involve the United States.

2. B

Students are expected to understand the concept of point of view in a cartoon and recognize that many Americans were opposed to the United States' decision to return to isolationist policies.

B. The cartoonist is attempting to point out that the decision of the United States' Senate not to ratify the Treaty of Versailles made a lasting peace unlikely.

A. The pointing finger of humanity and the dead body of the Versailles Treaty are a clear condemnation of the American policy of isolationism.

C. There is nothing in the cartoon to indicate anything to do with loans to European nations. This is an attempt to confuse students with the policies of the Marshall Plan following the Second World War.

D. Nothing in the cartoon refers to any dispute involving democracies and dictatorships.

3. D

Students are expected to be familiar with the disintegration and collapse of the Hapsburg (Austria–Hungary) and Romanov (Russia) dynasties that occurred as a result of the First World War, and the profound changes that occurred in the power structure of Europe as a result of this collapse.

D. The new states of Finland, Estonia, Latvia, Lithuania, Poland, Czechoslovakia, and Yugoslavia emerged as a result of the collapse of the Romanov and Hapsburg dynasties.

A. The appeasement policies of the 1920s and 1930s were not related to the collapse of the Romanov or Hapsburg dynasties.

B. Since the League of Nations did not come into existence until after the disappearance of the Romanov and Hapsburg dynasties, it cannot have been affected by this event.

C. The only nation that disarmed after the First World War was Germany, and only because disarmament was forced upon her.

4. C

Students are expected to understand the origins of the Weimar Republic and the problems faced by the new German democracy.

C. Many Germans blamed the leaders of the Weimar Republic for signing the Treaty of Versailles. Even though this treaty was forced upon Germany, this act seriously weakened the credibility of the new Weimar government.

A. Following the First World War, Germany was not allowed membership in the newly formed League of Nations because of being a defeated nation.

B. As a result of the disarmament provisions of the Treaty of Versailles, the Weimar Republic was limited in its military spending.

D. The Weimar Republic made no such treaty with the Soviet Union. There is an attempt in this answer to confuse the student with the details of the Nazi–Soviet Non-Aggression Pact, which was not signed until after the demise of the Weimar Republic.

5. B

Students are expected to understand the consequences of the policy of **appeasement** that was followed by Britain and France in the 1930s, and its consequences for the state of Czechoslovakia.

B. The Munich Conference involving Germany, Britain, France, and Italy resulted in Germany receiving territorial concessions in Czechoslovakia that ultimately resulted in all of Czechoslovakia being absorbed by Germany.

A. The Yalta Conference took place in February 1945. By this time, it was clear that Germany was certain to lose the war and the conference was an attempt to formulate a policy that would deal with conditions following Germany's defeat.

C. The Potsdam Conference in July of 1945 occurred after the defeat of Germany and was concerned with the war against Japan.

D. The Casablanca Conference took place in January 1943. A result of it was an agreement between the Allied powers to offer Germany only unconditional surrender.

6. B

B. Churchill constantly spoke out against making concessions to Germany during the 1930s, believing that it would only encourage Hitler to ask for more.

A. Churchill made it clear during the interwar period that he would have favoured a confrontational approach to relations with Hitler's Germany.

C. Churchill favoured collective security as a method of dealing with Germany. Unfortunately this approach was ignored until it was too late to avoid war.

D. Peaceful coexistence was a term used by Nikita Khruschev during the Cold War to describe a peaceful approach to relations between the Soviet Union and the United States.

7. A

Students are expected to understand the limitations of the League of Nations.

A. Members of the League believed that international pressure would dissuade aggressors from continuing their aggressive actions. No military action was possible.

B. The League could apply economic sanctions against an aggressor, and did so after Italy's invasion of Ethiopia in 1935.

C. Discussion of world issues was a right of all member nations, and was expected to solve most world problems.

D. The aggressive actions of nations like Japan and Italy were condemned by the League, but with little result.

8. B

Students are expected to understand Hitler's goals and match them correctly with events that actually took place when he was in power.

B. Elimination of possible rivals was furthered by the Night of the Long Knives during which Hitler slaughtered over 1500 of his political rivals in the Nazi Party.

A. The goal of attaining racial purity was not helped by the Enabling Act, which essentially gave Hitler dictatorial powers.

C. The goal of improving Germany's economy would not have been helped by the Nuremberg Laws, which were aimed at preventing intermarriage between Germans and so-called non-Germans such as the Jews.

D. Achieving territorial expansion would not have been helped by the Final Solution, which aimed to eliminate all of the Jews in Europe.

9. C

Students are expected to understand the purposes of the various wartime conferences that took place.

C. All of the conferences mark various stages in Allied planning and were aimed at defeating the Axis powers as quickly as possible.

A. All of the conferences were concerned with the events of the Second World War and the goal of defeating the Axis powers. The question of a replacement for the League of Nations was of secondary importance to winning the war.

B. There was little concern over Soviet expansion in Europe until the conclusion of the war, and that did not occur until after the Yalta Conference.

D. The nuclear weapons program was top secret, and was not a topic for discussion at any of the conferences.

10. B

Students are expected to recognize various developments and events of the Cold War.

B. All of the developments were initiated by the United States and clearly indicated that the United States was not going to retreat into isolationism following the Second World War.

A. All of the developments mentioned in the question were aimed at containing possible Soviet expansion.

C. The policy of détente did not develop until later in the Cold War. All of the developments listed occurred during the early years of the Cold War.

D. By 1949, the Soviet Union had established complete control over the nations of Eastern Europe.

11. C

Students are expected to be able to interpret point of view in a cartoon, in this case, the point of view of the Soviet Union toward Nazi Germany in 1936.

C. The dollar signs, the words "Shares" and "Shares in Arms industry," plus the almost fatherly appearance of the figures around the cradle indicate that the cartoonist believed that Hitler was strongly supported by Western capitalists.

A. The benign appearance of the figures surrounding the crib does not indicate that the cartoonist perceived the wealthy as a threat to Hitler.

B. Each of the figures is probably intended to represent a particular nation, such as Britain and the United States. These figures appear to be gently rocking Hitler's cradle. Rather than containing Hitler, the figures appear to be helping him.

D. In 1936, Hitler had not yet turned his attention to any of his neighbours.

12. B

Students are expected to understand the change in relations between Germany and the Soviet Union that took place in 1939.

B. The Nazi–Soviet Pact temporarily changed the official relationship between the Soviet Union and Germany from one of hostility to one of friendship. Until Hitler's attack on the Soviet Union in June of 1941, there was no further criticism of Germany in the Soviet Union.

A. The signing of the Munich Pact, in which Hitler received major concessions from the British and the French, was viewed by the Soviet Union as encouraging Hitler to continue his expansionist policies.

C. The invasion of the Soviet Union by Germany resulted in a return to the previous official animosity in the Soviet Union toward all things German.

D. Prior to the advent of war between Germany and the Soviet Union, Stalin had no plans to invade Germany.

13. A

Students are expected to display knowledge of various historical maps. In this map, a number of clues point to a time between the First World War and the Second World War. Note the names Estonia, Latvia, and Lithuania. These are countries that existed in the interwar period, but disappeared after 1939. In addition, East Prussia is separated from the rest of Germany by Poland, a condition that existed only between 1919 and 1939. As a result, the map must represent 1929.

14. D

D. None of the shaded countries existed before the First World War and all came into existence as a result of the war.

A. Given that the map depicts Europe in 1929, The Iron Curtain did not yet exist.

B. In 1929, Hitler had not yet taken power in Germany, therefore, there was no Nazi Germany.

C. In 1929, there were no pro-German fascist governments in Europe.

15. C

Students are expected to understand the viewpoint of the Soviet Union following the Second World War.

C. The Soviet Union attempted to insure its own security through the establishment of a pro-Soviet buffer zone that could be used to shelter the country against any future aggression.

A. A major motive in the Soviet occupation of Eastern Europe was a fear of invasion from the West. Despite the huge size of the Soviet army, Russia was not confident that she could win a war against the West.

B. It was clear in 1945 that Nazism had been crushed. The continued occupation of Eastern Europe was not necessary to maintain this situation.

D. Following the Second World War, the Soviet Union actually looted many of the territories it occupied. This hardly aided in their economic restoration.

16. A

In this question, students are expected to understand the background of the role of the United Nations in several of the conflicts that occurred between 1950 and 1995. The key to the answer is understanding that in three of the conflicts, the United Nations attempted to contain a conflict between two combatants. In the fourth conflict, it was the United Nations itself that participated in the conflict.

A. In the Korean War, the United Nations attempted to defeat the forces of North Korea and force unity on a divided Korea.

B. The Suez Crisis was the first conflict in which the United Nations assumed a peacekeeping role.

C. In Cyprus, the role of the United Nations has been to keep the two warring parties apart by applying the techniques developed in the Suez Crisis.

D. In Bosnia, the failure of the United Nations to halt the conflict was casued in part to the fact that the warring parties would not conform to the United Nations' traditional peacekeeping techniques.

17. B

Students must possess knowledge of the events of the Cold War and the relation of the various Iron Curtain nations to the Soviet Union.

B. The Czech government's attempts to introduce democratic reforms alarmed the leaders of the Soviet Union, who feared that such ideas might spread to other Soviet dominated nations.

A. By 1968, Czechoslovakia was already part of the Warsaw Pact, although not by choice.

C. Not all Soviet states completely collectivized agriculture, therefore this would not have been sufficient excuse for invading Czechoslovakia.

D. Czechoslovakia had no Russian minority.

18. A

In this question, students must be familiar with the terms **sovereignty** and **national security**. A clue to the answer is that in order to satisfy both of the objectives of sovereignty and national security, a nation must attempt to defend itself without participation in international organizations.

A. The policy of deterrence requires a nation to establish a military force strong enough to frighten off a potential enemy. An arms buildup and the creation of ICBMs would achieve this purpose.

B. The policy of deterrence would not be served by the reduction of arms even if it would be supported by an initiative such as SDI.

C. The policy of containment would not be served by means of peacekeeping initiatives or by the formation of a free trade organization like the EU.

D. The policy of containment would be served by means of a regional alliance, but the UN is not an example of a regional organization.

19. D

Understanding the diagram requires a knowledge of the European nations during in the Cold War. The clue in the answer is to understand that all of the nations listed except two belonged to either NATO (the left circle) or the Warsaw Pact (the right circle).

D. Czechoslovakia (Warsaw Pact) is incorrectly placed in NATO. Austria was neutral and did not belong to either alliance.

A. Italy (NATO) and Poland (Warsaw Pact) are correctly placed.

B. Belgium (NATO) and Hungary (Warsaw Pact) are correctly placed.

C. Great Britain (NATO) and Bulgaria (Warsaw Pact) are correctly placed.

20. D

The key to this question is in understanding that the position marked by the question mark is that of neutrality.

D. Yugoslavia was neutral.

A. Norway was a member of NATO.

B. Greece was a member of NATO.

C. Denmark was a member of NATO.

21. A

A. Romania was a member of the Warsaw Pact.

B. Sweden was neutral.

C. Turkey was a member of NATO.

D. France was a member of NATO.

22. B

Students must have an understanding of the terms **independent, bipolar, multipolar,** and **supranational**.

B. The Cold War between the dominant powers of the Soviet Union and the United States fits Model II.

A. Model I fits the model of the balance of power. Nations form a temporary grouping to meet a temporary threat.

C. Model III resembles a number of the regional economic alliances that have emerged during the 20th century, such as the EU.

D. Model IV is based on the existence of an international organization like the United Nations.

23. A

A. The loose grouping of nations in the coalition that defeated Iraq fits the description of Model I.

B. By the time of the Gulf War, the bipolar confrontation of the Cold War had ended.

C. The nations opposing Iraq in the Gulf War formed a temporary grouping that does not fit the description of the multipolar world of Model III.

D. The confrontational approach taken toward Iraq does not fit the model of international cooperation suggested in Model IV.

24. C

Students are expected to understand the parallels between the problems faced by the United States in Vietnam and those faced by the Soviet Union in Afghanistan.

C. Soviet military intervention in Afghanistan parallels all of the difficulties listed.

A. No such conditions existed during the period of military cooperation between the Soviet Union and Cuba.

B. The Soviet military intervention in Hungary only lasted a very short time.

D. The Soviet invasion of Czechoslovakia crushed all opposition within a few hours.

25. D

Students are expected to understand the domino theory and its application to the foreign policy of the United States.

D. American foreign policy in Latin America was strongly motivated by fear of the spread of communism through an American sphere of influence.

A. British policy in Africa during the 1930s was aimed at integrating its colonies ever more closely into the seemingly indestructible British empire.

B. French imperialist policy in the Pacific in the 1950s was primarily concerned with continued control over its colonial possessions.

C. Israeli foreign policy in the Middle East was mainly concerned the maintenance of secure boundaries.

26. D

Students are expected to understand that the anti-Soviet policies of Ronald Reagan pushed the level of military spending to the point where the Soviet Union could no longer compete.

D. Under Ronald Reagan, American defence spending increased by 120%. This was a level of expenditure that the Soviet Union, with its more limited economy, could not match.

A. Preservation of the American position in the Middle East did not contribute measurably to the end of the Cold War.

B. Throughout his term in office, President Reagan attempted to strengthen the NATO alliance, viewing it as a necessary bulwark against the Soviet Union.

C. Reagan made no secret of the fact that he viewed the United Nations as a weak and ineffective institution.

27. A

Students are expected to understand the political developments that have occurred most recently in Western Europe. This question is a little tricky because students are asked to choose between four real events. As a result, students are asked to judge which of the four events is the most important. This is indicated in the question by the words **most significantly** in bold type.

A. The reunification of Germany after being divided into East and West Germany since 1945 has and will continue to have significant influence on Europe and the rest of the world.

B. Because of the relatively small influence of Czechoslovakia both economically and politically, this event does not have the impact of German reunification.

C. This answer is a reference to the breakup of Yugoslavia. Although this is an important event, it could be argued that Yugoslavia is not Western Europe and, therefore, does not fit the question. In addition, Yugoslavia cannot be said to have the same economic or political importance that Germany has.

D. Although isolated acts of terrorism by radical nationalists still occur in Europe, they are nowhere near as frequent as they once were.

28. A

In this question, a considerable amount of information is given to the student to help with the correct answer. The student is expected, however, to display some knowledge of events in Yugoslavia since 1991.

A. All of the sources point to aggressive nationalism as a destabilizing force. Students should recall that Serbian nationalism was one of the key causes of the First World War.

B. In the case of Yugoslavia, self-determination (the right of a people to govern themselves as a nation) has led to ethnic conflict as the various ethnic groups in the country have broken away.

C. There are very few examples of the United Nations successfully determining ethnic divisions. Most ethnic divisions this century have been determined by force, not diplomacy.

D. This statement may well be true, but there is no reference to it in any of the sources.

29. B

In this question, it would be useful for the student to know who Marshall Tito was and a little bit about the post-Second World War history of Yugoslavia. It was Tito, a hero of the Second World War, who held Yugoslavia's various ethnic factions together.

B. The threat posed by the Soviet Union acted as a unifying force on Yugoslavia. With the collapse of Soviet power and the end of the Cold War, that unifying factor was removed.

A. The United Nations attempted, with limited success, to halt the ethnic strife that erupted between the Serbs and the various other ethnic groups that had once comprised a united Yugoslavia. The United Nations did nothing to intensify the problems created by the breakup of Yugoslavia, but sought rather to establish a peaceful solution to the problem.

C. Only the United States has threatened force against Yugoslavia and then only after violent acts against breakaway ethnic groups.

D. Diplomatic efforts by Western powers were aimed at restoring some semblance of stability to the Balkans, not encouraging a further breakup of Yugoslavia.

30. C

C. In states with Serb minorities, violent clashes occurred between members of the new states and the Serb minorities, supported by the Yugoslav army. Over 200,000 people died in ethnic violence.

A. The former Yugoslavia has broken into five separate sovereign states. At the time that this question was administered, a sixth state, Kosovo, was attempting to assert its independence. Since this time, Yugoslavia has ceased to exist as an independent nation.

B. Although the Serbs attempted to unite all territories with Serb populations, it has been forced to accept that some Serbs will have to live as minorities in some of the breakaway states.

D. The Yugoslav military has not attempted to seize power in what is left of Yugoslavia.

31. A

Students are required to have a basic understanding of the events of the Berlin Blockade, the Cuban Missile Crisis, and the Hungarian Uprising. The key to understanding the question is to realize that the three events have been mixed up in both statements. Statement I is false because the two events are separated by 14 years. The Berlin Blockade occurred in 1948 and the United States blockaded Cuba in 1962. In addition, the Soviet blockade of Berlin occurred before the American naval quarantine of Cuba, so it could not be a response to the American action. Statement II is false because the Soviet Union crushed the Hungarian Uprising. The United Nations was helpless to intervene in this crisis because the Soviet Union held veto power in the Security Council. **As a result, both statements are false, and the correct answer is "A."**

32. B

Students are expected to use the sources to answer the three following questions. A careful study of the sources should reveal that they are all concerned with the frequency of wars since the Second World War and the inability of the world community to deal with them in more than a fragmented and disjointed manner.

B. The sources examine the number of conflicts and the seeming inability of the United Nations and the World powers to deal with them.

A. Source I deals with the number of deaths in wars since 1945, but it is not intended to compare the rate of casualties today with the number from previous wars.

C. The United Nations is discussed only in the context of its inability to preserve world peace.

D. There is a reference to the superpowers in Source I, but there is no attempt to define their role in the maintenance of world peace.

33. C

C. Sources I and III are concerned with the number of armed conflicts in the world in 1993–94. Source II, by inference, shows those countries where such conflicts are taking place in these years.

A. Clearly, the various sources do not deal with the emergence of the world's new democracies. The word "democracy" is not even mentioned in any of the sources.

B. There is no information in any of the sources dealing with what type of government might exist in any of the countries listed on the map in Source II.

D. The United Nations did not send peacekeeping forces to many of the countries shown on the map in 1993–94.

34. A

The challenge in this question is for the student to go beyond the sources and use knowledge of world events to determine what the phrase "crisis of internationalism" refers to.

A. A serious problem of maintaining peace in the modern world is that many of the conflicts occur in areas of the world that are often considered unimportant to those nations that have the capability of enforcing world order. As a result, many conflicts are allowed to continue for months or even years without resolution.

B. As a result of the instability in the world, alliances such as NATO have maintained their membership, and even increased it, by adding former members of the Warsaw Pact such as Poland.

C. There is nothing in Source III that is in any way concerned with the environment.

D. Few of the world's nations need to rebuild their armed forces. Most nations have military forces that exceed their needs in a time of so-called peace.

35. C

For this question, students are expected to display their knowledge of various international organizations.

C. Amnesty International attends to the problems of human rights violations and abuses of political power in countries whose citizens are denied due process of law.

A. Greenpeace is an organization that is concerned almost entirely with protection of the world's environment.

B. The Red Cross, or Red Crescent in Muslim countries, functions as an emergency organization in the case of international disaster. In many nations, it also functions as the collection centre and repository of the blood supply for medical purposes.

D. The World Health Organization is concerned with improving health in nations around the world.

36. B

Both of these 1919 speeches address the issue of whether or not the USA should ratify the Treaty of Versailles and join the League of Nations.

A. either source mentions the divisiveness of partisan (party) politics.

C. Lodge is skeptical of collective security. Wilson, in contrast, heartily endorses it.

D. It is evident from his statement that President Wilson is opposed to a policy of isolationism. Senator Lodge, however, expresses isolationist views in his statement.

37. A

Lodge was a prominent Republican Senator and an arch-enemy of Wilson, who was a member of the Democratic Party. At the time of Lodge's speech, members of the Republican Party favoured isolationism and opposed Wilson's dream of American involvement in the League of Nations. Because Republicans made up a majority of the Senate, the Senate ultimately refused to ratify the Treaty of Versailles, which contained the covenant of the League of Nations.

B. Democrats did not support Lodge or the Republican position on the League issue.

C. The Republican majority in Congress did support Lodge's position, but it did not favour US participation in future European conflicts.

D. Senators who believed in the principle of collective security would not have supported Lodge's isolationist stance. They would have favoured Wilson's position.

38. B

Why did Germany walk out of the disarmament conference? It did so because it wanted to rearm. When it began to do so, other countries followed suit. The acknowledgment that rearmament accelerated after 1933 would be an effective conclusion for Source I.

A. The League did pursue Wilson's ideas about disarmament. Source I states that disarmament "was a major objective of the League of Nations during the 1920s and 1930s." A statement that contradicts Source I would not make an effective conclusion for that source.

C. Source I builds toward the conclusion that efforts at disarmament were being undermined and abandoned in the 1930s. A statement mentioning the naval arms limitation agreement of 1938–39 would not make an effective conclusion for the source.

D. Nations did not agree on disarmament on the eve of the Second World War. In fact, they were rushing to re-arm in 1938–39. A false statement would not make an effective conclusion for Source I.

39. A

In Source II, "The World" is saddened by the death of the League of Nations. This suggests that nations of the world were sympathetic toward the principles of supranationalism (international cooperation) upon which the League was based.

B. The main objectives of the League were to resolve international disputes, preserve global peace, and provide collective security—not to preserve economic prosperity.

C. The League was not essentially an economic organization. It did little or nothing to achieve an economic balance of power between nations or national groupings.

D. In the cartoon, "The World" is mourning, not celebrating, the passing of the League.

40. D

Personification is "the representation of a thing or abstraction in the form of a person, as in art." In Source II, the world is represented in the form of a crying man. The cartoonist uses this personification to represent the irony that the League's death was necessary to advance the cause of global peace. Irony is "an expression of meaning, often humorous or sarcastic, by the use of language of a different or opposite tendency." The use of irony is evident in the cartoon by the contradictory use of a saddened world and the joyful message "Peace at Last!" The cartoonist ironically presents the pitiful death of the League as a good thing for humanity.

A. The League actually failed to get major powers to support its efforts.

B. The League did not accomplish its mandate. It did not prevent another world war.

C. The League did not sacrifice itself to maintain peace. Firstly, it did not prevent the Second World War. Secondly, it died only when nations abandoned it for the new United Nations Organization in 1945–46.

41. D

The main point of Source II is that the League was a noble failure. Source I suggests that the League made notable efforts to promote arms reduction and arms limitation and disarmament—but that its efforts were ultimately a failure. Both sources represent the League's efforts as ultimately futile.

A, B, and C. None of the other three generalizations are mentioned or supported by the two sources.

42. B

Between 1920 and 1936, France constructed the Maginot Line (a line of defensive fortifications along its border with Germany) to defend itself from an anticipated German attack. The Maginot Line proved to be obsolete in the new era of highly mobile blitzkrieg warfare that was used beginning in 1939. The Germans caused the fall of France in 1940 by outflanking the Maginot Line with fast-moving tanks and motorized infantry.

A. France did not foolishly assume that an isolationist USA would come to its assistance. The neutral USA did nothing to protect France in 1939–40.

C. France did not concentrate on building up its air force in the way that Germany and Britain did. At the outbreak of the Second World War, Germany had a much larger air force than France. France was in no position to conduct a major bombing campaign against Germany's industrial centres.

D. The fall of France had nothing to do with French naval policy. It was conquered in a land campaign by the German army.

43. D

The Treaty of Versailles (1919) gave much of eastern Germany to Poland. This land came to be known as "the Polish Corridor" because it gave Poland an pathway (corridor) to the Baltic Sea through German territory. Agreements made at the Yalta and Potsdam Conferences in 1945 redrew the Polish–German border along the "Oder–Neisse Line." As a result, Poland acquired the German territories of Pomerania, Silesia, and East Prussia.

A, B, and C. The Munich Pact, Truman Doctrine, Locarno Pact, Helsinki Accords, and Atlantic Charter were not concerned with the re-drawing of Poland's boundaries.

44. B

Collective security is "a policy in international relations, designed to preserve world peace, according to which countries collectively guarantee the security of individual countries, as by sanctions or multilateral alliances against an aggressor." Through their common membership in the League of Nations (a supranational organization for collective security) Britain, France, and Czechoslovakia pledged to defend one another from aggression. Rather than supporting Czechoslovakia by promising to defend it from attack by an aggressive Germany (as they had pledged to do according to the League of Nations Covenant), Britain and France chose to yield to the threats and demands of Germany. Britain and France allowed Germany to annex northwestern Czechoslovakia (the Sudentenland) rather than risk going to war with Germany over Czechoslovakia.

A. Appeasement was actually an attempt to satisfy strongly pacifistic British and French citizens. The Munich Agreement was very popular in Britain and France in 1938.

C. Actually, Britain and France appeased Hitler because they did not feel adequately prepared for a military confrontation with Nazi Germany.

D. Actually, the British and French were reluctant to go to war over the Sudentenland because they believed that this ethnically German region of Czechoslovakia rightly belonged to Germany.

45. B

Japan pursued a policy of autarky (economic self-sufficiency) during the 1930s and 1940s. Its invasions of East Asian territories (such as the Dutch East Indies and Malaya) in 1941 were designed to make Japan self-sufficient in natural resources.

A. Abyssinia was a poor country that had few resources that could have benefited Fascist Italy. In the 1930s and early 1940s, the quest for natural resources was less of a motivation for Italian imperialism than it was for Japanese imperialism.

C. North Korea sought to unite Korea under communist rule in 1950. Acquiring South Korea's natural resources was, at best, a secondary goal of the North Korean invasion.

D. The USSR invaded Afghanistan to support the puppet-dictatorship that it had established there. It did not invade the country to seize its natural resources.

46. C

President Truman claimed that, without the use of atomic weapons, the Pacific War would have lasted into 1946 and would have had to culminate in an Allied invasion of the Japanese home islands. He projected that a million American lives and millions more Japanese lives would have been lost in a prolonged war fought with conventional weapons.
In contrast, less than 200,000 Japanese lives (and no American lives) were lost in the A-bomb drops on the two Japanese cities that brought a quick end to the war.

A. Although historians suspect that the dropping of the two A-bombs was, at least partly, designed to contain Soviet expansionism, the U.S. government did not mention this aim in its official justification of the two atomic bombings.

B. Germany had already surrendered unconditionally in May 1945. The atomic bombs were dropped on Japan three months later in August 1945.

D. Although some Americans probably felt that the A-bomb drops were just punishment for the sneak attack on Pearl Harbor, the U.S. government did not mention this motivation in its official justification of the A-bomb drops on Japan.

47. C

The map shows the final Allied offensives against Axis forces in Europe during the last months of World War II. These attacks resulted in the fall of Nazi Germany (the Third Reich) in May 1945.

A. The earlier period of 1939–1942 was the time of Nazi Germany's imperialist conquests.

B. "Operation Barbarossa" was the German code-name for Germany's invasion of the USSR in June 1941.

D. The map does show successful American campaigns in North Africa, Italy, and Western Europe—but it also shows successful Soviet offensives against the Germans. Thus, the title "American Successes in the Second World War" is not as comprehensive or appropriate as "The Destruction of the Third Reich."

48. B

The 1945 Yalta Conference resulted in an agreement for the division of Germany into American, British, French, and Soviet zones of occupation. It also gave formal approval for the occupation of eastern Europe by Soviet troops. The border between the Soviet zone of occupation and Western Europe subsequently became the famous "Iron Curtain" boundary that divided the European continent into two hostile camps during the Cold War. Western Europe would be part of America's sphere of influence. Eastern Europe found itself in the Soviet sphere.

A. The Marshall Plan did not change the Iron Curtain boundary between East and West. It merely sought to contain Soviet communism.

C. The Yalta and Potsdam Conferences in 1945 redrew the map of Europe that had been established in 1919 by the Treaty of Versailles. Europe's Cold War borders did not correspond to the boundaries set in 1919.

D. The 1938 Munich Conference altered the German-Czech border. But the 1945 Yalta and Potsdam Conferences established a new border between the Czechoslovaks and Germans that would exist for the duration of the Cold War.

49. B

The excerpt is from the Tripartite (Axis) Pact that was signed in September 1940. A collective security agreement is "a communal commitment whereby each member-state promises to defend the others from acts of aggression." Since the three nations involved in the Axis Pact were, in fact, aggressors that were invading and conquering other nations—the pact cannot accurately be described as a collective security arrangement. Common defence and the preservation of world peace— both goals of collective security—were not aims of this treaty.

A. The term *alliance* (a formal agreement between two or more nations) is an appropriate label for the Tripartite Pact.

C. Articles 1 and 2 give approval for German, Italian, and Japanese expansionism.

D. Articles 1 and 2 provide for the establishment of an Italo-German sphere of influence in Europe and of a Japanese sphere of influence in Asia.

50. A

In 1940, Germany, Italy, and Japan were nations that used war and military might as a primary means of pursuing their political ends. The governments of all three states exhibited the classic traits of fascism—authoritarianism, imperialism, ultra-nationalism, reactionism, and anti-communism.

B. All three nations were aggressive but not socialist. In fact, they were extremely hostile to socialism.

C. All three nations favoured a (controlled) free enterprise economy. None of them, however, were isolationist (opposed to the formation of alliances and/or international commitments). They did, after all, sign the Tripartite Pact.

D. All three states wanted to acquire additional territories from other countries. None of them, however, were communist countries.

51. C

The Common Market (European Economic Community) was established in the 1950s to stimulate economic prosperity through the encouragement of trade, the reduction of trade barriers, and the freer movement of labour and capital between member countries.

A. The goal of the Common Market was to promote economic cooperation between Western European states. It was not designed to encourage stiffer economic competition.

B. The halting of communist expansion was more of a concern of the Marshall Plan and the NATO alliance. The Marshall Plan and NATO both preceded the European Common Market. The EEC lacked the anti-communist political agenda of the Marshall Plan and NATO.

D. The EEC was in place by 1957. NAFTA did not come into effect until 1994.

52. B

The Truman Doctrine was an American pledge to support governments that were combating communist rebels and/or communist threats to national security; it was designed to contain the spread of communism. American involvement in the Korea War was another attempt to contain communist expansionism. The Cuban Missile Crisis was the traumatic event that ushered in the era of détente (a period of reduced hostility between the superpowers). One example of the fruits of détente was the Strategic Arms Limitation Agreement signed by the USA and USSR in 1972.

A and D. Appeasement was not a foreign policy strategy that was used in any of the events listed.

C. Both superpowers used brinkmanship in the Cuban Missile Crisis—but not in the SALT I negotiations or agreements.

53. A

The use of nuclear weapons is implied in Dulles' threat to "massively retaliate" against communist expansionism or intervention.

B. The era of communist expansion had not ended by 1953. Soviet Russia was, for example, supporting communist insurgents in Vietnam at the time.

C. Dulles was speaking of the US commitment to containing global communism—not just preventing its spread in Europe through NATO.

D. The fact that the USA was actively engaged in establishing alliance systems such as NATO and SEATO during the 1949–1954 era suggests that it (and other nations) did not have much faith in the UN's promise of collective security.

54. B

Rhetoric is "language designed to persuade or impress—often with an implication of insincerity or exaggeration." Dulles' promises were revealed to be rhetoric when the USA did nothing to help the Hungarians during their anti-Soviet rebellion in 1956. The Hungarians had believed Dulles when he said, "you can count on us"—and they felt betrayed when the Americans did not come to their assistance in 1956. The USA was simply not prepared to risk a war with the USSR over Hungary.

A, C, and D. Dulles's pledge of support to "all those suffering under Communist slavery" was not proved to be a hollow promise by any of the other three events listed.

55. D

The two maps focus on violations of national sovereignty by the two superpowers during the Cold War era. For example, Source I features the controversial American invasion of Cambodia that compromised Cambodia's sovereignty. Source II features the Soviet invasion of Afghanistan—a violation of Afghani independence.

A, B, and C. Neither source deals with appeasement, diplomatic activity, neutrality, economic developments, or UN involvement.

56. A

Guerrilla warfare (warfare consisting mainly of hit-and-run attacks by small bands of soldiers) was a mainstay of both the Vietnam War and the war in Afghanistan. In Vietnam, the Americans and South Vietnamese fought against Viet Cong guerrillas. In Afghanistan, the Soviet Red Army and Afghani communists fought against Islamic fundamentalist guerrillas called the mujahedeen.

B. Naval engagements were not a major part of the Vietnam War. They were non-existent in the war in Afghanistan.

C. The powers resorted to diplomacy in the Vietnam and Afghanistan conflicts very infrequently and then, only as a last resort.

D. The superpowers never directly fought against each other in either the Vietnam or Afghanistan wars.

57. B

A sphere of influence can be defined as:

- **"the claimed or recognized area of a state's interests"**
- **"any area in which one nation wields dominant power over another or others"**
- **"a region which is dominated and exploited by a powerful imperialistic state"**

In the Vietnam War, the USA was unsuccessful in preventing the loss of its sphere of influence in southeast Asia. The Soviets intervened in Afghanistan in order to bring the nation within their sphere of influence.

A, C, and D. Neither war was a real attempt by either superpower to upset the balance of power, to appease the other superpower, or to use an alliance to achieve foreign policy goals.

58. C

The author of Source III suggests that a nation should never enter into a war without giving serious thought to what might result. He would have criticized both superpowers for entering into costly wars that they should have known were unwinnable.

A, B, and D. In Source III, Karl von Clausewitz does not condemn foreign intervention as selfish, defend the principle of national sovereignty, or mention superpower confrontations.

59. B

Since the end of the Cold War, the two superpowers have entered into disarmament talks and agreements. The issue of how far they should go in this regard continues to be seriously debated in both the USA and Russia. Nuclear proliferation is another major concern in the New World Order. In the 1990's, several nations attempted to acquire nuclear weapons or nuclear weapons capabilities. For instance, the most recent example of proliferation was the development and testing of nuclear weapons by Pakistan in 1997. There is a heated debate in the international community about whether more nations should be allowed to join the "nuclear club."

A, C, and D. The collapse of communism in the USSR brought an end to the ideological tensions that were at the heart of the Cold War conflict. Improved relations between Russia and the United States has made Cold War terms such as *brinkmanship, escalation, détente, peaceful coexistence, deterrence, and containment* less relevant.

60. A

The focus of the quotation is the Marshall Plan (the European Recovery Program of 1947–52)—a program of American financial aid for war-torn Europe. The author suggests that the United States used the plan to gain economic supremacy in the European market.

B. Keeping Western European countries within the capitalist world was not a primary aim of the UN in the years immediately after the Second World War.

C. Although the NATO alliance was designed to contain communism—it was primarily a military alliance—not an economic program.

D. The Common Market (a.k.a., the European Economic Community) was established in 1958. The USA was not a member of this economic organization.

61. C

The author feels that the national sovereignty (independence) of European states was threatened by the Marshall Plan. He believes that the plan made European countries too dependent on American goods and services. He suggests that Europeans were surrendering control over their own national economies to banks, corporations, and investors from the USA.

A, B, and D. The author makes no mention of concerns about global prosperity, national prestige, or international cooperation.

62. C

The crushing of the Prague Spring liberalization movement in Czechoslovakia caused an increase in tensions between the superpowers. Détente is "an easing of tension between states."

A. Refusing to ratify the Treaty of Versailles—a treaty that included the League of Nations Covenant—is consistent with isolationism (withdrawal from or non-participation in the affairs of other countries).

B. NATO was a military alliance designed to defend Western Europe against Soviet aggression. It was, therefore, designed for containment (restricting the territorial growth or ideological influence of a hostile nation).

D. SDI was an American defence system intended to protect the USA from the long-range nuclear missiles (ICBMs) of the USSR. A deterrent is anything that discourages an enemy from attacking. The SDI missile screen, had it ever been developed, would probably have deterred a Soviet ICBM attack—because such an attack would have been blocked and closely followed by a retaliatory strike of American nuclear missiles. SDI also promised to deter the Soviets from launching a preemptive first-strike with ICBMs.

63. B

Speaker II recommends increased support for collective security. Collective security is "a policy or principle of international relations, designed to preserve world peace, according to which countries collectively guarantee the security of individual countries." At the present time, this concept is most closely associated with the United Nations Organization and its peacekeeping efforts. Peacekeeping is "the maintenance of international peace and security by the UN through military force."

A. NORAD is a military alliance for protecting Canada and the USA from an enemy aerospace attack; NORAD is not a UN body.

C and D. Speaker III recommends a policy of military isolationism—not supranationalism; the UN is a supranational organization. Speaker IV recommends forging a new alliance system rather than relying on collective security and the UN.

64. C

The two speakers whose views differ the most are speakers II and III. Speaker II supports the UN and the principles of collective security, internationalism and supranationalism. Speaker III is an isolationist; he wants to remove his country from alliances and commitments with other nations.

A. Speakers I and II both support involvement in a supranational organization.

B. Speakers I and IV both support membership in alliances.

D. Speaker III is an isolationist. Speaker IV is a supporter of supranationalism, but not of internationalism; he is only concerned about an alliance for Western security—not global security. The gulf between Speaker II's internationalism and Speaker III's isolationism is greater than the gulf between Speaker IV's supranationalism and Speaker III's isolationism.

65. C

Post-1989 political and territorial changes in Eastern Europe include the break-ups of Czechoslovakia, Yugoslavia,and USSR. A number of new nation-states have been formed as a result of the disintegration of these states—Russia, Ukraine, Latvia, Lithuania, Estonia, the Czech Republic, Slovakia, Slovenia, Bosnia, Croatia, etc.. Ethnic nationalism was the force that broke down the three multi-national states into these independent nation-states. The same force has been transforming the map of other continents— particularly that of Asia.

A. Support for socialism has significantly declined in Eastern Europe since 1989.

B. The USSR's sphere of influence in Eastern Europe was lost in 1989 and the Soviet superpower itself ceased to exist in 1991. There has been no subsequent restoration of a Russian sphere of influence in Eastern Europe.

D. Democracy, not authoritarianism, has been on the rise in Eastern Europe and other parts of the globe since 1989.

66. D

The proposals in Source II do not address the root cause of terrorism (which Source I identifies as injustice).

A, B, and C. Those who believe that the best means of combating terrorism is to combat injustice would not have misgivings about the Source II proposals because of the reasons given.

67. A

The term injustice refers to "any violation of the rights of others." Political oppression (the unjust persecution of individuals because of their political beliefs) is a form of injustice. The message assumes that injustice is the root cause of terrorism.

B, C, and D. The cartoon does not suggest that terrorism is caused by insufficient policing—or that terrorism is a major cause of ethnic conflict or unfairness in the global community.

68. D

In the 1990's, Russia reacted very negatively to NATO's recruitment of former Warsaw Pact member-states such as Hungary, Poland, and Czechoslovakia.

A, B, and C. Russia did not have any serious reservations about the European monetary union, the UN's selection of Kofi Annan for Secretary General, or the efforts to promote free trade in the Western Hemisphere.

69. C

The UN's supervision of the Iran–Iraq ceasefire is a classic example of peacekeeping. Peacekeeping is "the maintenance of international peace and security by the UN through military force." Involvement in any peacekeeping mission demonstrates a commitment to the principle of collective security. Collective security is "a policy or principle of international relations, designed to preserve world peace, according to which countries collectively guarantee the security of individual countries."

A, B and D. The efforts of Canada's UN peacekeepers in the Middle East do not demonstrate Canada's commitment to global prosperity, its own national security, or international equality. The Canadian peacekeepers were simply trying to prevent hostilities from breaking out again between Iraq and Iran.

70. D

An internationalist is devoted to the principle of cooperation among nations, for the promotion of their common good. Internationalists also support internationalist organizations, such as the UN, that work for the general benefit of the human race. Consequently, he would most likely favour a UN-brokered and -supervised peace process.

A, B, and C. An internationalist would not support Serbian domination of other Balkan peoples or unilateral intervention by a major military power. An internationalist would promote collective security and international peacekeeping as the best means of promoting and preserving world peace.

KEY STRATEGIES FOR SUCCESS ON EXAMS

Success on Exams

KEY STRATEGIES FOR SUCCESS ON EXAMS

There are many different ways to assess your knowledge and understanding of course concepts. Depending on the subject, your knowledge and skills are most often assessed through a combination of methods which may include performances, demonstrations, projects, products, and oral and written tests. Written exams are one of the most common methods currently used in schools. Just as there are some study strategies that help you to improve your academic performance, there are also some test writing strategies that may help you to do better on unit test and year-end exams. To do your best on any test, you need to be well prepared. You must know the course content and be as familiar as possible with the manner in which it is usually tested. Applying test writing strategies may help you to become more successful on exams, improve your grades, and achieve your potential.

🕮 STUDY OPTIONS FOR EXAM PREPARATION

Studying and preparing for exams requires a strong sense of self-discipline. Sometimes having a study buddy or joining a study group

- helps you to stick to your study schedule
- ensures you have others with whom you can practice making and answering sample questions
- clarifies information and provides peer support

It may be helpful to use a combination of individual study, working with a study buddy, or joining a study group to prepare for your unit test or year-end exam. Be sure that the study buddy or group you choose to work with is positive, knowledgeable, motivated, and supportive. Working with a study buddy or a study group usually means you have to begin your exam preparation earlier than you would if you are studying independently.

Tutorial classes are often helpful in preparing for exams. You can ask a knowledgeable student to tutor you or you can hire a private tutor. Sometimes school jurisdictions or individual schools may offer tutorials and study sessions to assist students in preparing for exams. Tutorial services are also offered by companies that specialize in preparing students for exams. Information regarding tutorial services is usually available from school counsellors, local telephone directories, and on-line search engines.

Exam Question Formats

There is no substitute for knowing the course content. To do well in your course you need to combine your subject knowledge and understanding with effective test writing skills. Being familiar with question formats may help you in preparing for quizzes, unit tests or year-end exams. The most typical question formats include multiple choice, numerical response, written response, and essay. The following provides a brief description of each format and suggestions for how you might consider responding to each of the formats.

Multiple Choice

A multiple choice question provides some information for you to consider and then requires you to select a response from four choices, often referred to as distracters. The distracters may complete a statement, be a logical extension or application of the information. In preparing for multiple choice questions you may wish to focus on:

- studying concepts, theories, groups of facts or ideas that are similar in meaning; **compare and contrast their similarities and differences**; ask yourself "How do the concepts differ?", "Why is the difference important?", "What does each fact or concept mean or include?" "What are the exceptions?"
- **identifying main ideas, key information**, formulas, concepts, and theories, where they apply and what the **exceptions** are
- memorizing important definitions, examples, and applications of key concepts
- learning to **recognize *distracters*** that may lead you to apply plausible but incorrect solutions, and ***three and one splits*** where one answer is obviously incorrect and the others are very similar in meaning or wording
- **using active reading techniques** such as underlining, highlighting, numbering, and circling important facts, dates, basic points
- making up your own multiple choice questions for practice

NUMERICAL RESPONSE

A numerical response question provides information and requires you to use a calculation to arrive at the response. In preparing for numerical response questions you may wish to focus on:

- memorizing formulas and their applications
- completing chapter questions or making up your own for practice
- making a habit of **estimating the answer** prior to completing the calculation
- paying special **attention to accuracy** in computing and the use of significant digits where applicable

WRITTEN RESPONSE

A written response question requires you to respond to a question or directive such as "explain", "compare", contrast". In preparing for written response questions you may wish to focus on:

- ensuring your response **answers the question**
- recognizing **directing words** such as "list", "explain", "define"
- providing **concise answers** within the time limit you are devoting to the written response section of the exam
- identifying subject content that lends itself to short answer questions

ESSAY

An essay is a lengthier written response requiring you to identify your position on an issue and provide logical thinking or evidence that supports the basis of your argument. In preparing for an essay you may wish to focus on:

- examining **issues** that are relevant or related to the subject area or **application of the concept**
- comparing and contrasting two points of view, articles, or theories
- considering the merits of the opposite point of view
- identifying **key concepts**, principles or ideas
- providing **evidence**, examples, and **supporting information** for your viewpoint
- preparing two or three essays on probable topics
- **writing an outline** and essay within the defined period of time you will have for the exam
- understanding the "marker's expectations"

KEY TIPS FOR ANSWERING COMMON EXAM QUESTION FORMATS

Most exams use a variety of question formats to test your understanding. You must provide responses to questions ranging from lower level, information recall types to higher level, critical thinking types. The following information provides you with some suggestions on how to prepare for answering multiple choice, written response and essay questions.

MULTIPLE CHOICE

Multiple choice questions often require you to make fine distinctions between correct and nearly correct answers so it is imperative that you:

- begin by answering only the questions for which you are certain of the correct answer
- read the question stem and formulate your own response before you read the choices available
- read the directions carefully paying close attention to words such as "mark ***all*** correct", "choose the ***most*** correct" and "choose the ***one best*** answer"
- use active reading techniques such as underlining, circling, or highlighting critical words and phrases
- watch for superlatives such as "all", "every", "none", "always" which indicate that the correct response must be an undisputed fact
- watch for negatives such as "none", "never", "neither", "not" which indicate that the correct response must be an undisputed fact
- examine all of the alternatives in questions which include "all of the above" or "none of the above" as responses to ensure that "all" or "none" of the statements apply *totally*
- be aware of distracters that may lead you to apply plausible but incorrect solutions, and 'three and one splits' where one answer is obviously incorrect and the others are very similar in meaning or wording
- use information from other questions to help you
- eliminate the responses you know are wrong and then assess the remaining alternatives and choose the best one
- guess if you are not certain

WRITTEN RESPONSE

Written response questions usually require a very specific answer. In answering these questions you should:

- underline key words or phrases that indicate what is required in your answer such as "three reasons", "list", or "give an example"
- write down rough, point-form notes regarding the information you want to include in your answer
- be brief and only answer what is asked
- reread your response to ensure you have answered the question
- use the appropriate subject vocabulary and terminology in your response
- use point form to complete as many questions as possible if you are running out of time

ESSAY

Essay questions often give you the opportunity to demonstrate the breadth and depth of your learning regarding a given topic. In responding to these questions it may be helpful to:

- read the question carefully and underline key words and phrases
- make a brief outline to organize the flow of the information and ideas you want to include in your response
- ensure you have an introduction, body, and conclusion
- begin with a clear statement of your view, position, or interpretation of the question
- address only one main point or key idea in each paragraph and include relevant supporting information and examples
- assume the reader has no prior knowledge of your topic
- conclude with a strong summary statement
- use appropriate subject vocabulary and terminology when and where it is applicable
- review your essay for clarity of thought, logic, grammar, punctuation, and spelling
- write as legibly as you can
- double space your work in case you need to edit it when you proof read your essay
- complete the essay in point form if you run short of time

KEY TIPS FOR RESPONDING TO COMMON 'DIRECTING' WORDS

There are some commonly used words in exam questions that require you to respond in a predetermined or expected manner. The following provides you with a brief summary of how you may wish to plan your response to exam questions that contain these words.

- **EVALUATE** (to assess the worth of something)
  - Determine the use, goal, or ideal from which you can judge something's worth
  - Make a value judgment or judgments on something
  - Make a list of reasons for the judgment
  - Develop examples, evidence, contrasts, and details to support your judgments and clarify your reasoning

- **DISCUSS** (usually to give pros and cons regarding an assertion, quotation, or policy)
  - Make a list of bases for comparing and contrasting
  - Develop details and examples to support or clarify each pro and con
  - On the basis of your lists, conclude your response by stating the extent to which you agree or disagree with what is asserted

- **COMPARE AND CONTRAST** (to give similarities and differences of two or more objects, beliefs, or positions)
  - Make a list of bases for comparing and contrasting
  - For each basis, judge similarities and differences
  - Supply details, evidence, and examples that support and clarify your judgment
  - Assess the overall similarity or difference
  - Determine the significance of similarity or difference in connection with the purpose of the comparison

- **ANALYZE** (to break into parts)
  - Break the topic, process, procedure, or object of the essay into its major parts
  - Connect and write about the parts according to the direction of the question: describe, explain, criticize

- **CRITICIZE** (to judge strong and weak points of something)
  - Make a list of the strong points and weak points

- Develop details, examples, and contrasts to support judgments
- Make an overall judgment of quality

- **EXPLAIN** (to show causes of or reasons for something)
  - In Science, usually show the process that occurs in moving from one state or phase in a process to the next, thoroughly presenting details of each step
  - In Humanities and often in Social Sciences, make a list of factors that influence something, developing evidence for each factor's potential influence

- **DESCRIBE** (to give major features of something)
  - Pick out highlights or major aspects of something
  - Develop details and illustrations to give a clear picture

- **ARGUE** (to give reasons for one position and against another)
  - Make a list of reasons for the position
  - Make a list of reasons against the position
  - Refute objections to your reasons for and defend against objections to your reasons opposing the position
  - Fill out reasons, objections, and replies with details, examples, consequences, and logical connections

- **COMMENT** (to make statements about something)
  - Calls for a position, discussion, explanation, judgment, or evaluation regarding a subject, idea, or situation
  - Is strengthened by providing supporting evidence, information, and examples

- **DEMONSTRATE** (to show something)
  - Depending upon the nature of the subject matter, provide evidence, clarify the logical basis of something, appeal to principles or laws as in an explanation, supply a range of opinion and examples

- **SYNTHESIZE** (to invent a new or different version)
  - Construct your own meaning based upon your knowledge and experiences
  - Support your assertion with examples, references to literature and research studies

(Source: http://www.counc.ivic.ca/learn/program/hndouts/simple.html)

TEST ANXIETY

Do you get test anxiety? Most students feel some level of stress, worry, or anxiety before an exam. Feeling a little tension or anxiety before or during an exam is normal for most students. A little stress or tension may help you rise to the challenge but too much stress or anxiety interferes with your ability to do well on the exam. Test anxiety may cause you to experience some of the following in a mild or more severe form:

- "butterflies" in your stomach, sweating, shortness of breath, or a quickened pulse
- disturbed sleep or eating patterns
- increased nervousness, fear, or irritability
- sense of hopelessness or panic
- drawing a "blank" during the exam

If you experience extreme forms of test anxiety you need to consult your family physician. For milder forms of anxiety you may find some of the following strategies effective in helping you to remain calm and focused during your unit tests or year-end exams.

- Acknowledge that you are feeling some stress or test anxiety and that this is normal
- Focus upon your breathing, taking several deep breaths
- Concentrate upon a single object for a few moments
- Tense and relax the muscles in areas of your body where you feel tension
- Break your exam into smaller, manageable, achievable parts
- Use positive self-talk to calm and motivate yourself. Tell yourself, "I can do this if I read carefully/start with the easy questions/focus on what I know/stick with it/. . ." instead of saying, "I can't do this."
- Visualize your successful completion of your review or the exam
- Recall a time in the past when you felt calm, relaxed, and content. Replay this experience in your mind experiencing it as fully as possible.

KEY STRATEGIES FOR SUCCESS BEFORE AN EXAM – A CHECKLIST

Review, review, review. That's a huge part of your exam preparation. Here's a quick review checklist for you to see how many strategies for success you are using as you prepare to write your unit tests and year-end exams.

KEY Strategies for Success Before an Exam	***Yes***	***No***
Have you been attending classes?		
Have you determined your learning style?		
Have you organized a quiet study area for yourself?		
Have you developed a long-term study schedule?		
Have you developed a short-term study schedule?		
Are you working with a study buddy or study group?		
Is your study buddy/group positive, knowledgeable, motivated and supportive?		
Have you registered in tutorial classes?		
Have you developed your exam study notes?		
Have you reviewed previously administered exams?		
Have you practiced answering multiple choice, numerical response, written response, and essay questions?		
Have you analyzed the most common errors students make on each subject exam?		
Have you practiced strategies for controlling your exam anxiety?		
Have you maintained a healthy diet and sleep routine?		
Have you participated in regular physical activity?		

KEY STRATEGIES FOR SUCCESS DURING AN EXAM

Doing well on any exam requires that you prepare in advance by reviewing your subject material and then using your knowledge to respond effectively to the exam questions during the test session. Combining subject knowledge with effective test writing skills gives you the best opportunity for success. The following are some strategies you may find useful in writing your exam.

- Managing Test Anxiety
    - Be as prepared as possible to increase your self-confidence.
    - Arrive at the exam on time and bring whatever materials you need to complete the exam such as pens, pencils, erasers, and calculators if they are allowed.
    - Drink enough water before you begin the exam so you are hydrated.
    - Associate with positive, calm individuals until you enter the exam room.
    - Use positive self-talk to calm yourself.
    - Remind yourself that it is normal to feel anxious about the exam.
    - Visualize your successful completion of the exam.
    - Breathe deeply several times.
    - Rotate your head, shrug your shoulders, and change positions to relax.

- While the information from your crib notes is still fresh in your memory, write down the key words, concepts, definitions, theories or formulas on the back of the test paper before you look at the exam questions.
    - Review the entire exam.
    - Budget your time.
    - Begin with the easiest question or the question that you know you can answer correctly rather than following the numerical question order of the exam.
    - Be aware of linked questions and use the clues to help you with other questions or in other parts of the exam.

If you "blank" on the exam, try repeating the deep breathing and physical relaxation activities first. Then move to visualization and positive self-talk to get you going. You can also try to open the 'information flow' by writing down anything that you remember about the subject on the reverse side of your exam paper. This activity sometimes helps you to remind yourself that you <u>do</u> know something and you are capable of writing the exam.

GETTING STARTED

MANAGING YOUR TIME

- Plan on staying in the exam room for the full time that is available to you.
- Review the entire exam and calculate how much time you can spend on each section. Write your time schedule on the top of your paper and stick as closely as possible to the time you have allotted for each section of the exam.
- Be strategic and use your time where you will get the most marks. Avoid spending too much time on challenging questions that are not worth more marks than other questions that may be easier and are worth the same number of marks.
- If you are running short of time, switch to point form and write as much as you can for written response and essay questions so you have a chance of receiving partial marks.
- Leave time to review your paper asking yourself, "Did I do all of the questions I was supposed to do?", "Can I answer any questions now that I skipped over before?", "Are there any questions that I misinterpreted or misread?"

USING THE FIVE PASS METHOD

- **BROWSING STAGE** – Scan the entire exam noting the format, the specific instructions and marks allotted for each section, which questions you will complete and which ones you will omit if there is a choice.
- **THE FIRST ANSWERING PASS** – To gain confidence and momentum, answer only the questions you are confident you can answer correctly and quickly. These questions are most often found in the multiple choice or numerical response sections of the exam. Maintain a brisk pace; if a question is taking too long to answer, leave it for the Second or Third Pass.
- **THE SECOND ANSWERING PASS** – This Pass addresses questions which require more effort per mark. Answer as many of the remaining questions as possible while maintaining steady progress toward a solution. As soon as it becomes evident the question is too difficult or is tasking an inordinate amount of time, leave it for the Third Answering Pass.
- **THE THIRD ANSWERING PASS** – During the Third Answering Pass you should complete all partial solutions from the first two Passes. Marks are produced at a slower rate during this stage. At the end of this stage, all questions should have full or partial answers. Guess at any multiple choice questions that you have not yet answered.
- **THE FINAL REVIEW STAGE** – Use the remaining time to review the entire exam, making sure that no questions have been overlooked. Check answers and calculations as time permits.

USING THE THREE PASS METHOD

- **OVERVIEW** – Begin with an overview of the exam to see what it contains. Look for 'easy' questions and questions on topics that you know thoroughly.
- **SECOND PASS** – Answer all the questions that you can complete without too much trouble. These questions help to build your confidence and establish a positive start.
- **LAST PASS** – Now go through and answer the questions that are left. This is when you begin to try solving the questions you find particularly challenging.

KEY EXAM TIPS FOR SELECTED SUBJECT AREAS

The following are a few additional suggestions you may wish to consider when writing exams in any of the selected subject areas.

ENGLISH LANGUAGE ARTS

Exams in English Language Arts usually have two components, writing and reading. Sometimes students are allowed to bring approved reference books such as a dictionary, thesaurus and writing handbook into the exam. If you have not used these references on a regular basis, you may find them more of a hindrance than a help in an exam situation. In completing the written section of an English Language Arts exam:

- plan your essay
- focus on the issue presented
- establish a clear position using a thesis statement to direct and unify your writing
- organize your writing in a manner that logically presents your views
- support your viewpoint with specific examples
- edit and proof read your writing

In completing the reading section of an English Language Arts exam:

- read the entire selection before responding
- use titles, dates, footnotes, pictures, introductions, and notes on the author to assist you in developing an understanding of the piece presented
- when using line references, read a few lines before and after the identified section

Mathematics

In some instances, the use of calculators is permitted (or required) to complete complex calculations, modeling, simulations, or to demonstrate your use of technology. It is imperative that you are familiar with the approved calculator and the modes you may be using during your exam. In writing exams in mathematics:

- use appropriate mathematical notation and symbols
- clearly show or explain all the steps involved in solving the problem
- check to be sure you have included the correct units of measurement and have rounded to the appropriate significant digit
- use appropriate labelling and equal increments on graphs

Sciences

In the Sciences written response and open-ended questions usually require a clear, organized, and detailed explanation of the science involved in the question. You may find it helpful to use the acronym **STEEPLES** to organize your response to these types of questions. STEEPLES stands for **S**cience, **T**echnological, **E**cological, **E**thical, **P**olitical, **L**egal, **E**conomical, and **S**ocial aspects of the issue presented. In writing exams in the sciences:

- use scientific vocabulary to clearly explain your understanding of the processes or issues
- state your position in an objective manner
- demonstrate your understanding of both sides of the issue
- clearly label graphs, diagrams, tables, and charts using accepted conventions
- provide all formulas and equations

Social Studies, History, Geography

Exams in these courses of study often require you to take a position on an issue and defend your point of view. Your response should demonstrate your understanding of both the positive and negative aspects of the issue and be supported by well-considered arguments and evidence. In writing exams in Social Studies, History or Geography, the following acronyms may be helpful to you in organizing your approach.

- **SEE** – stands for **S**tatement, **E**xplanation, **E**xample. This acronym reminds you to couple your statement regarding your position with an explanation and then an example.

- **PERMS** – stands for **P**olitical, **E**conomic, **R**eligious or moral, **M**ilitary, and **S**ocietal values. Your position statement may be derived from or based upon any of these points of view. Your argument is more credible if you can show that recognized authorities such as leaders, theorists, writers or scientists back your position.

SUMMARY

Writing exams involves a certain amount of stress and anxiety. If you want to do your best on the exam, *there is no substitute for being well prepared.* Being well prepared helps you to feel more confident about your ability to succeed and less anxious about writing tests. In preparing for unit or year-end exams remember to:

- use as many senses as possible in preparing for exams
- start as early as possible set realistic goals and targets
- take advantage of study buddies, study groups, and tutorials
- review previously used exams
- study with positive, knowledgeable, motivated, and supportive individuals
- practice the material in the format in which you are to be tested
- try to simulate the test situation as much as possible
- keep a positive attitude
- end your study time with a quick review and then do something different before you try to go to sleep on the night before the exam
- drink a sufficient amount of water prior to an exam
- stay in the exam room for the full amount of time available
- try to relax by focusing on your breathing

If you combine your best study habits with some of the strategies presented here, you may increase your chances of writing a strong exam and maximizing your potential to do well.

NOTES

DIPLOMA EXAMINATIONS

A Guide to Writing the Diploma Examination

The *Diploma Examination* section contains all of the questions from the June 2001 and January 2002 diploma examinations. The questions presented here are distinct from those in the Unit Review section. It is recommended that students work carefully through these exams as they are reflective of the format and difficulty **level of the final exam that students are likely to encounter**.

THE KEY contains detailed answers that illustrate the problem-solving process for every question in this section.

When writing practice exams, students are encouraged to simulate actual Diploma Exam conditions. This will help students become:

- *aware of the mental and physical stamina required to sit through an entire exam*
- *familiar with the exam format and how the course content is tested*
- *aware of any units or concepts that are troublesome or require additional study*
- *more successful in managing their review effectively*

To simulate the exam conditions, students should:

- *use an alarm clock or other timer to monitor the time allowed for the exam*
- *select a quiet writing spot away from all distractions*
- *place their picture ID on the desk or table where the exam is being written*
- *assemble the appropriate materials that are allowed for writing the exam such as pens, HB pencils, calculator, dictionary*
- *use "test wiseness" skills*
- *complete as much of the exam as possible within the allowable time*

In writing the practice exam, students should:

- *read instructions, directions, and questions carefully*
- *organize writing time according to the exam emphasis on each section*
- *highlight key words*
- *think about what is being asked*
- *plan their writing; once complete, proof for errors in content, spelling, grammar*
- *watch for bolded words such as most, least, best*
- *in multiple-choice questions, cross out any choices students know are incorrect*
- *if possible, review all responses upon completion of the exam*

June 2001 Diploma Examination

1. Which of the following government actions best reflects an emphasis on the promotion of self-reliance and competitiveness in the Canadian economy?

   A. Eliminating subsidies to small independent businesses

   B. Raising the goods and services tax on consumer spending

   C. Nationalizing natural resource production and distribution

   D. Regulating fees charged by Crown corporations

2. Which of the following characteristics would be present in a model public enterprise system?

   A. Investment capital for entrepreneurship

   B. Private ownership of resources

   C. Income inequality

   D. Price stability

Use the following statements to answer question 3.

Statement I	Statement II
The largest single source of revenue for the Government of Canada is taxes levied on the income of corporations.	Generally, in Canada, the rate of taxation on personal income rises as total taxable income increases.

3. Which of the following observations regarding the above statements is correct?

   A. Both statements are true.

   B. Both statements are false.

   C. Statement I is false and Statement II is true.

   D. Statement I is true and Statement II is false.

4. Supporters of a mixed economy argue that governments should attempt to moderate the effects of the "boom-and-bust" business cycle by

   A. raising interest rates during boom periods and raising taxes during recessions

   B. encouraging industrial production during boom periods and during recessions

   C. reducing tax rates during boom periods and restricting investment during recessions

   D. restraining expansion during boom periods and stimulating growth during recessions

Use the following sources to answer questions 5 to 8.

Source I

Selected Arguments For the Welfare State

1. Economic equality is the foundation on which basic freedoms rest. The welfare state can insure a basic economic equality for everyone.
2. Society has a moral responsibility to provide a minimum subsistence level for those citizens who are not able to provide it for themselves.
3. The welfare state represents a "compromise system" midway between an authoritarian government that satisfies everyone's minimum economic needs and a capitalistic system that leaves this task solely to the individual's initiative and ability. . . .
6. The sickness of any member of a society will adversely affect the whole society. For this reason, it is in society's best interests to help individuals in need of assistance.

Source II

Selected Arguments Against the Welfare State

1. The government has no right to give away the tax dollars of hard working people to those who are unable or unwilling to work.
2. Individual citizen's qualities of initiative and ambition will be destroyed in a "something for nothing society." . . .
5. The welfare state is incompatible with democracy and may lead to socialism or communism or some other form of totalitarian government.
6. The welfare state will foster an immense bureaucratic monster that will be buried in its own red tape.

Source III

—all sources from *The Welfare State: Opposing Viewpoints*

5. Which of the following issues is raised by these sources?
   - **A.** Should governments encourage individual incentive through welfare programs?
   - **B.** To what extent should governments regulate profit-oriented economic production and distribution?
   - **C.** Should governments assume responsibility for the economically disadvantaged?
   - **D.** To what extent should governments be responsible for maintaining the stability of an economy?

6. The belief that human activity is best served by the principles of the marketplace is suggested by
   - **A.** Source I
   - **B.** Source II
   - **C.** both sources I and II
   - **D.** neither Source I nor Source II

7. A neoconservative would agree with the suggestion in the cartoon that the welfare state is a demoralizing force because in a welfare state,
   - **A.** recipients of welfare may lose the initiative to provide for their own needs
   - **B.** the state should provide financial support for all citizens rather than just welfare recipients
   - **C.** welfare payments cannot provide the financial resources necessary to maintain an acceptable quality of life
   - **D.** the private sector has a moral obligation to provide employment for all members of the labour force despite the additional production costs

8. The arguments in Source II represent the views of someone traditionally associated with which position on the economic spectrum?

   A. Ultra left-wing

   B. Ultra right-wing

   C. Slightly left of centre

   D. Slightly right of centre

9. Adam Smith argued that collusion and agreement among producers of the same product to artificially raise selling prices would be

   A. acceptable, as long as such actions occurred in a market economy

   B. acceptable, as long as the government regulated the quality of the product

   C. unacceptable because the government has the right to determine market prices

   D. unacceptable because such actions interfered in the functioning of a free market

Use the following information to answer questions 10 and 11.

Perceived Advantages of an Economic System

- Individuals use their spending power to influence the production of goods and services.
- Economic freedom allows individuals to make their own decisions in the marketplace.
- Unrestricted competition guarantees the quality of goods and controls prices.
- Profits and tax exemptions provide business owners with the incentive to improve productivity and expand the workforce.

10. A Marxist would argue that these "Perceived Advantages"

    A. encourage individual greed rather than egalitarianism

    B. exploit the middle class to the benefit of the working class

    C. establish an equality of income that restricts individual initiative

    D. encourage government nationalization rather than increased entrepreneurship

11. These "Perceived Advantages" would be supported **most strongly** by

    A. Communist party supporters in China

    B. democratic socialist voters in Sweden

    C. Labour party supporters in Great Britain

    D. conservative economists in the United States

12. Which of the following statements identifies a dilemma faced by many democratic socialists during the Cold War?

    A. They were sympathetic to the American system of government and Soviet economic planning, yet hostile to American capitalism and Soviet dictatorship.

    B. They favoured using peaceful methods to achieve some economic goals, yet accepted violence to achieve others.

    C. They favoured privatizing primary industries but opposed nationalizing certain key industries.

    D. They were critical of the welfare state but supportive of the Soviet Union's centrally planned economy.

Use the following graph to answer questions 13 and 14.

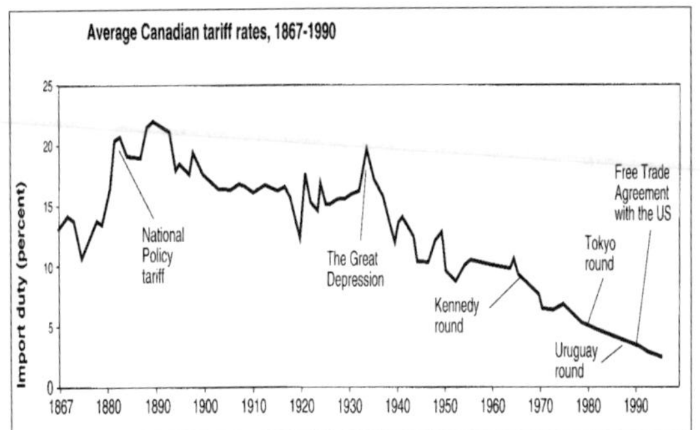

— from *Economics: A Canadian Perspective*

13. The trend indicated in the graph suggests that Canadian trade has become more

A. protectionist in nature

B. subject to currency fluctuations

C. integrated with other economies

D. dependent on world commodity prices

14. The graph provides information that supports the conclusion that government tariff policy since the Depression era has encouraged Canadian manufacturers to

A. rely more on domestic sales and less on the export market

B. become more competitive with producers in other nations

C. rely more heavily on foreign sources for resource materials

D. become more dependent on capital goods production

15. Government decisions to grant tax breaks to corporations, to ease restrictive regulations in the private sector, and to privatize state assets would **most likely** occur in

A. an economy based on public enterprise principles

B. a mixed economy using supply-side mechanisms

C. an economy based on social democratic principles

D. a command economy employing demand-side policies

Use the following editorial excerpt to answer questions 16 to 18.

If [governments are] looking for a road map [to economic recovery], they could do worse than to return to the old economics. The Americans [have started] to. Many of [Clinton's] key economists . . . grew up with the old economics. ... It goes like this: governments should spend when the economy is bad, and restrain spending when the economy is good.

Many western countries got into trouble because they kept on spending when the times were good....

It is not too late to return to what once worked. ... [Galbraith* recently stated], "The tendency of the modern market economy to periods of despondency and depression must be specifically addressed.... This requires positive government intervention."...

How should governments intervene? "Lower interest rates may help, but there is no magic in monetary policy ... In times of recession governments must move aggressively to employ people [and relieve] economic distress. ... Then, when recovery is assured, there must be the discipline that brings restraint and allows the reduction of government expenditure."

— John Kenneth Galbraith,
Canadian-born economist
—from *The Edmonton Journal*

16. In the excerpt, what is meant by the "old economics"?

A. Classical liberal theories

B. Laissez-faire theories

C. Supply-side theories

D. Keynesian theories

17. The concept in this editorial that would **most** alarm supporters of " 'the modern market economy' " is that of

    A. " 'positive government intervention' "

    B. " 'Lower interest rates' "

    C. " 'monetary policy' "

    D. " 'reduction of government expenditure' "

18. Since the 1980s, Western governments have had difficulties following Galbraith's advice to " 'move aggressively' " because of

    A. shortages of available investment capital

    B. the lack of initiative in a security-minded workforce

    C. pressure from the electorate to raise taxes on corporations

    D. the necessity of reducing accumulated budget deficits and debt loads

Use the following information to answer questions 19 and 20.

Various Political and Economic Beliefs

1. Economies should be planned and regulated by the state.
2. The principles of the free market should be promoted.
3. International economic agencies should regulate world trade.
4. Government intervention in an economy should be kept to a minimum.
5. Radical reform should be used to correct the abuses of capitalism.
6. The right of individuals to own property should be protected.
7. The rights of the collective should be preserved at all costs.

19. The beliefs that are consistent with moderate right-wing ideologies are

    A. beliefs 2, 4, and 6

    B. beliefs 1, 3, and 5

    C. beliefs 2, 6, and 7

    D. beliefs 1, 4, and 5

20. The beliefs that are consistent with the ideas of Marxist–Leninists are

    A. beliefs 2, 3, and 6

    B. beliefs 1, 5, and 7

    C. beliefs 2, 4, and 7

    D beliefs 4, 5, and 6

21. *Only a few people possess the intelligence and ability to rule effectively.*

    A fascist would support this generalization by rationalizing that

    A. the state must be concerned with community and family values rather than the selfish goals of a few individuals

    B. peoples' beliefs and opinions should be widely disseminated to encourage social cohesion and participation

    C. the state must recognize and allow for the basic fact of human nature that only the strong survive

    D. the privileges of the individual must prevail over the collective welfare of society

Use the following cartoons to answer questions 22 to 24.

Source I

—from *World Press Review*

Source II

—from *The Globe and Mail*

22. The focus of these cartoons from the early 1990s is the

- **A.** changing political landscape in eastern Europe
- **B.** growing popularity of left-wing doctrines in western Europe
- **C.** strong condemnation of capitalism as a workable system in formerly communist economies
- **D.** diminishing appeal of proportional representation as an alternative to one-party totalitarianism

23. Which of the following nations have resisted the ideological shifts referred to in these two sources?

- **A.** Poland and the Czech Republic
- **B.** North Korea and Cuba
- **C.** Iraq and Saudi Arabia
- **D.** Albania and Romania

24. The assumption underlying both sources is the belief that

- **A.** popular movements in former communist countries have been focused more on national unity than on political stability
- **B.** totalitarian socialist practices have been strongly condemned by right-wing extremist youth
- **C.** Marxist-Leninist theories have been criticized unfairly
- **D.** extreme leftist ideals have lost their appeal

25. According to democratic theory, active interest groups and a free press ensure that

- **A.** tyranny of the majority is prevented
- **B.** minority rights do not become entrenched
- **C.** bureaucratic decisions are given greater credibility
- **D.** elections reflect the wishes of mainstream political parties

26. Extreme political right-wing reactionaries and left-wing radicals would agree with which of the following aspects of societal change?

- **A.** Change is needed to improve the lives of the economically disadvantaged.
- **B.** Political power and authority must eventually rest in the hands of all citizens.
- **C.** Violence may be necessary if there are forces that resist proposed changes.
- **D.** A new society must eliminate all traditional elements of the society it has replaced.

Use the following graph to answer questions 27 and 28.

The Changing Political Landscape in Nation X:

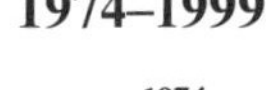

1974–1999

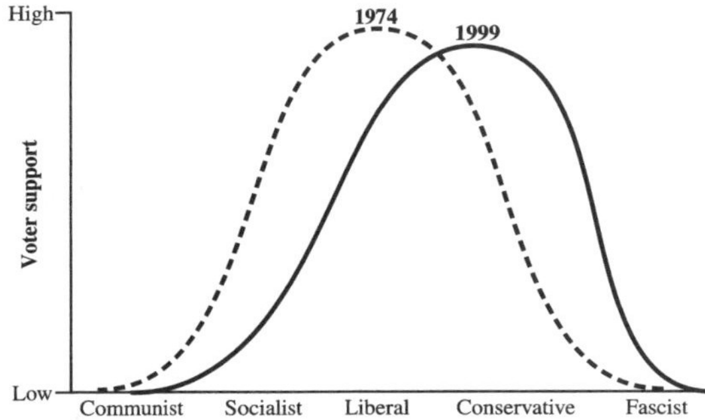

27. In 1999, most citizens of Nation X would **likely** have voted for political parties that promised

A. less government intervention in the economy

B. less opportunity for workers to be exploited

C. higher taxes on large corporations

D. increased welfare benefits for all

28. The information provided by the graph supports the conclusion that in Nation X,

A. public interest in political issues has declined

B. a movement toward reforming the electoral system has occurred

C. a shift in the social values held by the general population has occurred

D. the number of diverse political parties vying for power has increased

Use the following chart to answer question 29.

Proposal	Expected Benefit	Possible Negative Result
Canada should adopt an electoral system of proportional representation.	Political party representation in Parliament will more accurately reflect voter preference.	?

29. Which of the following statements completes the chart?

A. New laws will reflect the beliefs of an elite group.

B. Voter choice will be reduced as a result of fewer political parties.

C. Elections will occur more frequently if parties fail to win a majority vote.

D. Citizens will become more apathetic about politics, leading to low voter turnout.

Use the following excerpt to answer question 30.

The threat to individual liberties from the whims of the majority has traditionally provided a justification for the ruling classes to restrict the right to vote to their own circle. For centuries British Members of Parliament were elected by the small fraction of the population which met the voting qualification of owning a large amount of property. The laws were such that only men with private wealth or access to government patronage could afford to sit in Parliament.

— from *Royal Bank Letter*

30. The system described in this excerpt provides a historical example of

A. an aristocracy with a coalition government

B. an oligarchy with limited franchise

C. a minority government

D. a direct democracy

31. In Canada, an action that would represent a movement away from the practice of traditional representative democracy and movement toward the practice of direct democracy would be

A. a prime minister calling for a national referendum to determine government policy on the abortion issue

B. the House of Commons amending a private member's bill on abortion

C. a prime minister allowing members of Parliament to vote by conscience on a controversial abortion bill

D. an anti-abortion group disrupting question period in the House of Commons

32. Which of the following statements describes the functions of the legislative, judicial, and executive branches of government in a democracy?

A. The legislative branch suggests the law, the judicial branch enforces the law, and the executive branch applies the law.

B. The legislative branch administers the law, the judicial branch makes the law, and the executive branch carries out the law.

C. The legislative branch passes the law, the judicial branch interprets the law, and the executive branch carries out the law.

D. The legislative branch interprets the law, the judicial branch applies the law, and the executive branch develops and passes the law.

Use the following information to answer question 33.

Selected Socioeconomic Conditions

- Political instability and extremism
- Homelessness and extreme poverty
- Rampant inflation and unemployment
- Currency devaluation and market collapse
- Organized crime and political corruption

33. The "Socioeconomic Conditions" listed above are characteristic of

A. Great Britain during the 1920s

B. Canada in the 1930s

C. West Germany in the 1980s

D. Russia during the 1990s

Use the following charts to answer question 34.

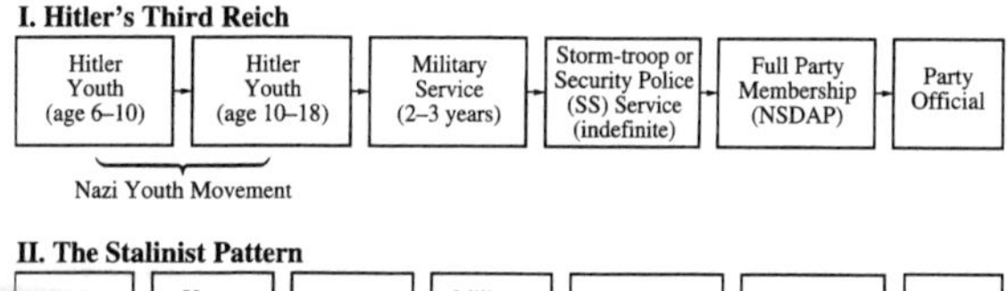

—from *Ideologies in World Affairs*

34. Which technique of dictatorship is illustrated in the charts above?

A. Purging dissidents

B. Terrorizing opponents

C. Scapegoating enemies

D. Indoctrinating supporters

35. The popular appeal of fascism in both Italy and Germany during the interwar years can be attributed largely to the emphasis fascist ideology placed on

A. racial discrimination

B. ultranationalistic fervour

C. isolationist foreign policies

D. class struggle between rich and poor

Use the following map to answer questions 36 and 37.

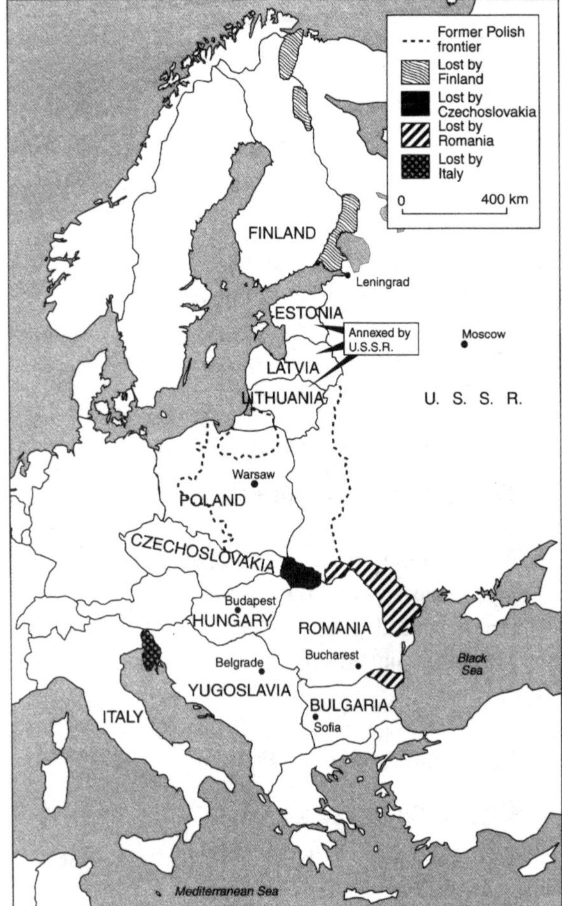

36. This map indicates major frontier changes in eastern Europe that resulted from the

A. First World War

B. Nazi–Soviet Pact

C. Second World War

D. end of the Cold War

37. Most of the nations shown to have lost territory did so **primarily** because of their

A. proximity to the Soviet Union

B. dissatisfied national minorities

C. authoritarian communist governments

D. refusal to pay reparations to the United States

Use the following quotation to answer questions 38 and 39.

There shall be no annexations, no contributions, no punitive damages. Peoples are not to be handed about from one sovereignty to another by an international conference or an understanding between rivals and antagonists. National aspirations must be respected; peoples may now be dominated and governed only by their own consent. . . . [This] is an imperative principle of actions which statesmen will henceforth ignore at their peril.

—President Woodrow Wilson's address to Congress, February 11, 1918

38. The "imperative principle" that Wilson was referring to is

A. open diplomacy

B. self-determination

C. collective security

D. national expansion

39. The idea that "Peoples are not to be handed about from one sovereignty to another" was **most clearly** disregarded in 1919 with the creation of

A. Austria

B. Finland

C. the Baltic states

D. the Polish Corridor

40. The optimism that greeted the League of Nations at its inception was shattered when the organization failed to fulfill its mandate and control the

A. imperialist tendencies of fascist dictators

B. domestic human rights abuses in Nazi Germany

C. economic consequences of the Great Depression

D. isolationist foreign policies of several great powers

Use the following information to answer questions 41 and 42.

Developments in Great Britain During the Interwar Years, 1919 to 1939

- Strong pacifist movements opposed involvement in European affairs.
- Many British leaders felt that the peace treaties following the First World War dealt too harshly with the defeated powers.
- The economic disaster of the Great Depression led to large cuts in military spending.
- Public opinion was strongly against military confrontation.

41. These developments encouraged the British government to adopt a foreign policy of

A. appeasing fascist demands

B. deterring communist expansion

C. supporting American isolationism

D. withdrawing from continental affairs

42. These developments created a climate that fostered public support for Great Britain's signing of the

A. Treaty of Versailles

B. Balfour Declaration

C. Yalta Agreement

D. Munich Accord

43. The League of Nations' imposition of economic sanctions to punish Italy for its invasion of Abyssinia influenced Mussolini's decision to

A. withdraw his troops from East Africa

B. form an alliance with Nazi Germany

C. remain neutral during the interwar years

D. support fascism as an alternative to democracy

44. The governments of Great Britain and France maintained a policy of non-intervention in the Spanish Civil War in the hope that the

A. conflict would remain contained to Spain

B. fascist rebels would achieve victory in Spain

C. League of Nations would declare a ceasefire in Spain

D. Republican government of Spain would maintain legitimacy

Use the following excerpt to answer question 45.

. . . the two factors which were probably decisive for the League's final failure were the lack of universality in its membership and the reluctance even to consider the use of force. [The latter] was understandable enough after the slaughter of the [First World War], but it was a fatal weakness. In the [UN] Charter we have tried to learn from this experience.

—from *Vital Speeches of the Day, 1951*

45. The ability of the United Nations to "learn from this experience" has been undermined by the

A. voting procedures in the General Assembly

B. creation of a bureaucracy to act upon major decisions

C. provision of a veto for permanent members of the Security Council

D. creation of special agencies to coordinate and administer humanitarian projects

Use the following diagram to answer question 46.

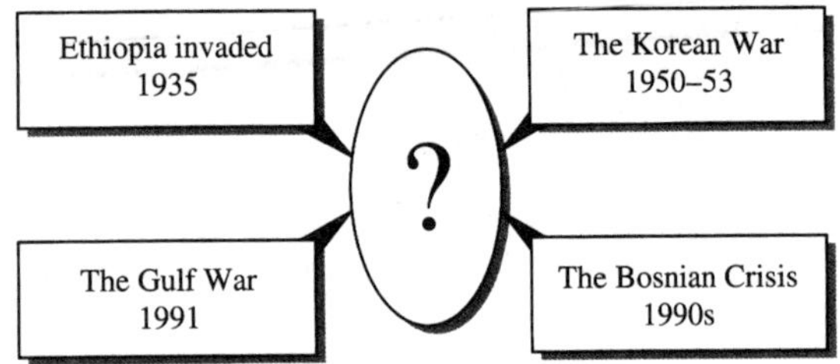

46. Which of the following generalizations completes this diagram?

A. Maintaining spheres of influence prevents hostilities.

B. Collective security achieves varying degrees of success.

C. Deterrence effectively prevents aggression between nations.

D. Diplomacy is primarily motivated by imperialist tendencies.

47. By supporting the terms of the Munich Agreement, France abandoned commitments made to

A. Great Britain in the Treaty of Versailles

B. Czechoslovakia in the Little Entente

C. the United States in the Dawes Plan

D. Germany in the Locarno Pacts

Use the following map to answer questions 48 and 49.

Major Battles of the Second World War

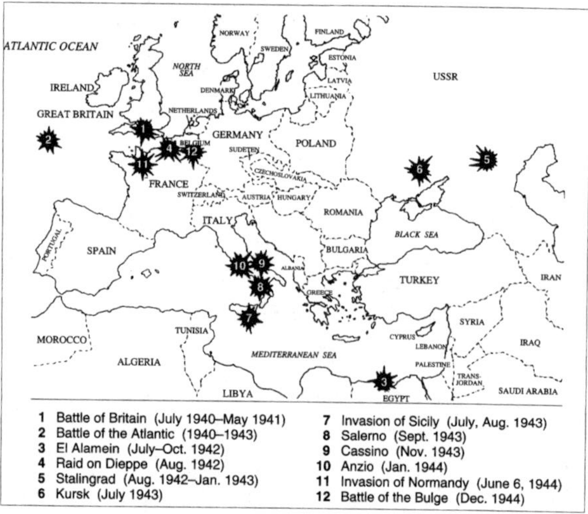

— from *The Rise of the Global Village*

48. Which of the battles indicated above had the **most significant** Canadian involvement?

A. Battles 1 and 12

B. Battles 2 and 3

C. Battles 4 and 11

D. Battles 5 and 7

49. Which of the following battles is correctly matched with its outcome?

	Battle Number	Outcome
A.	3	Germany gains control of Egypt until 1944.
B.	5	Valuable Soviet oil and grain reserves are ceded to the Axis alliance.
C.	11	Allied liberation of Nazi-controlled northern Europe begins.
D.	12	Germany initiates a plan of genocide against European Jews and other "non-Aryans."

50. During the Cold War, the United States and the Soviet Union directly demonstrated authority over territories perceived to be in their immediate spheres of influence during the

A. Gulf War and the Vietnam War

B. Berlin Airlift and the Suez Crisis

C. Korean War and the Six-Day War

D. Cuban Missile Crisis and the Hungarian Revolution

51. A feature common to the Korean War and the Vietnam War was that in both conflicts,

A. Soviet soldiers and equipment were tested against American soldiers and equipment

B. the United States became militarily involved because of a foreign policy of containment

C. the final result was a stalemate; neither side gained nor lost significant territory

D. communist forces successfully unified a divided nation

52. Which of the following events **best** illustrates the practice of brinkmanship?

A. The signing of the Kellogg–Briand Pact, 1928

B. The introduction of the Marshall Plan, 1947

C. The enforcement of the Berlin Blockade, 1948–49

D. The signing of the SALT I Agreement, 1972

Use the following excerpt to answer questions 53 and 54.

Thus the primary consideration soon became not the importance of a noncommunist South Vietnam in itself but the repercussions to be expected from reneging on this commitment. As concerns the impact internationally, the fear was of disillusionment with the worth of the alliances contracted by the U.S. and the encouragement of other Communist-led "wars of national liberation" which might follow a retreat from Southeast Asia. With regard to the domestic scene, the steadfast defense of South Vietnam was to preempt the charge of being soft on communism, an accusation to which Democratic presidents, mindful of Yalta and the "loss of China," were particularly sensitive.

—from *The Vietnam War: Opposing Viewpoints*

53. The writer suggests that American involvement in South Vietnam during the 1960s and 1970s was motivated **mainly** by

A. fear of the consequences of withdrawal

B. popular support in the United States for the war

C. the attempt to negotiate new military alliances in Asia

D. the desire to impose democracy on dictatorial governments

54. The writer's references to the " 'loss of China' " and being "mindful of Yalta" are made **primarily** in relation to the

A. traditional policy of isolationism and neutrality practised by the United States

B. spread of communist influence immediately following the Second World War

C. era of détente with China and the Soviet Union that was inaugurated by President Nixon

D. ideological break between the Soviet Union and China that occurred during the Khrushchev years

55. Which of the following issues emerging from the Second World War has generated the **most** debate and controversy?

A. How effective were intelligence-gathering agencies in ending the war?

B. Should the Allies have opened a second front in Europe sooner than they did?

C. How aware of Nazi atrocities were the German population and the rest of the world?

D. What were the secret, additional protocols that were a part of the Nazi–Soviet Pact of 1939?

Use the following information to answer questions 56 and 57.

Some Articles from the Treaties of Rome

- A common agricultural policy shall be established among Member states.
- A common transportation policy shall be created for Member States.
- A common tariff and trade policy among Member States shall be pursued.
- Tariff and trade restrictions among Member States shall be abolished.
- People, capital, and services shall move freely between Member States.

56. These articles were to serve as the basis for the formation of the

A. Allied Control Council in 1946

B. North Atlantic Treaty Organization in 1949

C. Council for Mutual Economic Assistance in 1949

D. European Economic Community in 1957

57. By accepting and acting upon these articles, a government demonstrated its commitment to the principle of

A. national sovereignty

B. ultranationalism

C. supranationalism

D. national security

Use the following information to answer question 58.

Vietnam 1954–1975	Afghanistan 1979–1989	Balkans 1992–?

58. Taken together, the above situations demonstrate the difficulties associated with superpower efforts to

A. restore their spheres of influence

B. coordinate peacekeeping operations

C. maintain control over foreign markets

D. resolve wars of national liberation or civil conflict

Use the following sources to answer questions 59 to 62.

Source I

After almost half a century, the communist world's leader, President Mikhail Gorbachev, has undertaken dramatic changes within the Soviet bloc that give the free world's leader, President George Bush, another historic opportunity to enhance the West's security and to effect a sea change in the U.S.–Soviet relationship. Gorbachev's policies of glasnost and perestroika have been hailed, even by some hard-line Western leaders, as heralding the end of the cold war. While his reforms give reason for a reappraisal of the West's policy toward the Soviet Union, we must bear in mind that the causes of the cold war—Moscow's domination of Eastern Europe and aggressive foreign policies around the world—still endure. Those who urge the West to "help Gorbachev" with low-interest loans and subsidized credits fail to realize that such actions are not in our interest until he makes an irrevocable break with the Kremlin's past policies.

— Richard Nixon, former U.S. president, 1989

Source II

A large segment of the American population has the need to cultivate the theory of American innocence and virtue—which must have an opposite pole of evil. ... I feel very strongly that the extreme military anxieties and rivalries that have marked the high points of the Cold War have increasingly lost their rationale. Now, they are predominantly matters of the past. The Cold War is outdated. Of far greater importance are areas which demand collaboration between the Soviet Union and the United States. ... What worries me more than whether Gorbachev has changed the Soviet Union for the better is the American media's persistent dramatization of Cold War myths and sterotypes. The Soviets dropped the Cold War mentality. Now, it's up to us to do the same thing.

— George Kennan, former U.S. diplomat, 1988

Source III

—all sources from *The Superpowers: A New Détente*

59. Some of the doubts expressed in Source I were alleviated later in 1989 when

- **A.** the people of the Soviet Union re-elected Gorbachev as president
- **B.** the two superpowers agreed to eliminate their land-based nuclear missiles
- **C.** hard-line communists used armed force to bring down Gorbachev's regime
- **D.** satellite states such as Poland, Hungary, and East Germany asserted their full autonomy from the Soviet Union

60. The speaker in Source II argues that the greatest impediment to ending the Cold War was

- **A.** American distrust of the Soviet Union
- **B.** Soviet refusal to participate in bilateral arms talks
- **C.** Gorbachev's inability to control the pace of reform in the Soviet Union
- **D.** American foreign policy that placed too much emphasis on conciliation of Soviet demands

61. Which of the following messages is suggested in Source III?

- **A.** American business interests hope to sell arms to the Soviet Union.
- **B.** American business investment may lead to the continuance of the super power arms race.
- **C.** Gorbachev's economic reforms have made the Soviet Union a stable place to invest.
- **D.** Gorbachev's reforms have focused on reviving the economy while reforming military spending

62. Which of the following statements about the sources is accurate?

- **A.** Source I and Source II offer similar points of view.
- **B.** Source III focuses on the central theme of Source II.
- **C.** Source III offers a message consistent with Source I.
- **D.** All three sources offer opinions that essentially support the same conclusion.

Use the following excerpt to answer questions 63 and 64.

Note: In this excerpt, the writer is responding to the 1997 French trial of Maurice Papon. Papon was charged with crimes against humanity during the Nazi occupation of France. Papon served as a bureaucrat in the collaborationist Vichy Government of France during the Second World War.

Justice must follow its course without interference. However, I do have a feeling of uneasiness. More than 50 years have elapsed, and much of the evidence is based on the imprecise recollections of a few witnesses. I also perceive the danger of a second trial. The Court of Assizes is working under the scrutiny of the outside world. The international press has devoted a great deal of coverage to this case. Many in the media, particularly the Anglo-Saxon media, would be very glad to hear a public admission or acknowledgment of guilt by the French nation. The media forget that France was an occupied nation. One can't blind oneself to the facts. There is an expectant pause and a desire to hear the French people hold themselves accountable. I cannot agree to this wish or the comparisons that are made with Germany. The Germans were responsible for their actions. The French people were subject to an occupying army that imposed its will upon them.

Did the French fail to show solidarity with their Jewish compatriots? It is in our own best interest to tell the truth. The Germans issued the orders for the arrests and deportations, but they were frequently carried out by French officials. As soon as the consequences had been determined, these agents should have refused to obey these orders.
Setting forth the truth should remain the province of academicians, historians, and the courts, rather than of the political arena, which is tempted to take whatever position it deems most advantageous.

—former French President Valéry Giscard d'Estaing

—from *World Press Review*

63. The writer suggests that war crimes committed in France differed from those committed in Germany in that French citizens responsible for such crimes

A. did not recognize the seriousness of their actions

B. did not participate in actions based on racist doctrines

C. were few in number and often fanatical in their beliefs

D. were following orders given by a foreign occupation force

64. The "uneasiness" of the writer arises, in part, from a concern that a war crimes trial would

A. reignite historic Franco–German enmity

B. be prejudiced by influences outside the legal system

C. place the guilt of the French nation on the accused person

D. reopen historic problems that are better left to political solutions

Use the following source to answer question 65.

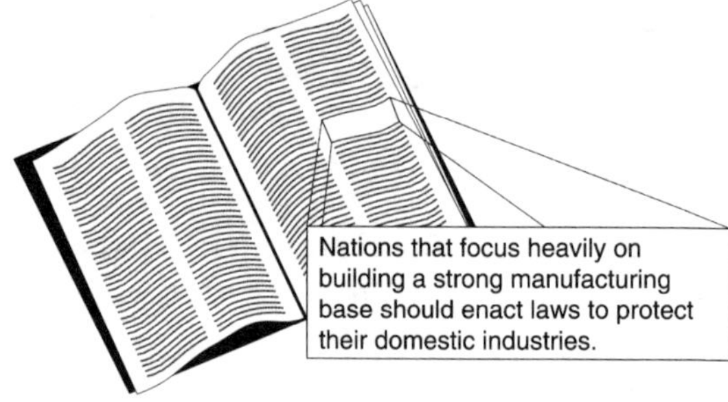

65. A proponent of the writer's beliefs would support a policy of

A. protectionist tariff barriers

B. interventionist social policies

C. regional cooperative alliances

D. international free-trade agreements

66. Organizations such as the WTO and the IMF encourage government actions designed to promote greater

A. ultranationalism

B. global integration

C. collective security

D. national sovereignty

67. To Marxist supporters, imperialist economic activity is **most clearly** exemplified by the

A. re-emergence of colonial empires

B. development of military spheres of influence

C. operation of transnational, global corporations

D. presence of supranational political organizations

Use the following source to answer question 68.

When faced with an international crisis, leaders of modern democratic governments have often referred to the "lesson of Munich."

68. What is the "lesson of Munich"?

A. Diplomacy is the best way to guarantee territorial security.

B. Nations should not interfere in each other's domestic affairs.

C. Agencies of collective security should not mediate in multinational disputes.

D. A hard-line stance must be taken by nations negotiating with an aggressor state.

Use the following cartoon to answer questions 69 and 70.

—from *Best Editorial Cartoons of the Year, 1994 Edition*

69. The details of the cartoon suggest that under the leadership of President Boris Yeltsin, Russia was seeking to

A. restore control over former Soviet republics

B. return to the traditional Soviet foreign policy of détente

C. establish an alliance system that includes states in western Europe

D. extend the policies of perestroika and glasnost to neighbouring states

70. In response to the threat depicted in the cartoon, most eastern European states have

A. adopted a policy of conciliation toward Russia

B. sought to establish formal links with NATO

C. declared their territories to be nuclear-free zones

D. begun programs to develop conventional deterrent forces

Written Response—Essay Assignment

Choose **one** of the following issues for your essay.

Topic A

Some people believe that poverty can most effectively be reduced through government spending on social programs. Others argue that poverty can most effectively be reduced when the government requires citizens to be self-reliant.

Should the state take an active role in the reduction of poverty?

In your essay, take and defend a position on this issue.

Or

Topic B

Some people believe that great power nations should act on their own to resolve crisis situations. Others argue that crisis situations should be resolved by the collective efforts of the international community.

Should crisis situations be resolved by the individual actions of great power nations?
In your essay, take and defend a position on this issue.

January 2002 Diploma Examination

1. In a democracy, the primary purpose of periodic elections is to ensure that

   A. new candidates are chosen as a means of preventing majority tyranny

   B. the legitimacy and accountability of the government is maintained

   C. one leader does not monopolize control of a political party

   D. minority groups are guaranteed political representation

2. *During a crisis situation, should parliamentary governments have the right to invoke emergency legislation that restricts personal freedoms?*

   Which of the following arguments supports an affirmative position on this issue?

   A. Strong direction is required to prevent egalitarianism.

   B. Preserving minority rights can sometimes prevent majority rule.

   C. Undemocratic means are sometimes needed to preserve democratic ends.

   D. Force is the most effective way to restrict dissenting views in a democracy.

3. Because important decisions are made in both the legislative and executive branches of the American government, there is significant opportunity for

   A. special interest groups to exert influence

   B. party leaders to win primary nominations

   C. citizens to participate in election campaigns

   D. mainstream political parties to elect candidates

4. To consolidate their control over government, totalitarian leaders typically

   A. restrict party membership to the wealthiest classes

   B. demand public ownership of most industry and production

   C. relegate opposition parties to the role of debating minor issues

   D. prevent any judicial or legislative review of executive decisions

5. Which of the following justifications for dictatorship would be least objectionable to most supporters of democracy?

   A. People should be willing to sacrifice personal freedoms to the will of the leader.

   B. The state should be concerned with conformity of thought and the ideological control of education.

   C. The collective welfare of society should prevail over the privilege of any individual whenever the two conflict.

   D. People should accept government control as a means of stimulating more thought and creativity than does individual freedom.

Use the following information to answer the next question.

Source I
Unemployment in Germany: 1929 – 1933

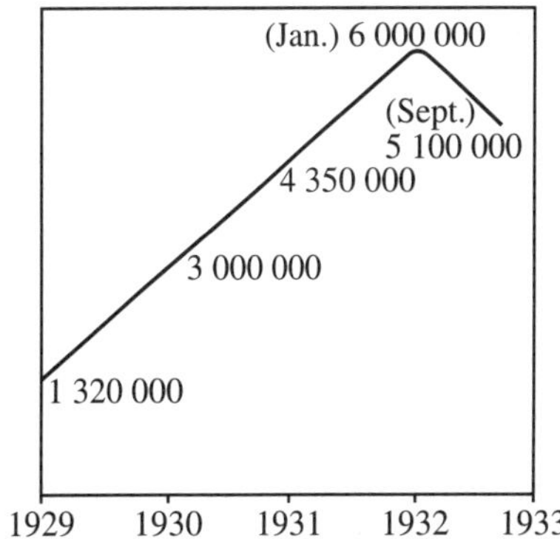

Source II

Occupation	% of Nazi Party Memberships	% of total populatio n
Blue-collar workers	28.1	45.9
White-collar workers	25.6	12.0
Self-employed	20.7	9.0
Officials and civil servants	14.9	9.3
Teachers	1.7	0.9
Farmers	14.0	10.6
Others	3.3	17.4

—from *Nazi Culture*

Source III

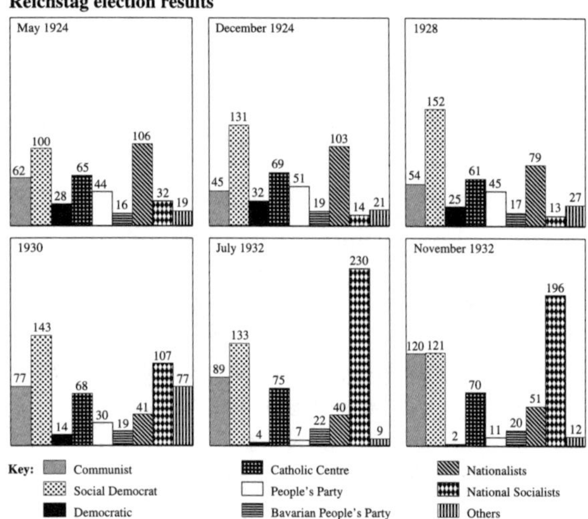

—sources I and III from *The World This Century*

6. The information in Source III supports the conclusion that

   A. Europe was politically stable prior to 1928

   B. National Socialist support peaked prior to 1928

   C. German politics became increasingly polarized after 1928

   D. German left-wing parties suffered a loss of support after 1928

7. Taken together, the sources would be most effective in researching which of the following questions?

   A. How was Germany affected by the economic boom of the 1920s?

   B. Was National Socialism a broadly based, popular political movement?

   C. Why was Germany able to recover so quickly from the First World War?

   D. Why did the Communist Party fail to achieve power in the Weimar Republic?

8. Which of the following statements regarding the sources is accurate?

   A. The data found in Source I represent a major cause of the trend shown in Source III.

   B. The information in Source II helps to explain the causes for the employment trend between 1929 and 1931 shown in Source I.

   C. The details in Source III contradict the expected voting patterns of "white-collar" Nazi Party members as shown in Source II.

   D. The election results shown in Source III and the number of unemployed shown in Source I did not effect the distribution of party memberships shown in Source II.

9. Which of the following actions would illustrate reactionary political forces at work in Canada?

   A. Parliament introduces reforms allowing for an elected Senate

   B. A federal government apologizes for earlier mistreatment of an ethnic minority

   C. A political party mandates that one-half of its candidates for election must be women

   D. The ruling party creates legislation allowing for the reinstatement of capital punishment

10. In non-democratic countries, elections are held **primarily** as a means of

A. reinforcing the perceived legitimacy of the regime in power

B. providing an opportunity for citizens to effect political change

C. meeting the legal requirements imposed by legislated constitutions

D. providing the elite with an insight into popular attitudes and beliefs

Use the following cartoon to answer questions 11 and 12.

—from *Best Editorial Cartoons of the Year, 1997*

11. The cartoon focuses on an issue in contemporary Russia that is related to the

A. absence of voter choice in a one-party political system

B. entrenched extremism of the typical Russian voter

C. unstable and volatile nature of Russian politics

D. variety of possible market-oriented ideologies

12. Which of the following generalizations about the nature of politics does the cartoon reinforce?

A. It cannot be assumed that an ideology will be rejected permanently.

B. It is necessary for dictatorships to rely on force and terror to stay in control.

C. Political leaders focus on promoting a positive image of themselves to the public.

D. Democratic systems of government usually create a stable political environment.

Use the following diagram to answer questions 13 and 14.

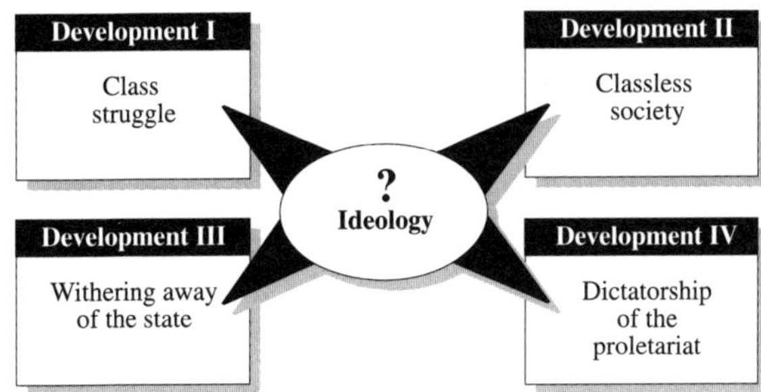

13. Which ideology is associated with these developments?

A. Fascism

B. Marxism

C. Utopian socialism

D. Democratic socialism

14. A radical left-wing revolutionary would argue that the historical order in which these developments occur is

A. I, II, III, IV

B. IV, II, I, III

C. IV, I, III, II

D. I, IV, III, II

Use the following chart to answer question 15.

Votes and Seats, 1974 and 1980 Elections in Nation X				
	1974		1980	
Party	% of Votes	% of Seats	% of Votes	% of Seats
Party A	43.5	53.5	44.5	54.1
Party B	35.7	36.1	32.7	34.5
Party C	15.4	6.0	19.7	11.4
Party D	5.0	4.1	1.7	0
Others	0.4	0.3	1.4	0

15. Supporters of the electoral system of Nation X would argue that this system

A. prevents tyranny of the majority

B. discourages the formation of majority governments

C. promotes political stability and legislative efficiency

D. encourages the formation of broadly based coalition governments

Use the following diagram to answer question 16.

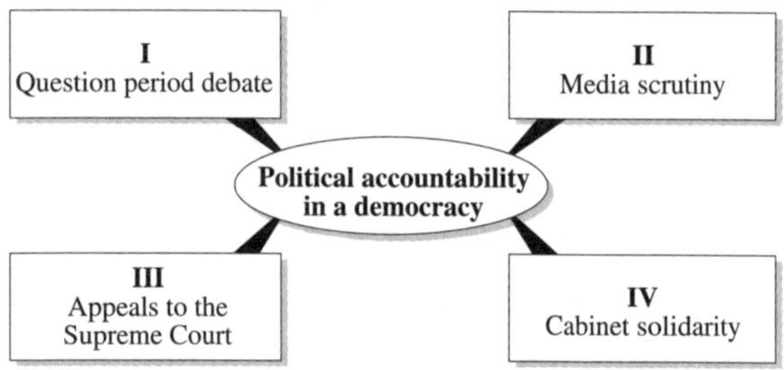

16. Which box in the diagram identifies a characteristic that is inconsistent with the diagram's central theme?

A. Box I

B. Box II

C. Box III

D. Box IV

Use the following excerpt to answer question 17.

> New Zealand seems to have found it. So have Germany and Sweden. It is, quite simply, a mixed system: half the members are elected from constituencies, the same way they are now; half are drawn from party lists, according to their share of the popular vote.
>
> —from *The Edmonton Journal*

17. The excerpt interprets the "mixed system" as combining aspects of both

A. federalism and a system of revolving minority governments

B. proportional representation and single member plurality

C. proportional representation and a coalition government

D. single member plurality and a congressional system

Use the following editorial excerpt to answer questions 18 and 19.

> The result, 15 years after the Thatcher Revolution began, is double digit unemployment in most western countries. Growth is slow. Recessions have resembled depressions. Why? Left to its own devices, the market has functioned as it should. The players have maximized profits where they could. There has been an even greater concentration of wealth in the hands of the wealthiest. And it has not trickled down from there, as the Thatcherites and Reaganites predicted, to create jobs and wealth for all.
>
> —from *The Edmonton Journal, 1994*

18. The writer of this editorial is critical of the belief that

A. employment can be created through government-funded programs

B. recessionary trends can be offset by major monetary and fiscal reforms

C. economic recovery can be achieved naturally through free enterprise principles

D. economic restructuring can be achieved with government direction and control

19. The writer's views would be **most strongly** opposed by

A. social democrats

B. liberal moderates

C. left-wing radicals

D. right-wing conservatives

Use the following graph to answer questions 20 and 21.

Economic Trend Indicators: Nation X, 1990–98

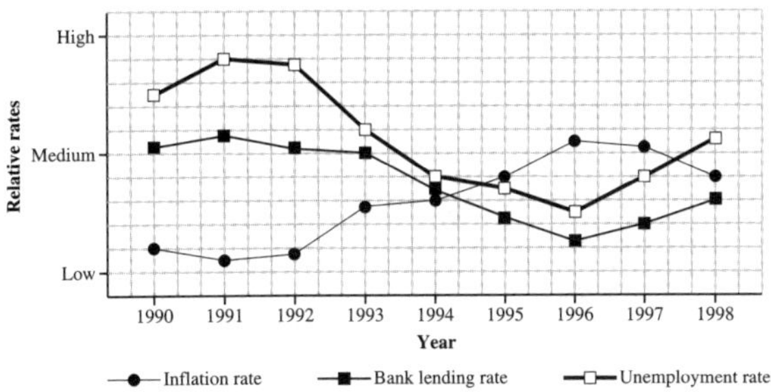

20. The information in the graph suggests that a rising bank lending rate results in

A. reduced rates of inflation and increased levels of unemployment

B. increased rates of inflation and reduced levels of unemployment

C. increases in both the level of employment and the rate of inflation

D. reductions in both the level of employment and the rate of inflation

21. Based on the trends revealed by the graph, skilled workers would have **most likely** received the largest salary increases during which of the following periods?

A. 1990–91

B. 1993–94

C. 1995–96

D. 1996–97

22. Supporters of public enterprise systems view competition as a negative force because they believe that competition

A. leads to inefficient use of goods and services

B. encourages a more equal distribution of wealth

C. thwarts the operation of supply and demand in an economy

D. distributes more wealth to the consumer than to the producer

23. Supporters of the type of command economy that existed in Nazi Germany believe that the

A. majority of a nation's resources should be state-owned and publicly controlled

B. majority of a nation's citizens should be involved in entrepreneurial enterprises

C. private enterprise system provides efficient production but requires overall objectives set by the state

D. private enterprise system can solve most economic problems if the government refrains from interfering in the economy

Use the following excerpt to answer questions 24 and 25.

> Along with the constant decrease in the number of capitalist magnates, who usurp and monopolize all the advantages of this process of transformation, the mass of misery, oppression, slavery, degradation and exploitation grows; but with this there also grows the revolt of the working class, a class constantly increasing in numbers, and trained, united and organized by the very mechanism of the capitalist process of production.
>
> —from *Economics Explained*

24. The ideas expressed in the excerpt are most closely associated with those of

A. John Maynard Keynes

B. John Stuart Mill

C. Adam Smith

D. Karl Marx

25. The claim that wealth becomes concentrated in the hands of a few is conveyed in the phrase

A. "the constant decrease in the number of capitalist magnates"

B. "the mass of misery"

C. "the revolt of the working class"

D. "the capitalist process of production"

26. Social democrats have traditionally opposed government policies that

A. emphasize the common good over individual profit

B. regulate business practices to protect consumers

C. provide social programs for low-income groups

D. reduce income taxes for high-income earners

27. Economist John Maynard Keynes would have been critical of governments that rigidly apply supply-side economic policies because he believed that such policies attempt to stimulate economic growth exclusively by

A. providing financial incentives to the business sector

B. providing financial incentives to low-income earners

C. controlling inflation through wage and price controls

D. controlling inflation through the adjustment of lending rates

28. *His reforms ushered in increased production of consumer goods, diversified and privatized agricultural programs, and decentralized economic planning and government services.*

The Soviet leader with whom these developments are **most strongly** associated is

A. Josef Stalin

B. Vladimir Lenin

C. Nikita Khrushchev

D. Mikhail Gorbachev

29. Laissez-faire capitalists oppose the formation of unions **primarily** because they believe that unions

A. restrict consumer confidence and spending

B. fail to act in the long-term interests of their members

C. encourage governments to spend lavishly on public works

D. distort the labour market and increase the cost of production

Use the following excerpt to answer questions 30 to 32.

> ...business likes tax cuts. It is another way of reducing the role of government. Like the deficit scare, tax cuts constrain government spending on public services. This opens the door to private sector profit-making activity in education, health and child care. Of course, public spending in these sectors holds out the promise of creating a more equal society. Private spending increases access for the wealthy to more privileged services that only they can afford, while reducing access for everybody else.
>
> —from *The Canadian Forum*

30. The writer suggests that businesses advocate tax cuts primarily as a means to

A. combat the growth of the public debt

B. create economic opportunities in the private sector

C. implement fiscal policies during periods of recession

D. encourage equal economic opportunity for most citizens

31. Given the point of view of the writer, which of the following statements could be added to the excerpt?

A. The revenues thus saved could be used to pay down the massive national debt.

B. Once again, the common good would be sacrificed to the practices of a market ideology.

C. The tax burden of the welfare state has for too long been a crushing deterrent to the well-being of citizens.

D. Individuals, for example, would no longer be frustrated by an overly inefficient health-care system.

32. Members of which contemporary Canadian political party would most fully endorse the position taken by the writer?

A. Liberal Party

B. Canadian Alliance

C. New Democratic Party

D. Progressive Conservative Party

33. Policies of massive deficit reduction and extensive privatization in the global marketplace differ from the economic policies recommended by most

A. left-wing economists

B. capitalist economists

C. laissez-faire economists

D. neoconservative economists

Use the following cartoon to answer questions 34 and 35.

—from *The Political Spectrum*

34. As depicted in the cartoon, "Liberalism" most likely represents the cost of

A. deregulating business practices

B. privatizing government agencies

C. providing tax incentives for the wealthy elite

D. financing welfare programs for low-income earners

35. Which of the following individuals would agree with the central message of the cartoon?

A. A left-wing voter

B. A fiscal conservative

C. A democratic socialist

D. A Keynesian economist

36. The American Senate refused to ratify the Treaty of Versailles because a majority of senators believed that specific terms of the treaty

A. were excessively lenient toward the defeated powers

B. jeopardized the United States' independence as a sovereign state

C. largely disregarded recommendations in Woodrow Wilson's Fourteen Points

D. failed to place blame on those nations regarded as responsible for causing the war

Use the following map to answer question 37.

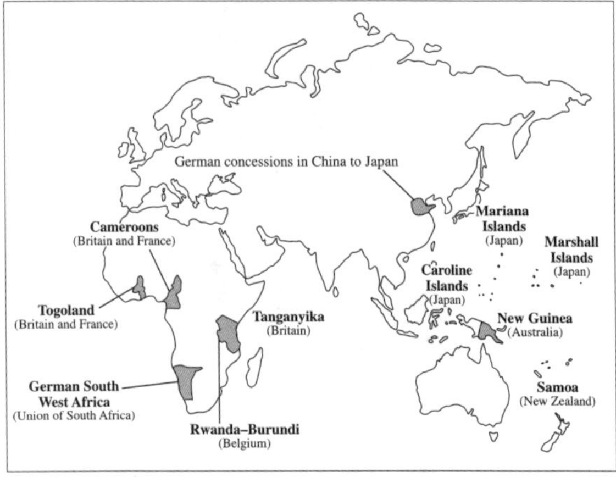

37. The **best** title for this 1920 map is

A. *Nazi Imperial Expansion*

B. *Self-Determination in Practice*

C. *The Balance of Power in Africa and Asia*

D. *League Mandates of Former German Colonies*

38. Which of the following actions was regarded by Hitler as an initial test of France's resolve to enforce the terms of the Treaty of Versailles?

A. The *Anschluss* of Austria

B. The annexation of the Sudetenland

C. The remilitarization of the Rhineland

D. The blitzkrieg launched against Poland

39. From the perspective of a German nationalist who supported the Nazis, the results of the Munich Agreement simply represented the fulfillment of the Wilsonian principle of

A. collective security

B. self-determination

C. appeasement

D. disarmament

Use the following excerpt to answer question 40.

Looking back to the 1930s for guidance, would the League of Nations have used force against Hitler's Germany if the league had understood where the Nazi campaign against the Jews was heading? The answer is no. Should it have done so? The answer is yes, on moral and practical grounds, moral because the killing of Jews was a crime against a people and against humanity; practical because millions of lives could have been saved, Jewish and others, and the Second World War might have been shortened, restricted, or even avoided by forcible action against the Nazis. But the internment and killing of German Jews was regarded as "an internal matter" by the League.

—from *The Edmonton Journal*

40. The writer suggests that in the 1930s, the League of Nations faced the dilemma of whether to

A. respect national sovereignty or protect a persecuted minority

B. mediate boundary disputes or impose binding territorial changes

C. prevent the formation of military alliances or maintain diplomatic neutrality

D. place sanctions on dictatorial states or encourage national self-determination

41. The League of Nations' failure to take strong and decisive action during the Manchurian Crisis challenged the credibility of the League's

A. adherence to collective security principles

B. application of the principle of open diplomacy

C. commitment to alliances among its weaker members

D. reliance upon summit conferences involving the Great Powers

Use the following sources to answer questions 42 to 44.

Source I

In principle and doctrine, Hitler was no more wicked and unscrupulous than many other contemporary statesmen. The state of German rearmament in 1939 gives the decisive proof that Hitler was not contemplating general war, and probably not contemplating war at all. The war of 1939, far from being premeditated, was a mistake, the result on both sides of diplomatic blunders.

Source II

Let us consider briefly the programme which Hitler laid down for himself. It was a programme of Eastern colonisation, entailing a war of conquest against Russia. . . . In order to carry it out, Hitler needed a restored German army which, since it must be powerful enough to conquer Russia, must also be powerful enough to conquer the West if that should be necessary. And that might be necessary even before the attack on Russia . . . it was always possible that a war with the West would be necessary before he could march against Russia. And in fact that is what happened.

—both sources from *The World This Century*

42. Hitler's "programme of Eastern colonisation" (Source II) was founded on the concept of

A. kristallnacht **B.** lebensraum

C. blitzkrieg **D.** Anschluss

43. According to the writer of Source I, Hitler's diplomatic success prior to 1939 was **primarily** based on his ability to

A. use collective security as a means to end a crisis

B. conscript millions of German soldiers

C. bluff vulnerable opponents

D. form aggressive alliances

44. Despite their different perspectives, the writer of Source I and the writer of Source II would agree that historians must carefully research

A. issues of morality

B. the art of diplomacy

C. questions of motivation

D. the consequences of treaties

Use the following quotation to answer question 45.

> … the German dictator, instead of snatching the victuals from the table, has been content to have served to him course by course.… A disaster of the first magnitude.… has befallen Britain and France.
>
> —*Sir Winston Churchill*

45. This comment was made by Churchill in direct reference to the terms of the

A. Locarno Pacts

B. Munich Agreement

C. Treaty of Versailles

D. Kellogg–Briand Pact

Use the following time-line to answer question 46.

The signing of the Rome–Berlin Axis	The creation of the Anti-Comintern Pact	?	The invasion of Poland

46. Which of the following interwar events completes the time-line?

A. The signing of the Kellogg–Briand Pact

B. The remilitarization of the Rhineland

C. The signing of the Nazi–Soviet Pact

D. The formation of the Little Entente

Use the following events from the Second World War to answer question 47.

V. Operation Barbarossa

W. Fall of Poland

X. Allied victory in North Africa

Y. Fall of France

Z. Attack on Pearl Harbor

47. The chronology of the events listed above is

A. events V, W, Z, Y, X

B. events W, Z, V, X, Y

C. events V, Y, W, Z, X

D. events W, Y, V, Z, X

Use the following map to answer question 48.

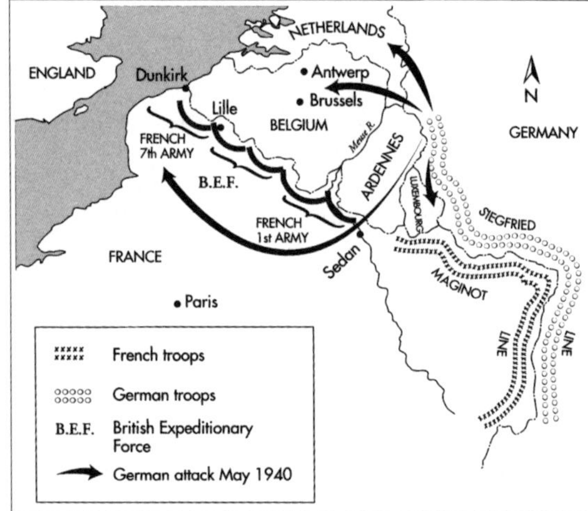

—from *Twentieth Century Viewpoints*

48. An appropriate title for this map is

A. England Falls to the Axis Powers

B. Maginot Line Stalls German Attack

C. Allied Disaster Culminates at Dunkirk

D. Siegfried Line Collapses under Allied Offensive

Use the following cartoon to answer questions 49 and 50.

WHO'S NEXT TO BE LIBERATED FROM FREEDOM?

—from *An Illustrated History of Modern Europe*

49. The above cartoon was drawn in the historical context of the

A. Soviet response to the Hungarian Revolution

B. threat of fascist expansion in Europe during the late 1930s

C. Soviet participation in the Marshall Plan during the late 1940s

D. threat of worldwide communist expansion during the Cold War

50. The American government's reaction to the situation depicted in the cartoon was to follow a foreign policy of

A. containment of real and perceived enemies

B. isolation from developments in Europe

C. withdrawal from regional alliances

D. aggressive military expansion

51. During the Cold War, the condition necessary for the success of superpower deterrence was the

A. advanced conventional weapons capability of both superpowers

B. export of conventional weapons from the superpowers to their allies

C. retaliatory capability of either superpower following a nuclear first strike

D. nuclear capability of one superpower that would make opposing weapons useless

52. In 1944, Churchill and Stalin agreed to a postwar division of Eastern Europe. Included in the agreement was the provision that the Soviet Union and Britain have an equal say over the postwar fate of Yugoslavia and Hungary.

This agreement is an illustration of the concept of

A. enforcing mutual deterrence

B. establishing spheres of influence

C. eliminating economic imperialism

D. encouraging national self-determination

53. A significant consequence of the discussions among the Allied leaders at the Yalta and Potsdam conferences was that

A. the fate of fascist Italy was settled

B. relations improved among the major Allied powers

C. American domination of global politics was guaranteed

D. tensions escalated between the Soviets and the Western Allies

54. Nikita Khrushchev's call for peaceful coexistence with the West and his denunciation of Stalin were major factors that contributed to

A. the emergence of anti-Soviet activism in Hungary and Poland

B. encouraging American determination to resist communism

C. establishing the formation of the Warsaw Pact

D. the escalation of the superpower arms race

55. The establishment of the Washington–Moscow "hotline" and the signing of the Partial Test-Ban Treaty marked the significant shift in superpower relations that occurred shortly after the

A. conclusion of the Suez Crisis

B. ending of the Berlin Blockade

C. negotiation of the Korean ceasefire

D. resolution of the Cuban Missile Crisis

Use the following information to answer questions 56 to 57.

Source I

What was at stake in Berlin was not a contest over legal rights, although our position was entirely sound in international law, but a struggle over Germany and, in a larger sense, over Europe. ...the Kremlin tried to mislead the people of Europe into believing that our interest and support would not extend beyond economic matters and that we would back away from any military risks. The abandonment of Berlin would have a disastrous effect upon our plans for Western Germany. It would also slow down European recovery, the success of which depended upon more production. ...We should be prepared to go to any lengths to find a peaceful solution to the situation, but we had to remain in Berlin. The main question was: How could we remain in Berlin without risking all-out war?

—American President Harry S. Truman
—from *Basic Documents in United States Foreign Policy*

Source II

—from *A Cartoon History of United States Foreign Policy*

56. Source I indicates that in dealing with the Soviet Union, the United States favoured a foreign policy of

A. appeasement rather than détente

B. diplomacy rather than confrontation

C. isolationism rather than containment

D. collective security rather than brinkmanship

57. The cartoon in Source II suggests that the Allied response to the Berlin Blockade was successful in

A. weakening Soviet morale in the city

B. allowing Soviet citizens to flee the city

C. driving the Soviet military from the city

D. breaching the Soviet barrier that closed the city

58. *Demands for national self-determination threatened superpower control over their respective spheres of influence.*

Within the context of the Cold War, this statement is **best** illustrated by the

A. signing of the Korean armistice in 1953

B. Hungarian Revolution in 1956

C. construction of the Berlin Wall in 1961

D. Cuban Missile Crisis in 1962

59. The United Nations Security Council is organized so that the

A. Secretary General has veto power over Security Council decisions

B. individual permanent members have ultimate decision-making authority

C. General Assembly controls which issues will be considered during a crisis

D. individual non-permanent members are selected exclusively from the developing world

60. Which of the following goals is **not** associated with the function of the World Trade Organization?

A. Encouraging protectionist trade blocs

B. Establishing rules governing trade among nations

C. Providing a forum for discussions to reduce trade barriers

D. Resolving trade disputes by international arbitration and adjudication

Use the following diagram to answer question 61.

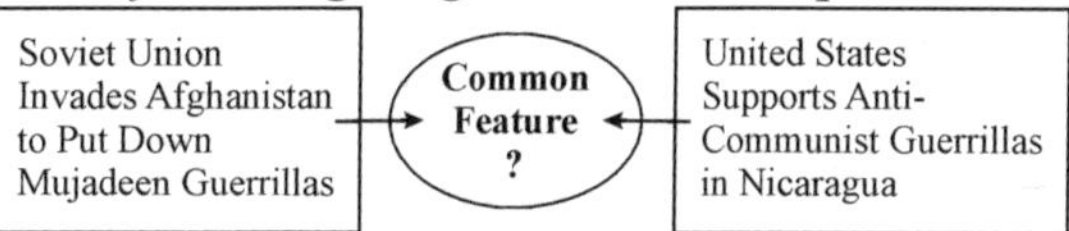

61. A feature common to the superpowers' actions described above is that of the

A. preservation of spheres of influence

B. defence of the principle of collective security

C. deployment of forces to stop guerrilla warfare

D. protection of the right to national self-determination

Use the following sources to answer questions 62 to 64.

Source I

Armed conflicts will continue to plague the world if some people interpret the right to self-determination to mean the right to create a racially homogeneous nation. It will be a perilous future if "democracy" is interpreted to mean the freedom of an ethnic majority to impose its will on ethnic minorities.

Source II

—from *Portfoolio 9*

62. The comments in Source I can be verified most convincingly by reference to the

A. increase in the number of United Nations' peacekeeping operations

B. breakthrough in the peace process between Palestinians and Israelis

C. shift in superpower relations that resulted from the end of the Cold War

D. numerous violent and ongoing civil conflicts in many parts of the world

63. The cartoon in Source II is ironic in that it illustrates the problem associated with ethnic conflict by

A. juxtaposing the goal of fellowship with the inability to coexist peacefully

B. emphasizing sports events as a way to bring people together in fellowship

C. presenting the Olympics as an event where people are often uncooperative

D. portraying the coordinator of the event as overreacting to potential conflicts

64. Both sources focus **primarily** on the problems

A. associated with brokering lasting peace settlements

B. of accommodating tensions created by demands for autonomy

C. of minority groups using force to overthrow authoritarian governments

D. related to coordinating international events with many diverse participants

Use the following diagram to answer question 65.

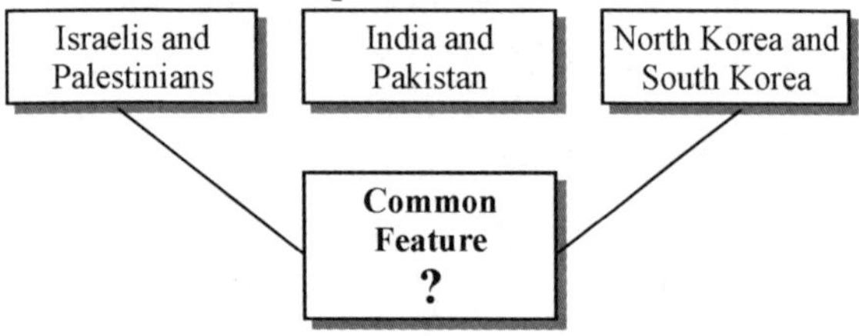

65. Which of the following "features" is common to the situations alluded to in the diagram?

A. Armed conflict continues to extract a heavy toll on civilians.

B. The United States has hosted talks between the political leaderships.

C. Long-standing animosity continues to impede the resolution of conflict.

D. The United Nations has deployed peacekeeping forces to protect a fragile peace.

Use the following excerpt to answer questions 66 and 67.

> In a world where the vast majority of conflicts now rage *within*, rather than between nations, increased UN activism may at times be the only viable alternative to the world standing in mute witness to mass slaughter. But that activism cannot be defined solely in military terms, and success in the long term will depend on a currently out-of-reach independence of action on the part of the UN. If its role in the world is to defend democracy, the UN's own democracy must be reclaimed. Otherwise, with the reality of a US dominated United Nations torn by North-South divisions, UN intervention, under the guise of peacekeeping, peacemaking or peace-enforcing, will be indistinguishable from the US interventions it is so often used to legitimate.
>
> —from *Twentieth Century Viewpoints*

66. The United Nations' involvement in mediating conflicts that "rage *within*, rather than between nations" is **best** illustrated by its deployment of forces to

A. Egypt in 1956

B. Kashmir in 1965

C. Kuwait in 1991

D. Bosnia in 1992

67. In this excerpt, the major criticism of the United Nations is that the organization has

A. become a pawn of American foreign policy

B. not acted quickly enough to stop mass slaughter

C. tried to impose settlements upon nations unwilling to accept American interference

D. been prevented from taking action by the veto power of permanent members of the Security Council

68. The European Union originated in the 1950s through efforts to

A. reduce trade barriers between Member States

B. integrate the foreign policies of Member States

C. create a multinational military force to protect Member States

D. prevent dictatorial regimes from gaining power in Member States

For questions 69 and 70, consider the following issue and the four positions.

Issue:	Should the United States have intervened militarily to stop the civil war and violence in the Balkans?
Position I	Yes, as a global superpower, the United States has a moral obligation to maintain world peace and security wherever trouble occurs. It was the only country capable of forcing the opposing Balkan factions to resolve their conflicts.
Position II	No, the United States had no national interests in the area; therefore, it was not worth sacrificing American lives. Neither the United Nations nor the United States should expand its mandate and responsibility for resolving conflicts like this.
Position III	Yes, civil and factional war in the Balkans posed a serious regional threat that would have escalated into an international conflict unless a decisive response was taken to stop it. The United States had the power to act effectively.
Position IV	No, only a negotiated peace brokered by the European Union would have resulted in a lasting settlement. An externally imposed solution would never have been accepted by any of the combatants locked in ethnic struggle.

69. Which position is correctly matched with an approach to global politics?

A. Position I → Appeasement

B. Position II → Internationalism

C. Position III → Interventionism

D. Position IV → Brinkmanship

70. Which position on this issue **best** parallels the American government's official policy toward international involvements during the 1930s?

A. Position I **B.** Position II

C. Position III **D.** Position IV

Written Response

Choose one of the following issues for your essay.

Topic A

Some people believe that society is best served when consumer demand alone influences production decisions. Others believe that governments, acting in the public interest, must control production decisions.

To what extent should production decisions be influenced by consumer demand?

In your essay, take and defend a position on this issue.

Or

Topic B

Some people believe that, when dealing with nations determined to extend their boundaries, diplomacy and negotiation are preferable to war. Others believe that a nation's efforts to expand its territory must be met with force, or the threat of force, when necessary.

To what extent should nations respond with diplomacy to the expansionist policies of other states?

In your essay, take and defend a position on this issue.

NOTES

Answers and Solutions
June 2001 Diploma Examination

1.	A	11.	D	21.	C	31.	A	41.	A	51.	B	61.	B
2.	D	12.	A	22.	A	32.	C	42.	D	52.	C	62.	C
3.	C	13.	C	23.	B	33.	D	43.	B	53.	A	63.	D
4.	D	14.	B	24.	D	34.	D	44.	A	54.	B	64.	B
5.	C	15.	B	25.	A	35.	B	45.	C	55.	C	65.	A
6.	B	16.	D	26.	C	36.	C	46.	B	56.	D	66.	B
7.	A	17.	A	27.	A	37.	A	47.	B	57.	C	67.	C
8.	B	18.	D	28.	C	38.	B	48.	C	58.	D	68.	D
9.	D	19.	A	29.	C	39.	D	49.	C	59.	D	69.	A
10.	A	20.	B	30.	B	40.	A	50.	D	60.	A	70.	B

1. A

Self-reliance and competitiveness are values closely associated with capitalism. Capitalists support the elimination of subsidies (government grants) to private businesses. Capitalists view the economy as a struggle between companies for market share —where only the most industrious and innovative corporations should survive.

B, C, and D. A Canadian who believed in self-reliance and competitiveness would favour a free enterprise economy with low taxation, privatization (the sale of publicly owned businesses), and deregulation (relaxing government control of the economy). He would not support nationalization (the government takeover of resources and/or industries) or the establishment of Crown Corporations (government-owned and -operated Canadian industries).

2. D

A model public enterprise system is an economy based completely on the communist theories of Karl Marx. In such an economy, prices would not be set by the laws of supply and demand (as they would be in a capitalist economy); in an ideal Marxist economy, stable and fair prices would be set by the state.

A, B, and C. Entrepreneurship (competition between risk-taking private businessmen), private ownership of resources, and economic inequality between rich and poor are not features that would exist in an ideal communist state; you would find these things in a free market (capitalist) economy.

3. **C**

Statement I is false. In the budget year 2000-2001, the largest single source of federal government revenue was personal income taxes ($141,463,000,000 or 32.4% of government revenue); corporate income taxes accounted for only $41,584,000,000 (9.5% of government revenue). Statement II is true; Canada has a system of progressive income tax in which wealthier Canadians must give the government a greater percentage of their total income than poorer Canadians.

4. **D**

Supporters of a mixed economy believe that the government should intervene in the economy to prevent or end recessions and depressions. They would suggest stimulating economic growth during recessions through that application of supply-side, demand-side, or monetarist strategies. Similarly, they would favour restraining expansion during boom periods by using fiscal policy and/or monetary policy to control inflation.

A, B, and C. Adherents of mixed economic theory might support raising interest rates during boom periods (to control inflation) or encouraging industrial production during recessions (to create jobs and consumer confidence). They would not, however, favour raising taxes during recessions, encouraging industrial production during boom periods, reducing taxes during boom periods, or restricting investment during recessions; they would see such moves as counterproductive measures or as unwarranted meddling with a healthy economy. Supporters of mixed economic theory believe in the free market; however, they think that the free market needs some help when a downturn in the economy has occurred or is about to occur.

5. **C**

A welfare state is a country in which the government provides economic support to the poor. The question "Should governments assume responsibility for the economically disadvantaged?" is raised by all three sources.

A, B, and D. The other questions are not directly and/or collectively addressed by the three sources.

6. **B**

Source II suggests that the welfare state should be dismantled and that society would be better off if people were left to fend for themselves in a free market governed by the laws of supply and demand.

A, C, and D. Source I supports the welfare state and calls for substantial government intervention in the economy—contrary to the market principles favoured by capitalists.

7. **A**

A neoconservative is a strong supporter of a free enterprise economy. He would agree with the suggestion that welfare programs corrupt the morals and values of recipients of government assistance. A neo conservative would maintain that government handouts erode the work ethic and self-sufficiency of recipients.

B, C and D. A neoconservative would not support government support for all citizens or increasing welfare benefits. Nor would a neoconservative believe that the private sector (privately owned businesses) have a responsibility to provide full employment.

8. B

The ultra-right position on the economic spectrum is laissez-faire capitalism. Considering that the author of Source II does not support welfare programs whatsoever, he appears to be a laissez-faire capitalist.

A, C, and D. The views of Speaker II are not typical of ultra-leftists (communists), socialists (left-of-centre supporters of a large social safety net), or welfare-capitalist conservatives (those slightly right-of-centre who support welfare programs for the poorest of the poor).

9. D

Adam Smith is the founder of the capitalist ideology. He argued that the formation of oligopolies (cartels) should be prevented by the state because they negated many of the benefits of the free market by eliminating business competition and driving up prices.

A. Firstly, Smith believed that cartels were incompatible with free enterprise and were never acceptable.

B. Secondly, Smith opposed government regulation of the economy—except in order to prevent the formation of monopolies and oligopolies.

C. Finally, Smith felt that prices should always be set by the free interaction of buyers and sellers in the marketplace—never by the government.

10. A

The list presents the perceived advantages of a capitalist economic system. A Marxist (communist) would argue that capitalism encourages individual greed rather than economic equality between citizens. B, C and D. A Marxist believes that capitalism exploits the working class, causes income inequality, and encourages private ownership of resources and industries—not public (state) ownership.

11. D

The list presents the advantages of a free enterprise economy (capitalist economy). This type of economy would be strongly supported by a conservative economist in the USA.

A, B, and C. Chinese communists (even those who support Red Capitalism) would favour more government control over the economy than would exist in a free market economy. Swedish democratic socialists and Labour Party supporters in Great Britain are strong supporters of the welfare state and are, therefore, further to the left on the economic spectrum than conservatives.

12. A

Democratic socialists admired American democracy but felt that American-style capitalism resulted in unacceptable poverty and exploitation. At the same time, they detested the oppressive government of the USSR but felt that some degree of government intervention in the economy was necessary.

B, C, and D. Unlike communists, democratic socialists condemn the use of violence to achieve economic goals. Democratic socialists generally favour private ownership of resources and industries; they generally embark on nationalization of industries only as a last resort—usually as a means of saving jobs that would otherwise be lost. Finally, democratic socialists support the welfare state and oppose central planning.

13. C

The trend shown in the graph indicates that Canadian trade has become less protectionist in nature; as a result of this freer trade with other countries, Canadian trade had become more integrated (interconnected) with other economies.

A, B, and D. The lowering of duties (tariffs) on foreign imports to Canada indicates that Canada has become less protectionist in nature. The graph does not provide any information about currency fluctuations or commodity prices.

14. B

The graph supports the conclusion that the reduction of tariffs (import duties) has forced Canadian manufacturers to become more competitive with foreign manufacturers. In a system of freer trade, Canadian companies cannot count on import taxes to make foreign products less appealing.

A, C, and D. In a system of freer trade, Canadian manufacturers have more access to foreign markets and rely less on sales within Canada. Canada is a resource-rich nation; freer trade has probably not made Canada more dependent on foreigners for natural resources; it has, however, probably made Canadians more dependent on manufactured goods from other nations. Canada has developed a service-based economy that has become less dependent on the manufacturing of machinery and equipment (capital goods).

15. B

Supply-side economic theory recommends tax breaks for businesses, deregulation, and privatization (the sale of state-owned industries).

A, C, and D. The given practices would occur in a right-wing, market-oriented economy that had adopted the trickle-down theory. These practices would not be found in a public enterprise (communist) economy, a democratic socialist state like Sweden, or a fascist economy (a command economy employing demand-side policies).

16. D

In the excerpt, the term "old economics" means Keynesian (demand-side) economics. The author sums up "old economics" as being those in which governments spend when the economy is bad, and restrain spending when the economy is good." This is a very concise summary of John Maynard Keynes' demand-side theory.

A, B, and C.

Classical liberals (laissez-faire capitalists) and supply-side economists would not recommend more government spending during recessions.

17. A

Supporters of a capitalist economy (market economy) would be most alarmed by the editorial's recommendation of government intervention in the economy. Capitalists view government intervention in the marketplace as unnecessary and/or harmful.

B, C, and D. The use of monetary policy (the manipulation of the money supply and interest rates) as a means of directing the economy and the reduction of government expenditure are both right-wing economic policies that are more palatable to a capitalist than left-wing economic interventionism.

18. D

Because of massive debts and deficits, Western governments have not been as free to aggressively intervene in the economy to prevent or combat recessionary pressures.

A. Aggressive government intervention requires massive government spending on such things as public works projects and social welfare programs. Government intervention requires available public funds; it does not depend on the availability of private investment capital.

B. A security-minded workforce with a lack of initiative would most likely exist in a communist economy; Western governments do not have communist economies.

C. In Western nations during the past two decades, voters have not pressured their governments to raise corporate taxes; in fact, governments have been allowed to reduce business taxes during the past twenty years.

19. A

Moderate right-wingers (conservatives) would support free market principles (capitalist theories), minimal government involvement in the economy, and private property rights.

B, C, and D. Conservatives do not believe in central planning, state regulation of the economy, economic radicalism (communism), or collectivism.

20. B

Soviet-style communists (Marxist–Leninists) believe in central planning, economic radicalism, and collective (group) rights.

A, C, and D. Communists oppose free market economics (capitalism), economic deregulation and non-intervention, and private property rights.

21. C

The generalization supports elitism—a sub-ideology of fascism. A fascist would support the view that "Only a few people possess the intelligence and ability to rule effectively" by appealing to the theory of Social Darwinism (which holds that "the state must recognize and allow for the basic fact of human nature that only the strong survive").

A, B, and D. A fascist would not justify his elitism (support for political inequality) with egalitarian collectivist ideas or faith in the wisdom of ordinary people. At the same time, fascists believe that the elite must serve the collective good (the interests of the state and community) not simply individual interests. According to the Fuhrer Principle (fuhrerprinzip), only the dictator truly understands the needs and interests of the nation.

22. A

The two cartoons focus on the collapse of communism in eastern Europe in the post-1988 era.

B. Firstly, after the collapse of communist regimes in eastern Europe in 1989 and the fall of the USSR in 1991, left-wing (communist) beliefs became less popular in Europe—not more popular.

C. Secondly, in the 1990s, capitalist (market) reforms were implemented in the formerly-communist nations of eastern Europe and received general support from eastern Europeans.

D. Finally, in the 1990s, democracy and the democratic proportional representation electoral system replaced totalitarianism in most ex-communist eastern European countries.

23. B

North Korea and Cuba are still communist dictatorships today. They have not yet experienced the democratization and economic liberalization movements that swept through eastern Europe in the 1990s.

A, C, and D. Iraq and Saudi Arabia were never communist dictatorships. All of the other nations listed (Poland, the Czech Republic, Albania, and Romania) moved away from communism in the 1990s.

24. D

Both cartoons suggest that extreme leftist (communist) ideals have lost their popularity. In the first cartoon, an East German no longer knows anything about Karl Marx (the founding father of communism). In the second cartoon, a toppled statue of Lenin (the founding father of Russian communism) is undergoing psychotherapy to deal with rejection by his former followers.

A, B, and C. Nothing in the two cartoons suggests that they are based on these assumptions.

25. A

Democratic theory holds that pressure groups and freedom of the press help to prevent majority tyranny (the trampling of the rights of minorities).

B. Firstly, democrats believe in the entrenchment of minority rights.

C. Secondly, the decisions made by bureaucrats (government officials) may and do come under attack from pressure groups and a free press in a democracy.

D. Finally, interest groups (pressure groups) and the media sometimes support alternative parties instead of traditional parties.

26. C

Fascists (extreme right-wing reactionaries) and communists (left-wing radicals) are willing to use violence to achieve their social and political goals.

A. Fascists accept economic inequality—but communists do not.

B. Communist believe that political power should be exercised by the masses—but fascists do not.

D. Communists are radicals who want to eradicate all aspects of traditional society; fascists, however, are reactionaries who want to revive lost traditions.

27. A

According to the graph, in 1999, the greatest number of voters would have voted for political parties with conservative views. Conservatives believe in less government involvement in the economy.

B, C, and D. Conservative voters would not support increased workers' rights, higher corporate taxes, or more public spending on social welfare programs.

28. C

The graph shows that, over time, the ideological views of voters have shifted toward the right side of the political-economic spectrum. This indicates that the general population has changed its social values.

A, B, and D. The graph does not suggest that public interest in political issues has declined—only that political views have changed. No information is provided about the number of political parties or views on election reforms.

29. C

Possible negative effects of adopting a PR electoral system include frequent minority and/or coalition governments. Since these governments are unstable and liable to fall because of non-confidence votes or failures to pass government bills, elections would likely occur more often in a PR system than under Canada's existing first-past-the-post (plurality) electoral system.

A, B, and D. It is unlikely that the adoption of the PR electoral system would result in elitist laws, a decrease in the number of political parties, more political apathy, or a lower voter turnout rate. In fact, opposite outcomes would probably occur. Such outcomes would generally be regarded as positive results of PR—not negative outcomes.

30. B

The excerpt describes a system of "rule by the few" (oligarchy). Before Britain adopted a system of universal suffrage, only men of wealth and property had the franchise (the right to vote)—and only men of wealth and property were elected.

A, C, and D. The excerpt makes no mention of aristocracy (rule by nobles), coalition government (a temporary alliance between two or more political parties), minority government (parliamentary rule by a government party with a minority of legislative seats), or a direct democracy (democracy through mass assemblies instead of elected representatives).

31. A

A referendum (the practice of referring measures proposed or passed by a legislative body to the vote of the electorate for approval or rejection) is a technique of direct democracy. Holding such a referendum would take ultimate decision-making power away from elected representatives and give it to the wider citizenry.

B. Firstly, only elected representatives are involved in the amending and passing of a private member's bill (a bill introduced by a MP who is not a member of the Cabinet); therefore, this is an example of representative democracy—not direct democracy.

C. Secondly, a free vote in the House of Commons would only involve elected representatives—not the direct vote of the citizenry as a whole; again, this would be an example of representative democracy.

D. Finally, although protestors might temporarily disrupt question period in the House of Commons (the time set aside in the House of Commons for the formal questioning of Cabinet members by opposition critics), these protestors would still not be directly participating in a government process. Neither this type of protest nor question period qualifies as an example of direct democracy, because neither action involves direct decision-making by the wider citizenry.

32. C

In a democracy with a separation of powers, the legislative branch makes laws, the judicial branch interprets the law, and the executive branch enforces the law.

A, B and D. The executive branch—not the legislative branch—suggests (proposes) new laws. The executive branch—not the judicial branch—enforces laws. The executive branch—not the legislative branch—administers the law. The legislative branch—not the judicial branch—makes laws. Judges—not legislators—interpret the law. The executive branch—not the judicial branch—applies the law. The legislative branch—not the executive branch—passes laws.

33. D

The given social and economic conditions existed in Russia during the 1990s.

A, B, and C. This set of conditions did not exist in Great Britain in the 1920s, in Canada during the 1930s, or West Germany in the 1980s. For instance, organized crime, political corruption, currency devaluation, and market collapse were not major trends in any of these countries during the given periods.

34. D

The technique shown in the two charts is indoctrination (teaching a person or group systematically or for a long period to accept partisan ideas uncritically). Government-directed youth groups and party organizations were important vehicles of indoctrination in both Nazi Germany and the USSR.

A, B, and C. No information is provided about purges (the elimination of political rivals), terror, or the direction of popular discontent (scapegoating).

35. B

The fascists used nationalism to attract the support of the intensely nationalistic German and Italian peoples. Many Italians and Germans were impressed by the extreme nationalist fervour (ultranationalism) that was on display at every fascist rally and ceremony.

A. Racism was not a major ingredient of Italian fascism and, even in Germany, ultranationalism gained the fascists more supporters than their racial policies.

C. Neither Italian fascists nor German fascists embraced isolationism (non-participation in alliances or in the affairs of other states); Mussolini's Italy and Nazi Germany both entered into alliances and intervened in the affairs of other states—in the Spanish Civil War, for example.

D. Finally, both German and Italian fascists promoted nationalism as the ultimate remedy for class divisions; fascists, unlike communists, do not encourage the class struggle between rich and poor; fascists encourage both rich and poor members of the nation to see each other as national brothers; fascists see the world as an arena for the struggle between nations—not classes.

36. C

The border changes shown on the map resulted from the Second World War. At the end of the war, the USSR annexed territories that once belonged to Poland, Czechoslovakia, and Romania. Similarly, in 1945, the borders of Poland and Yugoslavia were extended westward into German and Italian territories; this was done to punish the defeated Axis powers.

A, B, and D. The border changes shown on the map did not result from the First World War, the 1939 Nazi–Soviet Pact, or the end of the Cold War.

37. A

Josef Stalin, the dictator of the USSR, ordered most of the border changes shown on the map. Because Soviet troops occupied and controlled many eastern European nations (Poland, Estonia, Lithuania, Estonia, Romania, Czechoslovakia, Hungary, East Germany, and Bulgaria) at the end of the Second World War, the USSR was able to unilaterally change the borders of the occupied territories.

B. First of all, Stalin did not consider the wishes of national minorities before redrawing the borders of eastern Europe; in fact, the Soviets and their communist allies carried out brutal ethnic cleansing operations to drive minorities out of various border territories. For example, millions of Germans were driven out of the German territories that were given to Poland.

C. Secondly, the authoritarian governments that were set up in eastern European countries at the end of the war were puppet governments. These governments took their orders from Moscow; the puppet dictators played no real part in redrawing the boundaries.

D. Finally, none of the border changes shown resulted from refusals to pay reparations; in fact, the USA did not force any nation to make payments for the damages and costs of the Second World War.

38. B

The "imperative principle" referred to by Woodrow Wilson is self-determination (the right of a nationality to govern itself without outside interference). According to this principle, "national aspirations must be respected."

A, C, and D. It is obvious that Wilson's imperative principle does not refer to open diplomacy (non-secret international negotiations and agreements), collective security (common defence against aggression), or national expansion (adding adjacent territories to an existing nation state).

39. D

The idea that "Peoples are not to be handed about from one sovereignty to another" was most clearly disregarded in 1919 with the creation of the Polish Corridor. The Polish Corridor (the area between the Baltic Sea and the centre of Poland) was an ethnically German territory that was given to Poland so that the landlocked Polish nation would have access to the sea.

A, B, and C. Although the Austrian Germans were denied self-determination in 1919 (when they were not allowed to unite with the Germans of Germany), they were still allowed to have a separate state of their own. The Austrian part of Germany was not handed over to a non-German nation-state (like the Polish Corridor and the Sudentenland). Finland and the Baltic States (Estonia, Latvia, and Lithuania) were granted national independence in 1919.

40. A

The League of Nations failed to fulfill its mandate (the preservation of peace through collective security) when its member-states neglected to take effective action against fascist imperialism (empire-building) in Asia and Europe. For instance, the League did not stop the Japanese invasion of Manchuria or the Italian invasion of Ethiopia (Abyssinia).

B, C, and D. The League of Nations did not have a mandate to control domestic human rights abuses in Nazi Germany, to deal with downturns in the global economy, or prevent nations from adopting isolationist foreign policies.

41. A

The given developments encouraged Britain to adopt a foreign policy of appeasement (giving into an aggressor-nation in the effort to placate it and avoid a confrontation). Strong pacifism in Britain, among other things, made Britain reluctant to confront Germany or Italy during the 1930s. Instead, Britain sought to appease the fascist powers through the Hoare-Laval Pact and the Munich Pact.

B, C, and D. The given developments did not change Britain's relations with the USSR. Nor did they lead Britain to support American isolationism (non-participation in international affairs) or withdraw from continental (European) affairs.

42. D

The developments created a climate for appeasement that resulted in the Munich Accord (the 1938 agreement in which Germany was given the Sudentenland in Czechoslovakia in return for the assurance that Hitler would not seek to annex or invade other European territories).

A, B, and C. The given developments had no impact on public support for the 1919 Treaty of Versailles (peace treaty between Germany and the Allied Powers), the 1917 Balfour Declaration (a British statement of support for a Jewish homeland in Palestine), or the 1945 Yalta Agreement (the deal struck by Stalin, Roosevelt, and Churchill at a First World War summit meeting).

43. B

Mussolini responded to the League of Nations' limited (and ineffective) economic sanctions by establishing closer ties with Nazi Germany (in the Rome–Berlin Axis).

A, C, and D. The League's economic sanctions did not result in an Italian withdrawal from Ethiopia or Italian neutrality. Furthermore, Mussolini had supported fascism as an alternative to democracy for more than a decade before the League imposed sanctions; the sanctions had no effect on Mussolini's ideological beliefs.

44. A

The governments of Great Britain and France chose not to intervene in the Spanish Civil War for several reasons. One of these was the fear that the war could escalate into a wider European conflict.

B, C, and D. The British and French policy of non-intervention was not based on the hope that the fascists would win the war, that the League of Nations could resolve the conflict, or that staying out of the conflict would help the Republican side.

45. C

The UN Charter committed the organization to the maintenance of global peace through collective security (a policy of discouraging aggression by presenting an aggressor-nation with the real threat of a collective armed response). However, the use of veto power by the permanent members of the UN Security Council prevented the UN from using force to stop aggression on many occasions.

A, B, and D. UN collective security operations have not been undermined by the UN General Assembly, UN Secretariat, or UN special humanitarian agencies—because the Security Council has the final say over the deployment of UN troops—not these other bodies.

46. B

The four events demonstrate that international collective security organizations do not always provide the promised support. The League did not stop Italy from conquering Ethiopia. The UN sent troops to Korea and the Persian Gulf to maintain the sovereignty of South Korea and Kuwait. But the UN did not effectively act to protect Croatia, Bosnia, or Kosovo from Serbian aggression.

A, C, and D. None of the other generalizations completes the diagram.

47. B

By supporting the terms of the 1938 Munich Agreement, France abandoned commitments made to Czechoslovakia in the Little Entente. France's connection to the Little Entente (the 1920–38 alliance between Czechoslovakia, Romania, and Yugoslavia) stemmed from a 1924 treaty with Czechoslovakia in which France promised to defend Czechoslovakia's independence and territorial integrity. In the Munich Agreement, France broke this promise by agreeing to Germany's annexation of the Sudentenland (northwest Czechoslovakia).

A, C, and D. In the Munich Pact, France did not abandon its commitments to Great Britain, the USA, or Germany.

48. C

Canadians played a major role in Battle 4 (the raid on Dieppe) and Battle 11 (D-Day).

A, B, and D. In the Second World War, Canadians participated in the Battle of Britain, the Battle of the Atlantic, and the invasion of Sicily. Canadian units did not take part in the Battle of the Bulge (Americans versus Germans), the Battle of El Alamein (British versus Germans and Italians), or the Battle of Stalingrad (the Soviet Red Army versus Germans).

49. C

D-Day (the invasion of German-occupied Normandy) marked the beginning of the liberation of northwestern Europe by American, British, and Canadian troops.

A, B, and D. German troops were forced to abandon North Africa immediately after the Battle of El Alamein in 1942; they never occupied Egypt during the Second World War. The Germans were defeated in the Battle of Stalingrad and did not gain any Soviet resources in their unsuccessful attempt to seize the Russian city. Nazi Germany initiated the Holocaust in June 1941—not in December of 1944.

50. D

A sphere of influence is "a claimed or recognized area of a state's interests." Communist Cuba and Hungary fell within the Soviet sphere at the time of the 1956 Hungarian Uprising and the 1962 Cuban Missile Crisis. In both situations, the USSR ignored American challenges and acted to preserve its sphere of influence.

A, B, and C. The USA and USSR did not clash with one another in the Gulf War, Suez Crisis, or Six-Day War. Furthermore, they only indirectly confronted one another in the Korean War and Vietnam War.

51. B

In both the Korean War and the Vietnam War, the USA attempted to contain the spread of communism in Asia.

A. Firstly, Soviet troops did not fight against American soldiers in Korea or Vietnam.

C. Secondly, the Korean War resulted in deadlock, but the Vietnam War was won by the communist side.

D. Finally, communist forces successfully unified a divided Vietnam but failed to unite the two Koreas.

52. C

Brinkmanship is "the art of taking big risks in the pursuit of foreign policy goals—even to the brink of war—in the hope that opponents of one's goals will back down." The Soviet Union risked war with the USA when it cut off American access to West Berlin in 1948–49; this event is a good example of brinkmanship.

A, B, and D. The concept of brinkmanship is not illustrated by the Kellogg–Briand Pact (the international agreement in which nations renounced war as a foreign policy option), the Marshall Plan (the American program of economic assistance for war-torn Europe), or SALT I (the bilateral USA–USSR nuclear weapons limitation treaty).

53. A

The writer suggests that the American intervention in Vietnam continued for so long because Americans feared the international and domestic consequences of withdrawal from Vietnam. He states, for instance, that pulling out of Vietnam would have led to disillusionment among America's other allies.

B, C, and D. The writer does not suggest that American involvement in Vietnam was motivated mainly by the popularity of the war in America, the desire to establish new military alliances in Asia, or the wish to impose democracy on dictatorial governments.

54. B

The writer is referring to the spread of communist influence following the Second World War when he refers to "Yalta" and "the loss of China." The Soviet Union gained control of North Korea as a result of the Yalta Agreement of 1945 and set up a communist dictatorship there. At Yalta, Stalin also consolidated his control over eastern Europe and established more communist regimes there. Later, with Soviet backing, the communists won the Chinese Civil War and established a Marxist dictatorship in China in 1949.

A, C, and D. When the writer makes references to Yalta and China, he is not commenting on American neutrality or isolationism, détente (the easing of tensions between the USA and the communist dictatorships in Russia and China), or the Sino–Soviet split.

55. C

One of the most controversial issues of the Second World War is the question: "Who was responsible for the Holocaust?" Opinions vary as to how complicit the German people, Europeans, and humanity were in the mass murder of six million Jews during the Second World War.

A, B, and D. Neither the Nazi–Soviet Pact nor the Second World War spying have generated enduring controversy; there is considerable agreement among historians about these subjects. Differing viewpoints exist on the question of whether or not the western Allies should have invaded Nazi-occupied western Europe prior to D-Day; however, this question is not as hotly debated as the given question about the Holocaust.

56. D

The Treaties of Rome (25 March 1957) created the European Economic Community (European Common Market)—the forerunner of today's European Union.

A, B, and C. The given articles are not related to the formation of the Allied Control Council , NATO, or the Council for Mutual Economic Assistance.

57. C

Supranationalism is support for the creation of laws and institutions that are above the level of the nation state. By seeking economic integration and creating common economic policies, the member-states of the EEC were promoting supranationalism.

A. Membership in the European Common Market (EEC) necessitated the surrender of some national sovereignty; when a nation joins together with other nations to create common economic policies, it will no longer have complete control over its own economy.

B. Ultranationalism (extreme or excessive nationalism) is not the same thing as supranationalism (support for the creation of international laws, agreements, and organizations by national governments).

D. The European Economic Community brought about economic integration, it did not enhance the national security of western European nations.

58. D

The Vietnam War and the War in Afghanistan were both civil wars in which members of the same nationality (Vietnamese nationals/Afghans) fought against one another. The Balkan Wars of the 1990s were also civil conflicts in which former citizens of Yugoslavia battled for control of Yugoslav territories. All three wars (Vietnam, Afghanistan, and Yugoslavia) were also wars of national liberation in which nationalities fought to break free of outside control. The Viet Minh and Viet Cong rebels fought to drive French and American soldiers out of Vietnam. The Afghan rebels fought to drive Soviet troops out of Afghanistan. In the Balkan Wars, Slovenes, Croats, Bosnian Muslims, and Albanian Kosovars fought to break free of domination by Serbia. All three wars dragged on for many years, despite the efforts of the USA and Russia to end the conflicts.

A, B, and C. The Balkans (mountainous territories in southeastern Europe) were not an area in which superpowers tried to restore a sphere of influence in the 1990s. No UN peacekeeping forces were sent to Vietnam or Afghanistan. The primary aim of superpower involvement in each of these three wars was not to maintain control over foreign markets.

59. D

In early 1989, Richard Nixon doubted that the Cold War was ending because the USSR still controlled several eastern European nations. His doubts were challenged later in that year when these eastern European nations gained their independence from the Soviet Union.

A. Firstly, Mikhail Gorbachev was never elected (never mind re-elected) by the people of the Soviet Union in a fair and open election.

B. Secondly, the two superpowers did not agree to eliminate all land-based nuclear missiles in 1989.

C. Finally, the hard-line communist coup attempt took place in 1991—not 1989; in any case, this attempted overthrow of Gorbachev would have reinforced—not alleviated—Richard Nixon's doubts about the good intentions of the USSR.

60. A

George Kennan (the speaker of Source II) argues that the greatest obstacle to ending the Cold War was American distrust of the USSR. He notes that Americans "must have an opposite pole of evil" and clung to "Cold War myths and stereotypes" that represented the Soviet Union as an evil empire.

B, C, and D. George Kennan does not suggest that the major barrier to better relations between the USA and USSR was a Soviet refusal to participate in bilateral arms talks, the pacing of reform in the USSR, or American appeasement of the Soviet Union.

61. B

The cartoon suggests that American business investment may lead to the continuance of the superpower arms race. The cartoonist shows that, if American assistance helps to repair the stalled economy of the USSR, Soviet military production will begin moving again.

A, C, and D. Nothing in the cartoon suggests these three messages.

62. C

Source I and Source III both suggest that it is not in the interest of the USA to provide the USSR with economic assistance.

A, B, and D. These statements are inaccurate. Source II's point of view differs substantially from that of sources I and III.

63. D

The writer comments that French war criminals in the Second World War were following orders given by a foreign occupation force. He notes, "The Germans were responsible for their actions. The French people were subject to an occupying army that imposed its will upon them."

A, B, and C. The writer does not directly suggest any of these things.

64. B

The source of the writer's unease is his concern that a war crimes trial would be prejudiced by influences outside the legal system. In his closing statement, the writer notes that "Setting forth the truth should remain the province of...the courts, rather than of the political arena, which is tempted to take whatever position it deems most advantageous."

A, C, and D. The writer fears political interference with France's justice system—not the political problems that might result from a war crimes trial.

65. A

The writer expresses support for protectionism (the practice of protecting domestic industries from foreign competition through import duties).

B, C, and D. The writer does not recommend that nations adopt leftist social policies, enter into alliances, or conclude free trade agreements.

66. B

The World Trade Organization and the International Monetary Fund are UN bodies that strive for greater economic cooperation between the world's nations. Both organizations are trying to integrate dozens of different national economies into one global marketplace.

A, C, and D. The WTO and IMF do not promote extreme nationalism (ultranationalism) or national sovereignty. In fact, membership in either organization requires the surrender of some national economic sovereignty. Neither the IMF or the WTO is a collective security organization like NATO or the UN.

67. C

Present-day Marxists allege that multinational corporations now dominate and exploit the developing world in the same way that imperial powers (such as Britain and France) did in the nineteenth century. They use the term "neo-colonialism" to describe the economic dominance of the Third World by transnational corporations.

A, B, and D. Economic imperialism (the domination of the economy of a weaker nation by a stronger nation) is not exemplified by the creation of colonial empires (political imperialism) or the development of military spheres or influence (political or military imperialism). Supranational organizations (such as the EU or the UN) need not be imperialist in nature.

68. D

The lesson of Munich is that a hard-line stance must be taken by nations negotiating with an aggressor state. At the 1938 Munich Conference, Neville Chamberlain mistakenly believed that appeasing Hitler (conceding to Hitler's demands) would stop future German aggression.

A, B, and C. None of these lessons relates to the mistake made by Neville Chamberlain at the Munich Conference.

69. A

The cartoon suggests that Boris Yeltsin wanted to regain control over the former Soviet republics of Ukraine, Belarus, Moldova, Estonia, Latvia, and Lithuania—and, possibly, over Russia's former satellite states (Poland, Hungary, Romania, etc.).

B, C, and D. Nothing in the cartoon suggests that Yeltsin's Russia desired to revive détente, enter into alliances with western European nations, or resurrect the obsolete policies of glasnost (political liberalization) or perestroika (economic restructuring).

70. B

In response to the Russian military threat, most eastern European nations have sought to establish formal links with NATO. Some have already become full-fledged NATO partners.

A, C, and D. None of these strategies is the preferred way of dealing with the Russian threat to national sovereignty in eastern Europe.

Answers and Solutions
January 2002 Diploma Examination

1. B	11. C	21. C	31. B	41. A	51. C	61. A
2. C	12. A	22. A	32. C	42. B	52. B	62. D
3. A	13. B	23. C	33. A	43. C	53. D	63. A
4. D	14. D	24. D	34. D	44. C	54. A	64. B
5. C	15. C	25. A	35. B	45. B	55. D	65. C
6. C	16. D	26. D	36. B	46. C	56. B	66. D
7. B	17. B	27. A	37. D	47. D	57. D	67. A
8. A	18. C	28. D	38. C	48. C	58. B	68. A
9. D	19. D	29. D	39. B	49. D	59. B	69. C
10. A	20. A/D	30. B	40. A	50. A	60. A	70. B

1. B

One of the fundamental principles of democracy is that government is responsible (accountable) to the people. Government is held accountable for its actions.

B. In a democracy, the government is accountable to the voters. They have the choice of voting for the present government or for a new government. The government that wins the election has received its legitimacy (right to govern) from the people. Elections must be held every few years to ensure that government leaders are accountable to the citizens.

A. In a democracy, constitutional safeguards for minorities are the primary means of preventing tyranny of the majority. Elections might also help to protect minorities, but a party that wins a large enough majority can govern as it pleases without much regard for minority rights.

C. Regular elections cannot prevent party leaders from dominating their political parties. Such domination can only be prevented through regular leadership reviews, leadership conventions, and policy conventions.

D. Minority groups only gain representation if they can elect representatives to the legislature. Depending on the voting system used in the country, a minority group may not have representation.

2. C

The given issue is about emergency legislation during a crisis. The affirmative (positive) position on the issue is that in a time of danger or great difficulty, the government should have the right to proclaim emergency legislation (such as the War Measures Act or the Emergencies Act) that restricts civil liberties.

C. Using undemocratic means (restricting freedoms) to preserve democracy (during an emergency) does support an affirmative answer to the statement.

A. No one in a democracy would argue that egalitarianism (equality) could be a crisis requiring emergency legislation.

B. Preserving minority rights would be the opposite of restricting rights. Thus, this statement does not support an affirmative answer to the question.

D. This response is about the effectiveness of force. Thus, it does not support an affirmative answer to the question.

3. A

The executive branch of the American government consists of the president, the vice-president, the cabinet, and the civil service (bureaucracy). The legislative branch of the American government is called Congress and consists of two legislative houses: the Senate and the House of Representatives.

A. In the American political system, special interest groups—pressure groups and lobby groups— can exert pressure on a various elected representatives who wield significant political power. They can try to influence both representatives from the legislative branch (senators and congressmen) and the executive branch (the president).

B. The balance of power between the legislature and the executive does not provide greater opportunity for party leaders to win nominations for primary elections.

C. The organization of the American political system does not affect the ability of citizens to participate in elections. Citizens in all democracies can participate in elections.

D. In 2002, only two members of Congress were not also members of the two mainstream American political parties, the Democrats and Republicans. However, existence of equally powerful executive and legislative branches of government does not affect how the voters choose their representatives.

4. D

Totalitarian leaders are extremist dictators who attempt to completely control all aspects of public and private life.

D. Totalitarian leaders often make a show of elections and of speaking for the people, but have no intention of allowing criticism or dissent. The legislature must rubber-stamp executive decisions and the judiciary can only enforce the laws that result.

A. Party membership is often widespread and includes members of all classes. This is because the party is held to be the only legitimate representative of the people.

B. Ownership of industry and production can be public or private depending on the kind of totalitarian party. In Mao's China, ownership was public, while in Hitler's Germany, ownership was private.

C. If opposition parties are tolerated at all, their role is restricted and minor. However, control of opposition parties is part of the larger tactic of controlling the legislature and judiciary.

5. C

This question requires an understanding of democratic and authoritarian values and principles.

C. Democrats would have the least objection to the collective good prevailing over individual privilege. Democrats are supporters of equal rights for all citizens and generally oppose privileges (special rights or advantages) for particular individuals or select groups.

A. Democrats want to limit the will of the leader, or at least they want to hold the leader accountable for the exercise of that will.

B. If the state controls thought and uses the education system to promote a particular ideology, then democracy is undermined and the government cannot be held accountable. A supporter of democracy would strongly object to this kind of indoctrination.

D. Democrats think government control will stifle thought and creativity.

6. C

This question requires understanding of the word *polarized* (divided between two extremes). It also requires the ability to make inferences (conclusions based on evidence) from election results presented in a graph.

C. *Polarized* means divided between two extremes. After 1928, the Social Democratic Party and the Communist Party (both far-left parties) together held 222 seats of the 608 in the Reichstag, or Parliament. The National Socialist, or Nazi Party (a far-right party), held 230 seats. The remaining five significant parties, along with the "others," shared only 146 seats.

The political power was divided between the far left and the far right. Thus, German politics became increasing polarized.

A. the political stability of Europe cannot be referred from data that refer exclusively to Germany.

B. The election results show that support for the National Socialist Party peaked in July 1932 when it had 230 seats in the Reichstag. By the time of the November election, Nazi support had dropped, and the party won only 196 seats. The two far-left parties (the Communists and Social Democratics) had a combined total of 241 seats.

D. In 1932, the two far-left parties held significantly more seats than the Nazis. The overall support for the left wing had not declined.

7. B

As in the last question, it is necessary to make inferences (conclusions based on evidence) from data. To decide which question would be most useful in researching, the sources must be taken together.

B. Two of the three sources have information that can be used to research whether or not the Nazi party had popular support: the Nazi party membership data and the Reichstag election results.

A. Source I has the only economic data. Also, data beginning in 1929 would not be useful for researching the 1920s.

C. None of the sources gives any information about German recovery after the First World War. The unemployment data only begin in 1929, ten years after the war ended.

D. We might be able to infer that the Communist Party was unable to unite the left-wing vote, but more than one source out of three is required. Thus, B is the best answer.

8. A

Students are expected to draw conclusions from data.

A. Source I shows that the rate of unemployment increased drastically from 1929 to 1932. The trend shown in Source III is the increasing polarization of politics in Germany. Thus, there is reason to believe that the statement is accurate: a huge increase in unemployment represented a major cause of polarization. In other words, the Great Depression eroded support for democratic parties and caused citizens to turn to non-democratic parties for economic solutions.

B. There is nothing in the party membership data to explain why unemployment grew. (Unemployment might be used to explain why membership in the party grew, but that is not the question).

C. The chart cannot be used to interpret voting patterns. First, there is no date given for the Nazi Party membership data. We cannot assume that party membership remained unchanged through all the elections. Second, there is no way to tell from the election results whether or not all white-collar Nazis voted for the party. We do not know how many party members there were, or how many other German citizens voted for the Nazi party, or whether some party members voted against the party. Even party members do not always vote for their party.

D. High levels of unemployment and a polarized electorate did affect the distribution of party memberships: the increasing popularity of the Marxist parties did push businessmen, professionals, and white-collar workers toward the Nazis. Thus, the data do not show "no effect."

9. D

Students are expected to understand that a reactionary favours a return to a pre-existing state of affairs. A reactionary is someone who wants to turn back the clock and bring back practices of the past.

D. The restoration of the death penalty would bring back a practice that has been abandoned. Therefore, it would be a reactionary action.

A. Electing senators would be something new (and therefore progressive)—not a restoration of a past practice.

B. In the past, the federal government refused to apologize for the mistreatment of ethnic minorities. So, apologizing would be a recent and unprecedented trend.

C. Mandating a certain percentage of female candidates is a novel (and therefore progressive) reform—not an idea from the past.

10. A

Some dictatorial and totalitarian governments do hold elections. The usual patterns of control remain.

A. The governments of non-democratic countries, if they allow elections at all, hold rigged elections. The intent is to make it appear that the government has popular support and thus legitimacy. In dictatorships, such elections are an example of the dictatorial technique of controlled participation.

B. Citizens are only allowed to effect change in democratic countries.

C. Sometimes, non-democratic countries have legislated constitutions, and one purpose of holding elections is to meet the requirements of constitutional law. However, since dictators violate constitutional law whenever they wish, meeting constitutional requirements is never a primary reason for staging elections.

D. In a dictatorship, the results of an election are predetermined and opposition is severely punished. Dissenters know that their ballots have probably been monitored and that a vote against the regime will be punished. Voters will rarely express discontent by voting the wrong way. Therefore, an election in an authoritarian regime—unlike an election in a democracy—will not provide insight into the real attitudes and beliefs of citizens. Dictators understand this, and do not hold elections for the purpose providing insight.

11. C

There are three elements in this cartoon. One is the oversized statue of Lenin, which represents the totalitarian communist regime. One trait of totalitarian regimes is the cult of the leader, and toppling oversized statues of the leaders is a common response to the ending of a regime. The second element is the salesman, representative of the new free-market economic system. The third is the bemused Russian citizen holding a newspaper with election headlines suggesting a close race between Boris Yeltsin and the Communist Party. The voter is presented in beard, fur hat, and long coat— the traditional costume of the working-class Russian.

C. The hinges are the key image. The statue can be raised or lowered according to the change of the party in power. If the communists win, the statue of Lenin can be quickly re-erected. The cartoonist is commenting on the instability of Russian politics.

A. There is no voter choice in a one-party system, but the election headlines mention Yeltsin. The communist regime has already ended and the communists are just one party running in genuine elections.

B. The Russian voter is not represented as an extremist. He is drawn as a very old-fashioned, traditional Russian. It is possible that extremism is the cause of the political instability of Russia, but there is nothing in the picture to suggest it.

D. The salesman might represent entrepreneurial innovation, but there is no other comment on market ideologies.

12. A

See the solution for question 11.

A. The hinges are the key image. The statue can be raised or lowered, depending on who wins the next election, and the next, and the next. Perhaps the communist ideology has not been rejected permanently.

B. Nothing in the cartoon suggests the use of force and terror. We know that Lenin (and totalitarian leaders in general) used force and terror, but the question is to be answered from the details of the cartoon.

C. It is true that political leaders promote positive images of themselves, but the totalitarian cult of the leader goes far beyond ordinary images. It is one means of establishing control over the population. This cartoon does not apply to leaders in general, only to Russian leaders.

D. Democratic systems of government often do create political stability. The point of this cartoon is the lack of stability in Russia, even though it now has a democratic system.

13. B

This question tests knowledge of the core beliefs of fascism and Marxism and of utopian and democratic socialism.

B. Marxism teaches that human history must be understood in terms of economic struggle between classes. The final stages of this process would be a class struggle between capitalists and the proletariat, or the workers. The struggle would end in violent revolution and the overthrow of capitalism. The dictatorship of the proletariat would follow. All classes except the proletarian class would be eliminated, and the state would then gradually disappear. A classless society would follow. This last condition was sometimes called "the workers' paradise."

A. The core beliefs of fascism include support for dictatorship, a controlled private enterprise economy, militarism, and extreme nationalism.

C. Utopian socialists were nineteenth century reformers who believed that persuasion would be enough to bring about a more just and equitable economy and society. Although utopian socialists differed greatly in their ideas and in their strategies for overcoming the abuses of capitalism, none of them called for a violent struggle, the eradication of the bourgeoisie as a class, or a dictatorship of the proletariat. Although the Marxist vision of the withering away of the state is a utopian (impossibly ideal) vision, it is not a utopian socialist vision.

D. Democratic socialism does not aim for complete economic equality (a classless society); it only wishes to narrow the gap between rich and poor by a partial redistribution of wealth. Nor do democratic socialists advocate a violent class struggle, a dictatorship of the proletariat, or the dismantling of the state.

14. D

This question is about Marx's doctrines on history and economics.

D. Marx believed that the communist system would unfold according to a fixed and deterministic plan. First, class struggle, then a violent revolution. Next would be the dictatorship of the proletariat, followed by the elimination of classes. After that, the state would disappear and a classless society would be the final stage of the process.

15. C

This question requires an understanding of different electoral (voting) systems used by democratic nations. The main electoral systems are plurality and proportional representation. Plurality voting gives the legislative seat to the candidate with the most votes in a geographical area called a constituency, even if that number is less than 50% of the total. Proportional representation voting divides the seats in the legislature between parties according to the percentage of the total vote won by the party. It is clear from the chart that Nation X uses the plurality system since there is no direct correspondence between the percentage of votes and seats received by a party. Party A received less than half of the votes in both elections but won over half the seats. Thus, it forms a majority government and it can pass legislation without consulting the other parties.

C. Majority governments are generally stable and can legislate efficiently. Plurality electoral systems produce majority governments more frequently than proportional representation systems do.

A. The plurality system does not, by itself, prevent tyranny of the majority. Once elected, Party A can pass any legislation it wishes, at least until the next election.

B. This plurality system actually encourages the formation of majority governments.

D. If the seats in the legislature were divided proportionally, then no party on the chart would have a majority (over half the seats). Party A would have to form a government in partnership with another party. Such governments are called coalition governments. Party A would have to consult with the other parties. But in this case, the plurality system has given Party A virtually all the power. Coalition governments are less likely under a plurality system than under a proportional representation system.

16. D

The diagram illustrates political accountability in a democratic system of government. Three of the given items are means of holding elected representatives accountable for their actions. One of the items is an obstacle to political accountability.

D. Cabinet solidarity means that the members of the cabinet may disagree and debate in private; however, in public, they will always support government decisions. In practice, cabinet solidarity tends to erode political accountability, as citizens cannot determine which cabinet members actually proposed or supported a particular policy. Cabinet solidarity means cabinet secrecy. Politicians can only be held accountable when their actions are open, public, and transparent—not when their actions are private and taken behind closed doors.

A. The question period allows opposition members of the legislature to question cabinet ministers.

B. Media scrutiny means that the actions of the government are published and commented on.

C. Appeals to the Supreme Court are challenges to laws and sometimes they result in changes to laws.

17. B

Elections are essential in a democracy. There are two main electoral systems. In a plurality voting system, candidates run for office in constituencies. In each constituency, the candidate who wins the largest number of votes—even by one vote—represents that constituency in the legislature. In a proportional representation system, the members of the legislature are chosen from lists made by the party. A party receives the same percentage of legislative seats as the percentage of votes that it won in the election.

B. The "mixed system" described is a combination of a plurality system ("half of the members are elected from constituencies") and a PR system ("half are drawn from party lists according to their share of the popular vote").

A. Federalism is a system dividing power between two or more levels of government in country. In such a system, the federal government has power over matters affecting the entire country. Regional matters are the responsibility of provincial (in some countries, state) governments. Nothing in the excerpt suggests federalism.

Revolving minority governments can be a weakness of the PR system of voting. In some countries, no party can get ever get a majority, and the parties cannot agree for long. Frequent elections are the result. The excerpt is not about a pure PR electoral system.

C. Proportional representation often results in coalition governments. However, the mixed system described is an attempt to avoid the weaknesses of the PR system.

D. The congressional system is a way of organizing the government. The chief executive is not part of the legislature and is not answerable to the legislature and the members of the legislature have more independence in passing legislation. In a congressional system, plurality voting is the system for awarding seats in the legislature. Seats are not allotted from party lists or according to the popular vote.

18. C

The excerpt criticizes the supply-side economic ideas associated with Prime Minister Margaret Thatcher and President Ronald Reagan. "Thatcherites and Reaganites" believe in "trickle down" economics. They favour low taxes for the wealthy and for corporations. The idea is that free markets are the most efficient and produce the most wealth—and that wealth spreads throughout the nation by natural economic forces. They want as little government control of the economy as possible, and do not favour a redistribution of wealth through social programs.

C. The writer asserts that the free enterprise principles of Thatcher and Reagan did not result in job-creation, general prosperity, or economic recovery.

A. Government-funded employment programs are not part of the free-enterprise principles that the writer is criticizing. They are part of socialist principles that "Thatcherites and Reaganites" oppose.

B. The writer is not criticizing anti-recessionary monetary and fiscal reforms in general, but only the supply-side reforms used by the Thatcherites and Reaganites. The writer might support the Keynesian (demand-side) monetary and fiscal reforms that are rejected by supply-siders.

D. The writer seems to favour more government intervention in the economy. He criticizes Thatcherism and Reaganomics for being too laissez-faire.

19. D

The labels "left wing" and "right wing" are imprecise, but it is necessary to understand the political ideas that are usually associated with each label.

D. The writer is criticizing what are termed right-wing ideas. Right-wing conservatives (supporters of capitalism) form the group that would most strongly disagree with the writer.

A. Social democrats and democratic socialists are generally in favour of government control of many (but not all) aspects of the economy.

B. Liberal moderates are close to the "centre," and are likely to approve of a mixture of free-market and socialist principles. They would not strongly disagree with the writer.

C. Left-wing radicals (communists) would be in favour of very strong government intervention in the economy. Being extremists, they would favour complete government ownership of the means of production.

20. A or D

Study all graphs carefully. It is easy to misread the data.

A. The graph shows the bank rate rising from 1990 to 1991 and from 1996 to 1998. During these periods, the unemployment rate rose and the inflation rate fell.

D. Response D is actually a rewording of A. Both answers are correct.

B. Inflation increased and unemployment dropped when the bank rate was dropping from 1991 to 1996.

C. At no time did inflation and unemployment increase together.

21. C

There can be a relationship between inflation and salary increases. Large wage increases for many skilled workers can lead to inflation if businesses increase prices to offset the costs of the wage increases. Inflation can also be caused by the increase in the prices of raw materials for industry. In this case, workers demand pay increases to offset the rising cost of living. Skilled workers are mentioned specifically. This is because they are the most likely to belong to unions and to be in a position to be able to bargain for large increases.

C. 1995–96: The inflation rate increased sharply. This could have been caused by large wage increases among skilled workers. On the other hand, wages might have increased because skilled workers demanded more pay to make up for inflation.

A. 1990–91: The inflation rate decreased. Neither of the above reasons for wage increases applies.

B. 1993–94: The inflation increased, but only slightly. Large wage increases are less likely.

D. 1996–97: The inflation rate decreased. Neither of the above reasons for wage increases applies.

22. A

This question tests understanding of the values and principles underlying public enterprise (communist) systems.

A. Supporters of public enterprise would criticize the economic competition characteristic of capitalism for wasting valuable economic resources on competitive advertising, catering to wants instead of supplying needs, producing luxury goods rather than basic necessities, and encouraging planned obsolescence and a throw-away mentality.

B. Supporters of public enterprise are communists who want a completely equal distribution of wealth. They believe that capitalism causes economic inequality and an unfair distribution of wealth.

C. Competition is the operation of supply and demand. Supporters of public enterprise systems do not want to allow supply and demand to run the economy.

D. If competition distributed more wealth to the consumer than it did to the producer, then it would encourage a more equal distribution of wealth. Supporters of public enterprise do not believe that this actually results from free-market competition.

23. C

Nazi Germany had a controlled private enterprise economy. Private businesses were induced to produce the military equipment that Hitler wanted. (However, extensive production of consumer goods was allowed even during the first years of the Second World War.)

C. Private enterprises (privately owned businesses) produced goods in Nazi Germany, although they took direction from Nazi overlords and were subject to plans, such as the Four-Year Plan, for the economic development of the Third Reich.

A. The majority of Nazi Germany's resources and industries were privately owned and operated.

B. The entrepreneurial class (capitalist risk-taking businessmen) in Nazi Germany represented only a small minority of the total population. Hitler made little or no effort to encourage more Germans to become entrepreneurs.

D. The Nazis did not take a laissez-faire economic approach. Instead, they regularly intervened in the economy through job-creation schemes, public works projects, and subsidies and incentives to armaments manufacturers.

24. D

The main ideas in the excerpt are the exploitation of the working class by a small number of capitalists and the eventual revolt of the working class.

D. Two of Marx's main ideas were that an increasingly small group of capitalists oppressed the working class and that class warfare would lead to the triumph of the working class. The ideas in the excerpt are most closely associated with Karl Marx.

A. John Maynard wanted government to use limited economic intervention to eliminate the problems caused by capitalism's boom-and-bust cycle. He was a liberal economist who wanted to save capitalism, not to destroy it. He did not call for a proletarian (workers') revolution.

B. John Stuart Mill was a reform liberal who supported social welfare legislation and labour unions as ways of reducing the inequities of 19th century laissez-faire capitalism. He did not advocate a communist-style workers' revolution or call for the overthrow of the bourgeoisie.

C. Adam Smith was the father of laissez-faire capitalist theory. The criticisms of laissez-faire capitalism in the excerpt have nothing to do with Smith's ideas.

25. A

The excerpt refers to the ideas of Karl Marx. It is necessary to interpret the words of the excerpt.

A. The phrase "the constant decrease in the number of capitalist magnates" means that there are fewer capitalist magnates (rich owners of capital who control the means of production). These capitalists are the only ones who have any large amount of wealth. So the decrease in their number means that wealth is concentrated in the hands of fewer and fewer people.

B. The phrase "the mass of misery" refers to the numerous workers, who are being exploited by the capitalists.

C. The phrase "the revolt of the working class" refers to the final step in the struggle between workers and the capitalists. After the capitalists have been destroyed and the dictatorship of the proletariat has reorganized society, all classes will disappear and there will be no more wealth or poverty.

D. The phrase "the capitalist process of production" refers to the modern factory system of organizing workers and equipment to increase production.

26. D

This question examines the beliefs of social democrats. Three of the responses are supported by social democrats.

D. Social democrats believe in progressive income tax, which taxes high-income earners more than lower-income earners. It is supply-side economists and neo-conservatives who support the reduction of income taxes for high-income earners.

A. Social democrats emphasize the common good over individual profit.

B. Social democrats want to regulate business practices to protect consumers.

C. Social democrats wish to provide social programs for low-income groups.

27. A

This question tests knowledge of the differences between Keynesian economic theory and supply-side economic theory.

A. Providing financial incentives to business can mean several things, but in the context of this question, it means supply-side economics. In this case, financial incentives to the business sector mean cutting the high taxes on high incomes in order to encourage business expansion, more capital investment, and increased production. (Remember that high-income earners can be businesses as well as individuals.)

Keynes believed that governments should stimulate economic growth during a recession by encouraging consumer spending through increased spending on social welfare programs and on public works projects. He did not believe that economic growth would result from encouraging suppliers to produce more by reducing taxes for corporations and the wealthy.

B. Providing financial incentives to low-income earners means tax cuts, tax rebates, or personal transfers through welfare program spending. Keynes believed that money in the hands of low-income earners would be spent on consumer goods. This spending would stimulate the economy by directly stimulating demand, which would stimulate supply (increased production).

C. Controlling inflation through wage and price controls is not part of supply-side economics. Instead, supply-side economists support economic growth through encouraging higher productivity—that is, increased production without increased costs of production. This means that there is no pressure on business to increase prices and thus increase inflation.

D. Controlling inflation through the adjustment of lending rates is part of monetarism, the theory that recommends regulating the economy solely through manipulation of bank interest rates and the money supply. Supply-side economic theory does not favour monetary policy. Instead, it favours fiscal policy taxing and spending policies as the primary means of stimulating economic growth. (In this context, taxing and spending policies mean reducing taxes and reducing government spending.)

28. D

Soviet economic policy changed over the seventy years of the existence of the Soviet Union. Each of the four Soviet leaders named made changes to economic policy. Which of the leaders ushered in increased production of consumer goods, diversified and privatized agricultural programs, and decentralized economic planning and government services? Notice that these reforms represent an enormous change from traditional Soviet policy.

D. In 1986, Mikhail Gorbachev began reforming the centrally planned system. He legalized individual and family enterprise and the ownership of joint stock companies, and gave enterprises more control over their own budgets. Agriculture was privatized. Gorbachev was the Soviet leader most strongly associated with the developments outlined in the question.

A. When Josef Stalin gained absolute power in 1929, he imposed a command economy and established rigid central control of all aspects of life in the Soviet Union. For example, Stalin collectivized agriculture—he expropriated (seized without paying for) the privately owned farms of Soviet peasants and combined them into state-owned collective farms. His policy was one of nationalization (government take-over of land, resources, and equipment), not privatization (selling off of government-owned property and resources).

B. In 1921, Vladimir Lenin allowed a temporary and limited compromise with capitalism. The National Economic Plan allowed private agriculture and limited small trade. He did not decentralize government planning. Nor did he privatize agriculture—most farms were already privately owned by peasants.

C. Nikita Khrushchev came to power in 1953. Although he made limited changes to the centralized planning system, he did not privatize agriculture or significantly change centralized control of government planning or services.

29. D

Loosely translated, *laissez-faire* means "leave alone." Laissez-faire capitalists would like government to leave business alone as much as possible. All of the responses given could be used to argue against unions. Only one is a primary objection of laissez-faire capitalists.

D. Laissez-faire capitalists oppose labour unions primarily because unions restrict the economic freedom of workers and capitalists to set wages and prices through the laws of supply and demand. They also increase the costs of production of private enterprises and tend to erode worker productivity. Finally, they often cause prices to rise for consumers.

A. If inflation eats away at people's earnings, then consumer confidence and spending might well be reduced. But this is not the laissez-faire capitalists' primary argument against unions.

B. Unions sometimes do not act in the long-term interests of their members; however, it is likely that a laissez-faire capitalists would think that is a matter for union members to vote on themselves—a kind of self-determination.

C. Unions might encourage government to spend lavishly on public works because public works projects are usually unionized and thus union workers get jobs. Laissez-faire capitalists would generally be opposed to lavish government spending, but public works such as roads and bridges are on the whole good for the economy and encourage business and trade.

30. B

It is important to read the excerpt carefully.

B. To create economic opportunities in the private sector means to make it possible for businesses (the private sector) to sell services (economic opportunities) that were once paid by government out of tax monies collected. The writer is saying that business primarily wants government to cut taxes so that business can make money selling education, health, and childcare.

A. The "deficit scare" is the only reference to public debt. When a government runs a deficit, it spends more than it raises in taxes. Thus the public debt (money owed by the government) rises. Cutting government spending will cut the deficit and combat the growth of debt. But in this excerpt, the deficit is mentioned only in passing as an another excuse for forcing the government to spend less on services.

C. Fiscal policy refers to a government's attempts to regulate the economy (and prevent recessions) through its taxing and spending practices. The writer suggests that businesses want tax cuts not merely as a temporary anti-recession measure, but also because such tax cuts lead to greater opportunities for private enterprise.

D. The only mention of equality is that government spending may produce ("holds out the promise of") a more equal society. The writer does not suggest that businesses favour tax cuts because they desire equal economic opportunity for most citizens.

31. B

One of the statements supports the writer's viewpoint on tax cuts.

B. This statement fits the writer's position. The common good would be a more equal society in which everyone has the same access to publicly funded services. The market ideology would be the desire of business to make a profit selling services like education to the public. The common good would be sacrificed if only the rich have full access to services.

A. Cutting taxes does not save revenues because taxes are the revenues. Cutting expenditure when income from taxation remains constant saves revenues. Also, the writer calls the deficit (government overspending that leads to public debt) the "deficit scare," which, in this context, means that the writer believes that the deficit is not a major problem.

C. Businesses would say that the welfare state is a crushing burden. The writer expresses support for government spending on universal social programs (welfare programs).

D. Businesses would say that the health-care system is inefficient and should be changed by allowing free enterprise and competition to make the system efficient. The writer supports public health care, not private health care.

32. C

The views expressed in this excerpt would generally be called left wing. Leftists generally support bigger government, public health care, public education, and publicly funded day-care. Therefore, the most left-wing party would be the one that would most fully endorse (approve of and give public support to) the writer's position.

C. The New Democratic Party is considered to be a left-wing party.

A. The Liberal Party is generally considered to be a centrist party at this time.

B. The Canadian Alliance was considered to be a right-wing party.

D. The Progressive Conservative Party was considered to be a right-of-centre party.

33. A

Read this kind of question carefully as it is possible — under the pressure of an exam—to read hastily and reverse the meaning. The word "differ" is not bolded, and "differ" is the key word. The question asks which group of economists opposes extensive privatization and massive deficit reduction.

A. Left-wing economists favour government spending to influence the economy and they also favour government delivery of public services. Depending on how left wing they are, they may also favour government control or even ownership of resources and industries. They distrust global capitalism and favour government control of the global marketplace.

The following groups of economists would hold similar (but not identical) views on debt reduction, privatization, and the global economy.

B. Capitalist economists believe that capital (property or money, especially property or money that is used for production) should be privately owned.

C. Laissez-faire economists favour government leaving business alone as much as possible. They would want to see government downsized and government-owned corporations privatized.

D. Neoconservative economists favour capitalism. They strongly support government cutbacks and the privatizing of state-owned industries.

34. D

In the cartoon, the heavy man labelled "Liberalism" is crushing the slight man labelled "Taxpayer." The taxpayer is being crushed by the revenues that are necessary to pay for the social welfare programs that liberals support.

D. Welfare programs for low-income earners are paid for by taxes. Liberals support these taxes and the greater tax burden that results from them.

A. Government uses tax revenues to pay for the government agencies that regulate business. Deregulation would mean less expenditure, and presumably less of a burden on the taxpayer.

B. Similarly, privatizing government agencies would mean lower taxes.

C. Providing tax incentives for the wealthy elite means lowering taxes for the rich only. This cartoon suggests that all taxpayers are overtaxed—not just the richest. Furthermore, liberals generally favour a system of progressive income taxation in which the rich would pay a higher (not a lower) percentage of their income to the government than middle-class or lower-class taxpayers.

35. B

This cartoon criticizes economic liberalism and the welfare state that modern liberals favour. Given this, one can assume that the cartoon would be supported by a person who is right wing (a conservative or laissez-faire capitalist).

B. A fiscal conservative is someone who wants to see government spending reduced and government downsized. The cartoon supports fiscal conservatism by calling for government cutbacks.

A. A left-wing voter would be in favour of the government using revenues to support low-income earners.

C. A democratic socialist would support social welfare programs and the higher taxes that are needed to pay for these programs.

D. A Keynesian economist would support social welfare spending, particularly as a means of preventing downturns in the economy or of promoting economic recovery during recessions.

36. B

This question requires an understanding of the details of the Treaty of Versailles and also of the causes of American isolationism between the two world wars.

B. The first part of the Treaty of Versailles was the Covenant of the League of Nations. Article X (sometimes written as Article 10) of the Covenant required all the member states to act together militarily and economically against an aggressor nation. If the United States had ratified (agreed to the terms of) the treaty, it would have been agreeing to limit some of its sovereignty (freedom to act). A majority in the American senate voted against the treaty because of Article X.

A. The Americans did not refuse to ratify the Treat of Versailles because they thought that the treaty let the Germans off easily. In fact, the treaty punished Germany quite severely.

C. President Woodrow Wilson was a Democrat who supported internationalism. The American Senate was controlled by Republicans who opposed Wilson and embraced isolationism. The Republican senators did not block ratification of the treaty because it did not strictly adhere to Wilson's internationalist principles. The senators despised these principles.

D. Since Article 231 (the "War Guilt Clause") of the Treaty of Versailles did blame Germany and its allies for causing the war, the American Senate would not have refused to ratify the treaty for this reason.

37. D

This question focuses on pre-war German colonies and the concept of League mandates. In theory, the ex-German colonies were to be governed by a colonial power that would prepare them for eventual self-government. (The mandate system also applied to parts of the Turkish Empire, but only former German colonies are shown on the map.)

D. The map shows the League mandates of former German colonies, which gives the best title for the map.

A. This cannot be a map of Nazi conquests. The date is 1920, and the Nazis did not gain power in Germany until 1933. Also, Germany's 1939–1942 conquests were largely in Europe and in North Africa—not in sub-Saharan Africa, Asia, or the Pacific.

B. The principle of self-determination was part of the mandate system. The former German colonies were supposed to be prepared for eventual self-government. However, in 1920, none of the colonies had achieved independence. Thus, this map does not show self-determination in practice.

C. Giving Germany's colonies to other imperial powers did not create a balance of power in either Africa or Asia. A balance of power exists when powerful nations have roughly equal power. Britain, the dominant imperial power in Africa, became more powerful in that region; and Japan, the dominant imperial power in East Asia, became more powerful in that region.

38. C

Hitler took certain steps to increase Germany's power. It is necessary to know the chronological order of these steps, since all four actions violated the terms of the Treaty of Versailles, and the first step was the initial test of France's resolve. (To prepare for the exam, it is also necessary to understand the nature each event.)

C. The Treaty of Versailles forbade Germany to station troops in the Rhineland, on the border with France. France was strong enough to enforce the treaty, but Hitler thought the French government would back down. In 1936 he tested French resolve by sending in German soldiers. They had orders to retreat at the first sight of French troops, but the French did nothing. Hitler became bolder.

A. The *Anschluss* (union) with Austria took place in March 1938. The Treaty of Versailles forbade union with Austria, but Hitler already knew that no one would stop him.

B. The annexation of the Sudetenland, a part of Czechoslovakia, occurred in September 1938. Hitler had the Munich Agreement, signed by France and Britain, to assure him that no action would be taken against him.

D. The blitzkrieg against Poland in September 1939 began the Second World War.

39. B

It is necessary to understand each of the foreign policy terms in the four responses and to understand the background of the Munich Agreement (Also referred to as the Munich Conference and the Munich Accord.)

B. In his famous Fourteen Points, Woodrow Wilson defended the principle of self-determination (the right of all peoples to govern themselves). The majority of the inhabitants of the Sudetenland region of Czechoslovakia were ethnic Germans who wanted to live in the same state as other Germans. Hitler claimed the right to make them part of Germany. A pro-Nazi German nationalist would say that annexing the Sudetenland was justified by the Wilsonian principle of self-determination for every nationality.

A. Collective security is security from attack that is achieved through defensive alliances. No defensive alliance was negotiated or signed at the 1938 Munich Conference.

C. Appeasement is the policy of giving in to an aggressive nation in the hope of avoiding war. It was the policy that led Britain and France to sign the Munich Agreement. It was not a policy of Woodrow Wilson.

D. Disarmament is the policy of reducing or eliminating weapons. The Munich Agreement was an agreement to transfer the Sudetenland to Germany. It was not a disarmament agreement.

40. A

Sovereignty is a nation's right to self-government and freedom from outside interference. A nation can do what it likes within its borders; it is free from interference in internal matters. This question is about sovereignty and whether violating a nation's sovereignty is ever justified.

A. The main ideas in the excerpt are that the League of Nations should have used force against Germany to protect the Jews, and that the League did nothing because the persecution was an internal matter. Thus, the question of whether to respect Germany's sovereignty or to protect the Jews was decided in favour of not interfering in an internal German matter.

B. The question of mediating boundary disputes or imposing boundary changes was faced by the League of Nations in such incidents as the Sudetenland. (See solution to questions 38 and 39.) These were not internal matters subject to German sovereignty.

C. Military alliances and diplomatic neutrality are not mentioned in the excerpt.

D. Sanctions are military or economic actions used to stop a country from violating international norms of conduct. Sanctions are not mentioned in the excerpt. The author does not suggest that the dilemma faced by the League of Nations was a choice between placing economic sanctions on Germany and encouraging the Germans to govern themselves.

41. A

This question refers to why the League of Nations failed to defend China from Japanese aggression in 1931.

A. Article X (Article 10) of the League Covenant was based on the principle of collective security. If one member-state were to be attacked, then all the member-states would take military and economic action against the aggressor. When the League failed to take any action over the Japanese invasion of Manchuria, the credibility of the collective security principle was undermined.

B. The principle of open diplomacy meant that treaties between nations would not be kept secret. This was to avoid the kind of secret military alliance that helped to cause the First World War. Inaction over Manchuria had nothing to do with the principle of open diplomacy.

C. An alliance among the weaker members of the League refers to such alliances such as the Little Entente between Czechoslovakia, Romania, and Yugoslavia. The League of Nations was not committed to such alliances because they weakened the principle of collective security.

D. Summit conferences between the Great Powers—such as Britain, France, Italy, and Japan—were important to the function of the League. The importance of summit conferences (meetings of government ministers) was partly a result of reaction to the old-style pre-war diplomacy conducted by ambassadors. The old-style diplomacy had sometimes resulted in secret treaties that were blamed for causing the war. However, the League's failure to take action during the Manchurian crisis had little or nothing to do with the organization's over-reliance on summit diplomacy.

42. B

It is necessary to understand each term found in the responses, and then to apply the correct term to Source II.

B. *Lebensraum* (living space) was land in Eastern Europe that the Nazi government claimed as necessary for the continued political and economic development of Germany. This claim was the justification for attacking Poland and the Soviet Union as the first step in Hitler's "programme of Eastern colonisation." (This program was a plan to kill all the leaders of the Slavic peoples, keep a relatively small number of the peasants and working-class for slave-labour, and to replace the rest of the population with German settlers. The displaced Poles, Russians, and other groups were to be left to starve to death.)

A. *Kristallnacht* (Night of Crystal) was the night of November 9, 1938, when Nazis and Nazi sympathizers in Germany and Austria engaged in attacks on Jewish people and their property. The term refers to the broken glass from the windows of homes and businesses. It had nothing to do with Hitler's plans to invade Poland and the Soviet Union.

C. *Blitzkrieg* (lightning war) was the form of mobile warfare that Germany used in the rapid conquests of Poland, Western Europe, and Russia. Blitzkrieg is a strategy of mechanized warfare; it is not a form of colonialism.

D. *Anschluss* (union) was the political union of Germany and Austria that was brought about by Hitler in 1938. It was an important part of Hitler's plans, but separate from his plan to colonize Eastern Europe.

43. C

This question is about Hitler's diplomatic strategy before the Second World War. The answer to the question is not directly stated by the writer of in Source I. The correct response must be inferred from background knowledge of Hitler's foreign policy in the 1930's.

C. The writer states that Hitler did not intend to go to war, but only used the threat of war to make opponents give in to his demands. In other words, he used brinkmanship to bluff vulnerable opponents and achieve diplomatic successes like the Munich Agreement.

A. Hitler did not use collective security to end crises. Instead, he used the failure of collective security. He correctly judged that France and Britain would try to avoid the use of force. All of the western democracies remembered the horrors of the First World War and were unwilling to fight. Both Britain and France feared that force would lead to war.

B. The writer does not make a connection between Hitler's diplomatic successes and his forcing millions of Germans into military service.

D. The writer does not suggest that Hitler's diplomatic success resulted from aggressive alliances.

44. C

Sometimes it is necessary to interpret ideas that are not clearly stated in historical writings.

C. Both Sources deal with motivation, which in this context is used to mean intention. Source I argues from the state of German military preparedness that Hitler did not intend general war, and probably did not intend any war. Source II argues that Hitler planned for a war on two fronts as a means of gaining *lebensraum* (living space) in Eastern Europe. The sources disagree in their conclusions, but both consider that understanding Hitler's motivations is important for understanding the outbreak of war.

A. Only Source I mentions immorality, and only to assert that Hitler was no worse than many others.

B. Only Source I mentions diplomacy.

D. Treaties are not mentioned in either source.

45. B

This question deals with the concept of appeasement (the political strategy of avoiding war by giving in to the demands of an aggressor). In the 1930s, Britain and France gave in to Hitler's demands, hoping he would be satisfied and would not go to war.

B. The Munich Agreement (also Munich Accord, also Munich Pact): in 1938, Britain and France agreed that Germany could occupy the Sudetenland (the part of Czechoslovakia that had a majority population of ethnic Germans). Czechoslovakia was not invited to the conference. The Munich Accord became a symbol of appeasement. The "victuals" referred to are lands that Hitler wanted to add to Germany. The phrase "served to him course by course" is a reference to appeasement. In plain language, Churchill is saying that Hitler did not have to go to war to get the territories he wanted: Britain and France gave them to him one at a time, each time hoping that Hitler was telling the truth when he said he wanted nothing more.

A. The Locarno Pact (or Pacts) were several pacts (agreements between nations) signed at the Locarno Conference of 1925. Agreements on open diplomacy by means summit conferences, agreements to submit disputes to arbitration, and defence pacts entered into publicly were all thought to be signs of a new era of international cooperation and good will.

C. The Treaty of Versailles, signed in 1919, officially ended the First World War, and imposed harsh conditions upon Germany. The treaty certainly was not an attempt to appease Germany, and Churchill does not refer to the treaty in this excerpt.

D. The Kellogg–Briand Pact was signed in 1928. The signing countries renounced (gave up) recourse to war as a means of solving of international crises. All disputes were to be settled peacefully, by arbitration. Many nations signed, but the pact had little or no effect on world events. It did nothing to stop dictators and is not referred to by Churchill in this excerpt.

46. C

This question requires two understandings. First, it is necessary to know about the events leading up to the Second World War. Second, it is necessary to select the response that has a logical relationship to the other events in the time-line. All three events on the time-line are steps taken by Hitler and Nazi Germany on the road to the Second World War. In October 1936, Nazi Germany entered into an understanding with Italy (the Rome–Berlin Axis) that would eventually become a full alliance during the Second World War. In November 1936, Germany and Japan entered into the Anti-Comintern Pact to oppose the spread of communism beyond the borders of the USSR. Hitler's final step on the road to world war was the September 1939 invasion of Poland that triggered the Second World War.

The correct response to the question must be an action taken by Nazi Germany between November 1936 and September 1939 that contributed to the outbreak of the Second World War.

C. Nazi-Soviet Pact (or the Molotov–Ribbentrop Pact) signed on August 23, 1939, was treaty of non-aggression and friendship between Soviet Russia and Germany. It included a secret protocol that divided Poland and the Baltic states between Russia and Germany. It was Hitler's major action before the invasion of Poland.

A. Kellogg–Briand Pact (1928) was an international agreement that renounced war as a way of settling disputes. The date of the pact is too early for the given time-line and the pact was not a step taken by Hitler on the road to war.

B. The remilitarization of the Rhineland took place in March 1936 and so does not fit the empty place on the timeline.

D. The Little Entente (1920) was a defensive and economic treaty between Czechoslovakia, Romania, and Yugoslavia designed to make sure that there was no revival of the Austrian Empire, and no attempt by Hungary to alter the borders of 1919. The entente was not an action taken by Germany, and it predates all the other events on the time-line.

47. D

It is necessary to know the chronology of important events in the Second World War. A student must know the dates of these and other important events, or at least know the order in which they occurred.

Operation Barbarossa, June 1941; Fall of Poland, September 1939; Allied victory in North Africa, May 1943; Attack on Pearl Harbor, December 1941.

Thus, there is only one correct chronology:

D. Fall of Poland, September 1939; Fall of France, June 1940; Operation Barbarossa, June 1941; Attack on Pearl Harbor, December 1941; Allied victory in North Africa, May 1943

48. C

This question requires interpretation of a map. The map shows the German conquest of Holland, Belgium, and France in the spring of 1940.

C. The arrows representing the German attack show German armies surrounding the British Expeditionary Force and the French 1st and 7th Armies. In the following days, the British army and the elements of the French army made a fighting retreat to the coast and the port of Dunkirk, where 300,000 men were evacuated to Britain. The Allied Disaster culminated at Dunkirk.

A. England did not fall to a German attack in the Second World War. In fact, Germany never did invade England.

B. In the legend or key, a heavy black curving arrow is shown marking the path of German attack. It is clear from the map that the German armies bypassed the Maginot Line.

D. It is very clear that it was the German armies, not the Allies, that were on the offensive. The battles of 1940 were not fought anywhere near Germany's defensive Siegfried Line.

49. D

Recognition of the cartoon face of Josef Stalin–dictator of the Soviet Union from 1924 until his death in 1953–is essential. (The man spinning the globe is Molotov, Stalin's foreign minister.) The picture on the desk is of U.S. Secretary of State George C. Marshall. The Marshall Plan, or European Economic Recovery Program, is named after him. This clue suggests that the date of this cartoon is between 1948 and 1951. The Soviet Union would have nothing to do with the American Marshall Plan, which arranged economic cooperation among the countries of Western Europe and disbursed twelve billion dollars of American aid. One purpose of the plan was to counter the spread of communism and Soviet influence in Europe.

D. In the early years of the Cold War, the Soviet Union installed communist governments in Poland, Hungary, Bulgaria, Romania, and Czechoslovakia, and attempted to do the same in other countries. The "threat of worldwide communist expansion during the Cold War" fits the cartoon.

A. The Hungarian Revolution took place in 1956, after Stalin was dead.

B. Stalin was a communist dictator, not a fascist dictator. Also the cartoon is set in the late 1940s, not the 1930s.

C. The Soviets refused to participate in the Marshall Plan, although they could have done so. Stalin's pathological suspicion was one reason that the peoples of the Soviet Union could not benefit from the massive American aid.

50. A

During the Cold War, American foreign policy attempted to prevent the expansion of the Soviet sphere of influence.

A. The U.S.A. tried to contain (stop the expansion of) "real and perceived enemies"—namely, the Soviet Union and its communist allies. The Marshall Plan had a secondary objective of countering Soviet influence in Europe. The United States became part of NATO, entered into other military alliances, defended South Korea against invasion by communist North Korea, and became embroiled in the Vietnam War.

B. Isolationism is a policy of non-involvement in the affairs of other nations. The U.S.A. withdrew from developments in Europe after the First World War, not the Second.

C. During the Cold War, the United States entered into a number of regional alliances: NATO, NORAD, SEATO, ANZUS, and CENTO. It did not withdraw from such alliances as a response to perceived Soviet expansionism.

D. The United States built up its military as a defensive measure during the Cold War. It did not do so to aggressively attack or invade other countries.

51. C

This question refers to the doctrine of MAD (mutually assured destruction). The condition necessary for the success of superpower deterrence was the capability of each superpower to destroy the other with retaliatory nuclear weapons if ever attacked with an offensive nuclear strike.

C. The retaliatory capability of either superpower following a first strike was the reason for successful deterrence. No matter how much destruction might be caused by the country that struck first, enough nuclear weapons would survive the destruction to deliver a devastating counter-blow. (Undetectable nuclear-powered submarine fleets armed with nuclear missiles were an important part of MAD. Even if every land-based missile could be destroyed in a first strike, most of the submarines, which could be anywhere in any ocean, would survive to retaliate.)

A. No matter how advanced each power's conventional weapons, the destruction they would cause was not as frightening a deterrent as the prospect of a global thermonuclear holocaust.

B. The export of conventional weapons to allies did not deter an attack on a superpower in the way that nuclear weapons did.

D. To be successful, superpower deterrence required a balance of terror. If one superpower were able to defend itself against the other side's nuclear arsenal (by developing advanced anti-ballistic missile defences, for example), then there would be little to deter that superpower from attacking the other.

52. B

B. A sphere of influence is a territory or region over which an outside state claims control, influence, or a preferential status. In the 1944 agreement, both the USSR and Britain claimed Yugoslavia and Hungary as spheres of influence.

A. Mutual deterrence is a situation in which two enemies dare not attack each other. This concept is not illustrated in the excerpt.

C. Economic imperialism is the domination of the economy of a weaker nation by the stronger economy of another nation. The agreement does not suggest that either Churchill or Stalin sought economic domination of the economies of Hungary or Yugoslavia.

D. Encouraging national self-determination would consist of helping a nation to exert independent control of its own affairs. The 1944 agreement represents an infringement of the self-determination of Hungary and Yugoslavia as the USSR and Britain would be partly controlling the fate of Hungary and Yugoslavia.

53. D

This question requires an understanding of the outcomes of the Yalta and Potsdam conferences.

D. Tensions did escalate between the Soviets and the Western Allies at the Yalta and Potsdam summit conferences. The two sides distrusted each other and did not agree on many issues. For example, the Western Allies wanted free elections in the countries of Eastern Europe, while the Soviets were determined to install cooperative communist governments.

A. The fate of Italy was a relatively minor outcome of the conferences.

B. The relations among the Allied powers actually deteriorated. When the urgent necessity of defeating Germany was gone, the ideological tensions between the Western Powers and the Soviet Union resurfaced.

C. America did not dominate global politics during the Cold War era. The Soviet Union was a second superpower until its dissolution in 1991. The international political system from 1945 to 1991 was bipolar rather than unipolar.

54. A

This question deals with cause and effect. After Stalin died, Khrushchev gained power. In 1956, he made a secret speech to the 20th Party Congress. In his speech (which soon became widely known), he denounced Stalin's purges of the members of the Communist Party and the military. In the same year, he spoke of peaceful coexistence with the West and relaxed some of the control over satellite countries in Eastern Europe.

A. The signs of greater freedom encouraged Hungarians and Poles to seek greater independence from Russian control. Polish riots led to reforms in the Polish Communist Party, reforms that Khrushchev allowed, since the communists remained in control. The Hungarians rose in revolution, intent on complete freedom, and were crushed by Soviet tank divisions sent by Khrushchev.

B. Khrushchev's call for peaceful coexistence and his denunciation of Stalin's crimes tended to ease American fears of the USSR. They did not encourage the Americans to resist communism more strongly. The American government would be more likely to regard Khrushchev's words as hopeful signs.

C. The Warsaw Pact (1955) was a late response to the formation of NATO (1949), but it predated Khrushchev's call for peaceful coexistence and his denunciation of Stalin.

D. Khrushchev's two actions tended to slow down (de-escalate), not speed up (escalate), the arms race.

55. D

To respond successfully to this question, it is necessary to understand the nature and consequences of each of the crises mentioned and also of the telephone "hotline" and the Partial Test-Ban Treaty.

D. The 1962 Cuban Missile Crisis is considered to have been the point when the Soviet Union and the United States were closest to nuclear war. The United States discovered that the Soviets were installing missile bases in Cuba. President Kennedy demanded they be removed, and blockaded Cuba to stop Russian supply ships. After a tense week, Khrushchev agreed to withdraw all missiles and bombers in exchange for a guarantee that the United States would not invade Cuba. One result of this crisis was the subsequent installation of direct-link telephones in the Kremlin and in the White House to make emergency negotiations easier. Another result was the 1963 agreement to limit atmospheric testing of nuclear weapons. The world had been to the brink, and efforts were made to avoid another such crisis.

A. The Suez Crisis (1956), which involved Britain, France, Israel, and Egypt, caused tension between the superpowers, but did not directly lead to the establishment of the hotline or the signing of the treaty.

B. The Berlin Blockade (1948–49) ended in May 1949. The first Soviet nuclear device was tested in August 1949. It was years before the growing threat of nuclear war led to the Partial Test-Ban Treaty and the hotline link.

C. The negotiation of the Korean cease-fire took place in the early 1950's, not in the early 1960's when the hotline was established and the Partial Test-Ban Treaty signed.

56. B

This question requires the interpretation of original documents in the light of historical events. Vice-President Harry S. Truman became President of the United States upon the death of President Roosevelt in April 1945, before the war ended. President Truman was re-elected in 1948 and was president during the whole of the Berlin Crisis.

B. The statement, "We should be prepared to go to any lengths to find a peaceful solution to the situation" shows a desire for diplomacy. Truman's question, "How could we remain in Berlin without risking all-out war?" also shows a desire to avoid confrontation and an openness to negotiation. But as it turned out, the crisis was resolved not by diplomacy, but by doing something unexpected. The western Allies airlifted all necessary supplies into West Berlin for a year. The massive effort bypassed the Russian blockade without actually provoking confrontation. Finally, Stalin gave up and lifted the blockade.

A. Note the quotation "We had to remain in Berlin." There is no question of appeasement (giving in to an aggressor's demands) here. Although Truman did not want all-out war, he was determined not to give in. Détente (a relaxation of tension or hostility between nations) does not apply in this case. The Russian blockade of Berlin was a time of great tension.

C. Source I shows that the United States was actively involved in the recovery of Europe and had plans for West Germany and Berlin. This was the opposite of isolationism (non-participation in the affairs of other nations). Resisting the spread of Soviet influence and power was the policy of containment (prevention of the spread of an enemy ideology or the expansion of a nation's sphere of influence), which is suggested by Source I.

D. The United States did cooperate with its allies in resolving the Berlin Crisis, but that fact is not mentioned anywhere in Source I. The "we" used here refers to the Americans. Thus, collective security (a common defence against aggression) is not correct. Truman clearly states that he does not want to risk all-out war. Brinkmanship (pushing an opponent to the limit, even at the risk of war) was definitely not part of Truman's plans.

57. D

The cartoon in Source II strongly suggests the success of the Western Allies. The fingers, extended in the "V for Victory" symbol made famous by Prime Minister Winston Churchill during the Second World War, have broken the wall that symbolizes the Russian land blockade of West Berlin.

D. The cartoon suggests that as a result of the successful airlift, the hand of the Western Allies has breached the Soviet barrier that cut off access to West Berlin. Eventually, the Western Allies were able to get the USSR to open West Berlin to road traffic from West Germany.

A. The only sign of the Soviet presence in the Soviet sector (later East Berlin) is the communist flag flying. A flying flag does not suggest weakening of morale. In fact, it is a common symbol of strong morale.

B. There is no sign of anyone fleeing the city. The Soviets administered the sector granted to them by the Potsdam Conference, and they continued to do so. The hand of the Western Allies has kept West Berlin's supply lifeline open, but has not altered the agreement over administration. No Soviet citizens left East Berlin during the blockade as Soviet troops had totally cut off access to Western Europe during the crisis. In fact, the vast majority of the Soviet citizens who were at that time in East Germany were Soviet soldiers and officials who were blockading the city.

C. The Americans had no intention of driving the Soviets out of their sector of Berlin, and the cartoon does not suggest anything of the sort. East Berlin continued to be occupied by Russian troops until 1990.

58. B

This item requires the correct identification of an event in which demands for national self-determination (freedom from outside influence in a nation's internal affairs) threatened the USA's or the USSR's control over a dominated territory or region.

B. The Hungarian revolutionaries wanted freedom from Soviet control. In other words, they wanted national self-determination. Soviet forces crushed the revolution to ensure that Hungary remained part of the Soviet Bloc.

A. The signing of the Korean armistice ended the Korean War. North Korea remained communist and part of the communist sphere of influence. South Korea remained part of the Western sphere of influence.

C. The Berlin Wall was built to stop Germans from fleeing from East Berlin and East Germany to freedom and democracy in West Berlin and West Germany. The wall did not threaten, but rather it tightened, Soviet control over East Germany.

D. By the time of the Cuban Missile Crisis (October 1962), Cuba was within the Soviet sphere of influence. The crisis was caused by the establishment by Khrushchev and Castro of missile bases in Cuba that appeared to threaten American security. Cuba did not demand greater independence from Soviet influence during this crisis. Instead, Cuba moved closer to the USSR and remained a close ally until the dissolution of the Soviet Union in 1991.

59. B

The United Nations Security Council is organized so that the great powers have greater power than the smaller nations. Each of the five great powers, which are the five militarily strongest nations—the USA, Russia, China, France, and Britain—can, through the use of its veto power, stop the Security Council from taking action.

B. Individual permanent members have ultimate decision-making authority in the negative sense that there must be "great power unanimity" on substantive matters (issues that require the UN to take action). On such substantive matters, all five permanent members (the "great powers") must agree. A member that disagrees thus blocks any action. (Procedural matters are decided by a majority vote.)

A. Only the permanent members of the Security Council (the USA, Russia, China, France, and Britain) have veto power on substantive matters. (The actions of the Security Council are divided into procedural actions and substantive actions. Procedural refers to procedures, or the methods of doing things. Substantive refers to the actual actions of the Security Council.) The Secretary General has no veto power.

C. The Security Council, not the General Assembly, decides which issues will be considered during a crisis.

D. Non-permanent members are not selected exclusively from the poorer nations of the world. Richer nations such as Canada, Norway, and Ireland have won Security Council seats in UN elections.

60. A

The World Trade Organization (WTO) exists to promote global free trade.

A. Encouraging protectionist trade blocks would prevent free trade between nations, not promote global free trade.

B. The WTO establish rules for international trade.

C. The WTO does provide a forum for discussing how nations can reduce trade barriers such as tariffs.

D. Member states of the WTO agree to abide by WTO rulings on trade disputes between member nations.

61. A

This item requires students to identify the foreign policy goal that was pursued in the 1980s by the USSR in Afghanistan and by the USA in Nicaragua.

A. The Mujahedeen guerrillas were trying to overthrow a communist government friendly to the Soviet Union. The Soviets invaded in order to maintain the government. The communist government in Nicaragua was unfriendly to the United States. The US gave aid to anticommunist guerrillas, hoping the guerrillas would be able to overthrow the government and form a new government friendly to the United States. In both cases, the superpowers were trying to preserve their spheres of influence.

B. Collective security is a common defence—in the form of a defensive military alliance—against aggression. No such defensive alliance was involved in either the Soviet war in Afghanistan (1979–1989) or in the American-backed Contra movement in Nicaragua.

C. In one case, the guerrillas were attacked; in the other case, guerrillas were supported.

D. In neither case were nations left to sort out their problems on their own. Outside intervention such as that demonstrated here is a violation of national self-determination (freedom from external interference in a nation's internal affairs).

62. D

This item requires students to identify the situation in which ethnic majorities have caused armed conflicts by mistreating ethnic minority groups.

D. Many of the civil conflicts that have plagued the world in recent years are armed struggles between ethnic majorities and persecuted ethnic minorities. The comments in Source I are verified by these conflicts (in Sudan, Rwanda, Bosnia, Croatia, etc.).

A. The increase in the number of UN peacekeeping operations might be the result of conflicts between countries rather than conflicts within countries. Source I clearly refers only to the latter type of conflict. In other words, it is about civil war, not war between nations. Without knowing how much of the increase in UN operations is caused by civil conflict, the increase is not a convincing verification of Source I.

B. A breakthrough in peace negotiations between two warring ethnic groups would bring hope of peace. This would not support the comments about armed conflict continuing to plague the world.

C. Better relations between Russia and the United States are not the cause of the ethnic hatreds and extreme nationalism (ultranationalism) described in Source I.

63. A

Ironic humour exists in the incongruity between what actually happens and what might be expected to happen. In this cartoon, the banner proclaiming fellowship (friendly association) is contrasted with the fact that certain ethnic groups hate each other.

A. Olympic fellowship (friendly relationships among sporting nations) is the expected goal; the inability to live together peacefully is the unpleasant reality. The contrast is ironic.

Neither B, C, nor D contains a discrepancy between expectations and reality. Thus, they do not contain ironic humour.

64. B

Both sources focus on the tensions that exist between nations that lay claim to the same territory.

B. Both sources deal with the tensions that result when two or more nationalities want independent control of the same territory. Such conflicting demands for autonomy (independent control of national territory) are at the root of the ethnic hostilities described or depicted in the sources.

A. Brokering (helping to arrange) lasting peace settlements is a problem in all conflicts. The problem does not exist only in the case of the ethnic conflicts that are the topic of the two sources.

C. Neither source is about ethnic minorities rebelling against authoritarian states.

D. Neither source is about the complexities of staging international events. The cartoon uses an Olympic event only as a source of ironic humour.

65. C

Each of the three parts of the diagram shows two groups of people in conflict. Each of the conflicts is very different, but all of the conflicts have something in common: their intractability. They are ongoing, persistent, and seemingly impossible to settle.

C. Long-standing animosity (hatred, hostility) continues to impede (interfere with) the resolution of all three conflicts. All of these conflicts have remained unresolved since the late 1940s and none of them seems likely to be settled in the foreseeable future.

A. Armed conflict between Israel and the Palestinians and between India and Pakistan in Kashmir continue to take a heavy toll on civilians. There is no armed conflict between North and South Korea at the present time, although the two states are in an ideological conflict.

B. The United States has hosted talks between the Israelis and Palestinians only. (This is a tricky response. The United States has been involved in talks between the other nations mentioned. Hosted is the key word. To host talks is to arrange the talks and provide the necessary space and facilities.)

D. The UN has deployed peacekeeping forces in the Arab–Israeli conflict and in the Indian–Pakistani conflict. The UN action in Korea was a war to drive invading North Korean forces from South Korea. After the war, there were no UN peacekeepers in the Korean peninsula to preserve the ceasefire.

66. D

The references to conflicts that "rage within" nations refers to civil wars or to other internal conflicts. Only one of the conflicts listed was a civil war. The others were wars between two or more countries.

D. Bosnia in 1992: the combatants were Serbs, Croats, and Muslim Bosnians. This conflict was a civil war. The United Nations involvement was within the nation.

A. Egypt in 1956: the combatants were Egypt, Israel, Britain, and France.

B. Kashmir in 1965: the combatants were Pakistan and India.

C. Kuwait in 1991: the combatants were Iraq and Kuwait, and US-led Coalition forces.

67. A

The correct response to this item must be the major criticism made in the excerpt.

A. The "currently out-of-reach independence of action" of the UN means that the UN does not have independence of action. The "UN's own democracy must be reclaimed," means that the UN is not now democratic. The phrase "with the reality of a US dominated United Nations" means that the US presently dominates the UN. "UN intervention...will be indistinguishable from the US interventions it is so often used to legitimate" means that the US presently uses the authority of the UN to make American interventions in other countries seem to be legitimate. So, according to this excerpt, the UN is not independent, is not democratic, and is dominated by the United States, which uses the UN as a cover for its own actions. In other words, the UN has become a pawn of American foreign policy.

B. The first sentence suggests that UN intervention in the internal affairs of individual countries is a good thing. Nothing is said about the UN being too slow to act.

C. The writer states that the US has intervened in other countries and has used the UN to legitimate these actions. In other words, the US has acted and then used the UN to justify its actions. The UN is not described as having imposed settlements.

D. The Security Council and the veto power of its permanent members are not mentioned in this excerpt.

68. A

The European Union has evolved from previous cooperative agreements. One of these agreements—the Treaty of Rome—established the European Economic Community (also called the European Common Market) in the late 1950's.

A. The European Union began as a common market. Its purpose was to reduce, and eventually to eliminate, trade barriers between member states.

B. The primary purpose of the EEC (European Common Market) was to develop a common commercial policy, not an integrated foreign policy.

C. Since NATO had already been established in 1949 to defend Western Europe from aggression, the Western European nations made no real effort in the 1950's to create another multinational force for the defence of Western Europe.

D. In the 1950's, none of the original member states of the EEC was seriously concerned about an overthrow of democracy.

69. C

Students are expected to understand the terms used in the responses.

C. According to Position III, the US had the power to force an end to war in the Balkans and should have acted to prevent a more serious conflict. This is interventionism (political interference or military involvement by one country in the affairs of another). The position is correctly matched with the approach.

A. According to Position I, the US should have forced a solution in the Balkans. This is not appeasement (giving a hostile nation what it wants in the hope of avoiding war).

B. According to Position II, the US should not have become involved since it had no national interest in the Balkans. This is not internationalism (cooperation and mutual understanding between countries).

D. According to Position IV, only a negotiated peace brokered (arranged) by the European Union would have worked. The approach recommended here is diplomacy (the management of international relations through negotiation), not brinkmanship (taking a dispute to the verge of conflict in the hope of forcing the opposition to back down).

70. B

In the 1930's, the United States had an official policy of isolationism (avoiding entanglements in the affairs of other countries).

B. Position II maintains that the US should not have intervened because it had no national interest in the Balkans. Isolationism is a foreign policy of avoiding involvement in international affairs as long as the country's interests are not affected.

A. Position I suggests that the US should have intervened in the Balkans. Interventionism is not an approach taken under an isolationist foreign policy.

C. Position III suggests that the US should have intervened.

D. Position IV suggests that the US should not have intervened because it wouldn't have worked. This position does not advocate non-intervention for isolationist reasons.

APPENDICES

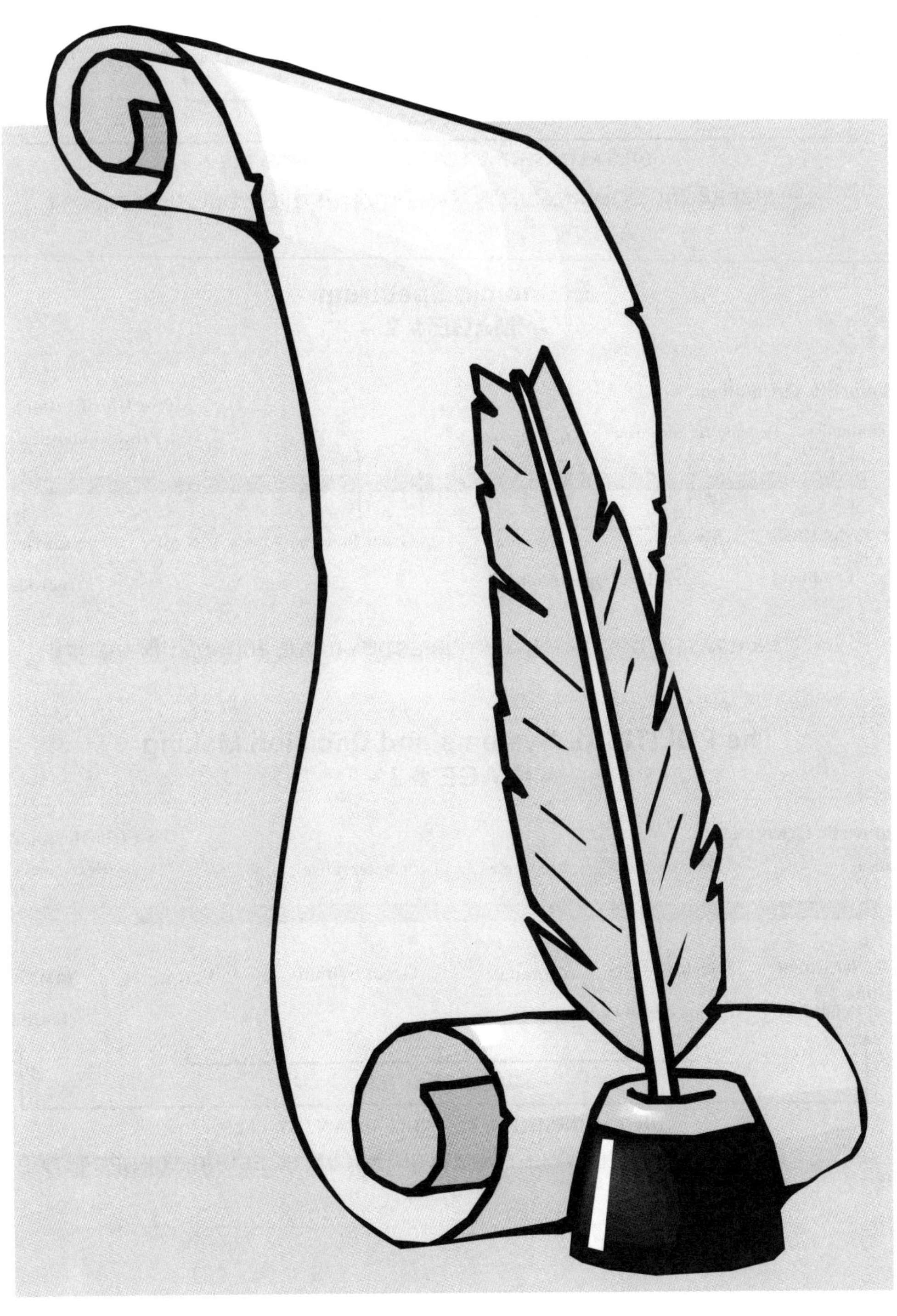

Appendix A

Political and Economic Spectrum
– IMAGE # 1 –

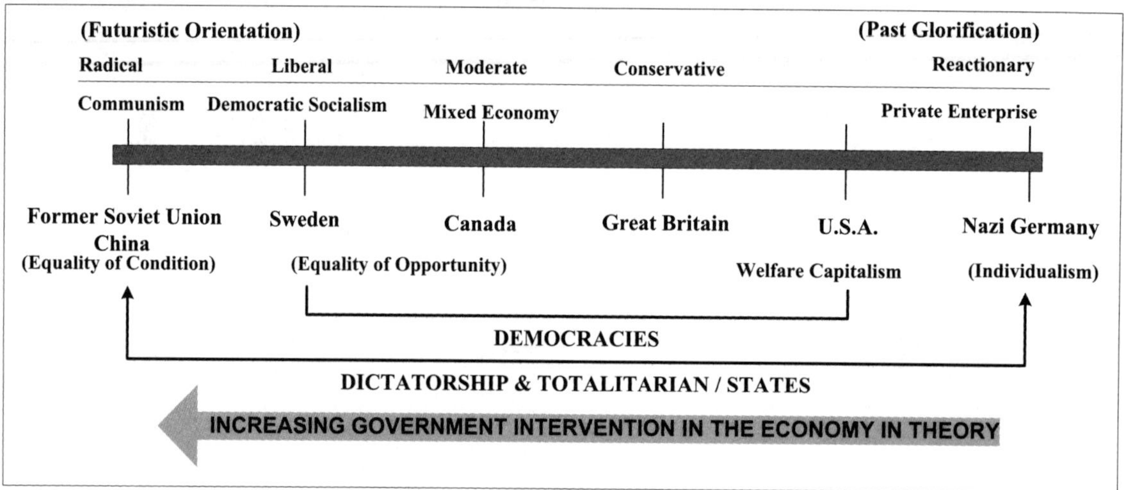

Economic Spectrum
– IMAGE # 2 –

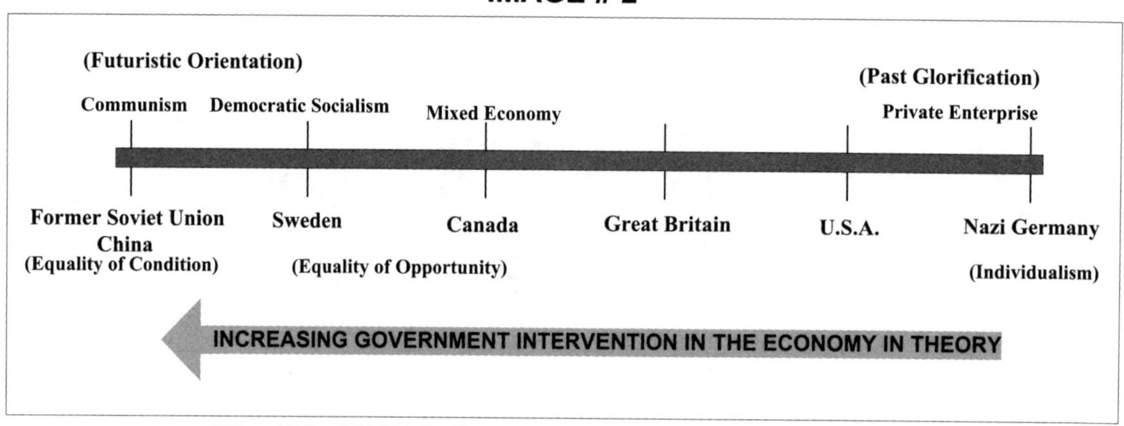

The POLITICAL Systems and Decision Making
– IMAGE # 3 –

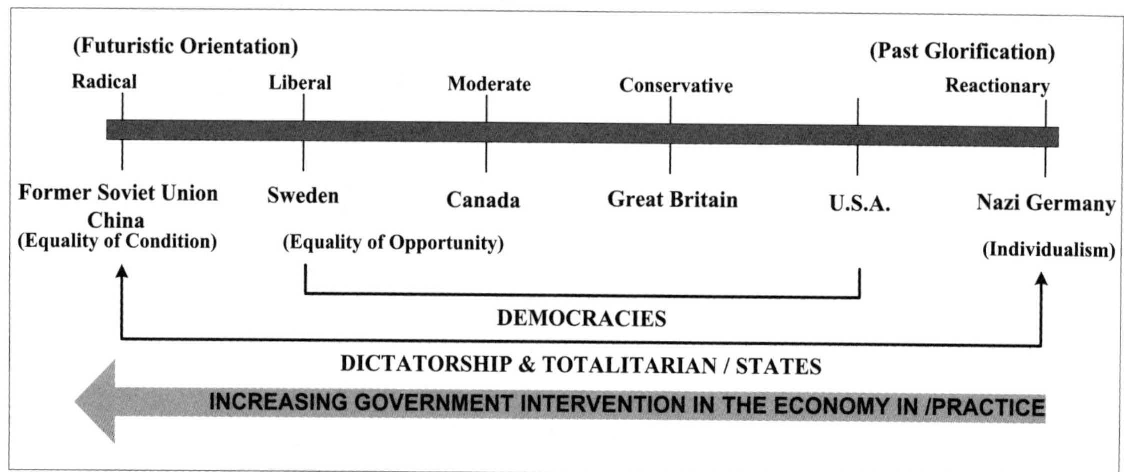

Political and Economic Spectrum
– IMAGE # 4 –

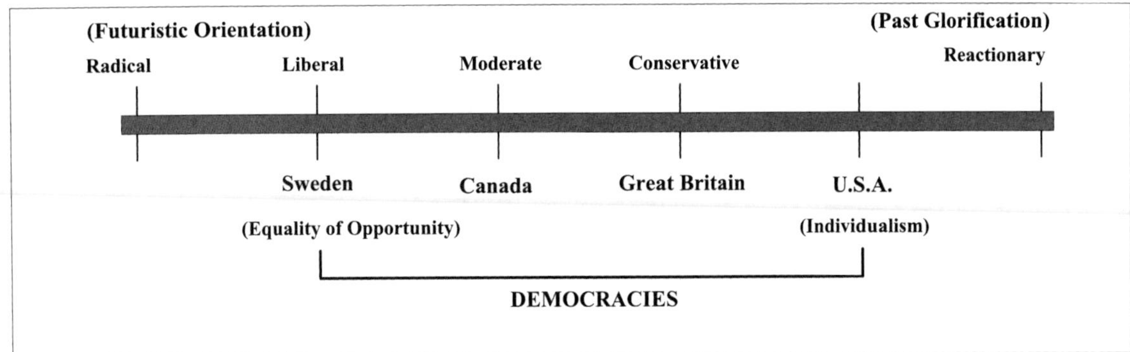

Dictatorships and the Political Spectrum
– IMAGE # 5 –

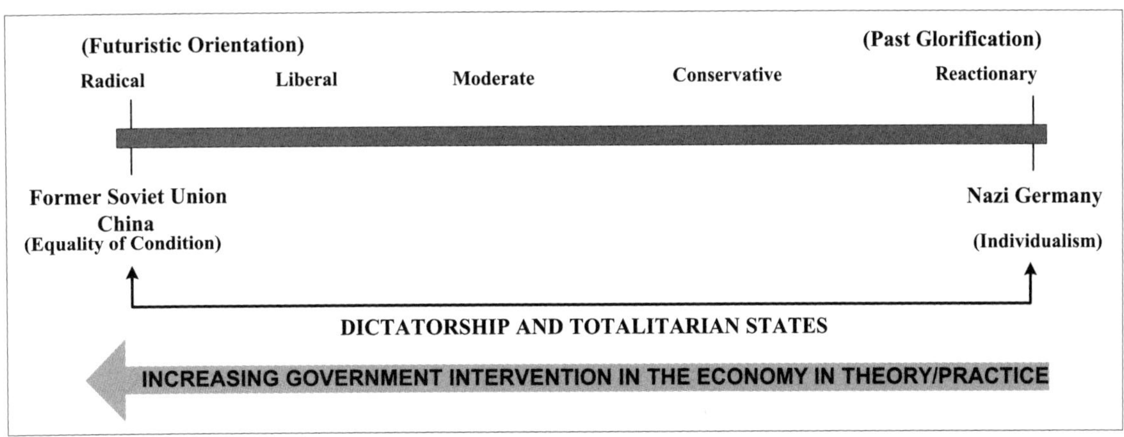

Scarcity
– IMAGE # 6 –

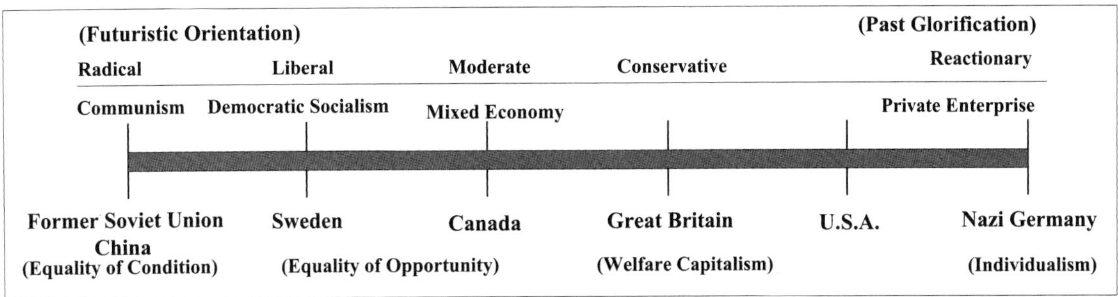

Private Enterprise
– IMAGE # 7 –

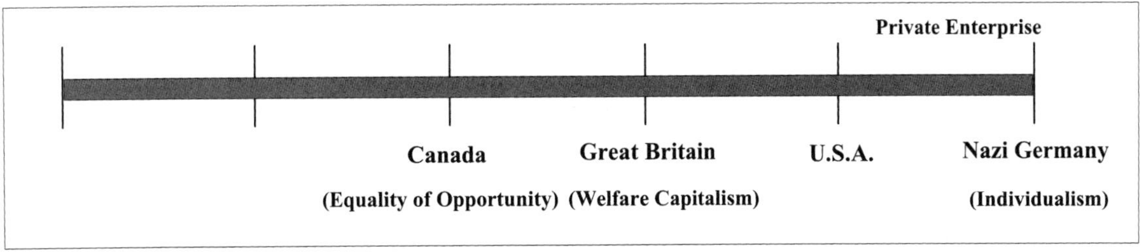

Public Enterprise
– IMAGE # 8 –

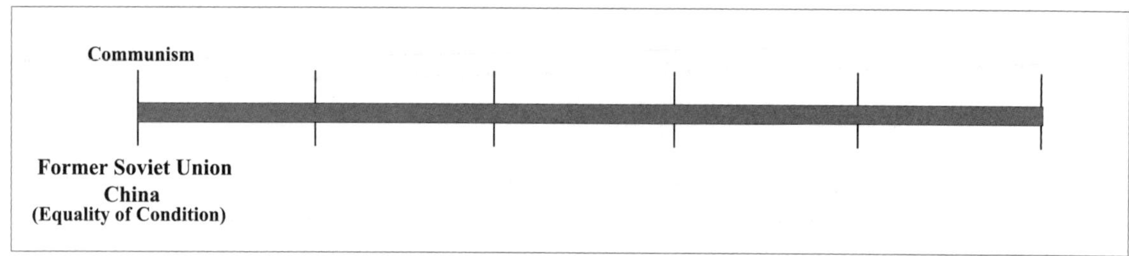

Political and Economic Spectrum
– IMAGE # 9 –

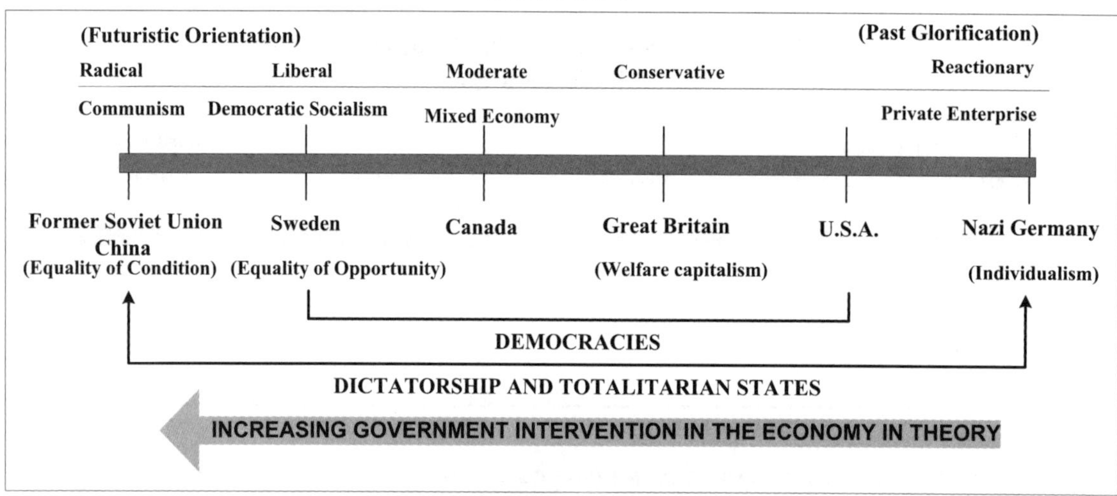

Political Spectrum
– IMAGE # 10 –

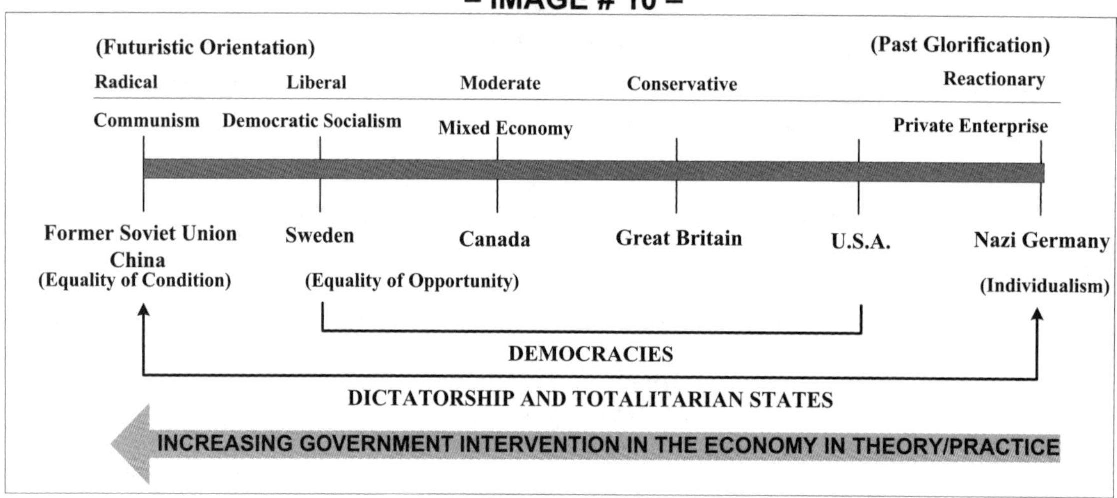

The Opposite Sides of the First World War
– IMAGE # 11 –

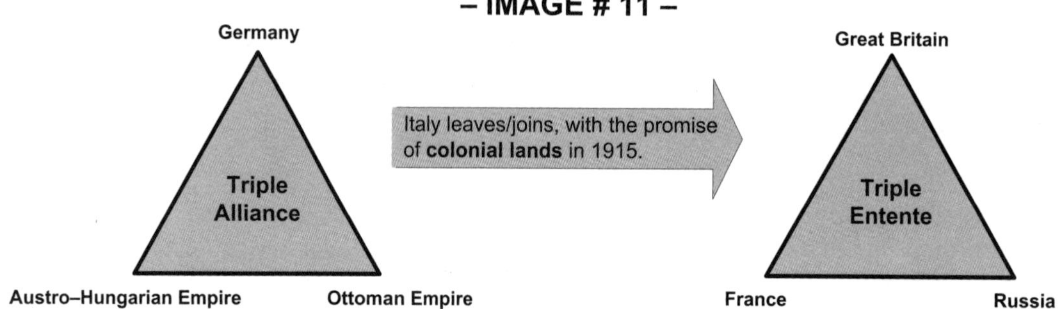

NOTES

Appendix B
Key Terminology

Global Interaction in the Twentieth Century

Confrontation
Nationalism
Self-determination
Sovereignty
Expansionism
Total War
Limited War
Guerrilla War
War Of Liberation
"Just" War
Terrorism
Brinkmanship
Collective Security
Internationalism
Balance Of Power
Humanitarianism
Alliances
Economic Blocs
Political Groupings
Regional Organizations
International Organizations
National Security
Treaty Of Versailles
League Of Nations
Little Entente
Isolationism
German/Soviet Non-Aggression Pact
Surrender
Sphere Of Influence
Containment Policy
Cold War
Iron Curtain
Marshall Plan
Warsaw Pact
Truman Doctrine
Berlin Blockade
NATO–North Atlantic Treaty Organization
Korean War
SEATO–Southeast Asia Treaty Organization
Decolonization
CENTO/Bagdad Pact
General Assembly
Security Council
UNO–United Nations Organization
Veto Powen
Peacekeeping Operations
Deterrence
Peaceful Co-existence
Arms Race
SALT I and II–Strategic Arms Limitation Talks
Cuban Missile Crisis
SDI – Strategic Defense Initiative
Summit Meetings
Pacific Rim
New Industrialized Countries:
South Korea
Singapore
Taiwan
ASEAN–Association of Southeast Asian Nations
Universal Declaration Of Human Rights
Helsinki Accord
Amnesty International
Green Peace
Anti-colonialism
Appeasement
Genocide
Blitzkrieg
Grand Alliance
Holocaust
Atlantic Charter
Yalta Conference
Potsdam Conference
Norad
Hamas

Here are some common names you are likely to encounter in Social Studies 30.

Emperor Hirohito
Fidel Castro
Jimmy Carter
Menechem Begin
Anwar Sadat
Yasser Arafat
Mao Tse -Tung
Chiang Kai-Shek
Ho Chi-Minh
Francisco Franco
Helmut Kohl
Haile Selassie
Saddam Hussein
Neville Chamberlain
Bill Clinton
George W. Bush
Edouard Daladier
B. Boutrous Ghali
Kofi Annan
Jean Chretien
Paul Martin
Clement Attlee
Harry S. Truman
Yuri Andropov
Mahatma Gandhi
Gamal Nasser
Mikhailn Gorbachev
Marshal Tito
Boris Yeltsin
Nikita Khrushchev
John Fitzgenald Kennedy
Leonid Brezhnev
Charles De Gaulle
Willy Brandt
Lloyd George
George Clemenceau
Woodrow Wilson
Benito Mussolini
Adolf Hitler
V.I. Lenin
Josef Stalin
F.D. Roosevelt

Political and Economic Systems

Scarcity
Natural Laws
Capitalism
Liberalism
Marketplace
Elite
Gross National Product (GNP)
Supply Schedule
Demand Schedule
Natural Price
Types of Government
Cartels, Trusts, Combines
Democracy
Wages, Interest, Rent
Constitutional Monarchy
Transfer Payments
Oligarchy
Monetary Policy
Junta
Exchange, Distribution
Indirect or Representative Democracy
Command Economy
Political Equality
Dollar Voting
Legal Equality
Central or State Planning Board
Gosplan
Glasnost
Techniques of Democracy
Kolkhoz
Interest/Pressure Groups
Subsidies
Lobbyists
Mixed Economy
Filibuster
Laissez-faire
Techniques of Dictatorship
Regulated Private Enterprise

One–party Dictatorship
Age of Enlightenment (Reason)
Indicative Planning
Elite Leadership
Democratic Socialism
Franchise, Suffrage, Vote
Nationalization
Indoctrination
Civil Disobedience
Propaganda
Controlled Participation
Entrepreneur
Direction of Discontent
Checks and Balances
Wealth of Nations
Majority Government
Minority Government
Communist Manifesto
Coalition
Das Kapital
Non-confidence Vote
Five Year Plans
Closure
Caucus
Perestroika
Bicameral Legislature
Cooperatives
Responsible Government
Multi-national Corporations (MNC'S)
Proportional Representation
Economic Cooperation and Development
Racism
Fascism
Council of Ministers
Congress of Peoples' Deputies
Politburo

First Secretary of the Communist Party
Octoberists, Young Pioneers, Komsomols
Revolutionary Stages
Supreme Soviet
Nazism
NAFTA–North American Free Trade Agreement.
Demand-side Economics
Supply-side Economics
Referendum
Polls (Gallop, Harris, Reid)
Ombudsman

Here are some common names you are likely to encounter in Social Studies 30.

John Stuart Mill
John Locke
John Maynard Keynes
Adam Smith
Karl Marx
Margaret Thatcher
Ronald Reagan

Appendix C
Written Response Topics: 1999-2001

January 1999

Topic A

Some people believe that certain groups in society are more capable of making fair and wise political decisions than are the majority of citizens. Other people believe that all citizens must be involved in political decision making.

To what extent should political decision making be restricted to a specific group in society?

Topic B

Some people believe that as we approach the end of the twentieth century, the world is entering an age of peace and stability unparalleled since the end of the First World War. Other people believe, however, that the post-Cold War era has ushered in an age of nationalist tension and conflict in many parts of the world.

As we approach the twenty-first century, has the world become a more dangerous place?

June 1999

Topic A

Some people believe that governments should implement policies that promote full employment during times of economic instability. Others believe that during times of economic instability, market forces should be relied upon to restore employment and prosperity.

To what extent should governments intervene in an economy to encourage full employment?

Topic B

Some people believe that all nations should support the establishment of a world government to encourage greater global cooperation and peace. Others believe that, despite the problems the world faces, a nation's sovereignty should not be subjected to the restrictions of a world government.

Should nations support a movement toward the establishment of a world government?

January 2000

Topic A

Some people believe that the right to voice minority opinions and viewpoints in a society should be protected at all costs. Others believe that the point of view of the majority should prevail over the opinion of minorities in the interest of preserving the stability of society.

To what extent should the right to express minority viewpoints be protected?

In your essay, take and defend a position on this issue.

Topic B

Some people believe that world peace and stability can best be preserved through the leadership of a single organization like the United Nations. Others believe that nations acting independently or together with other nations outside the sphere of an organization like the United Nations may preserve world peace more effectively.

Should the preservation of world stability and peace be the responsibility of a single organization like the United Nations?

In your essay, take and defend a position on this issue.

June 2000

Topic A

In some nations, there is only one political party or ruling elite, and it forms the government. In other nations, two or more political parties compete with one another to form the government.

To what extent should governments be formed through competition among political parties?

In your essay, take and defend a position on this issue.

Topic B

In order to preserve their national security, many nations have chosen to allocate a significant portion of their national budgets to military spending. Other nations have chosen to commit much less of their national budgets to military spending, preferring to depend on other means of preserving their national security.

To what extent should military spending be used by nations to preserve their national security?

In your essay, take and defend a position on this issue.

January 2001

Topic A

Some people believe that in order for an economy to prosper, individuals must be free to pursue profit making without restriction. Others believe that the unrestricted pursuit of profit benefits only a few and will create serious problems for society.

To what extent should governments encourage the unrestricted pursuit of profit?

In your essay, take and defend a position on this issue.

Topic B

Some people believe that political and military leaders must be held accountable for decisions and actions taken during times of war or civil unrest. Others believe that political and military leaders are justified in using extraordinary measures in an effort to end a conflict or restore order.

To what extent should political and military leaders be held accountable for decisions and actions taken during times of war or civil unrest?

In your essay, take and defend a position on this issue.

Note: In each exam, the student had a ***choice to answer either Topic A or Topic B.***

CREDITS

Political and Economic Systems

8 John K. Galbraith. From *Socialism: Opposing Viewpoints* (Greenhaven Press, Inc., 1978)

11–13 Arthur Meighen. From *Vital Speeches of the Day*, June 1950

15–16 From *World Press Review*, December 1994.

20 from *Approaches to Political and Economic Systems* (Globe/Modern Curriculum Press, 1983).

21–22 I. Cartoon by Ed McNally from *The Montreal Star*. II. Lester Pearson. From *Challenge of Democracy* (Nelson Canada, 1984).

27–30 Adapted from Baradat, *Political Ideologies, Their Origins and Impact*, 6/e, 1997, p.42.

43 Wayne C. Anderson. From *Vital Speeches of the Day*, December 1, 1991.

44 Quote by Barry Goldwater, as found in *Socialism: Opposing Viewpoints* by Bruno Leone (Greenhaven Press Inc., 1986).

45–47 Laura Winopol. From *The Edmonton Journal*, February 15, 1990.

50 Quote by Mikhail Gorbachev, as found in *The Struggle for Democracy* by Patrick Watson and Benjamin Barber (Lester & Orpen Dennys Ltd., 1988).

57–58 From *History at Source, Nazi Germany 1933-1945* by John Laver (Hodder & Stoughton, 1992).

59–60 I-III. Quotes by Aristotle, Thomas Jefferson, and Jeremy Bentham, as found in *Inside World Politics* by Diane P. Rogers and Robert J. Clark (The Macmillan Company of Canada Limited, 1969).
IV. Quote by Pierre Elliott Trudeau, as found in *Inside World Politics* by Diane P. Rogers and Robert J. Clark (The Macmillan Company of Canada Limited, 1969).

68–70 Andrew Coyne. From *The Globe and Mail*, October 1996.

75–78 I. Nick Loenen. From *Citizenship and Democracy: A Case for Proportional as found in The Edmonton Journal*, April 12, 1997. II./III. Norm Ovenden. From The Edmonton Journal, April 12, 1997.

85 Allen Bullock From "Hitler's Germany" as found in *History of the 20th Century* (Phoebus Publishing Co., 1973).

86 Cartoon by Bob Gorrell. From *The Richmond Times -Dispatch* as found in *Best Editional Cartoons of* the Year, 1996 Edition (Pelican Publishing Company, Inc. 1961).

89–90 Allan Chambers. From *The Edmonton Journal*, August 31, 1994.

92–95 I./II. Eric Kierans From "Corporations and the Cain Culture " as found in *Policy Options*, September 1989. III. Cartoon by James F Todd. From "Corporations and the Cain Culture" as found in *Policy Options*, September 1989.

99–100 I./II. Table by M.N Duffy. From *The 20th Century*, Second Edition (Basil Blackwell Publisher, 1983.

102 Terernce Corcoran from "How Subsidies Ate Atlantic Region" as found in *The Globe and Mail*, October 29, 1996.

Unit Test 1 – Political and Economic Systems

4 From *Royal Bank Letter* Commemorative Edition, January/February 1994.

5–7 Tables from *Canadian Political Facts* 1945–1976 (Methuen Publications).

15 Satya Das. From *The Edmonton Journal*, April 30, 1994.

16–17 R. N. Rundle. From *International Affairs 1890–1934* (Holmes & Meier Publishers, Inc., 1979).

19–20 II. David Bender and Bruno Leone. From *The Political Spectrum: Opposing Viewpoints Series* (Greenhaven Press, Inc., 1996).

24–25 T.L. Powrie. From *Political and Economic Systems* (J.M. Dent & Sons (Canada) Ltd.).

27–28 Cartoon by Brian Gable. From *The Globe and Mail*, January 26, 1996.

39 Ivan Laptev. From *Twentieth Century Viewpoints* (Oxford University Press, 1996). Public Domain.

40–41 Cartoon by Barney Tobey; © *The New Yorker Collection* 1970 Barney Tobey from cartoonbank.com. All Rights Reserved.

55–57 1. Neal Ascherson. From *World Press Review*, Sept. 1995.

64–65 Andrew Coyne. From *The Edmonton Journal*, October 17, 1996.

68–69 Gregory S. Mahler. From Canadian Parliamentary Review, Winter 1985–86.

Global Interaction

1–2 I./II. From *Internationalism: Opposing Viewpoints Series* (Greenhaven Press, Inc., 1978).

3–5 I./II. From *Twentieth Century History: The World Since* 1900 (Longman, 1987).

9 Adolf Hitler. Public domain.

15–16 Cartoon from *The World This Century, Working with Evidence* (Collins Educational, 1994).

20–22 I./II From *World Eagle*, March 1994.

25–27 I. Allan Chambers. From *The Edmonton Journal*, August 22, 1993 II. Jim Knudsen from *Best Editorial Cartoons of the Year* (Pelican Publishing Company, 1992).

30–32 I-IV From *Canadian Reference Guide to the United Nations* (Department of Foreign Affairs and International Trade, 1994).

35 Cartoon by Adrian Raeside from *The Edmonton Journal*, July 13, 1997, © Koko Press Inc.

39–40 Quote by A.J.P. Taylor, as found in *The World This Century* by Neil DeMarco (Bell & Hyman, 1987).

41–43 A Map History of the Modern World 1890 to the Present Day by Brian Catchpole (The Book Society of Canada Limited, 1973).

44–45 Republican National Platform. From *Internationalism: Opposing Viewpoints* (Greenhaven Press, Inc., 1978).

48–49 From *The Human Mosaic* by Terry G. Jordan and Lester Rowntree (Canfield Press, 1976).

53–55 Cartoon by David Low from *London Evening Standard.*

57–59 I–II. Quotes by Robert Kennedy and Nikita Khrushchev, as found in *History at Source, The Cold War* by E. G. Rayner (Hodder & Stoughton, 1992).

67–69 Alessandra Stanley. *The Edmonton Journal*, January 3, 1999.

71–72 Joseph Parrish. From *The Chicago Tribune* as found in *A Cartoon History of United States Foreign Policy* (Pharos Books, 1991) Chicago Tribune Company. All rights reserved.

73–75 Map from *The World Re-Made* by Josh Brooman (Longmun Group Limited, 1985).

78–79 From *The International Relations Dictionary* by Jack C. Plano and Roy Olton (Holt, Rinehart and Winston, Inc., 1969).

80 Quote by Hirohito. From "Japanese Foreign Policy, 1869–1942" as found in *Case Studies in Twentieth Century History* by Derek Heater (Longman Group UK Limited, 1988).

81–82 I. Quote by Edward Crankshaw. From "Gestapo" as found in *The Rise of the Nazi Horror: Who was Responsible*? by Bernard Feder (American Book Company. 1968).
II. Quote by C. Leonard Lundin. From "New Prospectives in World History" as found in *The Rise of the Nazi Horror: Who Was Responsible*? by Bernard Feder (American Book Company, 1968).

84–85 M.N. Duffy. From *The 20th Century, Second Edition* (Basil Blackwell Publisher, 1983).

88 Map by Regmarad. From *A Map History of the Modern World: 1890 to the Present Day* by Brain Catchpole (The Book Society of Canada Limited, 1973). Copyright (c) Regmarad.

90–91 Cartoon by Edwin Marcus. From *A Cartoon History of United States Foreign Policy Since World War* I (Vintage Banks).

92 Quote by Dwight D. Eisenhower. From "Public Papers of the Presidents of the United States: Dwight D. Eisenhower, 1954" as found in *Who's Been Counting My Fish? The Quotable Quotes of Dwight D. Eisenhower* from http://www.nps.gov/eise/quotes.htm. Public domain.

93 Illustration from *The Modern World Since* 1917 by Philip Sauvain (Basil Blackwell Publisher, 1983).

94–97 I., II., III. John Hay. From *The Ottawa Citizen* as found in *The Edmonton Journal*, May 30, 1992.
IV. From *The Japan Times* as found in *World Press Rewiew*, December 1991.

101–103 I. Jonathan Eyal. From *The Independent*, May 31, 1993.
II. Cartoon by Jeff MacNelly. From *The Chicago Tribune* as found in *The Edmonton Journal*, May 9, 1994. (c) Tribune Media Services, Inc. All Rights Reserved.

CREDITS

Unit Test 2 – Global Interaction

1–2 Cartoon by Kirby. From *Internationalism: Opposing Viewpoints Series* (Greenhaven Press, Inc., 1978). Public domain.

5–6 Winston Churchill. From *Our World This Century* (Oxford University Press, 1982). Public domain.

11–12 Russian cartoon, 1936, from *Evidence in Question: European History 1815–949* (Oxford University Press, 1980). Public domain.

13–14 Map from *History Scene in the Modern World* (Collins Educational, 1987).

28–30 I. Tony Howarth. From *Twentieth Century History: The World Since 1900* (Longman Group Ltd., 1979).
III. "Five Scenarios for Separation" from Review of International Affairs, Belgrade. As found in *World Press Review*, May 1991.

32–34 I. From *The Edmonton Journal*, November 10, 1993.
III. Stephen Rosenfeld. From The Washington Post © The Washington Post. As found in *The Edmonton Journal*, May 30, 1994.

36–37 I. Henry Cabot Lodge. From *Twentieth Century Speeches* (Penguin Books, 1992) Public Domain.
II. Woodrow Wilson. From *Twentieth Century Speeches* (Penguin Books, 1992). Public Domain.

38–41 I. Donald Johnston. From *The Bumpy Road to Disarmament* (Harper & Row, Publishers, 1973). Copyright @ 1973 by the New York Times Co.
II. Cartoon by Vaughn Shoemaker. From *The Bumpy Road to Disarmament* (Harper & Row, Publishers, 1973).

47 Map by Reg Piggott, John Blackman, Leslie Marshall. From *The Twentieth Century World* (Cambridge University Press, 1983).

49–50 From *Facts in Review* (German Library of Information, 1941). Public Domain.

53–54 Harriet Ward. From *World Powers in the Twentieth Century* (BBC and Heinemarm Educational Books Ltd., 1978).

55–58 I. Map from *The Modem World Since 1917* by Philip Sauvain (Basil Blackwell, 1983).
II. Map from *The Contemporary World* (Oliver & Boyd, 1983).
III. Karl von Clausewitz. From *On War*, translated by O.J. Matthijs Jolles (Random House, Inc., 1943).

60–61 F. Greene. From *The Cold War* by Hugh Higgins (Bames & Noble Books, 1974).

66–67 Cartoon by Auth, © *The Philadelphia Inquirer*.

June 2001 Diploma Exam

5–8 I and II. Excerpts from *The Welfare State: Opposing Viewpoints*, edited by David L. Bender Greenhaven Press, Inc., 1982.
III. Cartoon by Belva Detlof. From "Construction Action, Inc." as found in *The Welfare State: Opposing Viewpoints* (Greenhaven Press, Inc., 1982).

13–14 Graph from *Economics: A Canadian Perspective* (Oxford University Press Canada, 1992) by James P. Thexton.

16–18 Excerpt from an article by Satya Das. From *The Edmonton Journal*, A8, March 21, 1994.

22–24 I. Cartoon by Zel. From Berliner Morgenpost as found in *World Press Review* (The Stanley Foundation), page 30, July 1991.
II. Cartoon by Gable. From The *Globe and Mail*, September 3, 1991.

30 Excerpt from "The Essence of Democracy" as found in the *Royal Bank Letter*, vol. 72, no. 6, November/December 1991.

34 Illustration from *Ideologies in World Affairs*, by Andrew Gyorgy and George D.Blackwood, copyright © 1967 Blaisdell Publishing Company.

38–39 President Woodrow Wilson. From "President Wilson's Address to Congress, Analyzing German and Austrian Peace Utterances, "February 11, 1918, as found on http://www.lib.byu.edu. Public domain.

45 Anthony Eden. From *Vital Speeches of the Day*, vol. 17, no. 22 (1951): 675 (City News Publishing Co. Inc.).

48–49 Map from *The Rise of the Global Village* by Douglas Baldwin et al. (McGraw-Hill Ryerson Ltd., 1988).

53–54 Quote by Guenter Lewy. From "AMERICA IN VIETNAM" 1978 as found in *The Vietnam War: Opposing Viewpoints* (Greenhaven Press, Inc., 1984).

59–62 I. Nixon, Richard, "American Foreign Policy: The Bush Agenda" In: *Foreign Affairs*, v. 68:1 (1988/89)]. Paragraphs 2-3, 4–6.
II. Excerpt by George Kennan. From "New Perspectives Quarterly" as found in *The Superpowers: A New Détente Opposing Viewpoints* (Greenhaven Press Inc., 1989).
III. Cartoon by Henry Payne. From *The Superpowers: A New Détente Opposing Viewpoints* (Greenhaven Press Inc., 1989).

63–64 President Valéry Giscard d'Estaing. From *Le Monde*, Paris, October 28, 1997 as found in *World Press Review*, vol. 45, issue 1, January 1998.

69–70 Cartoon by Edmund Valtman. From *Best Editorial Cartoons of the Year* (Pelican Publishing Company, 1994).

January 2002 Diploma Exam

6–8 II: George L. Mosse. Table from *Nazi Culture: Intellectual, Cultural and Social Life in Third Reich* (Grosset & Dunlap, 1966). I and III: Graphs by George L. Mosse. From "Nazi Culture" as found in *The World This Century: Working with Evidence* by Neil DeMarco (Unwin Hyman Ltd., 1987).

11–12 Cartoon by Brian Gable. From *The Globe and Mail as found in Best Editorial Cartoons of the Year, 1997 Edition* (Pelican Publishing Company, Inc.).

17 Article by Andrew Coyne. From "Time for proportional representation in elections; Current system makes Canada a global oddity" as found in *The Edmonton Journal*, A19, October 17, 1996.

18–19 Article by Satya Das. From "Keynesian theory still the best road map for economic recovery" as found in *The Edmonton Journal*, A8, March 21, 1994.

24–25 Quotation by Karl Marx. From *Economics Explained* by Robert L. Heilbroner and Lester C. Thurow (Simon & Schuster, Inc., 1987).

30–32 Article by Duncan Cameron. From "Tax Cuts" as found in *The Canadian Forum* vol. 75, no. 853, Oct. 1996, page 3.

34–35 Cartoon by Don Hess. From *St. Louis Globe-Democrat* as found in *The Politican Spectrum: Opposing Viewpoints* (Greenhave Press, Inc., 1986).

40 Article by Christopher Young. From "UN troops need authority to fight; Peacekeepers in Bosnia" as found in *The Edmonton Journal*, A9, April 13, 1992.

42–44 I: Quotation by A.J.P. Taylor. From *The World This Century: Working with Evidence* by Neil DeMarco (Unwin Hyman Limited, 1987).
II: Quotation by Hugh Trevor-Roper. From *The World This Century: Working with Evidence* by Neil DeMarco (Unwin Hyman Limited, 1987).

45 Quotation by Winston Churchill. From *Blood, Toil, Tears and Sweat: The Speeches of Winston Churchill* edited by David Cannadine (Houghton Mifflin Company, Boston, 1989). Public domain.

48 Maps from *Twentieth Century Viewpoints: An Interpretive History* by Victor Zelinski et al. (Oxford University Press Canada, 1996).

49–50 Cartoon by David Low. From *An Illustrated History of Modern Europe 1789–1974* by Denis Richards (Longman Group Limited, 1977).

56–57 I: Harry S. Truman. From "Memoirs II" as found in *Basic Documents in United States Foreign Policy* (D. Van Nostrand Company Ltd, 1968).
II: Cartoon by Daniel Bishop. From the *St. Louis Star-Times* as found in *A Cartoon History of United States Foreign Policy Since World War I* (Random House, Inc., 1967).

62–64 II. Cartoon by Brian Gable. From *Portfoolio 9* (Macmillan Canada, 1993).

66–67 Phyllis Bennis and Michel Moushabeck. From "Altered States: A Reader in the New World Order" as found in *Twentieth Century Viewpoints* by Victor Zelinski et al. (Oxford University Press Canada, 1996).

Artwork by: Andrea Smereka

NOTES

NOTES

NOTES

ORDERING INFORMATION

All School Orders

School Authorities are eligible to purchase these resources by applying the Learning Resource Credit Allocation (LRCA – 25% school discount) on their purchase through the Learning Resources Centre (LRC). Call LRC for details.

THE KEY *Study Guides* are specifically designed to assist students in preparing for unit tests, final exams, and provincial examinations.

KEY *Study Guides* – $29.95 each plus G.S.T.

Senior High		Junior High	Elementary
Biology 30 Chemistry 30 English 30-1 English 30-2 Math 30 (Pure) Math 30 (Applied) Physics 30 Social Studies 30 Social Studies 33	Biology 20 Chemistry 20 English 20-1 Math 20 (Pure) Physics 20 Social Studies 20 English 10-1 Math 10 (Pure) Science 10 Social Studies 10	Language Arts 9 Math 9 Science 9 Social Studies 9 Math 8 Math 7	Language Arts 6 Math 6 Science 6 Social Studies 6 Math 4 Language Arts 3 Math 3

Student Notes and Problems (SNAP) Workbooks contain complete explanations of curriculum concepts, examples, and exercise questions.

SNAP Workbooks – $29.95 each plus G.S.T.

Senior High		Junior High	Elementary
Chemistry 30 Math 30 Pure Math 30 Applied Math 31 Physics 30	Chemistry 20 Math 20 Pure Math 20 Applied Physics 20 Math 10 Pure Math 10 Applied Science 10	Math 9 Science 9 Math 8 Math 7	Math 6 Math 5 Math 4 Math 3

Visit our website for a "tour" of resource content and features at
www.castlerockresearch.com

#2340, 10180 – 101 Street
Edmonton, AB Canada T5J 3S4
e-mail: learn@castlerockresearch.com

Phone: 780.448.9619
Toll-free: 1.800.840.6224
Fax: 780.426.3917

2006 (3)

SCHOOL ORDER FORM

THE KEY	QUANTITY
Biology 30	
Chemistry 30	
English 30-1	
English 30-2	
Math30 (Pure)	
Math 30 (Applied)	
Physics 30	
Social Studies 30	
Social Studies 33	
Biology 20	
Chemistry 20	
English 20-1	
Math 20 (Pure)	
Physics 20	
Social Studies 20	
English 10-1	
Math 10 (Pure)	
Science 10	
Social Studies 10	
Language Arts 9	
Math 9	
Science 9	
Social Studies 9	
Math 8	
Math 7	
Language Arts 6	
Math 6	
Science 6	
Social Studies 6	
Math 4	
Math 3	
Language Arts 3	

SNAP WORKBOOKS Notes and Problems/ Student Notes and Problems	QUANTITY	
	Workbooks	Solutions Manuals
Chemistry 30		
Chemistry 20		
Physics 30		
Physics 20		
Math 30 Pure		
Math 30 Applied		
Math 31		
Math 20 Pure		
Math 20 Applied		
Math 10 Pure		
Math 10 Applied		
Science 10		
Science 9		
Math 9		
Math 8		
Math 7		
Math 6		
Math 5		
Math 4		
Math 3		

TOTALS

KEYS	
WORKBOOKS	
SOLUTION MANUALS	

Learning Resources Centre

Castle Rock Research is pleased to announce an exclusive distribution arrangement with the Learning Resources Centre (LRC). Under this agreement, schools can now place all their orders with LRC for order fulfillment. As well, these resources are eligible for applying the Learning Resource Credit Allocation (LRCA) which gives schools a 25% discount off LRC's selling price. Call LRC for details.

Orders may be placed with LRC by
telephone: (780) 427-5775,
fax: (780) 422-9750,
internet: www.lrc.learning.gov.ab.ca
or mail: 12360 - 142 Street NW
Edmonton, AB T5L 4X9.

PAYMENT AND SHIPPING INFORMATION

Name: ______

School Telephone: ______

SHIP TO

School: ______

Address: ______

City: ______ Postal Code: ______

PAYMENT

☐ by credit card

VISA/MC Number: ______ Expiry Date: ______

Name on Card: ______

☐ enclosed cheque

☐ invoice school P.O. number: ______

#2340, 10180 – 101 Street, Edmonton, AB T5J 3S4 Tel: 780.448.9619 Fax: 780.426.3917
email: learn@castlerockresearch.com Toll-free: 1.800.840.6224

www.castlerockresearch.com